alias
bob dylan
r e v i s i t e d

Stephen Scobie

Red Deer PRESS

the publishers
Red Deer Press
813 MacKimmie Library Tower
2500 University Drive N.W.
Calgary Alberta Canada T2N 1N4

credits
Edited for the Press by Jill Fallis
Cover design by Duncan Campbell
Text design by Erin Woodward
Cover photograph © Bettmann / CORBIS / MagmaPhoto.com
Printed and bound in Canada by AGMV Marquis for Red Deer Press

acknowledgements
Financial support provided by the Canada Council, the Department of Canadian Heritage,
the Alberta Foundation for the Arts, a beneficiary of the Lottery Fund of the Government
of Alberta, and the University of Calgary.

National Library of Canada Cataloguing in
Publication Data
Scobie, Stephen, 1943–
Alias Bob Dylan revisited
Previously published under title: Alias Bob Dylan.
Includes bibliographical references and index.
ISBN 0-88995-227-2
1. Dylan, Bob, 1941– —Criticism and interpretation. I. Scobie,
Stephen, 1943– Alias Bob Dylan. II. Title.
ML420.D98S42 2003   782.42164'092   C2001-910213-5

5 4 3 2 1

contents

for Maureen

"Silvia, rimembri ancora . . ."

This book owes much to the many people who have, over the years, shared, encouraged, or tolerated my passion for Bob Dylan.

First then, and always, it is for Maureen, whom I abandoned on a Saturday afternoon in 1966 to go to Bellingham, Washington, in search of *Blonde on Blonde*.

Then it is for all the members of "Trainload of Fools," the Victoria Dylan discussion group—especially for Eric and Jane, who keep us keeping on, and for Renée, who is always on the road.

This book is for Martin, who taught the first Dylan course with me, and for Trevor with his marvelous gifts. It is for Simon, who had the unsurpassable good fortune to hear the first-ever live performance of "Blind Willie McTell." And it is for Robin, who always covers his tracks.

This book is also for Jean-Louis in the gardens at Versailles; and for Roger, Ken, and the Cat, "masters of the bluff and masters of the proposition."

It is for Rainer, "the intellectual fan"; for Uli in the Weinhof Zimmermann; for Karl with a *C;* and for Didi the Crazy DJ in the dungeons of Schloss Plankenstein.

It is for Peter and Kevin and Harvey and John and Arnie at Jimmy's Corner in New York; for Lloyd, who brought me to Madison Square Garden; and for Linn, who met me there.

This book is for all the internet fans with whom I have agreed, disagreed, fought, and collaborated on the topics of our shared obsession.

And it is for James—"heart of mine," heart of an unknown donor—who drove with me to Hibbing and Duluth, down Highway 61.

Q: What do you think of people who analyze your songs?
A: I welcome them with open arms.

. . . .

It's always silent where I am.

–Bob Dylan
Press conference, San Francisco
December 3, 1965

"God, rock 'n' roll, art, poetry, marriage, women, sex, Bob Dylan, poets, death . . ."

–Allen Ginsberg

note on the revised edition

Alias Bob Dylan was first published in 1991, to coincide with Bob Dylan's fiftieth birthday. That first edition went through several reprintings, until Dennis Johnson, publisher of Red Deer Press, and I agreed that it should be allowed to go out of print, with the understanding that a revised and updated edition would later appear.

Alias Bob Dylan Revisited is this new edition. It profits from over ten years of new material, not just in new recordings and performances by Dylan, but also in the exponential explosion of discussion about Dylan on the internet. As a result, this book is fundamentally different from its predecessor. At least half of the material is new, and everything that did appear in the first edition has been rethought, revised, and recontextualized. This is fundamentally a new book.

Chapter 1, "Prophet and Trickster: An Overview," outlines two sets of parameters—one chronological and one thematic—within which everything in this new edition may be situated. The chronology suggests a way of looking at Dylan's overall career in terms of three major phases. The thematic section proposes two images—"Prophet" and "Trickster"—as distinct but mutually implicated stances which persist throughout Dylan's career.

Chapter 2, "Glossary," consists of brief essays introducing a series of key terms, or recurring images and motifs—alias, mask, signature, self-portrait, ghost, quotation—which form the basis of my critical discourse on Dylan. Chapter 3, "Contexts," explicates some of the surrounding issues—the relevance of the author's biography, the status of the published text, whether or not Dylan's lyrics should be regarded as poetry, the nature of performance—which frame my discussion. Chapter 4, "Genres," deals with Dylan's major works in terms of continuing types of songs (self-reflexive songs, love songs, outlaw songs, religious songs). It is this chapter which derives most directly from the first edition.

Chapter 5, "Intertexts," presents two major figures whose work stands in intertextual dialogue with Dylan's. The first is Allen Ginsberg, whose whole body of work can fruitfully be read alongside Dylan's. The second is Greil Marcus, whose book *Invisible Republic* affords an opportunity for discussing the Basement Tapes. Chapter 6, "Movies," discusses two major cinematic projects with which Dylan has been involved: Sam Peckinpah's *Pat Garrett & Billy the Kid* and his own *Renaldo and Clara*. (The book has gone to press, alas, too early for me to include any comment on Dylan's highly problematic 2003 film, *Masked and Anonymous*.)

Interspersed between these chapters are a succession of brief takes, "Moments and Milestones," on major Dylan songs. The selection here is, I admit, quite arbitrary: this section could have been drastically expanded.

Chapter 7 is comprised of three major essays presented as "Summations" of the three chronological phases suggested in Chapter 1. The Years of Creation are represented by a detailed analysis of "Visions of Johanna," the Years of Commitment are represented by a discussion of "Brownsville Girl," and the Years of Performance are represented by a review of the 1997 album *Time Out Of Mind*. Finally, a "Postscript" looks, all too briefly, at Dylan's 2001 album, *"Love and Theft."*

Some sections of this book, then, are repeated (though always in revised form) from the first edition of *Alias Bob Dylan*, but a great deal of it is new. Some of the new material has previously appeared in the magazines *On the Tracks* (USA), *Parking Meter* (Austria), *Du* (Switzerland) and *Judas!* (Scotland). My thanks are due to the editors of these magazines, especially Mick McCuistion and Rainer Vesely. And thanks also to Dennis Johnson at Red Deer Press, whose faith in this book has sustained me, time out of mind.

Stephen Scobie

Victoria, British Columbia

April 2003

note on quotations

Works frequently cited have been identified by the following abbreviations:

L: Bob Dylan, *Lyrics, 1962–1985* (New York: Alfred A. Knopf, 1985)
T: Bob Dylan, *Tarantula* (New York: Macmillan, 1971)

Most of the quotations from Bob Dylan songs in this book are taken from *Lyrics*. All such quotations are noted parenthetically in the text; for example, "Blowin' in the Wind," found on page 53 of *Lyrics*, is noted here as (L, 53).

Any quotations from Bob Dylan lyrics given in the text without parenthetical page citations have been transcribed directly from recordings—either when I am quoting from a song not included in *Lyrics*, or when I am quoting from a recording in which the words of the actual performance differ significantly from the printed text in *Lyrics*. Such cases necessarily include all songs since 1985. Although a new edition of *Lyrics* has long been promised, it had not appeared, unfortunately, at the time of this book's going to press.

All quotations from the Bible are from the Authorized (King James) Version.

acknowledgements

All quotations from Bob Dylan songs used by permission of Special Rider Music.

Excerpt from "Who Be Kind To" from *Collected Poems 1947–1980* by Allen Ginsberg. Copyright 1965 Allen Ginsberg. Reprinted by permission of HarperCollins Publishers, Inc.

Excerpt from "Wichita Vortex Sutra" from *Collected Poems 1947–1980* by Allen Ginsberg. Copyright 1966 Allen Ginsberg. Reprinted by permission of HarperCollins Publishers, Inc.

Our grateful thanks to the Allen Ginsberg Office for permission to quote from previously unpublished manuscripts. Also, our grateful thanks to Anne Waldman for permission to quote from previously unpublished material.

Frank is the Key

The Chippewa called it The Hill of Three Waters. Long before precise topographical surveys, the Chippewa recognized the significance of this spot which we now, in our language, describe as a site two or three miles north of Hibbing, Minnesota. It is a triple continental divide. A raindrop falling onto this precise spot might divide into three parts, with three equal chances of flowing north (into the Hudson Bay), south (into the Mississippi River system and thus to the Gulf of Mexico), or east (by way of the Great Lakes to the St. Lawrence River and the Atlantic Ocean). Topographically, the town of Hibbing could be considered the center of North America.

The exact spot at which this triple divide occurs is no longer accessible to the public. It falls within the boundaries of the Hull Rust Mahoning Mine, the largest opencast iron mine in North America. "Since ore shipping began in 1895, more than 1.4 billion tons of earth have been removed . . . [leaving a] vast pit yawning more than three miles long, up to two miles wide, and 535 feet deep."[1] The pit of the Hull Rust Mine, now filled with water like a manmade lake, extends as far as the eye can see, its levels of red earth and ore exposed like a stratified geological map. At the observation complex a mounted sign records that the Chippewa name for this site meant "Hill of Three Waters." It does not record what the Chippewa word was.

Mining began in this area in the early 1890s. Legend attributes the origin to the moment when the German prospector Franz Dietrich von Ahlen "stuck his head out of a tent on a 40 degree below zero January morning in 1893 and said,

'I believe there is iron under me. My bones feel rusty and chilly.'" Within a couple of years the mine, and the town, were started, and von Ahlen, like so many immigrants before and since, had changed his name. Franz had become Frank; von Ahlen had become his mother's maiden name: Hibbing.

By 1912 Hibbing was a prosperous, thriving community laid out on a grid system over many blocks. It boasted an opera house and a grandiose library donated by Andrew Carnegie (Carnegie's U.S. Steel Corporation was the holding company for several Hibbing mines). Unfortunately, by 1912 it was also clear that the richest deposits of iron ore lay directly *under* the town site. The First World War (to the winning of which iron ore mined in Hibbing made no small contribution) delayed action, but from the early 1920s on, the town of Hibbing was, simply, moved.

Most wooden buildings—houses, hospitals, schools—were hoisted from their foundations, mounted on wheels, and moved two miles south to the suburb of Alice, which now became Hibbing. More ornate stone buildings, like the Lincoln School and the Carnegie Library, could not be moved. Some other buildings, like the Sellers Hotel, didn't make it, but collapsed spectacularly on the way. The move went on for thirty years. It was still happening in the late 1940s and early 1950s, when Bobby Zimmerman was growing up in the new town.

What is left of old north Hibbing today is minimal and eerie. The stone steps leading up to the Lincoln School, between Second and Third streets, are still there. Standing upon them you can see the remaining street signs and the cracked pavement outlines of the streets as they once were, lined by neat rows of trees. The corner of Second and Lincoln is clearly marked, but there are no buildings there. A couple of blocks to the north, the last signs of old Hibbing disappear into the vast open pit of the Hull Rust Mine.

Fifty years ago much more was still visible:

> old north Hibbing . . .
> deserted
> already dead
> with its old stone courthouse
> decayin' in the wind . . .
> the old school
> where my mother went to

rottin' shiverin' but still livin'
standin' cold and lonesome
arms cut off
with even the moon bypassin' its jagged body
pretendin' not t' see . . .

(L, 107)

Imagine the young Robert Zimmerman, alias Bob Dylan, walking through the ruins of old Hibbing. The Minnesota wind blows cold across the Mesabi Iron Range. The open pit of the mine lays the countryside bare, like the scar of open-heart surgery. The foundations of the old buildings disappear into another year's grass. Two miles to the south is the solid middleclass town of Hibbing. There his father, Abraham, works at Micka Electric, a furniture and appliance store (now called Brownie's) on Fifth Avenue. His mother, Beatty Stone Zimmerman, works at the Feldman's store on Howard Street. The family lives at 2425–East Seventh Avenue in a tiny, white, boxlike house on a corner lot close to Hibbing High School. This is where the legend, and the name, begin.

Hibbing is a displaced center.

Hibbing is a ghost.

Hibbing is a double of itself.

Hibbing is an alias, a pseudonym, written in the name of the mother.

In 1958 a band featuring Bobby Zimmerman played in the auditorium of Hibbing High School at the Jacket Jamboree Talent Festival.[2] According to school friend and fellow musician Bill Marinec, Bobby Zimmerman was a perfectionist, drilling and rehearsing the band for weeks beforehand. He knew exactly what he wanted.

For many readers of the standard biographies, "the auditorium of Hibbing High School" must evoke something quite modest: a school gymnasium, perhaps, with folding chairs set out over the lines of the basketball court. Nothing could be further from the truth.

Hibbing High School was built in 1926, financed by money from the mining companies as they moved the town southward. In 1920s money it cost $3.9 million. A picture of it was featured in the 1935 *National Geographic* (67:316). The auditorium, modeled on a Broadway theater, the Capitol, seats 1,825 spectators. The ceilings are of molded plaster, and the ornate walls feature paintings of decorous classical nudes. Two large, formal boxes flank the stage. The chandeliers are made of glass imported from Belgium and Czechoslovakia. The stage has a loft ninety feet high with room for more than sixty drops. The ceiling is covered in gold leaf to improve the acoustics, which are superb: even under the back balcony, every word from the stage is crystal clear. Every stage that Bob Dylan has played on over the forty-plus years since has been, after the Hibbing High School auditorium, an anticlimax.

Bob had his band well prepared. They were to hit their first notes at full volume the moment the curtains began to open. The front rows would be filled with jocks, the privileged elite of the school: the H-Club, the lettermen. They could be relied on not to understand. In 1958 few people in Hibbing had heard rock and roll; none had ever been played in as distinguished a setting as the Hibbing High School auditorium. Legends abound as to this performance. Some say that the audience laughed, some say that it booed. Some claim that the teachers tried to cut off the power—a claim identical to that made about the Newport Folk Festival seven years later. Some who were there, like Larry Furlong and Jackie O'Reilly, admit that they don't remember the audience's reaction. All remember Bobby though: pounding at the piano like a demented Little Richard, singing "Rock 'n' Roll Is Here To Stay."

Part of the legend is that Bobby Zimmerman broke the foot-pedal of the school's Steinway piano. The Steinway is still there, backstage, at the Hibbing High School. The pedal has been repaired.

In 1989, when I visited, no one in Hibbing said "Bob Zimmerman"; they all said "Bobby"—as in "My uncle beat up Bobby Zimmerman once and threw him in a trashcan for being such a wimp." For weeks after the concert, Bill Marinec recalls, people looked at Bobby strangely and didn't say a word.

First and foremost, even before being a songwriter, Bob Dylan is a performer. He exists on stage. He has never given any audience anything close to what they expected.

This book is about performance.

This book is about displaced centers, ghosts, doubles, aliases.

Franz Dietrich von Ahlen became Frank Hibbing; Robert Zimmerman became Bob Dylan. Hibbing was von Ahlen's mother's maiden name; Bobby's mother was Beatty Solemovitz, who became Beatty Stone. Like a rolling stone. The pseudonym suppresses the name of the father; eventually, in the figure of Isis, Bob Dylan returns to the name of the mother.

The liner notes to *John Wesley Harding* (1967) feature three kings, who believe that "the key is Frank!" (L, 265).

"Frank," says the first king, "Mr. Dylan has come out with a new record. This record, of course, features none but his own songs and we understand that you're the key."

"That's right," Frank replies. "I am."

I do not believe that there is any one "key" to the work of Bob Dylan, in the sense that any one fact or approach can unlock and explain all the mysteries of his career. But I do want to suggest, in another sense of the word, that this book is written "in the key of" Frank—Frank Hibbing.

Frank Hibbing's statue stands in a quiet park in Hibbing, Minnesota. Wearing his backpack and his hiking boots, he faces west and north, toward the mine, toward the Hill of Three Waters. There is as yet no statue of Bobby Zimmerman in Hibbing, Minnesota. Nor one of his alias either.

Prophet and Trickster:
An Overview

The popular image of Bob Dylan remains, to a great extent, confined to the ways he appeared in the 1960s. He is remembered for his early folk-protest songs and for his controversial move into rock and roll, "going electric." His image is fixed in the public's imagination somewhere between "Blowin' in the Wind" and "Like a Rolling Stone." If there is any awareness at all of his post–1960s career, beyond a mild surprise that the old man isn't dead yet, it too is fixed in an orthodox belief that Dylan's creative powers have steadily declined, and that, with the odd exception of an isolated album like *Blood on the Tracks* (1975) or *Time Out Of Mind* (1997), he has done nothing worth listening to in the last forty years.[1] Concert appearances have often been treated by reviewers as nothing more than opportunities for strained exercises of wit in finding bizarre comparisons for his voice. The fact that some people have found his career in the 1990s to be no less dynamic and challenging than his career in the 1960s is regarded with bemusement and condescension.

My argument in this book is that Dylan must be approached in terms of his whole career: indeed, that his longevity, his capacity for artistic survival and self-renewal, is one of his most remarkable accomplishments. There have been many changes in the course of that career, but there have also been core elements of consistency. This chapter will sketch out a general framework, both of the changes and of the consistency, in two ways: first, by suggesting an overview of Dylan's career divided into three shifting but complementary phases, and second, by attempting to define a complex artistic stance which persists throughout all three phases.

The Times They Are A-Changin'

I designate the three phases as the Years of Creation, the Years of Commitment, and the Years of Performance. Immediately, however, I must insist on certain important provisos. First, I do not for a moment mean to suggest that these three categories are exclusive of each other: that creative ability ceases after the first phase, or that performance has not always been central to Dylan's aesthetic. All three qualities—creation, commitment, and performance—coexist in all three phases. What I mean to suggest is that at different times one quality or another may usefully be regarded as dominant.

Second, I do not mean to suggest that these phases can be rigidly divided from each other. There is a good deal of overlap and transition. But I do think that one of the values of the division I am proposing is that it overrides what have conventionally been seen as turning-points in Dylan's career: "going electric," the motorcycle accident, the conversion to Christianity, and so on. My scheme suggests that there are deeper continuities, within which changes in musical style, from folk to rock, from country to gospel, are comparatively superficial.

Third, this scheme is entirely retrospective, imposed with the benefit of the hindsight of more than forty years. I am not suggesting that any of these phases was consciously planned or intended. The purpose of the scheme is solely to give some structure, chronologically, to the ways in which we think of Dylan's career, and to highlight both its changes and its consistency.

The Years of Creation

The first phase, the Years of Creation, begins with Dylan's emergence on the New York music scene in 1962 and lasts throughout the remainder of the 1960s. It is characterized by an extraordinary exuberance of creativity, a prolific overflowing of words and music. Artistic creation simply pours out of Dylan during this period, unceasingly and effortlessly, and without (seemingly, though it may be dangerous to exaggerate this point) very much in the way of conscious control.

He writes songs by the dozen, in a wide variety of styles, influenced by everyone from Woody Guthrie to Arthur Rimbaud. He writes poems, plays, and a kind of free-floating surrealist prose that hovers on the margins of poetry. Biographical accounts refer to him continually scribbling lines on odd scraps of paper, or sitting banging away at an old manual typewriter. Musically he seems incapable of confining himself within one mode. He shifts from traditional folk music to contemporary urban protest to psychedelic rock to old-time country without missing a beat. And all of this happens at an incredible speed. What we now see as three of the most important albums in the history of American popular music—*Bringing It All Back Home, Highway 61 Revisited,* and *Blonde on Blonde*—were recorded in a period of a mere fifteen months, from January 1965 to March 1966.

Throughout this period, performance is a central part of Dylan's artistic activity. It was as a performer on the stages of New York folk clubs and concert halls that Dylan forged his reputation. The confrontational electric concerts of 1965–66, backed by The Hawks, remain among the most thrilling moments of his career. Nor is there any reason to question the sincerity of his commitment to the causes he embraced, such as civil rights: it's simply that Dylan was moving so fast that no one position, aesthetic or political, could hold him for long. This was the period during which his fans waited impatiently to see what the next album would be like, sure only that it would not be like the one before.

Conventional wisdom would see this phase ending with Dylan's infamous motorcycle accident in July 1966 and his consequent withdrawal from public performing. There is some truth to this view: arguably this period of retrenchment, pulling back from the frenetic excesses of the previous few years, saved Dylan's life. If he had died in that accident, going out in a premature blaze of glory, he would have achieved the kind of apotheosis reserved for artists like John Keats or, closer to Dylan's own heart, James Dean. (One has the uneasy impression that many of his so-called admirers would have preferred it that way.) But his survival is a key indication that Dylan was, in fact, a very different kind of artist. Like his friend and mentor, Allen Ginsberg, Dylan was in this for the long run.

So I do not see this first phase ending in 1966. After only a brief pause, Dylan's creativity was again in overdrive, producing (albeit in private) the astonishing richness of both composition and performance in the recordings known as the Basement Tapes, and writing the whole of *John Wesley Harding* in a matter of weeks in late 1967. Even then he was still capable of the self-transformations in *Nashville Skyline* and *Self Portrait.* It is not until the early 1970s that this phase fully ends.

The Years of Commitment

What changed, I believe, was the quality of effortlessness. Dylan himself said that he had to learn "to do consciously what [he] used to do unconsciously." He could no longer automatically tap into that prolific, overflowing quality of his imagination. It became something that he had to work at, to which he had to make a conscious commitment. When I describe this second phase as the Years of Commitment, I am thinking not only of Dylan's commitment to social and religious causes, from Hurricane Carter to Jesus Christ; and not only of his (very impressive) commitment to certain large-scale artistic projects, such as the Rolling Thunder Revue and the film *Renaldo and Clara;* but also and primarily of his commitment to himself as an artist.

There is a transitional period, roughly 1971–73, during which Dylan drifts in uncertainty. He dabbles in other people's projects—some of them quite estimable, such as Sam Peckinpah's *Pat Garrett & Billy the Kid* and Allen Ginsberg's *First Blues*—but he lacks any clear sense of direction. What turned him around was, by his own account, the painting lessons he took from Norman Raeben, starting in the spring of 1974. The borders are a bit fluid here, since I see the beginning of this second phase as concurrent with the composition of *Planet Waves* in late 1973. But Raeben certainly confirmed his new sense of himself as a conscious artist, and it is to Raeben's instruction that Dylan explicitly attributes the method of writing *Blood on the Tracks.*

There follows a period of passionate commitment, in which Dylan works in a very clear and controlled way. It is, not coincidentally, the period of his most sustained and successful collaborations: with Jacques Levy on the songs of *Desire* and with Howard Alk on the painstaking, yearlong process of editing *Renaldo and Clara.* The ideal of the Rolling Thunder Revue, as a loosely organized community of traveling musicians, may also be seen as a collaboration, though it was only briefly and fitfully successful. But collaboration is a conscious act: it requires the artist to be answerable to someone other than himself, or even his audience. The collaborations with Levy and Alk are essential to Dylan's work at this period.

Again the conventional view would be that there is a decisive break in Dylan's career in late 1978 to early 1979, with his conversion to fundamentalist Christianity. But in terms of this phase, I see very little difference. Dylan brings to his Christian music exactly the same qualities of passionate commitment that he brought to Rolling Thunder and *Renaldo and Clara*. Even the awkwardness of his writing at this point, as he deliberately adopts the verbal style of his new faith, confirms the self-conscious quality of his commitment. The determination and intensity of Dylan's performances at this time remain quite stunning. But between a Rolling Thunder performance of "Tangled Up In Blue" and a gospel tour rendition of "When He Returns," there is very little to choose. Even at the height of his evangelism, Dylan is still a good pupil of Raeben, learning to do consciously what he used to do unconsciously.

This second phase lasts until 1983. Indeed, if I had to give a specific date for the end of it, I would place it in June to July of that year, when Dylan, remixing the album *Infidels*, chooses to leave off it such great songs as "Foot of Pride" and "Blind Willie McTell." After ten years of self-conscious confidence, Dylan's faith in his own material seems to waver. And again there is a brief period of drift: another, much less successful dabbling in commercial movies with *Hearts of Fire*, a few rather uncertain tours, and some wildly uneven albums. The 1986 album *Knocked Out Loaded* is emblematic: one brilliant song—"Brownsville Girl," in collaboration with Sam Shepard—surrounded by dreck.

The Years of Performance

Even at this intermediate stage, Dylan had the correct instinct: he needed to get back to live performance. But the mid-1980s tours with big-name collaborators—Santana, Tom Petty and the Heartbreakers, the Grateful Dead—weren't quite working out. However, in the shows with the Dead and in the second Petty tour in fall 1987, Dylan began to recover his zest for performance and to realize that he needed to do it on his own.[2] So in the spring of 1988 he scrapped the big bands and the female backing vocalists and returned to a stripped-down, three-piece group, playing hard-driving rock and roll surrounding a section of traditional acoustic music. The so-called Never Ending Tour had begun.

In this third phase, the Years of Performance, Dylan is certainly no less committed than he was before. Indeed, his commitment to the image of himself as a working musician, constantly on the road, playing more than one hundred concerts a year, is remarkable. And though he certainly writes fewer songs than he used to, he has nevertheless produced three of his finest albums in this period: *Oh Mercy* (1989), *Time Out Of Mind* (1997), and *"Love and Theft"* (2001). But the focus has certainly been on performance: in the continuous reworking and recreation of his own songs on stage, and also in his renewed commitment to the traditional music from which he began. His two albums of traditional material, *Good As I Been To You* (1992) and *World Gone Wrong* (1993), stand among his finest work. These traditional songs, he told *Newsweek* in 1997, "are my lexicon" (Gates, 64).

As he continues touring, past the age of sixty, Dylan confronts the problem that rock and roll has always been defined as the music of youth. "Unlike every other great genre of American pop," writes James Miller, "rock is all about being young. . . . Without an air of ingenuous freshness and earnest effort, rock as a musical form is generally coarse, even puerile—full of sound and fury, perhaps, but characteristically spurning the subtle creativity and seasoned craftsmanship that is the glory of such other mature vernacular pop music genres as jazz and the blues, country and gospel" (19).

This view is perhaps debatable—part of the problem is, of course, that we are still in the first generation of rock musicians. Only now, with people like Dylan, are we getting the chance to see what an old man's rock and roll might be like. But it's also suggestive, in that what Dylan has done in these last Years of Performance has been precisely to "season" his music with these more "mature" genres, especially the blues and the bluegrass/gospel of the Stanley Brothers. He still plays rock and roll—just listen to any late 1990s rendition of "Highway 61 Revisited"—but it is a rock and roll which very self-consciously displays its roots and allows them to nourish it.

Dylan's stage work has, of course, been uneven: no one plays a hundred masterpieces a year. There have been periods, such as early 1991, in which Dylan's performances were decidedly perfunctory, and periods in which the band has not quite gelled. But what is remarkable to anyone listening to a wide selection of performance tapes from these last ten or more years is how often he *has* succeeded in revitalizing a song or electrifying an audience. As far back as the renowned San Francisco press conference in 1965, disparaging any efforts to see him as a brilliant poet or the "spokesman of his generation," Dylan insisted that he was just "a song and dance man." He still has some work to do on his dancing, but the best performances of the Never Ending Tour confirm that the most vital locus of his art is still on stage, live, in front of an audience.

But it is always dangerous to try to pin Dylan down or to assume that any position is permanent. In 2001 Dylan produced a new album, *"Love and Theft,"* which is so remarkable that it immediately demands a retrospective rethinking of this whole chronology. Or perhaps it means that we are now entering a fourth phase, as yet undefined, but fully as promising and unpredictable as anything that has happened so far.

No Prophet's Son

Throughout his career and persisting through all these phases, certain aspects of Dylan's personal and aesthetic stance have remained constant. I attempt to define this stance in terms of an interaction between two personae: that of the prophet and that of the trickster. The prophet, deriving from biblical, national, and poetic traditions, is a relatively fixed position, the ground to which Dylan always returns. The trickster represents his equally strong temptation to undermine that position, to avoid fixity, and to embrace a fluid sense of self and identity—as revealed in his obsession with masks, doubles, shadows, false names, and mirror reflections.[3]

Early in his career, Bob Dylan declared (quoting the prophet Amos): "I know I ain't no prophet, an' I ain't no prophet's son" (L, 27). But even this disclaimer, as I have attempted to show elsewhere,[4] is, in the manner of the trickster, not to be taken entirely at face value. Certainly Dylan was familiar from an early age with the tradition of Hebrew prophecy, and all his work is steeped in biblical quotation.

The Hebrew prophet was a man[5] called by God, singled out by a special experience of inspiration and revelation to act as God's spokesman, to carry His word to the people. As such, the prophet spoke both personally and impersonally. As the vehicle of God's word, his individual personality was unimportant. Joseph Dheilly writes: "The prophet was a messenger of God, inspired by him and dedicated to carrying the revealed Word to the chosen people. . . . The prophet sometimes expresses himself as if there were a kind of confusion between his own person and God; his own individuality seems almost interchangeable with the divine" (33). What he says is more important than who he is.

Yet, at the same time, the prophet was a highly individualized figure. He bypassed the existing structures of both church and state; he rebuked priests and kings alike; he derived his authority not from any institution, but from the assertion of his personal vocation. According to Joseph Blenkinsopp, "the prophetic-charismatic figure is legitimated not by virtue of a socially acknowledged office like the priesthood, but solely through extraordinary personal qualities. The prophet is therefore neither designated by a predecessor, nor ordained, nor installed in office, but *called*" (35). Similarly, in a song like "A Hard Rain's A-Gonna Fall," Dylan speaks with the absolute authority of the impersonal prophet declaring the truth about a catastrophic situation,[6] and yet also grounds that authority in personal revelation: "I'll know my song well before I start singing" (L, 60).

The Hebrew prophet took on a public role, speaking about the moral and political health of a whole community. "A constant characteristic of Hebrew prophecy," writes Peter Southwell, "was its concern with matters of national morality and social justice, with the character of God and his purposes for Israel and all mankind" (92). At various stages in his career, Dylan's prophetic stance has been inflected in different ways: through his involvement with the civil rights movement of the early 1960s; through his explicitly Christian preaching of the late 1970s; and through the tradition of American music which gives him the words to proclaim, in 1994, that we live in a "world gone wrong." Always, however, the concern is public and, in a broad, nonpartisan sense, political. "Protest on behalf of the poor and disadvantaged," writes Blenkinsopp, ". . . is one of the most powerful strands in prophetic preaching" (5). Or, as Dylan sings on *Oh Mercy:* "We live in a political world." Again we see the paradox of im/personality: the prophet uses the authority of his personal charisma to speak to, and on behalf of, his community, his nation.

The popular image of the prophet is that of someone who foretells the future. Yet biblical prophecy is seldom concerned with prognostication, except in extremely general terms. Its true concern is with actuality, with an analysis of the present moment—though that moment is always seen within the larger context of God's plans, which certainly include the future. Prophecy, writes Dheilly, "consists of three elements: judgment upon the present, call to conversion (positive) and the threat of punishment (negative); these are concluded by the promise of deliverance and sometimes by a prospect of messianic times" (74).

This biblical balance between present and future, condemnation and promise, is carried over into the more secular and explicitly nationalist tradition of prophetic writing about America. Mark Ford links Dylan to Emerson, and claims that they share a view of America as "almost simultaneously ideal and degraded, utopian and apocalyptic"; the resut, Ford continues, is that many of Dylan's songs "might be said to continue the tradition of the American Jeremiad" (Corcoran, 136-7). In his definitive study, *The American Jeremiad,* Sacvan Bercovitch defines the jeremiad as

> a mode of public exhortation that originated in the European pul-
> pit, was transformed in both form and content by the New England
> Puritans, persisted through the eighteenth century, and helped sus-
> tain a national dream through two hundred years of turbulence and
> change. The American jeremiad was a ritual designed to join social
> criticism to spiritual renewal, public to private identity, the shifting
> "signs of the times" to certain traditional metaphors, themes, and
> symbols.
>
> (xi)

It shared with Hebrew prophecy the paradox of the speaker's im/personali-ty. The writers of jeremiads "could describe themselves as isolated representa-tives of the people—historian-seers whose representative qualities were enhanced by their hostility towards those they represented" (55). The jeremiad was the mode of Hebrew prophecy inflected through the political history of American nationalism, and its fusion of the secular and the sacred, of public and private identity, is everywhere to be found in Bob Dylan. A song like "Tears of Rage" belongs absolutely in this tradition: "We carried you in our arms on Independence Day" (L, 312). Dylan has frequently presented himself in the par-adoxical position of an "isolated representative."

Bercovitch writes:

> The traditional mode, the European jeremiad, was a lament over
> the ways of the world. It decried the sins of "the people"—a com-
> munity, a nation, a civilization, mankind in general—and warned of
> God's wrath to follow. . . . [But the Puritans saw themselves as] a
> "peculiar people," a company of Christians not only called but cho-
> sen, and chosen not only for heaven but as instruments of a sacred
> historical design. Their church-state was to be at once a model to
> the world of Reformed Christianity and a prefiguration of New

Jerusalem to come. To this end, they revised the message of the jeremiad. Not that they minimized the threat of divine retribution; on
the contrary, they asserted it with a ferocity unparalleled in the
European pulpit. But they qualified it in a way that turned threat
into celebration. In their case, they believed, God's punishments
were *corrective*, not destructive. . . . The Puritans' concept of errand
entailed a fusion of secular and sacred history. The purpose of their
jeremiads was to direct an imperiled people of God toward the
fulfillment of their destiny, to guide them individually toward salvation, and collectively toward the American city of God.

(7–9)

Thus Bercovitch defines a whole position of prophecy, in the American
social and political tradition, which might well be summed up in "Tears of
Rage," or in "Blind Willie McTell":

See the arrow on the doorpost
Saying this land is condemned
All the way from New Orleans
To New Jerusalem

To the biblical conception of the prophet, and to its particular American
inflection as the jeremiad, we must add the more strictly literary conception of
the *poet* as prophet. "At a certain stage in its development," writes Sir Maurice
Bowra, "poetry is largely concerned with the revelation of a special kind of
knowledge and is the task of prophets who get their information from the
Muses or a god or a familiar spirit or the strange voyages of their own disem-
bodied souls" (3). But Bowra too stresses that prophetic poetry is always political: "Prophetic vision differs from mystical in that it is concerned with the familiar world, and from sociological prognostications in that it moves not through
the laborious processes of analysis and calculation but through sudden moments
of illumination, when what lies beyond argument is seen in a fierce and disturbing flash of light" (6). Thus "the poet's vision is inspired by an overriding concern for mankind in its weakness or its wickedness. It is this which provokes
alike promises of ultimate felicity and warnings of annihilating doom" (13).

While the roles of poet and prophet have long been seen as analogous, the ideal of the poet as divinely inspired prophet really took off in the Romantic period, drawing on the writings of the mid-eighteenth-century critic Robert Lowth. James L. Kugel writes: "It is not much of an exaggeration to say that the great poet-prophets of Romanticism, as well as Romantic views of inspiration (and the descendants of these views, down to Surrealism and perhaps beyond), were all beneficiaries of Lowth's equation of poet and prophet" (25). This tradition began in English with William Blake, was given a specifically American inflection by Walt Whitman, and was most powerfully, for Dylan, inherited and proclaimed by Allen Ginsberg. Ginsberg's great trilogy of prophetic poems— "Howl," "Kaddish," and "The Fall of America"—synthesize the traditions of Hebrew prophecy, American jeremiad, and Romantic poetry, and bring them all immediately and forcefully into the milieu within which Bob Dylan began and continued his writing.

There has always been in Dylan's work a strong element of the prophetic stance: a sternly moralizing view of the world, a keen eye for social injustice and suffering, a demand for America to live up to its Puritan self-conception as "a city on a hill." In some of his early 1960s "protest" songs, this view could be seen as purely political; at its deepest, it has always had the added element of prophecy. Dylan's protest songs rarely espouse partisan political positions. The answer, he tells you, is there to be found, but it is "blowin' in the wind," not in the platform of any particular group or party.

This prophetic view was also shaded, right from the beginning, by an apocalyptic sense of living in the end times, initially in the quite literal form of the fear (very real in the 1950s and early 1960s) of nuclear war, and later, in the late 1970s and early 1980s, in a more traditional religious sense.[7] In more recent times Dylan's "prophetic" context is to be found not so much in the Bible or in contemporary political events, as in the whole tradition of American popular culture, and in what Greil Marcus calls "the old, weird America" (1997, 87) preserved in the idiosyncratic (and undeniably prophetic) synthesis of Harry Smith's *Anthology of American Folk Music*.[8] But if Harry Smith was a prophet, he was also, equally, a trickster. And so is Bob Dylan.

Coyote Impersonating Some Highway Rambler

The figure of the trickster has been widely studied in mythologies from around the world, from Hermes in ancient Greece to the Monkey King in China. In the stories of the native peoples of North America, the trickster turns up most often as Coyote, though on the West Coast he is Raven—"at my window with a broken wing" (L, 167). The most comprehensive recent study is Lewis Hyde's *Trickster Makes This World* (1998).

Trickster, says Hyde, "is the mythic embodiment of ambiguity and ambivalence, doubleness and duplicity, contradiction and paradox" (7). He is a transgressive force, a crosser of borders, a disrupter of order. He plays practical jokes—often obscene—and lies behind the workings of malign chance; Coyote is the divine agent of Murphy's Law. He fools others, yet is also fooled himself. As often as not, Coyote ends up as the butt of his own jokes. Yet he is also a Creator, a bringer of culture. He is the element of the unexpected, of productive change, which any culture needs in order to avoid rigidity and stagnation. Coyote brings life, and then shits in your watering hole.

The role of the trickster is, in some ways, similar to that of the prophet—both are messengers, both cross borders between the human and the divine—but while the prophet ultimately speaks to stability, the trickster exists precisely to disrupt that stability. Thus he seems at times almost like a parody of the prophet, or the prophet's black-comedy flipside. The prophet embodies what is most consistent and abiding in Dylan's career, while the trickster represents the constant shifts and changes, the underminings and reinventions, which have for over forty years kept that career dynamic and unpredictable. Dylan's 1981 song "Jokerman" is an almost systematic catalog of the trickster's reliance on "contradiction and paradox."

More specifically, three aspects of trickster mythology are especially apt for Dylan: (1) he is constantly in motion, (2) he is a thief, and (3) he is a master of disguises and changing identities.

In the Coyote stories, Coyote is almost always traveling. Rarely is he presented as being at home in one place. Hyde comments:

> To say simply that trickster lives on the road doesn't give the full nuance of the case, for the impression one often gets is that trickster travels around *aimlessly*. . . . Maybe the point of saying that

trickster is on the road is to say that he has "the context of no context," in George W. S. Trow's wonderful phrase. To be in a particular town or city is to be situated; to be on the road is to be between
situations.

(39)

Three times in six lines, Hyde uses the phrase "on the road," which of course
echoes the title of Jack Kerouac's novel of the same name, the definitive text of
the Beat Generation.9 Dylan has frequently acknowledged his debt to Kerouac;
a song on *Bringing It All Back Home* is explicitly called "On the Road Again."10
Images of travel are everywhere in Dylan's songs, which are populated by rov-
ing gamblers, by young men on a train going west, by older men who have
"been all around this world," by unknown riders approaching, and by singers
bidding a "restless farewell." And Dylan's recent commitment to incessant,
worldwide touring may seem in its way "aimless," an urge to be always "between
situations."

In 1971, after watching Dylan perform at the benefit concert for
Bangladesh—one of his rare appearances in the reclusive years between 1966
and 1974—and hearing him perform "Blowin' in the Wind" for the first time in
years, Jonathon Cott wrote in *Rolling Stone* magazine (September 2, 1971):
"What was this new incarnation? Lazarus rising from our dead memories?
Coyote impersonating some highway rambler? Was he really singing the lines
no one ever expected to hear him sing again?" Cott is exactly right to invoke
Coyote here, and to place him both on the highway ("on the road again") and
as an impersonator: a master of disguise, and a thief.

Why Must I Always Be the Thief?

The trickster is always in between, in what anthropologists call "liminal" situations. He is found at the border, the hinge, the crossroads. According to Hyde,
he is

> the adept who can move between heaven and earth, and between
> the living and the dead. As such, he is sometimes the messenger of
> the gods and sometimes the guide of souls. . . . Sometimes it hap-
> pens that the road between heaven and earth is not open, where-

upon trickster travels not as a messenger but as a thief, the one who steals from the gods the good things that humans need if they are to survive in this world.

(6)

So Prometheus stealing fire is a trickster, and also a creator of culture. Trickster "isn't a run-of-the-mill liar and thief. When he lies and steals, it isn't so much to get away with something or get rich as to disturb the established categories of truth and property and, by so doing, open the road to possible new worlds" (Hyde, 13).

Dylan has always been fascinated by the figure of the thief, and it is one of his recurring images for himself, which helps to explain the title of his recent album, *"Love and Theft."* He has always been attracted to the genre of the outlaw ballad, and the antiheroes of the American tradition appear throughout his work: Jesse James, Billy the Kid, Pretty Boy Floyd, John Wesley Hardin[g]. "Yes, I am a thief of thoughts," Dylan acknowledges in "11 Outlined Epitaphs" (L, 112), discussing his extensive intertextual borrowings, and looking forward to his 2001 title. In "Positively 4th Street" he envisages himself as a "master thief" (L, 211), while the chorus of "Tears of Rage" returns repeatedly to the self-addressed question "Why must I always be the thief?" (L, 312). And in "All Along the Watchtower," he juxtaposes two aspects of the trickster figure by staging a symbolic dialogue between a joker and a thief.

In few of these cases is the thief seen simply as criminal, but rather as productive, redemptive, even sacrificial. In the words of one of Dylan's most often-quoted lines, "To live outside the law, you must be honest" (L, 233). Theft is necessary transgression.[11] Hyde quotes Plato, from the *Cratylus*, meditating on the origins of the Greek trickster Hermes: "I should imagine that the name Hermes has to do with speech, and signifies that he is the interpreter *hermeneus*, or messenger, or thief, or liar, or bargainer; all that sort of thing has a great deal to do with language" (Hyde, 75). Note here how close *messenger* (the traditional role of the prophet) is to *thief.* All of these are liminal states: in between, at the hinge, at the Hermetic crossroads. Prophet and trickster both stand between worlds, crossing the borders back and forth, carrying with them their contraband cargo—which may be fire, or even, as Plato suggests, language itself.

One of the constitutive features of human language, as opposed to less complex sign systems, is its ability to lie. Hyde quotes Umberto Eco: "A sign is everything which can be taken as significantly substituting for something else. . . . Thus semiotics is in principle the discipline studying everything *which can be used in order to lie*" (Hyde, 60). So substitution, or theft, becomes the basis for language, and trickster, as thief, the inventor of language. "Both lying and thieving," Hyde notes, "multiply meanings" (65).

Again we return to the paradox of the necessary coexistence of the prophet and the trickster. The prophet proclaims the truth; the trickster tells lies. Yet both are, in their way, Hermeneutic messengers, speaking across the borderline, testifying to their privileged insights. "Trickster discovers creative fabulation, feigning, and fibbing, the playful construction of fictive worlds," Hyde writes. "It is trickster who invents the gratuitous untruth" (45). And in his fictive constructions, in his multiplying of meanings, trickster too attests that he will stand on the ocean until he starts sinking, but will know his song well before he starts singing.

A Face like a Mask

Precisely because he is so often a liar, a thief, or a player of practical jokes, it is necessary for Coyote—who is, like Bob Dylan, a great survivor—to be also a master of disguise. He is frequently presented as assuming other forms, changing his skin, imitating other animals. Hyde describes the trickster as "polytropic," a Greek word meaning "turning many ways, wily, versatile, much-traveled" (52). This ability, Hyde says, "raises serious puzzles about identity" (53). He compares the trickster to Herman Melville's Confidence Man, who

> appears in a series of masks and roles, never as himself. That being the case, can we rightly say he has a self? And if he does, how can we describe that self with any, well, confidence? . . . With some polytropic characters it is possible that there is no real self behind the shifting masks, or that the real self lies exactly there, in the moving surfaces and not beneath.
>
> (53–54)

All of which sounds very much like the man who took on the mask, or alias, of Bob Dylan.

The question of identity has been central to Dylan's career ever since its foundational gesture, Robert Zimmerman's assumption of the name "Bob Dylan." It is now a critical commonplace to speak of the ways in which Dylan has "reinvented" himself—as protest-folksinger, as Dionysiac rocker, as down-home country gentleman, as born-again preacher, as inveterate touring performer, as the living inheritance of the blues—each pose or invention being a new hypothesis of identity. "Can we rightly say he has a self?" Hyde asks, and the textual answer is No. What Dylan has always presented to us is a succession of "shifting masks" and "moving surfaces," or, in his own words, a "series of dreams." Identity, for Dylan, is always hidden: "Everybody's wearing a disguise / To hide what they've got left behind their eyes" (L, 393)—or, in the ubiquitous pun, behind their I's.

This trickster's play with identity is reflected, literally, in Dylan's fondness for *images of the self at one remove*, the self which is itself but not quite itself—rather, identity as doubled, divided, or deferred. These images include alias, mask, mirror, shadow, brother, ghost, and all the echo-effects of allusion and quotation. All of this book can be read as an extended meditation on these images, several of which are discussed in more detail in individual sections of Chapter 2. But what all of them have in common is the way in which identity is never unproblematic, never quite identical with itself. Identity is always something that comes back *from* the 'other,' reflection or shadow; identity is always constructed *for* the 'other,' mask or disguise.

In these three respects at least, then—as the highway rambler constantly on the road; as the culture-bringing thief; as the master of disguise whose identity is always in doubt—Dylan throughout his career has played the role of trickster. But remember that the trickster maintains a constant dialogue with the prophet, and thus the aesthetic stance which most fully defines Dylan must always be seen as an interplay between the two.[12] The prophet gives him the moral gravity and consistency which have sustained him through a career which is now, in the most apparently ephemeral of media, exceeding forty years. The trickster provides the stimulus of the unexpected renewal which has kept that career as dynamic now as it was when Robert Zimmerman first stumbled out of the Midwest and entered his alias.

"When the Ship Comes In"

In 1964, when I first heard "When the Ship Comes In" (L, 100–01), I interpreted it as a kind of love song. It seemed to speak of a moment of overwhelming happiness, when nature itself was transformed—all those laughing fish and smiling seagulls—and the whole environment shared in the exultant joy of two lovers coming together. Nothing could stop them:

> the words that are used
> For to get the ship confused
> Will not be understood when they're spoken.
> For the chains of the sea
> Will have busted in the night
> And will be buried at the bottom of the ocean.

I loved the exuberance of the colloquial *busted* as much as I loved its alliteration with *buried.* Even the shout of triumph over defeated "foes" in the final stanza seemed to be only the exaltation of young love overcoming all obstacles. What registered most strongly with me was the *mood* of the song: its exhilaration, its triumph, its happiness.

In other words, I ignored—despite its context within a very political album—all the public implications of the text, and chose to understand it as a purely personal exclamation. But, while I'm still partly convinced by this early reading, I do now see other dimensions to the song.

One is, alas, biographical. I say "alas" because this is not the most edifying Bob Dylan anecdote. In an interview with Anthony Scaduto, Joan Baez recalled that Dylan composed the song after an incident in which a hotel had refused to confirm to him a reservation in her name because he looked too scruffy. "He wrote it that night, took him exactly one evening to write it, he was so pissed. . . . I couldn't believe it, to get back at those idiots so fast" (Scaduto, 208). In this context, the song is the petty expression of spite in revenge for an equally petty expression of social snobbery. It's an almost perfect example of the inadequacy of biographical "explanations." The song goes so far beyond its occasion that the discrepancy is ludicrous. Tracing the song back to its origin provides only a definition of "reductiveness."

Except that the idea of "revenge," however petty, restores to the song an edge of vindictiveness which my initial reading of it as a joyful love song had certainly dulled. It *is* a rather mean and nasty song. There is a vindictive joy in its picture of those who "like Pharaoh's tribe / Will be drownded in the tide"; the emphasis on "pinch themselves and squeal" delights in even the smallest manifestation of physical pain. This sense of revenge becomes more resonant, however, when it is related to the intertextual model: Bertold Brecht's "Pirate Jenny."

In this song too, a mysterious ship—a "black freighter"—appears in a harbor. Its appearance signals a wholesale orgy of vengeful violence against the inhabitants of the town, with one woman (the singer of the song) determining who should die and who (none at all, it appears) should live. In Brecht, the song has implications of political revolution; the victims are clearly the bourgeoisie, and the avenging angel is more a representative of the militant proletariat than anyone with a purely private grudge. Seen in this context, Dylan's song more than ever transcends the circumstances of a private spite against a supercilious hotel staff. It becomes the expression of the triumph of a long-downtrodden oppressed class. The references to Pharaoh become more precise: here are the Children of Israel escaping their Egyptian bondage, both literally and in the time-honored metaphorical identification between the Jews and America's black slaves: "Let my people go."

"When the Ship Comes In" thus becomes a civil rights song, one worthy of being offered to Joan Baez—though there is still a lingering personal irony in the fact that the person who introduced Dylan to Brecht was his previous and by now abandoned girlfriend, Suze Rotolo.

But if Brecht is the most obvious intertextual inspiration for the song, there is also another linguistic context for it: namely, that it is another of Dylan's many explorations and rephrasings of common clichés. "When my ship comes in" is a common phrase, expressing the anticipation of wealth and success to come. It derives quite literally from the days when mercantile investments depended on the safe arrival of ship cargoes. B. J. Leggett comments:

> We know that the phrase is associated with long-awaited success and, even more pertinent to an apocalyptic text, that it is associated with the dream of a triumph that may never come—people who use the phrase are typically those whose ships will never come in. . . . That is, the phrase brings with it a wish-fulfillment element that the song extends with its own fantasy of laughing fishes and smiling gulls—one day all our troubles will be over, it says, but we need not be too specific about how or when this will take place.
>
> (156–57)

The cliché, then, subtly undermines the whole song. By its evocation of a "wish-fulfillment . . . fantasy" that may never actually happen, it *defers* the conclusion of both the love song (the ecstatic union of the lovers) and the revenge song (the satisfactory comeuppance of everyone from hotel clerks to Pharaoh's tribe). What matters is the desire itself, not any possible accomplishment of the desire. Indeed, psychoanalytic critics like Jacques Lacan argue that desire never can be fulfilled, that it always renews itself, as the movement of desire, beyond any apparent conclusion. And such an impulse of desire is the driving force of narrative itself, indeed of language.

Dylan's song always looks forward to the hour "when the ship comes in"—right to the last line, all the verbs are in the future tense—because it is never an event which can be regarded as accomplished or completed. The song, dashed off in an evening of feeling "pissed," must always remain open-ended and future—like love, and like the revolution.

chapter 2
Glossary

Alias

> *If I'm writ on your books, love,*
> *Just you blot out my name.*

"Waggoner's Lad" (trad.)[1]

I have spoken in Chapter 1 of Dylan's fondness for images of the self at one remove: alias, mask, mirror, shadow, ghost. Of all these images, perhaps the most fundamental is the *alias*, the definition of identity through the assumption of a new name.[2]

Bob Dylan came out of a milieu in which he was surrounded by instances of renaming. Even the name of the town in which Bobby Zimmerman grew up—the groundplan, as it were, for the geography of his imagination—is an alias: Hibbing, the assumed name of Franz Dietrich von Ahlen. Bob's mother's maiden name, Stone, had been changed by her father from the original Solemovitz. Such renamings were common among immigrant communities. Whether by deliberate choice, as gestures of assimilation, or by the chance impositions of immigration officials at Ellis Island, thousands of European immigrants changed their names to American forms. In their book *The Language of Names*, Justin Kaplan and Anne Bernays further note that for many Jewish families "conventional, fixed family naming was a relatively new thing. It dated from the late eighteenth and nineteenth centuries and had been forced on them by civil authorities [in Europe]" (57). So the surname was always potentially unstable.[3]

However, none of this context lessens the importance of the adoption of a pseudonym as the foundational moment of Bob Dylan's career. For him, it was more than a matter of convenience. It was a far-reaching gesture of self-definition, rooting his identity and signature in an archetypal trickster's move of self-disguise. But how, in the first place, did it actually happen?

The most commonly accepted version of the story is that in October 1959 young Bobby Zimmerman walked into a Minneapolis coffeehouse called the Ten O'Clock Scholar, looking for a job. The owner, David Lee, asked him his name, and on the spur of the moment he answered "Bob Dylan." Telling this story in later years, Dylan insisted that the name just popped into his head, and that there was no conscious intention of echoing the name of the great Welsh poet Dylan Thomas.

This version has been treated with a good deal of skepticism. Zimmerman had already shown a fondness for pseudonyms, appearing on stage, both in Hibbing and on tour with Bobby Vee, under the name Elston Gunn.[4] It seems more probable that he had the new alias prepared well before going to the coffeehouse, possibly before he had even left Hibbing. Dylan's childhood friend John Bucklen remembers Bob telling him that the name was indeed derived from the Welsh poet, and his girlfriend Echo Helstrom claimed that Bob was using it as early as 1958, and that he explained it to her by showing her a book of Dylan Thomas's poetry. (Daniel Karlin skeptically notes that Echo's story "seems to have been refined over the years" (Corcoran, 42).)

Alternative versions, especially those which remain skeptical about Dylan Thomas, also favour alternative spellings. In 1966 Dylan said that the name came from an uncle on his mother's side of the family who spelled it "Dillon" or perhaps "Dillion." Genealogical research on the Zimmerman and Stone families has failed to uncover any such relation, though there was indeed a pioneer family called Dillon in the Hibbing area. There has also been some speculation about the influence of the character Matt Dillon from the TV western series "Gunsmoke." This explanation is far from improbable. There is ample evidence in Dylan's later work of his interest in westerns, from *Pat Garrett & Billy the Kid* to "Brownsville Girl."

Another possibility relates the name to an American football player called none other than Bobby Dillon.[5] In Hibbing in the 1950s, before the Minnesota Vikings, the NFL "home team" would have been the Green Bay Packers from

Wisconsin. And throughout Zimmerman's teenage years, the star defensive back for the Green Bay Packers was Bobby Dillon.[6] Dillon was not just a run-of-the-mill journeyman football player. He was a major star, and it is impossible to conceive of any teenage boy in Minnesota who did not know his name. There is even one notable occasion—the opening of a new stadium at Green Bay in 1957—when the guest of honor was the "Gunsmoke" actor James Arness. So both Dillons, Bobby and Matt, were on the field at the same time, two years before the Ten O'Clock Scholar, and one year before he announced the name to Echo.

Then again, given Bobby Zimmerman's obsessive and well-documented interest in James Dean, we should not discount a 1956 pop single called "The Ballad of James Dean." The singer was, like Bob Dylan and James Dean himself, a midwesterner. His name was Dylan Todd.

There remains at least the possible scenario that the alias began as Dillon. The "Gunsmoke" character may be there in the background, but the echo of his own name, "Bobby," suggests that the football player, Bobby Dillon, would have been a more immediate influence (with Dylan Todd somewhere in the background). At some stage, either in Hibbing or in his early university days in Minneapolis, he would then have decided to change the spelling to "Dylan," in which case it is very likely that the Welsh poet was in his mind, if not when he originally adopted the name, then at least when he changed the spelling.

In the absence of reliable evidence, however, this scenario must remain a hypothetical speculation, albeit a tempting one, rather than a statement of fact. It is equally likely that, as John Bucklen and Echo Helstrom remember, he was Welsh-poet-Dylan right from the start and that all the "Dillon" references are further trickster moves of deflection and disguise, falsifying even the false name.

For Bobby Zimmerman in 1959, fresh out of Hibbing, the particular name he chose was perhaps less important than the simple gesture of assuming a new name. It was part of an extended program of self-recreation, along with the way he dressed, the way he talked, and the stories (largely fictional) he told about his past. "Bob Dylan" became the seal and signature of his new persona: it sealed him off definitively from Hibbing, from Robert Zimmerman, and from his father, Abraham Zimmerman. It was the signature that guaranteed the authenticity of what he had become. The name "Bob Dylan" is Bob Dylan's first and most enduring work of art.[7]

The choosing of a new name is also, necessarily, the repudiation of an old one. In a case like Dylan's—retaining the given name, changing the surname—it is specifically the rejection of the name of the father. It is not my intention here to undertake any Freudian speculations on the basis of Robert Zimmerman's actual biography. Far too little is known about the relations between him and his father for such dubious exercises in amateur psychoanalysis to be anything other than irresponsible.[8]

But there are repeated images and motifs in Dylan's *writing* (not his life) which might be seen as textual traces of an Oedipal conflict. Such moments include the intriguing evocation of Oedipus in *Tarantula;* the figure of the failed or dying father in many of the "outlaw" songs; and most obviously, Dylan's compulsive reenactment of the patriarchal father Abraham trying to kill his son in literally hundreds of concert performances of "Highway 61 Revisited." Highway 61 leads from Duluth, where Robert Zimmerman was born, down the Mississippi valley through Memphis to New Orleans. Traveling down Highway 61, then, Bob Dylan moves from an actual father to a metaphorical one, from Abraham Zimmerman in Hibbing down to the deepest roots of American song—folk, gospel, blues—which were to become the sources of his music. In a sense this song, this journey, *has to* start with a lethal confrontation with the name of the father—"God said to Abraham, 'Kill me a son' "—so that it can allow the son to continue, surviving in his pseudonym.

Our society's conventional notion of the proper name, especially the surname, ties the use of the word *proper* to the idea of "property." The proper name is the signal of inheritance, the name which guarantees the handing down of property from generation to generation—especially from father to son. For the proper name as surname is always the Name of the Father:[9] the patriarchal name of male succession. Hence the force which accrues to its denial—the breaking of taboo—in the assumption of an alias.

The name is thought of as property also in the sense that it is "my own," it belongs to me. It has a unique reference, it names *only* me, it is proper(ty) to me. Common nouns and names refer to many diverse things, so there is always a sense that the relationship between word and thing is precarious, arbitrary, open to (mis)interpretation. But the proper noun or name refers, we would like to believe, only to one thing or person; it is a signal of self-identity, of a personal *presence*. The divisions of language[10] do not apply to the proper name. I and my name are one.

However, these assumptions prove to be rather tenuous, and susceptible to deconstructive analysis, even for the ordinary "proper name," let alone the alias. A name may perhaps have a unique reference, but it can never be a unique instance. The name works only by repetition, that is, by the possibility of its repetition in another context. The name depends upon the possibility of some other person recognizing you by your name *again*. Like any other linguistic sign, a name has to be able to operate in the *absence* both of its referent and of its originator. Far from being a guarantee of presence, the proper name is dependent upon absence. Further, by being repeatable—not just in the sense that it *can* be repeated, but that it *must* be repeated—the proper name necessarily leaves itself open to all kinds of *im*proper uses: forgery, mistaken identification, citation in contexts far outside the control of the name-bearer.

The name is never identical with its bearer, because the name can still be cited (quoted, praised, abused, misused, given all glory or taken in vain) not only in the bearer's simple absence but in his absolute absence, his death. In a 1977 interview with Allen Ginsberg, Dylan said, "Nobody's Bob Dylan. Bobby Dylan's long gone. . . . Let's say that in real life Bob Dylan fixes his name on the public. He can retrieve that name at will. Anything else the public makes of it is its business" (Ginsberg 1989, 28). I think that Dylan is right to realize that his name, like all names, is "long gone"; but I think he is naive to suppose that anyone can "retrieve that name at will."

The name, then, is always in process. It asserts identity—it even *creates* identity—but it can never do so as anything fixed or controlled. The name must always be repeated, and repeated in new contexts in which its signification will shift. In this sense, the alias, far from being an exceptional category of naming, is the defining and foundational category. And similarly, of all Bob Dylan's aliases, the most instructive is the one he adopts in Sam Peckinpah's film *Pat Garrett & Billy the Kid*, where his alias is "Alias."

Usually an alias substitutes one name for another: "Bob Dylan" for "Robert Allen Zimmerman." But in Peckinpah's film the alias is doubled, because the name "Alias" refers not only to a character but also to itself as the process of naming and renaming, the gesture of displaced and disguised identity. In this process of substitution, one name slides into another, refusing to fix on any single name as authoritative or originary. What the name Alias denotes is the improperness of the proper name. More extreme than a simple pseudonym, it rejects not only the name of the father, but also the possibility of founding a new patronymic.

The alias is the archetypal gesture of *identity at one remove*—Dylan's trickster fascination with a sense of identity as always being elusive, always one step to the side of itself, always resisting the imposition of, in this case, the Name of the Father. As Alias, Bob Dylan is always someone else, always a deferral, always a ghost.

Another improper use of the proper name is to use it as if it were, indeed and after all, a common noun. Many names originated as common descriptions— once upon a time there was a Baker who actually baked bread—whose force was lost as they became absorbed into the institution of the proper name. But this process can always be reversed. "[The name's] inscription in language," writes Jacques Derrida, "always affects it with a potential for meaning, and for no longer being proper once it has a meaning . . . once it is reinvested with semantic content" (1984, 120).

So, if the assumption of an alias is one way to declare one's independence from the father's name, another way would be to render the name no longer proper by reinvesting it with semantic content. I propose, then, to round out this section with a brief discussion of the name that Bob Dylan left behind him, the name the alias replaced: Zimmerman.

The only direct appearance of the name Zimmerman in the text of Bob Dylan's writings is in the song "Gotta Serve Somebody," where it appears in diminutive form as "Zimmy." But here the whole point is that it *is* being used as a proper name—and it is on that basis that I discuss it in the section "Signature" later in this chapter. What happens, though, when "Zimmerman" ceases to be a proper name—when the word is returned to its common sense, in German, *Zimmermann* as "carpenter"?[11]

Actual carpenters are few and far between in Dylan's work. Indeed, there are only two major instances—and one of these is in a traditional song not written by Dylan, and of which there is only one documented performance. That is the ballad "House Carpenter," recorded in 1961 and finally released on *The Bootleg Series* thirty years later. In this ballad, the female protagonist is "married to a house carpenter," but is tempted away to the sea, and ultimately to her death, by the demonic ghost of a former lover.[12] The lover represents the dangerous, and indeed fatal, attractions of romance, travel, life on the road, forbidden relations. The carpenter represents safe, conventional married life: home, children, family, respectability—who could be more respectable, more devoted to the construction of a home, than a carpenter? In the song, the carpenter is the one who is left behind—just as "Bob Dylan" left "Zimmerman" behind in Hibbing as he followed the demon lover of his art and career off to Minneapolis and New York. Dylan's point of identification in this performance is certainly with the woman—and what he identifies with most is her eternal rejection of the fate of being a *Zimmermann*.

In Dylan's writing, the major occurrence of the translated name occurs in "Tangled Up In Blue," when the singer, reflecting on "All the people we used to know," states that "Some are mathematicians / Some are carpenter's *[sic]* wives" (L, 359). In the complex narrative of that song, identities and pronouns are more than usually fluid. The protagonist is sometimes "he" and sometimes "I"; the narrative sometimes suggests autobiographical elements, but other parts of it are clearly fictional. But in certain restricted senses, it would not be impossible to read this "carpenter's wife" as, quite literally, Mrs. Zimmerman. Indeed, Dylan himself has somewhat perversely encouraged this reading by the fact that, in most performances of this song since his divorce, he has changed the phrase to "truckdrivers' wives."[13] Once again, the Zimmerman is left behind.

Carpenter also carries obvious religious implications: like Jesus, son of Joseph, Robert Zimmerman was both a carpenter and a carpenter's son. None of the songs of Dylan's religious period refers directly to Christ as a carpenter, but this association does operate in the background of both the previously cited songs. In "House Carpenter," the woman is torn between damnation (the ghost of her former lover) and salvation (the carpenter who is her present husband). The roles may clearly be read allegorically as those of Satan and Christ. "Tangled Up In Blue" also suggests, somewhat more tenuously, an analogy between its protagonist and Christ. He works as a fisherman out of the port of Delacroix—literally, "of the Cross." A woman stoops to "tie the laces of [his] shoe" (L, 358)—like Mary Magdalene washing the feet of Jesus, like John the Baptist proclaiming that "There cometh one mightier than I after me, the latchet of whose shoes I am not worthy to stoop down and unloose" (Mark 1:7).[14] So if one possible reason for the change from "carpenter" to "truckdriver" is Dylan's 1978 divorce, another possible reason is his 1979 conversion: "carpenter's wife," as a reference to the Virgin Mary, may simply have seemed inappropriate, or even blasphemous.

But if *Zimmermann* as "carpenter" is rare in Dylan's work, its German root—*Zimmer* (room)—is everywhere. Dylan's songs are full of rooms: hotel rooms, haunted rooms, empty rooms, mirrored rooms (L, 300, 350, 403, 364). Often, again, they are places that he has left behind and looks back to. In "Bob Dylan's Dream," the already-old youthful protagonist wishes that he and his friends "could sit simply in that room again" (L, 62). In "One Too Many Mornings," "I turn my head back to the room / Where my love and I have laid" (L, 94). In "Wedding Song," "I've said goodbye to haunted rooms" (L, 350). Rooms are places of danger—the "felony room" (L, 244)—or of betrayal—when his lover leaves him, he knows he can find her "in somebody's room" (L, 356). The room may even be the site of death—"When the shadow comes creepin' in your room" (L, 73)—and it invites the obvious rhyme: "your room, his tomb" (L, 212).

As late as *Time Out Of Mind*, the room is still a dominant image, still associated with restriction and abandonment. "I've been pacing round the room, hoping maybe she come back," he sings in "Dirt Road Blues." "I've been praying for salvation, laying round in a one-room country shack." Most ominously, in "Not Dark Yet," "there's not even room enough to be anywhere." Here "room" is the very condition of existence, and it too has been taken away. There is no longer any room, any *Zimmer*, any Zimmerman. The name itself, whether patronymic or alias, has been lost.

Mask

> *He had a face like a mask . . .*
>
> "Man in the Long Black Coat"

Right at the beginning of Dylan's career, the mask makes a curiously accidental appearance. The famous review that Robert Shelton wrote for the *New York Times* (September 28, 1961) contains the phrase "his musicmaking has the mark of originality and inspiration."[15] When this review was reprinted on the back cover of Dylan's first album, *mark* was misprinted as *mask*. Bob Dylan has been wearing the mask of originality ever since.

Greek and Roman theater used the mask both to conceal identity and to express character. The mask hid the face of the actor, whose individuality was unimportant: he existed only to serve the role. At the same time, the stylized designs of the mask gave expression to the dramatic reality of the fictional character. Actor and character coexisted as each other's doubles; the voice was the ghost within the mask. Since the Latin word for mask, *persona,* evolved into the English *person,* the image of the mask is at the root of all ideas about personality and identity.

Dylan has commented on the classical mask:

> A long time ago they used to have these Greek plays . . . they had actors too, but they called them hypocrites. That's right. It'd be like a play, you know, like there'd be a play with about 30 people in it, but actually there'd be only four. They'd all just wear masks; they *[Dylan pretends to recite in a high pitched voice . . . to the crowd]* talk in another voice, and they'd just wear a mask. So four people could play the part of 30 people. That's a heavy responsibility. Keeps you on your toes. Never know who you are.[16]

In this particular context, Dylan puts a moralizing spin on the idea, emphasizing the etymological identity of *actor* and *hypocrite,* but what clearly concerns him is the problematic relation between the mask and identity. The mask multiplies identity—four people can play thirty parts—and thus puts identity itself into doubt—"Never know who you are." The mask enables identity itself to become an artistic construct.

In the same way, Ezra Pound used the classical mask, the *persona,*[17] as an image for what the poet does in the act of writing:

> In the "search for oneself," in the search for "sincere self-expression," one gropes, one finds some seeming verity. One says "I am" this, that, or the other, and with the words scarcely uttered one ceases to be that thing.
>
> I began this search for the real in a book called *Personae,* casting off, as it were, complete masks of the self in each poem. I continued in a long series of translations, which were but more elaborate masks.

These words provide an uncannily accurate description of the early Dylan "casting off"—the term means both *creating* and *discarding*—the masks of himself as protest singer, rock star, country gentleman, before embarking on the "translations" of other people's songs which he released in 1970 under the paradoxical title *Self Portrait.* And at various later stages in his career, especially during the 1990s, Dylan has returned to the idea of the "cover version" as both translation and mask.

There has always been an element of the Poundian *persona* in Dylan's work. In a strictly limited sense, a *persona* is an adopted voice: a poem in which the poet, though writing in the first person, is manifestly taking on the role of a fictional character. Famous examples include Robert Browning's "My Last Duchess," T. S. Eliot's "The Love Song of J. Alfred Prufrock," and Pound's "Homage to Sextus Propertius." In this strict sense, there are only a few prominent examples in Dylan—the miner's widow who sings "North Country Blues," the Mexican gunman who narrates "Romance in Durango"—but what Dylan will also do more subtly is to insert fictional details into apparently autobiographical texts. He thus problematizes any easy assumption of direct biographical reference and invites us to see the "I" of his songs, always, as a *persona,* as a mask. For example, the "sincere self-expression" of "Idiot Wind" must always be placed in the context of the blatant fictionality of the presentation of the "I" in the song's opening lines:

> They say I shot a man named Gray and took his wife to Italy,
> She inherited a million bucks and when she died it came to me.
> I can't help it if I'm lucky.

> (L, 367)

A few years later, as a member of the Traveling Wilburys, Dylan twisted this ironic fiction back against itself by adopting "Lucky" as another alias: fictionally claiming for himself an identity already marked as fictional, and wearing a mask which was openly acknowledged as a mask. "Keeps you on your toes," indeed. "Never know who you are." To say the least, it would never be safe to assume that the "I" of a Bob Dylan song is, in any unproblematical sense, "Bob Dylan."

Pound's use of quotation marks indicates a degree of skepticism about such phrases as "search for oneself" and "sincere self-expression." Later, postmodernist theory would argue strongly against any concept of the 'self' as a transcendent subject somehow preexisting discourse; rather, the 'self' is produced in and by discourse, in an act which Judith Butler specifically defines as "performance." Again, one comes back to Bob Dylan's supreme performative act: the *naming* of his own mask as an alias.

The mask always casts identity into doubt. To say "I am" something is already to cease to be that something. Bob Dylan has made frequent comments on the instability and indeterminacy of his projected identity. His 1983 song "I and I" explicitly thematizes the mask of divided identity and relates it to the indivisibility of God: "Jaweh, I AM THAT I AM" (Exodus 3:14). In a 1985 interview he commented, in relation to this song:

> Sometimes the "you" in my songs is me talking to me. Other times I can be talking to somebody else. . . . It's up to you to figure out who's who. A lot of times it's "you" talking to "you." The "I," like in "I and I," also changes. It could be I or it could be the "I" who created me. And also, it could be another person who's saying "I." When I say "I" right now, I don't know who I'm talking about.
>
> (Cohen 1985, 39)

The result is that the personal pronouns in Bob Dylan's songs tend to be highly mobile and indeterminate in reference. The most famous example is the shifting of the narration in "Tangled Up In Blue" between first and third persons, but there is also, always, a good deal of ambiguity in the address of "you." Anthony Scaduto quotes Dylan as saying, "when I used words like 'he' and 'it' and 'they' and talking about other people, I was really talking about nobody but me" (249).

In late 1985 Dylan commented, "I don't think of myself as Bob Dylan. It's like Rimbaud said, 'I is another.'"[18] "Bob Dylan," then, is not a secure statement of identity; the assumed name is the mask of the other. "It's Halloween," Dylan announced to a New York audience on October 31, 1964: "I have my Bob Dylan mask on." The context of the date specifically places the whole notion of identity within the carnivalesque tradition of acting and masking. Eleven years later, at another Halloween concert (October 31, 1975; Plymouth, Massachusetts), Dylan again wore a mask on stage, this time literally. The performance was filmed, and became the opening scene of *Renaldo and Clara*.

In *Rolling Thunder Logbook,* Sam Shepard gives a detailed account of the mask-effect at this concert:

> Tonight Dylan appears in a rubber Dylan mask that he'd picked up on 42nd Street. The crowd is stupefied. A kind of panic-stricken hush falls over the place. "Has he had another accident? Plastic surgery?" Or is this some kind of mammoth hoax? An impostor! The voice sounds the same. If it is a replacement, he's doing a good job. He goes through three or four songs with the thing on, then reaches for the harmonica. He tries to play it through the mask but it won't work, so he rips it off and throws it back into the floodlights. There he is in the flesh and blood! The real thing! A face-lift supreme! It's a frightening act even if it's not calculated for those reasons. The audience is totally bewildered and still wondering if this is actually him or not.
>
> (1977, 114)

As a dramatist, Shepard responds to the theatricality of the gesture and gives a brilliant analysis of the effect it might have on the audience—who are, not coincidentally, listening to a song which contains the line "You can almost think that you're seein' double" (L, 300). But the memory of the 1964 concert may have colored Shepard's reading of this mask. Other accounts describe it as not a Bob Dylan mask but a Richard Nixon mask, and both the film and the photograph in Shepard's book tend to confirm this identification. Either way, whether the outline of the face was Dylan or Nixon, this mask was semi-transparent. It did not really hide the face beneath it. Like the classical *persona,* the mask not only disguises but also gives expression to the man who wears it. This mask is, in the film, the character of Renaldo. And through Renaldo's transparent mask, the audience sees the face, the other mask, of Bob Dylan.

A great deal of *Renaldo and Clara* depends upon masks, disguises, assumed names, and shifting identities—all the trickster's strategies. The film revels in the theatrical traditions both of the classical mask and of the *commedia dell'arte* whiteface. In one of the many interviews he gave in relation to the film, Dylan was asked whether his obsession with such motifs didn't amount to evasiveness, a refusal of commitment. Dylan's answer is pure Coyote:

Ah, evasiveness is all in the mind. It's about what is beneath the mask. The mask in this movie isn't used to hide the inner self, it's used to show the inner self. The mask is more real than the face. It isn't hiding anything.[19]

"The mask is more real than the face": as good a one-line summary as could be found for the problem of identity in Bob Dylan.

Another suggestive commentary on masks is given by Derrida, who emphasizes that the mask is also a sign of death: "every mask announces the mortuary mask." For Derrida, "the mask dissimulates everything *save* (whence the blind and jealous fascination it exercises) the naked eyes, the only part of the face at once seeable, therefore, and seeing, the only sign of living nakedness that one believes to be shielded or exempt from old age and ruin" (1993, 72–73). Or as Bob Dylan puts it: "Everybody's wearing a disguise / To hide what they've got left behind their eyes" (L, 393).

The mask's eyeholes are both essential to its effect (enabling the wearer to see) and the exception to its effect (the one part of the face that is *not* hidden). Thus the eyes too take part in the mask's play of identity, not least through the central pun on *eye* and *I.* Eyes occur extremely frequently in Dylan's lyrics,[20] and there always exists the possibility of hearing the double meaning *I:* "My eyes are hazy"; "breaking my eyes"; "my warehouse eyes"; "eyes behind the mirror"; "one dying eye"; "violence in the eyes"; "a man who had no eyes." Many of these references involve problematic vision: the instability of the eye/I, or the uncertain mirroring of "looking in my baby's eyes" (L, 411). "A million faces at my feet," the singer reflects on his audience, "and all I see are dark eyes" (L, 500). But in "Highlands," the last song of *Time Out Of Mind,* he claims a tentative renewal: "I got new eyes," he says, though he immediately qualifies it: "everything looks far away."

"I cannot say the word *eye* any more," wrote Dylan in the liner notes to *Highway 61 Revisited* in 1965. ". . . when I speak this word *eye,* it is as if I am speaking of somebody's eye that I faintly remember . . . there is no eye—there is only a series of mouths—long live the mouths" (L, 210). So we return to the mask, for if the eyes are one opening in the mask, the mouth is the other. And the mouth is the medium for the singer, for the voice—and, of course, for the oral art in which *eye* and *I* are indistinguishable.

So far I have dealt with the mask mainly from the point of view of the trickster, insofar as it relates to the instability of identity. Perhaps it would only be fair to close this section by turning to Dylan as prophet, to the moral sense of the mask as that which dissimulates, and to the actor, indeed, as "hypocrite." In this sense, the most striking instance of the mask is in "Masters of War," where Dylan—or the figure of the young Dylan, in all his righteous prophetic fury— insists not only that "I can see through your masks" but also that "I can see through your eyes" (L, 56). Here, indeed, as Derrida says, the mask fails to shield the eyes (or the I's) of those who deal in war and ruin. The mask, the eye, and the I are all stripped away, leaving nothing but death.

Signature

> love an kisses
> your double
> Silly Eyes

(T, 11)

Thus does Bob Dylan "sign" one of the verse epistles in his book *Tarantula*. But what might it mean to sign oneself as the "double" of the other, of the person you're writing to? What might it mean to sign a false name? What might it mean if that name is "I," punned as "Eye," doubled as "Eyes"? In short, what might it mean to sign?

Recent critical theory has paid a good deal of attention to the concept of "signature." The author's name presented on a title page or copyright notice occupies a marginal site, not part of the text but not separate from it either. It reaches out from the text to that historical world where the "author" leads his biographical existence, yet it also brings the author's name into the text as part of its verbal structure and play. As Peggy Kamuf puts it, "At the edge of the work, the dividing trait of the signature pulls in both directions at once: appropriating the text under the sign of the name, expropriating the name into the play of the text" (13).

As a gesture of appropriation, the signature claims both the text and the name as property. It claims ownership of the text in the name of the author, a name to which certain legal and economic rights can be attached. The most obvious of these is copyright, an individual's claim to the ownership of a text. Only you can sign your signature; it seals the assertion our society makes of unique, inimitable individuality. The proper name is your property; it guarantees the authenticity of your claim to be, for example, "Stephen Scobie," or "Bob Dylan."

Yet at the same time, as Derrida has shown,[21] the signature depends for this very effect on its iterability: the fact that it is not a unique and singular event, but rather an event that must be able to be reproduced on various separate occasions. One signature can only be authenticated by reference to a different instance of the same signature. This iterability means that the signature can always be reproduced, forged, quoted, inserted into all the possible contexts of language. This is the gesture that Kamuf calls "expropriation": the signature enters the text and thus moves outside the sole control and intentionality of the author. The proper name is not just your property; it can no longer guarantee the authenticity of your claim to be, for example, "Bob Dylan."

The proper name lives on as that which exceeds individual identity. A public name like "Bob Dylan" is no longer within the control of the man who happens to bear it; it has gone beyond him. Recall Dylan's statement: "Nobody's Bob Dylan. Bobby Dylan's long gone" (Ginsberg 1989, 28). Once the name is signed, it is on its own.

The proper name "lives on," Derrida suggests, in both senses of that phrase. The name is a kind of parasite, which lives on the author and at his expense; it also lives on in the sense that it survives. Its effects continue after the author's death, and even while the author is still alive, the proper name accompanies him as a sort of ghost. "Lenny Bruce is dead," sings Bob Dylan, "but his ghost lives on and on" (L, 455). In the same way Frank Hibbing lives on, and in, the ghost town that bears his pseudonym.[22] The very act of signature is an acknowledgment of the possibility of the name living on. By signing, the writer is already distancing himself, as if he were dead, from the presence of the name. As late as *Time Out Of Mind*, Bob Dylan is still acknowledging this link: "When I'm gone," he sings, "you will remember my name."

The problem of the signature in Dylan's work may be approached by looking at a curious song from *Self Portrait*, the album whose very title invites the kind of puzzling self-reference involved in the deployment of the proper name. The copyright notice on the record label confidently attributes the song "Belle Isle" to the authorship of "B. Dylan." In the first edition of his book *Song and Dance Man*, Michael Gray accepted this attribution and wrote a wonderful commentary on the wittiness of what he took to be Dylan's parody of traditional folk-song modes. Unfortunately "Belle Isle" *is* a traditional folk song, which shows up in many different versions all over the world, especially in Newfoundland. The text that Dylan sings is almost identical with that contained in the magazine *Sing Out* or in Edith Fowkes's *Penguin Book of Canadian Folk Songs.* So Gray issued a massive *mea culpa,* a long article in which he traced the history and provenance of the song "Belle Isle," which was now regarded as definitively *not* by "B. Dylan."[23]

Still, it could well be argued that Gray's original reading is the better one. The signature "B. Dylan" on the record label is an illegitimate act of appropriation, a claim to legal ownership of a text to which he is not entitled. But equally, the text of "Belle Isle" now includes that false signature. Dylan may have failed to appropriate the song, but his claim to "authorship" has been expropriated into the play of its text. "Belle Isle," after all, is *about* mistaken and disguised identity. It tells of a young man who returns to the sweetheart he has left years before. Not revealing his identity, he attempts to seduce her, but she remains true to her memory of her absent love. He then reveals himself:

> Young maiden, I wish not to banter,
> 'Tis true I came here in disguise.
> I came here to fulfill our last promise,
> And hoped to give you a surprise.

She (improbably, I have always thought) forgives his deception, and they live happily ever after. In the song, the false identity, the "disguise," becomes the means of establishing the authenticity of the girl's love, and that love in turn guarantees the truth behind the false name. "B. Dylan" (alias Robert Zimmerman) then claims this song, on an album whose "self portrait" is largely made up of songs by other people. Dylan sings the overstated, sentimental verses with an air of seeming sincerity which, Gray argues, turns the whole performance into parody. The song resonates with Dylan's sense of the sheer instability of identity, the impossibility of self portrait, the paradoxes of signature.

It is unsurprising that many early "Bob Dylan" songs are filled with paradoxical references to names and naming. "You heard my voice a-singin'," he assures his audience, "and you know my name" (L, 30). But the name which the early

1960s listener would know, and which would seemingly guarantee the presence and authority of that singing voice, was, of course, "Bob Dylan," the assumed name that Robert Zimmerman was writing into the text of his own life.

Of particular interest here is "Advice to Geraldine on Her Miscellaneous Birthday," a poem written in 1964. The poem takes the form of an extended series of admonitions to an unspecified listener. In a typical paradox, Dylan's advice to her is not to take advice: "do Not create anything," he warns, "it will be / misinterpreted" (L, 125). The danger of creating any text is not just the risk of misinterpretation (which is seen here as an inevitable condition of textuality), it is that the text persists. It lives on and, like a parasite, it lives on you: "it will not change / it will follow you the / rest of your life." Thus the author's attempt to appropriate the text, to regard it as property over which he can exercise some control—the right, for instance, to specify what is or is not a misinterpretation—is bound to fail.

The appropriative gesture of the signature is itself expropriated by the text's capacity to survive beyond the control of the author's name. The echo of the two names suggests that even the name itself is split: *Dylan,* male author, is countersigned by "Ger*aldine,*" female audience. What remains is a strategy of resistance, not only to the demands of audiences, but also to the traditional modes of self-recognition and identification: "when asked / t' give your real name," Dylan's advice to Geraldine ends, "never give it."

Naming gives authority. By 1964 a "Bob Dylan song" had come to mean a style of writing that was recognizable, like a signature, and the name Bob Dylan lent authority to whatever its bearer had to say on social and political questions. "Blowin' in the Wind" (even if it is strikingly vague about specific courses of political action) had become his "signature tune." Dylan was to become increasingly uncomfortable with the role in which "Bob Dylan" had been cast, and he attempted a whole series of disclaimers of his imposed status as a prophet, a folk messiah, a spokesman for his generation.

The problem was that it appeared as if such disclaimers would also have to be disclaimers of the name Bob Dylan, which he had so urgently and carefully nourished as the basis of his career. Eventually he was successful in resolving this problem by making "Bob Dylan" stand not for any imposed role but for the very act of resistance to imposed roles. Traces of this struggle can still be read in the various references to names and naming in his early poems and songs.

Take, for instance, the opening lines of "With God on Our Side." Dylan's song is based on the Irish ballad "The Patriot Game," which begins by establishing the identity and thus the authority of its narrator: "Oh my name is O'Hanlon / I'm just gone sixteen." But Dylan deliberately refuses these specifics of naming. Instead, his opening—"Oh my name it is nothin' / My age it means less" (L, 93)—attempts to base the rhetorical authority of his song on the singer's anonymity, his representativeness, rather than on the personal charisma of "Bob Dylan." In terms of his advice to Geraldine, he is refusing to give his real name.

Again the paradox arises: what was Bob Dylan's "real" name? The evasion of "My name it is nothin'" did not return the original listener to anyone called Robert Zimmerman. At the time this song was written, in April 1963, that name was still unknown to the general public, and the singer's voice signs this song too with the authority of "Bob Dylan." The very gesture of refusing the name works inversely to increase the authority of the suppressed signature. Similarly, in "Tomorrow Is a Long Time," Dylan portrays a state of separation from the loved one as also an alienation from the self and from the name: "I can't hear the echo of my footsteps, / Or can't remember the sound of my own name" (L, 42).[24] Namely?

Most of this early equivocation was an internal drama intended, as it were, for Dylan's ears only. For the audience who heard "Tomorrow Is a Long Time" in 1962, "the sound of my own name" was still unproblematically "Bob Dylan." Robert Zimmerman, singing the song, must have been aware of the irony of what was being concealed. But from November 1963 on, the facts of Dylan's background as Zimmerman were widely known,[25] and the curious paradox is that they made it *easier* for Dylan to develop his assumed identity, his alias. The game was now being played with the audience's full knowledge. The mask could be worn in public and could be publicly displayed as a mask.

This is the point of Dylan's comment to the audience at the New York Philharmonic Hall on October 31, 1964. "Don't let that scare you," he says, referring to the song he had just finished, the decidedly scary "Gates of Eden." "It's just Halloween,"—pause—"I have my Bob Dylan mask on"—laughter, loud applause—"I'm mask-erading." And then he begins "If You Gotta Go, Go Now," with its wonderfully comic disavowal of prophetic status:

It ain't that I'm questionin' you
To take part in any quiz
It's just that I ain't got no watch
An' you keep askin' me what time it is.

(L, 158)

Now the audience can laugh with him at the idea of a Bob Dylan mask: Bob Dylan has become the name of this kind of disavowal.[26] Over the next year he was to break decisively with the folk music establishment and its demands for what "Bob Dylan" should be. In doing so, he was to create another mask of Bob Dylan, rock star, from which another escape would become necessary. This movement from one mask to another, rather than any achieved position within the movement, became what the name "Bob Dylan" signed and stood for.

In the 1965 song "Farewell Angelina," Dylan wrote: "Call me any name you like / I will never deny it" (L, 184). But in a typical gesture of evasion and deferral, he did not sing it himself. "Farewell Angelina" was given to Joan Baez to sing. Until 1991 there was no known recording—official or unofficial, studio, concert, or bootleg—of Bob Dylan singing those lines.

As Dylan moved into the kaleidoscopic imagery of 1965 and 1966, the concern with his own name was caught up in what Daniel Karlin calls the "carnival of names"—historical, fictional, legendary—of the hordes of characters who inhabit Highway 61 and Desolation Row (Corcoran, 38). Naming in these songs is so dispersed that there is no possibility of identification. "All these people that you mention," he concludes, "I had to rearrange their faces / And give them all another name" (L, 206). With so many names to choose from, no single name can exert the authority of the signature. The singer's signature appears only in the acrostic of the title *Blonde on Blonde:* BoB.

In *Tarantula*, written in 1965–66, naming and the changing of names are everywhere. "Invent me a signature," says one of the book's many characters (T, 130), and Dylan certainly obliges.

dear tom
have i ever told you that i
think your name ought to be
bill. it doesnt really matter

of course, but you know, i like
to be comfortable around people.
how is margy? or martha? or
whatever the hell her name is?
listen: when you arrive & you
hear somebody yelling "willy" it'll
be me that's who.

(T, 37–38)

(Incidentally, these lines display Dylan's considerable and underestimated skill as a poet. One might almost conclude that he'd been reading Robert Creeley.)

But who is "me that's who"? Each section of *Tarantula* ends with a verse letter, signed in a bewildering variety of names, the very first of which is "your double / Silly Eyes" (T, 11). In the next few pages, the narrator is warned that a woman will "split your eyes" (T, 15), and he admits that "my eyes are two used car lots" (T, 14). The eye/I continues to be doubled, and it comes like a used car, secondhand, from the other.

The most remarkable passage on naming in *Tarantula* is Dylan's self-composed epitaph:

here lies bob dylan
murdered
from behind
by trembling flesh
who after being refused by Lazarus . . .
was amazed to discover
that he was already
a streetcar &
that was exactly the end
of bob dylan
. . . .
here lies bob dylan
demolished by Vienna politeness—
which will now claim to have invented him . . .
boy dylan—killed by a discarded Oedipus

who turned

around

to investigate a ghost

& discovered that

the ghost too

was more than one person

(T, 118–20)

"When I sign," wrote Derrida, "I am already dead." When the name "Bob Dylan" finally appears in Bob Dylan's text, it is as an epitaph, a sign of death.

The naming here is explicitly linked to the Oedipal scenario of the father's murder, in which "Bob," already a diminutive, is further reduced to the childish *boy*. Naming is appropriated by the "Vienna politeness" of Sigmund Freud, which "will now claim to have invented" ("invent me a signature") the name Bob Dylan. As a rejection of the father's name, the adoption of a pseudonym always carries this Oedipal charge. Freud's account of the Oedipus complex attempts to describe the way in which desire is transferred from one object to another. In this passage the "trembling flesh" transfers from the dead Lazarus to the "murdered" Bob Dylan, only to find that he too has been transformed, into a streetcar (named, surely, Desire).

Simultaneously, Dylan casts himself in the role of the father killed by Oedipus. In Sophocles' play, Oedipus set out "to investigate a ghost" and discovered that the truth of the ghost lay in his own proper name: Oedipus, swollen foot, who bears as a scar the murderous signature of his father. Again we see the proper name as ghost, as that which lives on (Zimmerman, the carpenter). The ghost is "more than one person": involved here are the ghosts not only of Oedipus and Sigmund Freud but also those of Frank Hibbing, Abraham Zimmerman, and Bob Dylan.

Yet all these references also converge upon "one person," just as Oedipus discovered that the alien murderer he was seeking was himself. The gesture of Oedipus, upon discovering the truth, was to blind himself, the splitting of his eyes confirming the awful singularity of his *I*. The author of a self-composed epitaph views himself from the outside, as in Rimbaud's "Je est un autre." But he also must recognize that these doublings occur within himself, within the first person. As Dylan writes later in the book, "it is not that there is no

Receptive for anything written or acted in the first person—it is just that there is no Second person" (T, 134).[27] In Rimbaud's terms, there is only the impersonal third person. If there is no "I," there is no "you."

In the 1970s, this concern with signature and personal identity, the naming of the I, was largely deflected into fictional constructs (as in "Idiot Wind" and most of *Desire)*. It resurfaced forcefully in Dylan's Christian songs, most obviously in "Gotta Serve Somebody":

> You may call me Terry, you may call me Timmy,
> You may call me Bobby, you may call me Zimmy,
> You may call me R. J., you may call me Ray,
> You may call me anything but no matter what you say
> You're gonna have to serve somebody

(L, 424)

In one sense this is a restatement of "Farewell Angelina": "Call me any name you like / I will never deny it." The specific name, these lines insist, is unimportant; in the eyes of the Lord, all names are equal. Names are arbitrary signs with no inherent connection to the essential reality of the persons they signify. No matter what you call me, the ultimate truth of my existence remains unchanged. This argument is supported by the apparently random choice of most names on this list. There has never been any biographical motivation for associating Bob Dylan with Terry, Timmy, R. J., or Ray.[28]

But one name on the list—Zimmy—is more ambiguous in its effect. As the only appearance of the name Zimmerman in the entire Dylan canon, it both dismisses and appeals to the essential reality of the name behind the mask. This name too is unimportant, the song says, but in saying it, in quoting this name, the song reasserts that naming is not simply arbitrary. The proper name is not detachable from the character of its bearer but is written into the text of what and who the bearer has become. It is, again, a name of death, a dead man's name. *Zimmy,* after all, is not just the singer's name: it is also his father's name. In *Tarantula* "boy dylan" had been killed by a "discarded Oedipus," the man who in turn had killed his father. Here Bob Dylan reasserts the name of his dead father, in a boyish, contracted form, as, ironically, that which is immaterial to the Name of the Father.

The name "Bob Dylan," however, lives on, and for the songs of the religious period it is still a problem. These songs are full of the singer's troubling sense of his unworthiness, his division both from God and from himself. As in the earlier songs, this division often focuses on the singer's name. "Every Grain of Sand" associates it with temptation and sin: "I gaze into the doorway of temptation's angry flame / And every time I pass that way I always hear my name" (L, 462). One version of "Caribbean Wind" attempts to kill it off altogether:

> Stars on my balcony, buzz in my head, slayin' Bob Dylan in my bed,
> Street band playin' "Nearer My God To Thee."

Just as "Zimmy" is the only occurrence of "Zimmerman" in a Dylan song, so this is the only time that the actual name "Bob Dylan" appears in the text of a song.[29] As in *Tarantula,* the appearance of the signature is a signal of death. Moving nearer to God, Bob Dylan has to slay "Bob Dylan." Here he lies, murdered by trembling flesh.

Later, in the 1980s, "Bob Dylan" was slain in a more lighthearted way, as Dylan assumed yet more pseudonyms. As one of the Traveling Wilburys, he was again able to play Alias—and again the point of the play was that the audience was in on the joke. Although the names Harrison, Orbison, Petty, Lynn, and Dylan never appear on the albums, everyone knew who they were. The Wilbury masks are an ironic acknowledgment of the impossibility of anonymity. Dylan's chosen first name on the first album was "Lucky," and this name also resonates through his lyrics.

It is, for instance, the name of the "Minstrel Boy," who appears on *Self Portrait* as an image of the artist attempting to cope with the demands of a commercial audience: "Who's gonna throw that minstrel boy a coin? / Who's gonna let it down easy to save his soul?" (L, 280). At other times *lucky* appears not as a name but as an adjective. In retrospect, however, these references too speak to the later alias. *Lucky* is often an ironic adjective for Dylan, who is wary of all simple twists of fate. In "Pledging My Time" luck is lethal:

> Well, they sent for an ambulance
> And one was sent.

> Somebody got lucky
> But it was an accident.
>
> (L, 222)

And in "Idiot Wind," Dylan prefaces a song of intense personal anguish with a brief flight of fictional fancy:

> They say I shot a man named Gray and took his wife to Italy,
> She inherited a million bucks and when she died it came to me.
> I can't help it if I'm lucky.
>
> (L, 367)

Or in Wilbury terms, I can't help it if I'm Lucky.

When the second Wilbury album was released in 1990, everything had shifted again. All the Wilbury aliases had changed, as if the names themselves lacked inherent stability or permanence. Dylan now appeared as "Boo" Wilbury. The name evokes the Deep South, but it also responds ironically to Dylan's audience. Twenty-five years after Newport, Dylan adopts the audience's booing, *their* response to *him,* as his own new "name." The name comes back from the other: "I" am, once more, "your double / Silly Eyes." *Boooooo!* Thus the name is inscribed, on the album cover, as a signature—or perhaps more precisely, as a *counter*signature.

The *Oxford English Dictionary* defines the verb *countersign* as "to sign (a document) opposite to, or alongside, or in addition to, another signature; to add one's signature to a document already signed (by another) for authentication or confirmation; to confirm, sanction, ratify." Peggy Kamuf suggests that an author can and inevitably must countersign his own work, must add and keep on adding new instances of signature to confirm, sanction, and ratify what has already been claimed in its name. Because the play and structure of the text always expropriate the signature, no instance of signature can ever stand outside the text definitively enough to guarantee its authenticity. All signatures must be repeated, cited and recited, countersigned.

"Countersignature" is one way of describing what Bob Dylan has been doing obsessively since 1974: that is, performing his signature in concert. A signature must be, like a live performance, unique, the guarantee of presence and personality. Yet a signature must always be capable of being repeated, forged, reinscribed—in a word, countersigned. When I say that Dylan in concert is "performing his signature," I am saying that he is being both genuine and false, that he is simultaneously delivering us his presence and standing back from it, denying any possibility that he is really there. What we see and hear on the stage in front of us is not the singer but his alias, not the person but his name.

Each tour Bob Dylan has undertaken—and at times, it seems, practically each concert—has presented a new version of "Bob Dylan." Like a signature, each version is unique yet simultaneously recognizable, because it must refer to previous versions of the "same" signature. And by virtue of that very combination of sameness and difference, no version can be final. Each signature calls out for a countersignature. That is why the project that Dylan embarked on in 1988 has become known quite seriously as The Never Ending Tour. There can be no ending to it. The more concerts Dylan plays, the more necessary it becomes that he continues playing.

This project of countersignature might be seen as a limited, sterile, inward-turning one, especially in comparison to the flamboyant extroversion of Dylan's lyrics in the mid-1960s. What I have argued here is that signature, the staging and performance of the name Bob Dylan, has always been at the center of Dylan's career. Indeed it *is* his career. The simple strategy of disguise by which the young Robert Zimmerman attempted to make a name for himself, literally, has turned into the lifelong core of his invention of himself. The problem of Bob Dylan's signature is at the center of the fascination he continues to exert over all those who think that they know his name.

Self Portrait

"What is this shit?"

Rolling Stone, July 1970

Of all Bob Dylan's albums, perhaps none has been more controversial or divisive among his fans than *Self Portrait* (1970).[30]

The major problem is the disparity between the very casual and heterogeneous contents of the album and what seems to be promised by the title—a privileged moment of self-revelation. But should we really expect a "self portrait" to reveal any more than a mask or an alias does?

Portraiture is the representation of the body—and especially the face—as a sign. Thus it is always an ambivalent enterprise. The split between signifier and signified implies a fundamental division in our knowledge and perception of the world. Everything we are conscious of comes to us only in this mediated and divided form. A sign is always the sign of being's lack of identity with itself, of a division within our idealized self-presence. We see the portrait as an affirmation, and a confirmation, of identity. We use portraits to project images of ourselves. Some images, such as those an author puts on a book-jacket or a singer puts on an album cover, may be very carefully crafted and commercially calculated. As audiences, we like to see such images; we feel vaguely cheated when an author doesn't show us what he or she looks like.

Portraits also have a legal force. The identification photo on a passport or a driver's license operates in very much the same way as the signature, as a legal confirmation of identity. But such portraits are also subject to all the problematics of the signature, or of the proper name. To be effective, they must be *repeated;* the portrait is never identical with itself, but must always refer, in a differential network, to other instances of the "same" portrait.

Further, a portrait is someone *else's* image of *your* body; it is always an interpretation, and may well be received as a *mis*interpretation. Some sitters notoriously dislike their own portraits. Always there is in the portrait some sense of alienation, that distancing effect which most of us experience the first time we hear a tape recording of our own voice.

Part of the fascination of *self*-portraiture, then, may be the gesture it makes toward eliminating such feelings of division. At the very least, the self portrait cuts out the middle man: you are your own artist and interpreter. The self portrait reunites signifier and signified by eliminating the split, reasserting unity within the system of signification. We are fascinated by the idea of self-portraiture because it offers the illusion of not being a sign. If there is mediation here, it is of the self through the self, not of the self through the other.

However, recent studies of self-portraiture, like that undertaken by Derrida in *Memoirs of the Blind,* reveal the illusory nature of such ideas—though the fact that they are illusions does not render them any the less seductive. Indeed, far from mitigating the sense of splitting within the sign, self-portraiture multiplies it, and introduces new levels of paradox, new ways in which presence is divided from itself.

In the case of the self portrait as easel painting, the very position of the painter is paradoxical. The conventions of the genre place the artist in front of a space that is assumed to be occupied, simultaneously but impossibly, by both an easel and a mirror—and further, by extension, by the viewer. Each position cancels out the other, but is also the condition of the other's possibility. The artist, Derrida writes, "no longer sees himself, the mirror being necessarily replaced by the destinatory who faces him." His own eyes in the mirror are replaced "by other eyes, by eyes that see him, by our eyes. We are the condition of his sight . . . and of his own image" (1993, 62).

Thus the image of the self in the self portrait is split into at least these four positions: that of the artist himself; that of the reflection the artist sees of himself in a real or imagined mirror; that of the image on the canvas; and that of the spectator, who returns and enables the artist's gaze, and finally appropriates the artist's position in front of the canvas. The spectator is thus positioned within the "same" (imaginary) space as the self-portraitist. Far from being a pure condition of self-presence, the self portrait only exists by virtue of its detour through the gaze of the other.

Further, Derrida points out that it is only because of the conventions advanced by giving a work the *title* "self portrait" that we can identify it as such. Nothing in the image itself testifies that the face we see is the artist's own. Nor does anything confirm that the image we suppose the portrayed face to be looking at, in the (hypothetical) mirror, is in fact the same as the image painted on the canvas we now see.

> The identification remains *probable,* that is, uncertain, withdrawn from any internal reading, an object of inference and not of perception. An object of culture and not of immediate or natural intuition. . . . This is why the status of the self-portrait of the self-portraitist will always retain a hypothetical character. It always depends on the juridical effect of the title, on this verbal event that does not belong to the inside of the work but only to its parergonal border.
>
> (1993, 64)

This logic of the self portrait, then, extends far beyond the limited case of the easel painting. Derrida concludes: "If what is called a self-portrait depends on the fact that it is called 'self-portrait,' an act of naming should allow or *entitle* me to call just about anything a self-portrait, not only any drawing ('portrait' or not) but anything that happens to me, anything by which I can be affected or let myself be affected" (65). Again, the self portrait is not a pure, unmediated presentation of the self. All kinds of heterogeneous material may be "entitled" to be included, both in the sense that such material has a moral or legal right to be so regarded, and in the sense that this right is produced by the act of giving a title, of naming. Once more, the self portrait only reaches the self by means of a detour through the other, and through the other's name (or alias).

At the time when *Self Portrait* first came out, in June 1970, a new Bob Dylan album was still an eagerly expected event. In the years since Dylan's withdrawal from active touring in 1966, his fans had been puzzled and teased by a series of ambiguous events. Rumors flew about the precise consequences of his motorcycle crash. He had been in seclusion at his home in Woodstock and had made only one curiously perfunctory concert appearance at the Isle of Wight. He had produced one brilliant and enigmatic album, *John Wesley Harding,* then followed up its hints of country music with the pure and corny love songs of *Nashville Skyline*—a beautifully relaxed album.

The problem was that, for many of Dylan's most ardent followers, 1969 was scarcely the political time to produce a beautifully relaxed album of pure and corny love songs. *Nashville Skyline* was not the album you wanted to listen to as you shipped out to Vietnam. Actually, by the time *Self Portrait* came out, the most recent Dylan album that many people had heard was *The Great White Wonder,* the first bootleg, and the first glimpse of the majestic and mysterious songs later known as The Basement Tapes. So what was Dylan up to? Had he given up on politics altogether and lapsed into bourgeois domesticity? Was he writing masterpieces like "Tears of Rage" or trivial throwaways like "Country Pie"? Was he still the voice of his generation, or was he simply fooling around?

Given this context, it is little wonder that such intense anticipation was aroused by the announcement of an album called *Self Portrait.* Dylan's presentation of his "self" had always been devious and enigmatic, from his initial assumption of the alias through all the quicksilver changes of artistic stance which had flashed like a series of lightning bolts through the 1960s. Would he now, at the beginning of the new decade, step out from behind his masks and provide an honest, straightforward "self portrait"?

The initial critical response was one of extreme disappointment, summed up in a scathing critique in *Rolling Stone* (July 23, 1970), whose opening line, attributed to Greil Marcus, became the most famous putdown in Dylan criticism: "What is this shit?" More than thirty years later, *Self Portrait* remains one of Dylan's most problematical albums, widely despised and dismissed, though with a few determined and perverse admirers.

What was the problem? In the first place, there was the fact that so few of the songs were by Dylan. Of the twenty-four tracks, only eight could be credited as authentic Dylan compositions. Of these eight, two were purely instrumental, one consisted of a single repeated couplet, and two were very sloppy, casual concert performances of previously released songs. For anyone expecting a fresh treasure trove of meaningful Dylan lyrics, *Self Portrait* was slim pickings indeed.

The remaining sixteen tracks[31] were divided between traditional folk songs, some frankly schlocky pop and country tunes, and a couple of bows to contemporary songwriters, like Gordon Lightfoot and Paul Simon. The count was confused by the fact that Dylan blithely claimed composing credit for several traditional songs for which he was at best entitled to say "arranged by. . . ." Several selections—including "Blue Moon" and "Take a Message to Mary"— seemed to plunge to the depths of commercial banality from which Dylan and the 1960s were supposed to have redeemed popular music. In all, both the words and the music seemed to represent a headlong retreat from everything that the name "Bob Dylan" had come to stand for. And this terrible, lazy mishmash was supposed to be a self portrait? What is this shit?

Several possible explanations were suggested:

- *Self Portrait* is a cynical commercial exploitation of Dylan's reputation, pure "product," an attempt to cash in on what was left of a fading reputation and a bankrupt imagination.
- *Self Portrait* is totally without significance of any kind. It's simply Dylan fooling around with some tunes he enjoys. The title is a practical joke, played on precisely the kind of people who would take a title like that too seriously.

> • *Self Portrait* is a deliberate attempt at demythologizing—Dylan consciously trying to undermine his own messianic image by releasing a thoroughly awful album.
>
> • *Self Portrait* is a serious attempt to give a comprehensive view of all the musical influences which have gone into Dylan's career, including, with the concert recordings, some of his own classic songs.
>
> • *Self Portrait* is a series of masks, the "translation" phase of what Ezra Pound called *personae.*
>
> • *Self Portrait* is the final extension of the minimalism visible in Dylan's post-1966 work, to the extent that he has extinguished any concept of his own personality and is content to define himself entirely in terms of other people or his own past selves.
>
> • *Self Portrait* is a double image, a deliberate response to the bootleg *The Great White Wonder,* mimicking its structure and its song selection.

Part of the continuing fascination of *Self Portrait* is that all of these explanations are at least partly plausible as readings of the album. (Note that I am not talking here in terms of authorial intention. I have no idea what Bob Dylan thought he was doing with *Self Portrait* or how seriously he took the title. I'm talking only of ways in which the listener can respond to the actual text that emerged under that title.) But what unites them all are the ideas suggested above in more theoretical terms: that the force of *entitlement* compels us to read even the most heterogeneous material *as* a self portrait, and that this self portrait moves through the detour of the other.

When a new Bob Dylan record came out in the 1960s, and you eagerly took it home and put it on your turntable, the first question was always: what will the voice sound like this time? Because Dylan's voice had been different on each separate album: a rough growl, a high nasal whine, the faked Oklahoma tones of imitation Woody Guthrie, the surprisingly mellow sweetness of *Nashville Skyline.* The voice was Bob Dylan's signature, but what it signed was always a mask. Folksinger, protest bard, psychedelic rock star, relaxed country gentleman: each mask had its own voice. So what voice, you wondered, would announce itself on the first track of an album called *Self Portrait?*

The answer, devastating in its simplicity, was: no Dylan voice at all. The voice of the other.

As the track begins, you hear a chorus of women's voices singing a simple couplet:

All the tired horses in the sun
How am I supposed to get any riding done?

A nice backing vocal, you think; when will the lead voice come in? Or, an interesting chorus; how will the verses develop it? At the twenty-seven–second mark, on the third repetition, a solo guitar enters: good, that sounds like Bob. Then at the forty-three–second mark, a whole string orchestra of violins starts up in the background. Violins? On a Bob Dylan record?

And you keep on waiting. The guitar maintains its simple strummed accompaniment, but the violins soar to even cornier heights. And the women's voices keep on repeating, without variation, the same lines:

All the tired horses in the sun
How am I supposed to get any riding done?

Gradually it dawns on you that there will be no more. This *is* the song. There won't be any more words to develop the suggestions of that initial couplet. You won't hear Dylan's voice on this track. After what seems like an eternity, but is actually three minutes and eight seconds, the track fades to silence.[32]

So the first, and in some ways the most radical and definitive, gesture of *Self Portrait* is the denial of the self. The silencing of the voice. Instead of the idiosyncrasies of Bob Dylan's "own" vocal presence, we get this bland anonymity:[33] female, not male; chorus, not solo; a backing vocal taking over the lead role. Dylan has taken his single most characteristic feature—his voice—and annulled it. This track is, with a vengeance, "an act of naming [which] should allow or *entitle* me to call just about anything a self-portrait" (Derrida 1993, 65): the self portrait of the 'other.' Later selections on the album may reinforce this point— Dylan singing other people's songs, imitating Presley, double-tracking himself as both Simon and Garfunkel—but none of them makes the point as concisely or as forcefully as this initial *deferral* of his own identity.

Self Portrait begins by refusing what is, for a singer, the medium of self-portraiture. The voice is not there; so the singer is defined by his silence. But what about the *writer?* Many critics, both friendly and hostile, have noted the implied pun: "How am I supposed to get any *writing* done?"[34] If Dylan's "self portrait" for most of the 1960s had been defined in terms of his originality as a writer—as the author of everything from "Blowin' in the Wind" to "Visions of Johanna"—then this disavowal of writing, this lethargic disinclination of his Muse, is another radical deferral of his perceived "identity." Identity is no longer self-identical. That is the statement of *Self Portrait.* The singer portrays himself in the voice of the other; the writer takes refuge in repetition. As we listen to the same two lines, over and over, the refusal of thematic development becomes its own statement. There is no such thing as repetition, Gertrude Stein insisted. There is no such thing as repetition; there is only an increase in insistence.

But when all is said and done, there is the track itself. It is, I confess, one of my favorite "Bob Dylan" recordings. On those rare occasions when I succumb to the foolish temptation to compile a list of my "Ten Best Dylan Songs," I usually include, as a supplementary number eleven, "All the Tired Horses." I listen to it frequently, with pleasure. And I wish (though I know that the wish is utterly perverse), I wish that some day I could hear Bob Dylan singing it in concert.

The front cover of *Self Portrait* is, in the most traditional sense, a self portrait—an image of the artist painted by himself. Dylan has long been an amateur of the visual arts,[35] but at the time, his only widely known work was the cheerfully *naïf* cover illustration for The Band's *Music From Big Pink* (1968). The *Self Portrait* self portrait is also *naïf* and, indeed, crude in style: a roughly daubed sketch with little attempt at conventional craft or resemblance.

In fact, without the context provided by its title, it is unlikely that many viewers would identify it as a "likeness" of Bob Dylan. It eliminates one of his most characteristic features—the tremendous shock of curly hair—and obscures another—his hooked nose—by presenting it in frontal view. The face seems fuller and coarser than in most photographs, and his suspicious, narrow-eyed squint is replaced by a wide-eyed, raised-eyebrows stare. As a self portrait, it seems a deliberate contradiction of all the known or expected images.

Stylistically it owes something to *naïf* painting or folk art, though such styles usually strive for more verisimilitude. The thick brush strokes and the broad slabs of paint, such as the light blue-purple bulk of the nose, are perhaps more reminiscent of early Fauve or primitivist painting. And the extreme dislocation of style between the depictions of the two ears may even indicate a reminiscence of early Cubism. Indeed, it might not be too much of an exaggeration to suggest that this is a face which might have stared out from one of the studies for Picasso's *Les Demoiselles d'Avignon*.

What is intriguing about this image are its contradictions. On the one hand, it seems so rough and amateurish; on the other, the self-conscious deliberateness of this effect suggests a certain level of art-historical sophistication. In the same way as the songs on the album seem to sidestep the verbal sophistication of Dylan's earlier work in favor of the simple or even banal modes of popular songs, so this cover parades its own crudeness and dares the viewer to accept it as a "serious" painting. In the same way as the songs defer Dylan's identity as singer-songwriter behind a series of masks—and even appear, in "All the Tired Horses," to erase altogether the privileged signifier of that identity, Dylan's voice—so this painting, with its overstated *un*likeness to any previous images of Dylan, challenges the process of identification implicit in any notion of the "portrait" of a celebrity.

Dylan in the mid-1960s had been the embodiment of urban sophistication, of a knowing, hip, ironic style. In 1965 he was described as the coolest person on the planet. But nothing could be less "cool" than the self portrait on the cover of *Self Portrait*.

If this album is a "self-portrait of the other," what or who exactly are the "others" through whom it is detoured?

The first answer is: other singers, other writers. Dylan invites us to construct his "self portrait" as a composite of other musical artists: the anonymous composers of traditional ballads like "Belle Isle" or "Copper Kettle"; the commercial craftsmen who manufactured pop melodramas like "Take a Letter to Mary"; country singers and old bluesmen, the guardians and inheritors of American music; contemporaries like Gordon Lightfoot and Paul Simon; an echo of Elvis on "Blue Moon"; the anonymous female voices of "All the Tired Horses." And, of course, "Bob Dylan" himself—the Bob Dylan who wrote "Like a Rolling Stone" and who now playfully deconstructs that song in front of an audience at the Isle of Wight. Each of these other singers bears upon Bob Dylan but is not identical with him—just as the front cover image proclaims itself a "self portrait" while simultaneously distancing itself from any previous image of its painter's face.

But beyond this aspect, the further answer to the question "Who is the other through whom the self portrait must take its detour?" is: the listener.[36] Bob Dylan is, above all else, a performer, and a performer needs an audience. Without the presence of the audience, the performance is incomplete; reciprocally the audience *constitutes* the performance and the performer: in the line quoted earlier from Derrida, "We are the condition of his sight . . . and of his own image." If he is to give a complete portrait of himself-as-performer, then Dylan has to go through the detour of the audience. It is we, listening to this miscellaneous collection of songs, who are called upon to *entitle* it "Self Portrait."

Let me illustrate these points further, and in closing, with one more quotation from the album. Again, it's from a song which is not "by" Bob Dylan, despite the album credit. It's from "Days of '49," a traditional American folk song describing the San Francisco gold rush of 1849. The singer is portrayed as a derelict ex-miner, down on his luck, who looks back nostalgically to "the days of old, the days of gold." It's possible to see the dramatic situation as an ironic comment on Dylan himself, already, in 1970, looking back at a "golden age," 1965–66, which is now irretrievably behind him. Homeless, the miner moves from place to place, and his presence is perceived as, precisely, a *sign* of his absence:

> I wander round from town to town
> They call me the rambling sign
> There goes Tom Moore, a bummer sure
> And the Days of '49.

The signified "Days of '49" may be fixed, a period in the historical past, but the signifier, Tom Moore, is still "rambling," constantly on the move, semiotics in motion.

The line could stand as an image for Dylan's procedure throughout *Self Portrait*. If the album's signified is that absent, hypothetical, unknowable construct 'the self,' its signifiers are always fluid and unstable, "rambling from town to town": from "Copper Kettle" to "Blue Moon," from the assured complexity of "All the Tired Horses" to a ramshackle concert stumble through "Like a

Rolling Stone." All of the positions along this ramble—folk, rock, pop, country—bear upon the figure of "Bob Dylan," but none is identical with him. Indeed, he is never identical with himself. Like Tom Moore, Bob Dylan is always in motion, the trickster, "on the road again."

Self Portrait is a rambling sign, that is, an unstable sign. It twists and turns, never quite yielding what you expect. It detours through other styles, other voices, other ears. It shores its fragments against its own ruins. In the most casual and haphazard way, it assembles its oddments and echoes, bits and pieces of the other, into a compelling portrait of the self.

Ghost

The 1975 Joan Baez song "Diamonds and Rust," which is openly acknowledged to be about Bob Dylan, begins with the line: "Well, I'll be damned, here comes your ghost again." As well as being very acute about the importance of the image of the ghost in Dylan's own work, the line could also be taken as a concise summary of the situation and plot of the traditional ballad "House Carpenter."[37] This ballad was recorded by both Dylan and Baez in the early 1960s: Dylan in 1961 (though not released until *The Bootleg Series* in 1991) and Baez in 1962–63 (released on her first *In Concert* album).

"House Carpenter" forms an early link between the two artists, although a link not openly acknowledged until many years later. Baez regularly sang the song in concert, but Dylan's recording seems to have been a one-off; it was not part of his repertoire. His version is, you might say, the ghost behind Joan's.

In the traditional story of the ballad, an unnamed woman is in love with a sailor, usually called James Harris. They exchange vows and pledges, but are not legally married. He goes off to sea and disappears; she marries a carpenter. After seven years, Harris returns—or appears to. He reproaches the woman for breaking their vows, and persuades her to abandon her husband and children and come away with him. They are only briefly at sea before their ship sinks and the woman is drowned.

Thus, in its most secular form, the ballad is a stern warning for erring wives: the woman is punished for leaving her lawful husband. But in most of its earlier versions, there is a strong supernatural element. The returning lover, James Harris, is in fact dead. His apparition is only as a revenant, a ghost. In many versions he is identified as a "daemon lover," or indeed as the Devil himself, taking on the former lover's appearance in order to tempt the woman to damnation. Quite literally: "I'll be damned, here comes your ghost again." Many versions of the song end with a vision of "the hills of hell," where the doomed lovers will spend eternity. The punishment of the erring wife now comes with a religious sanction. But it is still possible to view the story in a Romantic light, and to conclude that the woman would rather be united with her original lover, even in hell, than survive as a dutiful wife to her safe, carpenter husband—echoes of Cathy and Heathcliff in *Wuthering Heights*.

As the ballad crossed the Atlantic, and as it flourished in nineteenth- and twentieth-century America, the supernatural element became less prominent. While the identity of James Harris as a ghost or a demon may still be implied in the story and in the tradition, it is no longer fully explicit in the text, to the extent that singers came to feel they had to explain it to the audience ahead of time, no longer being able to rely on the audience having the cultural knowledge to pick up the hints. Dylan, for instance, although he does include the "hills of hell" verse, still prefaces the song with a spoken introduction: "Here's a story about a ghost come back from out in the sea, come to take his bride away from the house carpenter." And even here, Dylan mentions only a ghost, not a demon; that is, the revenant is genuinely the ghost of the former lover, not the Devil in disguise.[38]

It is the ghost, I suggest, that really interests Dylan. "Ghost" is one of the images which I have been attempting to define, throughout Chapter 2, as images of identity at one remove: the self, but the self altered, slipped, exceeded, doubled, echoed, mirrored, shadowed, shifted to one side—all the trickster's maneuvers. The ghost is not the self but the image of the self, projected beyond the ego's control but somehow reclaimed, gone beyond death and then come back—the literal meaning of the word *revenant*. As Dylan puts it on *"Love and Theft,"* "you can come back, but you can't come back all the way."

In all these ways the ghost is very like the proper name (and this whole discussion should be read in close conjunction with the "Alias" and "Signature" sections of this chapter). "It is the name which comes back," writes Derrida. "Names are revenants" (1987, 98).[39] Robert Zimmerman (the carpenter) creates "Bob Dylan," but the name goes beyond him, far beyond his control. Like a ghost, it lives on; like a parasite, it lives on him. Things are done *in his name*—songs are sung, concerts are given, books are written, websites proliferate, all manner of claims are staked on immortality—but in the end they all *come back to* him: the voice, the performer, the identity, the name, the alias. It's like Bob Dylan said: "It's like Rimbaud said, 'I is an Other' " (Crowe, 1985).

For Dylan, the ghost is always revenant, the one who returns: like Angel in "Just Like Tom Thumb's Blues," who "looked so fine at first" but who "left looking just like a ghost" (L, 207).[40] The most direct reference is the evocation of the death, and yet the continued presence, of Lenny Bruce. "Lenny Bruce is dead but his ghost lives on and on" (L, 455). Ghosts always speak to this paradox of presence and absence. The dead are both here and not here, eternally cut off from us and yet always nudging our shoulders.[41] Even Dylan's "present" experience of Lenny Bruce—"I rode with him in a taxi once, only for a mile and a half"—has the unreal quality of a timeless apparition—"Seemed like it took a couple of months."

The song which most fully embodies this paradox is (as I argue in more detail in Chapter 7) "Visions of Johanna." Even the title suggests ghostliness. Johanna is never fully present, except as a vision. Yet in another sense all of the other characters are spectral compared to her. It is in this song, of course, that the ghost makes its most spectacular appearance in Dylan: "The ghost of electricity howls in the bones of her face" (L, 223). Here, Louise is described in terms of an energy which both asserts itself, howling, as a vivid and painful presence and yet also is absent, a mere ghost, just as all the characters in the song defer their existence to the always present absence of Johanna.

The idealized women of Dylan's mid-sixties songs escape the precise definitions of being fully present. The elusive Sad-Eyed Lady of the Lowlands resists all the questions imposed on her—she cannot be buried, carried, outguessed, impressed, mistaken, persuaded, employed, or destroyed. The ultimate image of her, in the last line of the song, is "your saintlike face and your ghostlike soul" (L, 240). Both saint and ghost are images of spiritual existence at one remove from the body. Again, it's a double remove, not fully a ghost but only *like* a ghost, the image always receding from the specifics of identity.

Saint and ghost are also paired in another line, ten years later: "My patron saint is a-fighting with a ghost," in "Abandoned Love" (L, 393).[42] Here one is tempted to take *patron* in terms of its etymology, as a presiding *paternal* spirit, and to see this fight as a rematch of "House Carpenter": the carpenter against the lover, Abe Zimmerman against the ghost. But even without this stretch, it is clear that the ghost is always connected to identity, and to the formation of identity in relation to the death of the father. I return (revenant) to the key lines from *Tarantula:*

> boy dylan—killed by a discarded Oedipus
> who turned
> around
> to investigate a ghost
> & discovered that
> the ghost too
> was more than one person

(T, 120)

What Oedipus discovers is a duplication of identity *within himself.* He is both son and husband, both father and brother. The ghost tormenting Thebes turns out to be himself; birth is complicated by murder.[43] Oedipus blinds himself, destroying his eye/I and creating a new mask for his identity. The blinding also repeats the ritual mutilation of his childhood (the piercing of his feet) which gave him, improperly, his proper name. *(Oedipus* literally means "swollen foot.") The Oedipal story establishes identity, but it also throws it into doubt. There was, for instance, no such person as "boy dylan": when Bob was a boy, he was Zimmerman. The ghost will always be "more than one person."

The closest Dylan comes in later years to repeating the story of "House Carpenter" is a curious scene in *Renaldo and Clara,* where the character called Ramon (played by Rob Stoner) argues fiercely with "Mrs. Dylan" (played by Ronee Blakley). It's as if the carpenter's wife is again being urged to sea by her lover. In interviews Dylan insisted that Ramon in this scene was indeed a ghost: "Ramon actually is the memory of the dead lover . . . the image of the dead lover. . . . You see him in the mirror. He's the Hanged Man—someone who's suspended" (Ginsberg 1989, 27). This ghost of Ramon prefigures the ultimate ghost in the film: the Woman in White, described by Dylan as "the ghost of Death" (18). That is, Dylan argues here that "Death" itself is not final,[44] that even Death must die, and must come back, like a ghost, revenant: "She won't leave. . . . She always seems to go . . . but she's always back" (19).

All of these ghostly scenes are played through the images of Bob Dylan's personal identity. Ramon's ghost (played by an actor called Rob) haunts the fictional character Mrs. Dylan. The Woman in White is played by Joan Baez, who elsewhere in the film actually sings, "Well, I'll be damned, here comes your ghost again." Death's ghost returns repeatedly to the room of Clara, played on screen by Sara, the actual Mrs. Dylan. Each of the actors in *Renaldo and Clara* has several identities: they are themselves, yet they play fictional roles. They appear in mirrors and they wear masks—whiteface makeup that gives them all, especially Renaldo, a saintlike face and a ghostlike soul. They are all "more than one person," damned and living on, exceeding their names, howling in the bones of Louise's face, riding in a taxi with Lenny Bruce, coming back like ghosts from out in the sea, to take their bride away from the house Zimmerman.

Quotation / Citation / Recitation

Throughout Chapter 2, I have tried to trace some of the key images which Dylan uses to express a sense of the self at one remove. Alias, mask, self portrait, ghost; one could add shadow, echo, mirror, brother, thief. Each projects an image which is the self but not quite the self; each shares the trickster's delight in disguise, in shape-shifting. And each repeats, over and over again, Bob Dylan's favorite line from Rimbaud: I is an other.

One of the most obvious techniques by which an author may present "I" as "an other" is quotation: the inclusion in his own work of images, phrases, lines (or, musically, tunes, riffs, arrangements) taken from other works. It's something that Dylan has done from his earliest days. Steeped in musical tradition, he has always alluded, quoted, or downright stolen from those who went before him; every album he has ever made could have borne the title *"Love and Theft."* Notoriously, he "borrowed" Dave Van Ronk's arrangement for "House of the Rising Sun"; he has repeatedly ransacked the treasures of Harry Smith's *Anthology of American Folk Music.* "Girl of the North Country" is a patchwork of quotations from traditional material. In one of his earliest compositions, "Song to Woody," Dylan fashions a tribute to Woody Guthrie which incorporates phrases and images from Guthrie's own songs, and sets it to one of Guthrie's own tunes. The opening song on *"Love and Theft,"* "Tweedle Dee and Tweedle Dum," lifts its whole musical arrangement, right down to the lead guitar solos, note for note from a 1950s pop song by Johnny and Jack, "Uncle John's Bongos." And recent research has shown that a surprising number of lines from the text of the album were lifted directly from a Japanese novel by Junichi Saga.

The effect is what I described previously as "the mask of originality." Dylan's original presentation of himself is achieved, to a surprisingly great extent, through quotation from other people. It is no aberration that an album of other people's songs should be entitled *Self Portrait*. "Bob Dylan," writes Nicholas Roe, "is apparently most himself as a sublimely capable alias, merged into a babel of others' voices" (Corcoran, 85). The self is reflected through the mask, alias, signature of the other. In a 1997 interview, Dylan described the old songs, the whole tradition of American music, as his "lexicon": quite literally, traditional songs provide the vocabulary, the constituent materials, of his original vision.

This effect is especially evident in his two most recent albums, *Time Out Of Mind* and *"Love and Theft."* Both of them are saturated with allusions, echoes, and direct quotations from traditional American songs, especially the blues and, increasingly, jazz.[45]

Quotation is explicitly acknowledged in the new title: it's not simply *Love and Theft* but, in quotation marks, *"Love and Theft."* Here, the quality of citation is itself cited, recited, and re-recited. I know of no other instance in which a title specifically cites itself as citation. That is, the title is clearly a quotation ("love"), but also an *unacknowledged* quotation ("theft"). The quotation marks proclaim its status as citation, and thus as tribute, as the acknowledgment of an intellectual debt; yet the lack of any specific attribution of source shades towards plagiarism, towards "theft."

Indeed, to this day Dylan has never explicitly, in public, admitted the source of the title. As with so many instances of love and theft in his songs, he has left it to the diligent efforts of his host of fans, especially on the internet, to root out the sources. In this case, most Dylan scholars agree that the source is a 1995 book by University of Virginia scholar Eric Lott, entitled *Love & Theft: Blackface Minstrelsy and the American Working Class*. Lott himself is both bothered and flattered to have had his title so ambiguously appropriated. He said in an interview with the Charlottesville *Daily Progress* (11/29/2001), "It's not like Dylan called and said, 'This is a great book. I'm going to use it for my record.' He used it and he won't fully 'fess up. In a weird way it's a love-and-theft relationship to my own title." Then he added: "I wouldn't be interested in suing anybody, but I'd be interested in coming onstage to play drums on the tour. But that's not going to happen." Such are the dreams of academics!

Lott's book explores the ways in which the white musicians of the American minstrel tradition appropriated, exploited, traduced, parodied, and yet paid tribute to the tradition of black music. His title phrase encapsulates the ambivalances of appropriation: it is theft, often in quite blatant terms; yet you only steal what you want to possess, what you, in some sense, love.

Incidentally, Lott points out that one of the major features of American minstrel shows was their fondness for including parody or pastiche versions of Shakespeare (another instance of love and theft). Dylan explicitly acknowledges this influence in a couple of songs on *"Love and Theft"*: one burlesque of *Romeo and Juliet*, and this splendid conflation of *Othello* and *Hamlet:* "Othello told Desdemona, 'I'm cold, cover me with a blanket. / By the way, what happened to that poisoned wine?' She said, 'I gave it to you, you drank it'" ("Po' Boy"). The whole point of the joke here is that listeners should both recognise the sources of the quotation, and realise how the quotation is being distorted (in this version, it is Desdemona who kills Othello, not the other way round; and the male hero, rather than Gertrude, who drinks the poisoned wine).

Dylan takes the idea of "love and theft" very seriously. T.S. Eliot once said that poor poets borrow, great poets steal. Dylan evidently sees himself as a great poet. *"Love and Theft"* is full of both love and theft; indeed, it is constituted by both. He loves this stuff, but he also unashamedly steals it. The songs on this album consistently run a fine line between postmodern intertextuality and old-fashioned plagiarism. At what point, we may ask, does allusion become quotation become theft?

The pairing of "love and theft" echoes the duality between prophet and trickster which I claim to be the continuing dynamic of Dylan's work. The prophet adheres to what he loves: "strengthen the things that remain" (L, 432). The trickster sees "the things that remain" as targets for theft. But the specific references to Lott's work may be less important than the simple quality of citationality in the album's title. The very fact that the phrase is enclosed by quotation marks on the cover of the album is itself the most striking acknowledgement of quotation in Dylan's work. He loves what he is stealing, and in this title, he places both the love and the theft front and centre, on display, surrounded—literally—by the graphic signs of citational appropriation.

Consider also Dylan's Oscar-winning song, "Things Have Changed," which intervenes between *Time Out Of Mind* and *"Love and Theft."* The song was written for the soundtrack of the Curtis Hanson movie *Wonder Boys,* and it is supposed to express the point of view of the film's main character, so it can't be taken *simply* as an expression of Dylan's own opinions. Rather, it has to be seen indirectly, as another alias, another mask. He is in effect "quoting" a fictional character.

It's a caustic and bitter song, summed up in its chorus:

> People are crazy and times are strange
> I'm locked in tight, I'm outta range
> I used to care, but things have changed

The language is by turns direct, imagistic, and whimsical, but it is always full of the implications of quotation (not least the self-citation by which it irresistibly calls to mind the much younger and more idealistic "The Times They Are A-Changin' ").

Reviewing the song in *Salon* (2000), Greil Marcus writes:

> Taking phrases out of the air (from the Carter Family's "Worried Man Blues," Duane Eddy's "Forty Miles of Bad Road"), to completely inhabit "I been all around the world, boys," a line from scores of old mountain songs and white blues, the person Bob Dylan thus begs leave to inhabit a fictional construct in which he imagines what it would mean to outlive oneself.

What Marcus stresses here is that the practice of quotation—the way in which, in Dylan's recent songs, almost every line seems to have its source in some older song—is a way to construct the self, or to "inhabit" a fictional self. Marcus uses the formal and slightly old-fashioned phrase "begs leave," not only because it is itself a citational phrase, but also because it implicates the listener. It is from his audience that "the person Bob Dylan"—that is, Bob Dylan as *persona,* as mask—"begs leave." We must become his collaborators, because the whole effect of citation depends on the quotations *being recognized as* quotations. Dylan wants that double awareness: the memory of the old context interacting with the awareness of the new. (It's not that we have to be good enough scholars to pin down a line to its specific source in the Carter Family or Duane Eddy: it's enough for us to be aware of the quality of the line *as* citation.)

For Jacques Derrida, this quality of citation is the condition of the sign. "Every sign," he writes, " . . . can be *cited*, put between quotation marks; in so doing it can break with every given context, engendering an infinity of new contexts in a manner which is absolutely illimitable" (1988, 12). Part of the effect of this structure is that "the intention animating the utterance will never be through and through present to itself" (18). The self is constructed through citation, but it is also divided by it. (Self portrait moves through the detour of the other; the proper name is an alias.) There can be no sign without the possibility of its being cited, but citation necessarily exceeds the control and intention of the "original" author. Citation leads to recitation. Dylan's cited words can be cited, in a new context and for new purposes, by Greil Marcus; I in turn can cite Marcus; other people (I hope) will cite me. Dylan repeatedly cites other singers, and thus recites himself. The citational self is always a divided one—like the alias, like the ghost.

The line in "Things Have Changed" which most clearly expresses what Marcus alludes to in his review, and which, ironically, comments on this whole practice of citation, is "I've been trying to get as far away from myself as I can." It's a line which speaks to the split self, the divided consciousness of Rimbaud's "I is another." But it also speaks to the nature of Dylan's creativity, not only as a writer but also as a performer. It might, indeed, act as a summary for that whole phase of Dylan's career which I have called the Years of Performance. For performance is quotation: citation as recitation. The performer on stage stands back from his own earlier work and begs leave to reinhabit it, from a distance, to revisit his own former self, as if he were a ghost. This is what Marcus means when he suggests that Dylan is "imagin[ing] what it would mean to outlive oneself": to become one's own ghost, revenant, living on one's name, but still living on.

And what remains in that situation, when all you are is a ghostly quotation? Dylan himself provides the answer, on *Time Out Of Mind:* "When I'm gone," he sings, "you will remember my name." What Dylan does in performance is to quote his own name, just as I try to do all through this second edition of this book, quoting the first edition, and still re-citing it:

"Alias Bob Dylan." Revisited.

"*Boots of Spanish Leather*"

Many of Bob Dylan's love songs turn on moments of reversal: moments when the roles assumed by the two lovers are shown to be equivalent, or exchangeable. "You're right from your side, / I'm right from mine," he sings, or: "Most likely you go your way (and I'll go mine)" (L, 94, 232). Such reciprocity is sometimes generous, as in "To Ramona," and sometimes rancorous, as in the ferocious conclusion to "Positively 4th Street," in which the gesture of standing in someone else's shoes—usually a basis for understanding and empathy—produces only "You'd know what a drag it is / To see you" (L, 211).

A particularly subtle exchange of roles occurs in "Boots of Spanish Leather" (L, 99). At first it seems like a straightforward ballad about a collapsing love affair, in which the speaker blames the woman for deserting him, for being more committed to the new attractions of "the country to where you're goin' " than to the old fidelities of their relationship. All through the song, the woman tries to compensate by offering to give him *things* ("made of silver or of golden") while he insists that he doesn't want material things. All he wants is her love.

But at the end of the song, as he finally gives up on the relationship, he decides rather cruelly to take her at her word. He, too, descends to the level of substituting material things for emotional truth. You want out? he says to her. Okay, buy your way out. You want to assuage your guilt for abandoning me? Here's my price. And then he asks for a rather expensive item: "Spanish boots of Spanish leather."

The irony is increased by the source of the phrase. In the folk-song tradition, the phrase "boots of Spanish leather" most often occurs in variants on the ballad "Gypsy Rover" or "Gypsy Davey" (which was a part of Dylan's early repertoire, and which he recorded on *Good As I Been To You*). The boots are the symbol of the domestic wealth and comfort which the lady gives up in order to follow her gypsy lover. In other words, boots of Spanish leather are usually associated with a woman's fidelity to love. Dylan deploys them in exactly the opposite sense.

The ending of the song, then, has a twist of bitter irony to it—but the bitterness is directed as much against the man as against the woman. She was just doin' what she's supposed to do. The real betrayal at the end of this song is his, not hers. By asking for the boots, he has betrayed the ideal vision of their love as much as she has. And once again, the lovers have changed places.

chapter 3

Contexts

Biography

Many Bob Dylan fans, myself included, have an almost obsessive (or "bobsessive") interest in the details of his biography. We can reel off birthdates, the names of his children, backup musicians in his various bands, and where exactly he was on almost any date in the past forty years—or at least, we know which book or website to go to for such information. The development of the internet has made it possible for details of his concerts to be posted as soon as the last encore has died away, so that now we fully expect to check this evening's set list before going to bed.[1]

But what real value does such extensive knowledge have, in terms of understanding and interpreting the songs? I have insisted, in previous chapters, that Bob Dylan's "identity" is never unproblematic: that in its most characteristic images (alias, mask, ghost) it is always divided and disguised. How, then, can the biography be related to the work?

For me, this problem is particularly acute since my critical and theoretical position (in literary terms) is deeply influenced by those forms of New Criticism, structuralism, and poststructuralism which have focused on the text to the exclusion of the author: an exclusion that reaches its rhetorical climax in Roland Barthes's essay "The Death of the Author" (1977, 142–48). If I follow this methodology, how can I then pursue an obsessive interest in everything connected with the figure of the biographical author Bob Dylan? How can I justify traveling to Hibbing, Minnesota, to gawk at his childhood bedroom?

The theory of the death of the author is, however, much more sophisticated than any simplistic dismissal of biographical information. At its most radical it calls into question the way we view not only authors but all so-called individuals. It depends upon a fundamental questioning of the notion of the self. In what sense can an author, or indeed anybody, be said to be an autonomous, coherent individual? Or to what extent are our selves and our images of ourselves the product of networks of intertextual traces—of language, of history, of society, of the unconscious? Such skepticism about individuality—the notion that we are not singular entities but variable and multiple personalities—is also a major concern of Bob Dylan's work, finding expression in such images as the mask and the alias. In this sense, far from being opposed to critical theory, Dylan's work thematizes one of its central questions.

What dies in "the death of the author" is not the literal author but his authority: that is, the position of the author as the final criterion by which every reading of a work is to be measured and judged. Traditional criticism saw its purpose as the recovery and restatement, "in other words," of the original intention of the author. If a reading could be proved to be consonant with what could be known, or more often surmised, of the author's original state of mind, then it was a good or valid reading. If a reading seemed to exceed or run contrary to authorial intention, then it was a bad or invalid one.

Such a position is very limiting. It has great difficulty in accounting for *un*conscious or accidental "intentions," or for any difference between the cultural contexts of the original author and the present reader. For instance, no twentieth-century reader of Sophocles' *Oedipus Rex* can avoid seeing Freudian psychology as at least part of the meaning of the text—but it is a part that clearly cannot be attributed to the intention of the author.[2] What is being disputed is not just what can be known of the author's biography and intentions (though these are problematic issues) but the *authority* accorded to such knowledge. The "author" becomes not so much the source or origin of his texts as *another text,* to be read with as much care, intelligence, and attention as one would devote to the reading of a poem.

What one can know about an author's life is thus a text, made up of all the formal biographies, newspaper stories, internet statistics, and just plain gossip that has entered into public circulation. Similarly, what one can know about the author's intentions is another text, derived from diaries, letters, interviews, discarded drafts, and so on. None of these texts can be taken simply. None, least of all works of fiction or poetry, can be accepted as reliable or unmediated statements of autobiography. All such texts take their place within the larger "text" to which we may attach, for the sake of convenience, an author's name—such as "Bob Dylan."

As an example of how this approach might operate in a particular interpretation, consider the suggestion that John Wesley Harding, the name of the outlaw, the song, and the album, is a reference to God, whose Jewish name Jehovah, or Jaweh, could be transliterated from Hebrew (which lacks separate letters for vowels) as the initials JWH. A strictly biographical approach would have to seek evidence that Dylan knew that JWH could stand for Jaweh—a reasonable surmise, since he was brought up within orthodox Judaism—that he remembered this contraction when he chose the name, and that he intended his listeners to make this connection. A subtler version would hold that both the memory and the intention were unconscious.

Evidence could be sought in interviews and other reported statements by Dylan about John Wesley Harding. Failing that, a scholar might hope that after Dylan's death some letter or diary entry might be found in his papers to corroborate the point. In any event, all these strategies refer the interpretation back to the author. As Barthes says, they seek an explanation grounded in "the author, his person, his life, his tastes, his passions" (1977, 143).

A post-Barthesian reading would not discount what could be known about Dylan's biography. It *is* relevant that he had a Jewish upbringing and that *John Wesley Harding* is a deeply religious album, which in many ways prefigures the Christian albums of ten years later. But such concerns would no longer dominate or determine the reading. Nor would the reading be proved "wrong" if Dylan himself were to scoff at it and say, "I never intended any such thing." The author's intention, writes Derrida, "is not annulled . . . but rather [inscribed] within a system which it no longer dominates" (1976, 243). As soon as such a reading has been suggested, it enters the textual system of *John Wesley Harding*. It must be evaluated in terms of what it can offer to a reading of that system, not in terms of what it has to offer for anyone's understanding of the biographical person Bob Dylan.

This is not to say that the biography or the public career is irrelevant to the songs. Dylan insists on their relevance, especially in the setting that has repeatedly proven the most vital and productive milieu for his art: live performance. Dylan's concerts over the years have played an endless series of variations on his public image, on what an audience expects of him. This was perhaps most clearly demonstrated in the self-consciously mythopoeic Rolling Thunder Revue, but it is no less evident in other tours. (The very concept of a "Never Ending Tour" piles self-reference upon self-reference, and invites the possibility of a radically open-ended process.) Any given concert, in its selection and arrangement of old songs, provides another "text" of Bob Dylan, another complete but momentary alias.

The necessity of reading Dylan as a text, rather than the text as Dylan, becomes even more acute when we deal with songs that are more ostensibly autobiographical, especially those that refer to Dylan's love life. Such songs should be approached as dramatic images, not as clues in some biographical crossword puzzle. Dylan claimed that his song "Sara" should be read in reference not to his wife but to the biblical wife of Abraham. A later section of this book, in Chapter 7, examines some ramifications of that intertextual chain, but the point to be made here is that, however one reads it, the interest of "Sara" is as a textual construct that includes both the biographical and the biblical references. What the song does not do, and should not be asked to do, is offer any simple, transparent report on the state of the Dylans' marriage in 1975.

In trying to write about Dylan's love songs, then, the critic's first temptation is to take a biographical approach: to identify the women about whom the songs were written, and thus to relate the interpretation of the songs to what is generally known of Dylan's private life.3 But this approach poses major problems, which fall into three main areas.

Firstly, the biographical material is incomplete and inadequate. There are too many details that, despite the prying of biographers (most recently, Harold Sounes), we simply do not know. The major figures in this story—Dylan and his wife Sara—have maintained a tight hold on their privacy. People who have spoken about their relationships with Bob Dylan have often done so from clearly self-interested and biased positions, either for or against him. Much of what can be said about the Dylans' marriage must remain pure, or impure, speculation. Further, the very notion of biographical "fact" is problematic. "Fact" is always the product of discourse and can seldom be appealed to in any direct or unmediated way. So how can any of this material be used as a basis for judging whether the songs give an accurate portrayal of what happened, or whether they are to be read as fictional variations?

Secondly, even in cases where enough biographical material is available to identify discrepancies or inventions in the songs, we have no way of knowing how or why those discrepancies arose. The writer may have forgotten details and may be making an honest mistake. He may be deliberately distorting the record in an effort at self-justification, or he may simply be using the facts as the foundation for a fictional construct. Nothing says that poetry has to be factually accurate. The very nature of linguistic utterance always involves a split between the I who writes and the I who is written: a certain degree of fictionalization is inevitable in any statement. The more complex the statement becomes—by being shaped into a song, for instance—the less reliable it is as a record of fact.

And thirdly, even if these problems could somehow be resolved with absolute or even relative certainty, the question remains: so what? What purpose has been served by determining a biographical reference? Does it really contribute anything worthwhile to our critical understanding and appreciation of the songs themselves? In cases where the biographical record may clarify an ambiguity in the text, does that clarification improve the text by making it more understandable, or does it diminish the text by reducing the possibilities of interpretation? If, for instance, we conclude that "She's Your Lover Now" is "really" about Edie Sedgwick and Bob Neuwirth, does that knowledge increase or diminish our enjoyment of the song's wit and intricacy? The purpose of criticism is not to pander to the curiosity of gossip but to respond to the complexity of the texts themselves.

Fair enough: but "the texts themselves" are not always as pure and self-enclosed as that phrase often suggests. The texts are caught up in the intertext of, for instance, proper names. When Bob Dylan sings about a woman called Sara, he is right to insist that the song need not and should not be taken as referring exclusively to his wife. Indeed, it may well be, at some level, "about" the biblical Sara. But it would be naive to claim also that Sara Dylan can be entirely excluded from the intertext of this song. Dylan's use of the name ensures her presence there.

In fact, for all his reticence about his private life, Dylan, especially in the 1970s, frequently "staged" it in his art. What I mean by "staging" is the process by which an actual person, identifiable to the audience either by name or by some publicly accessible biographical detail, is projected into the text as a quasi-fictional character. The effect is most obvious in a song like "Sara" or in the film *Renaldo and Clara*. In that movie two factors are of equal importance. One, it is about two fictional characters called Renaldo and Clara, and two, they are played by actors identified as Bob and Sara Dylan. An audience must balance these two elements. The film cannot be read as a transparent account of what went on between Bob and Sara—it must be approached as a work of fiction. Simultaneously, that fiction takes its particular shape, resonance, and authority from the identities of the actors. This kind of staging of autobiography takes place not only in *Renaldo and Clara* but also in many songs.

So, while admitting the force of the three problems, and while remaining unable to answer adequately any of the objections they raise, I still have to respond to the love songs at least partly in biographical terms, if only because those are the terms the songs themselves invite, both in their original recordings and in the history of their repeated concert performances.

Again, what I am doing is reading the total "Bob Dylan" system as a text—a text which includes both fact and fiction, both autobiography and imagination. To do justice to such a mixture, it is, of course, necessary to know, as accurately as possible, what the biographical facts are—not as ends in themselves, but as part of this complex text. Which is, I suppose, why I still read with fascination books like Dave Engel's *Just Like Bob Zimmerman's Blues: Dylan in Minnesota*—and why I probably will, before going to bed tonight, consult Bill Pagel's website for a set list of this evening's concert.

Poetry

Bob Dylan has never been very comfortable with the word *poet*. He has shied away from claiming it for himself, and he resisted or mocked other people applying it to him. In a 1966 interview he told Robert Shelton:

> I think a poet is anybody who wouldn't call himself a poet. Anybody who could possibly call himself a poet just cannot be a poet. . . . When people start calling me a poet, I say: "Oh, groovy, how groovy to be called a poet!" But it didn't do me any good, I'll tell you that. It didn't make me any happier. . . . Hey, I would love to say that I

am a poet. I would really like to think of myself as a poet, but I just can't because of all the slobs who are called poets.

(353)

Nor was he particularly complimentary or optimistic about the state of poetry in America in the mid-1960s. In a 1965 interview with Paul J. Robbins, he said:

You were asking about poetry? Man, poetry is just bullshit, you know? I don't know about other countries, but in this one it's a total massacre. It's not poetry at all. People don't read poetry in this country—if they do, it offends them; they don't dig it. You go to school, man, and what kind of poetry do you read? You read Robert Frost's "The Two Roads," you read T. S. Eliot—you read all that bullshit and that's just bad, man, it's not good. It's not anything hard, it's just soft-boiled egg shit.

(Benson, 50)

Similarly, references to poets in Dylan's own songs are often caustic and sarcastic. The most famous example is the description of "Ezra Pound and T. S. Eliot / Fighting in the captain's tower" of the *Titanic* as it goes down (L, 206). Here, Pound and Eliot—the definitive academic exemplars of modernism—are seen as irrelevant, mocked by calypso singers, trapped in their own pointless squabble for control of a cultural institution which is sinking under their feet.

At other times, however, Dylan has been more positive. In the interview with Cameron Crowe for the *Biograph* booklet (1985), he remembers with a good deal of fondness the cultural milieu of Minneapolis during his brief student career there in the winter of 1959–60:

I came out of the wilderness and just naturally fell in with the beat scene, the Bohemian, BeBop crowd. . . . There were always a lot of poems recited—*"Into the room people come and go talking of Michelangelo, measuring their lives in coffee spoons"* . . . *"What I'd like to know is what do you think of your blue-eyed boy now, Mr. Death."*

T. S. Eliot, e. e. cummings. It was sort of like that and it kind of woke me up.

(5)

Here, somewhat cavalierly quoted, is the "soft-boiled" Mr. Eliot. The same interview also cites Pound, Albert Camus, Gary Snyder, and William S. Burroughs. Dylan acknowledges that his New York girlfriend of a couple of years later, Suze Rotolo, introduced him to the French Symbolist poets, especially Rimbaud, who was to become an enormous influence. But first and foremost were the Beats:

> For then it was Jack Kerouac, Ginsberg, Corso and Ferlinghetti— *Gasoline, Coney Island of the Mind*...oh man, it was wild—*I saw the best minds of my generation destroyed by madness*—that said more to me than any of the stuff I'd been raised on. *On the Road,* Dean Moriarty, this made perfect sense to me.
>
> (Crowe, 5)

Ginsberg's poetry, especially "Kaddish," remained an inspiration throughout Dylan's career, but Ginsberg, with characteristic unselfishness, always insisted that the key influence was Kerouac. In a 1985 interview Ginsberg brushes aside a question about the influence of his own work in order to stress that of Kerouac's:

> I do know that he did read a lot of Kerouac's *Mexico City Blues,* Grove Press, 1959. He read that in '58-9 and it had a big influence on him, he said.
>
> *Do you think your works—*
>
> I'm telling you something specific. Somebody gave it to him and it influenced his poems—or "blew his mind," as he said—it being the first book of poetry which talked the American language to *him,* and so influenced his writings, or turned him on to poetry, as he said at Kerouac's grave. A specific book, a specific text at a specific time. 1958-59. *Mexico City Blues.* Grove Press.
>
> (Gray and Bauldie, 170)

What emerges from this all-too-brief survey is that Dylan did indeed read and take seriously *some* poetry. He created a kind of personal canon, made up of poets whom he had read at significant points in his early career, and of poets whose work fed directly into his own. Apart from occasional references to Shakespeare, they include few of the "classic" English poets, though Ginsberg again testifies to Dylan's interest in William Blake. (And in 2002, he unexpectedly quoted Oscar Wilde!) Rimbaud and the French Symbolists are clearly central to this canon. Dylan's view of Eliot (as we have seen above) was ambivalent. On the one hand, Eliot's affinity to French Symbolism provides the basis for an influence continuing from "Desolation Row" in 1965 to the more direct echo, "the waste land of your mind" (L, 496), in 1985. On the other hand, Dylan was deeply suspicious of Eliot's "establishment" character, the position of cultural dominance he had achieved by the 1950s, and that suspicion extended to other "established" or "academic" poets like Pound and Frost.4

This "personal canon" extends as far as the Beats, especially Ginsberg and Kerouac, but then it stops. There is little or no indication that Dylan has read any contemporary poetry, anything published in Britain or America since the early 1960s.5 (What on earth would he make of John Ashbery, or Anne Carson?) The reason may be quite simply that none of this work is directly useful to Dylan in terms of his own writing. It is noticeable, for instance, that all of the poets cited either work in rhyme or use free verse in ways suited to dramatic oral performance.

Even so, it does seem odd that someone as verbally adept as Dylan should so completely isolate himself from the most interesting writing being done around him. In this sense it is not even remotely possible to call Dylan "postmodernist." Indeed, despite his disdain for Pound and Eliot "fighting in the captain's tower," he is, in many ways, their inheritor. Poetically, he might well be described as the last of the great modernists.

Any discussion of Bob Dylan's "poetry" should start from the tricky question of whether it is, in fact, apposite to describe him as a "poet" at all, or whether it would not be more accurate to use some other term, such as "songwriter." In such a discussion *poetry* is all too often used in a sense which is more evaluative than descriptive: not as a neutral label or category, but as a way of claiming for "popular" art the cultural respectability of established literature.

In the late 1960s a lot of enthusiastic critics and editors proclaimed that artists like Dylan—as well as John Lennon, Leonard Cohen, Joni Mitchell, and others—had redeemed the banality of pop-song lyrics by elevating them to the status of "poetry."[6] This usage seems indefensible. It is a false compliment, based on the intellectual snobbery which assumes that "high culture" is innately superior to any work in a popular medium. "Songwriter" becomes, then, a term of denigration, implying either an inferior artistic form ("mere" songwriting) or commercial sellout (no record which sells a million copies can possibly be expressing a genuine personal vision).

It is precisely against the snobbery inherent in these uses of "poetry" that many critics have felt compelled to insist that Dylan is not a poet but, in a positive sense, a songwriter; that his words do not stand alone, but make sense only in combination with his music and with the idiosyncrasies of his vocal performance. This is basically the line I want to pursue, but I would not want to confine myself within an absolute, hard-and-fast distinction between poetry and song.[7] I am much more in agreement with Simon Frith when he argues that "the distinction between poetry and lyric . . . is aesthetically misleading. There is . . . a continuity between poetry and song, rather than a clear division. Between the two lie various sorts of 'performed' language" (178). This is a valid point, and it opens up a whole range of intermediate forms: poetry readings, performances of verse drama, sound poetry, poems set to music, and so on. While accepting in principle the idea of "a continuity . . . rather than a clear division," it is still possible to identify some significant dividing points along that continuum, and to make some distinctions which may be of practical use in trying to describe what it is that Bob Dylan actually does.[8]

The earliest poetry, so far as we can tell, was usually sung: folk ballads, bardic verse, the epic poems of Homer. But at some stage—the invention of printing is the decisive date—a split between poetry (printed) and song (performed) became established in the Western tradition.

"What is taken for granted," writes Frith, "is that (modern) poetry is something read, not something heard; that it is defined by page layout rather than by the performing voice" (78). To some extent, the work of songwriters like Dylan—or of poets like Ginsberg—has brought poetry back toward its oral roots. Still, it simply isn't possible to turn the clock back five hundred years, nor to ignore completely the effects of printed visual form on the nature and development of Western poetry.

In this context, then, the major distinction between poetry and song is that a poem is capable of functioning fully and perfectly as nothing more than words on the printed page. Other things can be added to it. One may well want to hear the poet reading it aloud. One may want to read it aloud oneself. One may enjoy a musical setting of it.9 But these are optional extras. Take them all away and the poem would still survive. A song, however, depends upon music and vocal performance. It does *not* function fully and perfectly as words on the printed page.

Often indeed, song lyrics printed as poetry will appear to be inferior poetry. Take, for example, a line from "Sad-Eyed Lady of the Lowlands": "And you wouldn't know it would happen like this" (L, 239). On the printed page, as a line of "poetry," among the verbal pyrotechnics of the rest of the song, it is nothing: flat, banal, dull, unaccented. But on the recording, in Dylan's vocal performance, it soars, it is glorious. Or take a line from "Precious Angel": "On the way out of Egypt, through Ethiopia, to the judgment hall of Christ" (L, 426). On the page, it looks impossibly clumsy, a clunky, unrhythmical line with far too many syllables in it. But in performance, Dylan exploits and transcends that very clumsiness, even adding an extra syllable in "Cheee-rist," and it works splendidly as song, not as poem.

Simon Frith gives an excellent account of the reasons for this effect:

> Good song lyrics are not good poems because they don't need to be: poems "score" the performance or reading of the verse in the words themselves, words which are chosen in part because of the way they lead us on, metrically and rhythmically, by their arrangement on the page (a poem is designed to be read . . . and such reading directions are just as much an aspect of "free" as of formally structured verse forms). Lyrics, by contrast, are "scored" by the music itself. For a lyric to contain its own musical (or performing) instructions is, as Ned Rorem observes, to overdetermine its performance, to render it infantile.
>
> (181)

In a song, then, the words are in continuous interaction with the music and with the vocal performance. There are things that the words *do not need* to do, and indeed *should not* do, since these effects are more naturally conveyed by the music or the voice.

Conversely, the effect of the music, though pervasive, can only partly be articulated. Music acts as "the unconscious of the text." I take this phrase from the French critic Catherine Clément. Although she is writing about the relation of words and music in opera, I believe that her account is also highly suggestive for song:

> A double, inseparable scene: the words give rise to the music and the music develops the language, gives it dialect, envelops it, thwarts or reinforces it. Conscious and unconscious: the words are aligned with the legible, rational side of a conscious discourse, and the music is the unconscious of the text, that which gives it depth of field and relief, that which attributes a past to the text, a memory, one perceptible not to the listener's consciousness but to his enchanted unconsciousnesses.
>
> (21)

The music is the context within which the text lives. It allows the text to be; it justifies the text's existence. The music provides a rhythm, a tonality, an emotional ambience. Its generic conventions—folk, rock, country, gospel—provide an intertextual basis which the words of a specific song may either contest or reinforce. But the music does not have to "say" anything itself. It just has to be there, in the background, on the threshold of the unconscious, like a ghost.

The voice, then, mediates between text and music, since the voice is the primary locus of Clément's "double . . . scene." Frith writes of

> the relationship between the voice as a carrier of sounds, the singing voice, making "gestures," and the voice as the carrier of words, the speaking voice, making "utterances." . . . The issue is not meaning (words) versus absence of meaning (music), but the relationship between two different sorts of meaning-making, the tensions and conflicts between them. . . . And what makes the voice so interesting is that it makes meaning in these two ways simultaneously.
>
> (186–87)

In the vocal performance words and music may reinforce each other or be held in tension against each other. "What Dylan 'means' in a song," writes John Herdman, "is not always what the words say: the sense may be conveyed through the tensions between words, expression and musical mood" (6). How a song "means" is always as much a function of the music and the voice as of the text.

In all these ways, then, songs differ significantly from poems, and it really isn't very useful to obscure these differences by claiming that Bob Dylan is "a poet." Having said that, however, I would also argue that there is, in the purely verbal aspect of Dylan's writing, a great deal of wit and invention that can be described in traditional poetic terms. So, bearing in mind all the qualifications expressed above, I will now identify a few of Dylan's more characteristic verbal strategies: by no means an exhaustive or comprehensive list, but some preliminary suggestions of what might constitute his "poetry."

The most obviously "poetic" aspect of Dylan's language is his gift for vivid and sometimes bizarre imagery. What struck the first listeners of "Blowin' in the Wind" was not its rather vague and conventional political sentiments, but the embodiment of these ideas in the images of a mountain being washed to the sea, or a white dove sleeping in the sand. Especially in the "psychedelic" years of the mid-1960s, it is this kind of imagery which flourishes in Dylan, pushing the symbolic into the surreal and the vivid into the grotesque. At times the sheer profusion of invention piles up images on top of each other until they topple on the edge of absurdity, preserved only by the sheer energy of their imagistic exuberance: "The motorcycle black madonna / Two-wheeled gypsy queen" (L, 175).

But at their best, the images are held in balance by other poetic elements, such as rhyme, assonance, alliteration. In "To dance beneath the diamond sky with one hand waving free / Silhouetted by the sea, circled by the circus sands" (L, 173), the use of *diamond* as an adjective transforms the natural scene into one of magic and revelation. This effect is reinforced by the pattern of alliteration between *dance* and *diamond, one* and *waving, silhouetted* and *sea, circus, sands.* And the obvious echo between *circle* and *circus* reflects the more subtle wordplay within the word *waving*—the action of the human arm which is also the action of the sea constituting itself as a series of waves.

Similarly the impact of "The ghost of electricity howls in the bones of her face" (L, 223) derives not only from the visual evocations of its imagery, or from its echo of Allen Ginsberg, but also from the balance between these four long vowels *(ghost, howls, bones, face)* and the five short vowels of *e-lec-tric-i-ty*.

The surreal landscape created by such imagery is populated by a no less vivid array of intertextual characters, whether derived from history, from other artistic works, or from pure imagination. On these streets, the Hunchback of Notre Dame walks alongside "Einstein disguised as Robin Hood" (L, 205), accompanied by assorted doctors, riverboat captains, Persian drunkards, and neon madmen. These figures are characterized by bizarre names—White Heap, Savage Rose, Fixable—or by brilliantly concise images—Ophelia summed up in the single line "She wears an iron vest" (L, 205). Such names and images appeal in the first place by their startling and even incongruous originality. But the best of them persist in the listener's own imagination, not only for their verbal wit but also for their cultural and psychological perceptiveness.

The profusion of such images tends to produce a rather loose, nonlinear structure. Image piles on image, and verse follows verse, without a great deal of consecutive necessity. In songs like "Desolation Row" and "Memphis Blues Again," the total effect of the song would not be greatly altered if there were one verse more or less, or if the verses were sung in a different order. Indeed, it is comparatively rare now for Dylan to sing "complete" texts of these songs in concert. All that holds them together is a repeated reference to a single controlling image, "Desolation Row" or "Gates of Eden," usually at the end of each verse. The effect is to de-emphasize the linear progression of the song and to see its structure more in spatial terms, as if all the images were laid out alongside each other in a continuous present tense. Or as if each verse were a separable unit in a modular, nonlinear structure.

In the 1970s, when he was studying painting with Norman Raeben and working on his film *Renaldo and Clara,* Dylan repeatedly said that his aim was to "stop time." That is, within the bounds of media that absolutely depend on temporal progression (music, film), he paradoxically sought after an ideal of stasis, of spatially arranged simultaneity, that sets up a counterforce to the very movement of the medium itself. Even his idiosyncratic guitar solos, which tend to reiterate single notes rather than extend into melodic lines, may be seen as a variation on this compulsion.

Dylan can certainly tell a story when he wants to, though his finest narrative songs tend to feature disconcerting gaps and ambiguities within the story lines. But in these image-dominated lyrics there is never a sense of strong linear progression. The images go nowhere, are repeatedly pulled back to the recurring lines at the end of each verse. The images are quite literally *arresting*. They draw attention to themselves as definitive statements of timeless essences.

This kind of vivid and flamboyant imagery is matched, in Dylan's writing, with aspects of a much plainer style, one that depends on colloquial or proverbial speech. Dylan excels in the use of a hip, street-smart language, often organized through a virtuoso display of rhyme.[10] The definitive example remains the opening stanza of "Highway 61 Revisited":

> God said to Abraham, "Kill me a son"
> Abe says, "Man, you must be puttin' me on"
> God say, "No." Abe say, "What?"
> God say, "You can do what you want Abe, but
> The next time you see me comin' you better run"
> Well Abe says, "Where do you want this killing done?"
> God says, "Out on Highway 61."

(L, 202)

The effect here derives from the contrast between the dignity of the subject matter, of the half-remembered biblical language, and the colloquial urban diction, emphasized by the speed of the exchange and the idiomatic slang of the dialogue, controlled by the tight pattern of the rhymes.

Dylan is indeed a master of rhyme: it was one aspect of his craft which Ginsberg really envied. Ginsberg hailed the couplet in "Idiot Wind"—"Blowing like a circle around my skull / From the Grand Coulee Dam to the Capitol" (L, 368)—as America's "grand national rhyme." Often Dylan's rhymes are quite outrageous—a word he rhymes with *contagious*—and seem to be offered for the sheer delight of their virtuosity: "What can I say about Claudette? Ain't seen her since January, / She could be respectably married or running a whorehouse in Buenos Aires" (L, 464). Only occasionally, as in "No Time to Think," is he overwhelmed by the demands of an overelaborate rhyme scheme.

At times the rhymes have a quite extraordinary thematic density. Take, for example, the moment in "Hurricane" which is printed rather blandly in *Lyrics* as "And though this man could hardly see / They told him he could identify the guilty man" (L, 375). What the written version obscures is that Dylan syncopates the rhythm so that the first syllable of *identify* is perceived as a rhyme for the last. To rhyme a word with itself might be mere virtuosity, but here it also underlines, precisely, the thematic ambiguity. The question is one of criminal identification (or, in the case of Hurricane Carter, *mis*identification): who is the "I" who is I-dentified? And who is the witness? A man who "could hardly see" is nevertheless required to "eye-dentify" the guilty man. All the irony of the narrative situation is condensed into the rhyme.

Dylan himself has on occasion identified the use of rhyme as key to the uniqueness of his style. In a 1992 interview with Robert Hilburn, responding to a question about all the "new Dylans" touted over the years, he states:

> That's never been a worry. There wasn't anybody doing my thing—
> though I'm not saying it was all that great. It was just mine and no
> one was going to cover that territory. No one frames the language
> with that same sense of rhyme. It's my thing, just like no one writes
> a sad song like Hank Williams or no one writes a bitter song like
> Willie Nelson. My thing is the forming of the lines.
>
> (Benson, 220)

Here he clearly sees the "framing" of his own language as a question of line and rhyme. I think this is one of the most perceptive comments he has ever made about his own writing.

Another major aspect of Dylan's use of a plain colloquial style may be seen in his variations on cliché. Dylan loves to use common phrases, often proverbial phrases, and render them with very slight alterations, so that the cliché phrase is renewed by the play of verbal wit. Often two phrases are blended into a new compound. In the line "Something there is about you that strikes a match in me" (L, 345), the expected "meets" or "finds" a match is crossed with the quite literal *striking* of a match, so that the abstract perception of similarity between two people flares like fresh fire.

Even in a verbally banal song like "Make You Feel My Love," the phrase "You ain't seen nothing like me" is transformed by the addition of "yet," again conflating two clichés into a new formulation. Similarly "Darkness at the break of noon" (L, 176) crosses the conventional "break of dawn" with "darkness at noon" (the title of Arthur Koestler's 1940 definitive statement on intellectual disillusionment with communism). The noon "breaks" (in all senses of that word) in the post-ideological vacancy of political ideals.

This effect is one which Frith sees as a traditional aspect of blues lyrics: "Common phrases which have lost their metaphorical power are taken seriously and so recharged . . . blues singers have certainly treated language like this, as cultural memory" (1996, 174). Increasingly in his later writing, Dylan has come to rely on this kind of "cultural memory." The songs on his latest albums, *Time Out Of Mind* and *"Love and Theft,"* are virtual compendia of quotations from traditional sources. Scarcely a line on these albums cannot be traced back to an old folk or blues song. But the effect is by no means derivative. There is a knowing irony to Dylan's use of such lines. He knows that these lines are quotations, and he knows that his audience knows that he knows.

The effect is to some extent similar (to return this discussion, one last time, to the captain's tower) to the use of quotation by Ezra Pound and T. S. Eliot. In *The Waste Land* Eliot assembles quotations (and, notoriously, footnotes them) from the whole range of world literature. In their scattered state they act as an image of the fragmented, ruined condition of modern civilization—what Dylan would call, in a phrase which is itself a quotation, a "world gone wrong." In their newly collaged structure they offer an uncertain foundation for the rebuilding of order. "These fragments," writes Eliot in the ambivalent ending of the poem, "I have shored against my ruins."

Dylan's archaeology of traditional lyrics on *Time Out Of Mind* and *"Love and Theft"* may also be read in a double sense. The use of the quotations signals Dylan's sense of continuity: his appreciation of the old masters of his tradition, his tribute to them, his wish to reassert the tradition in a contemporary context. But at the same time, his use of them *as quotations* signals his sense of distance from the tradition: his awareness that they seem quaint, old-fashioned, out of place in this world gone wrong, and his rueful acknowledgment that these modes can now be understood *only* as quotation, that it is no longer possible for anyone, even Bob Dylan, to "sing the blues like Blind Willie McTell." That is, the phrases which a blues singer like McTell could use with a kind of naive authenticity can now be used, by a postmodern singer like Bob Dylan, only in citational form—like the trickster, at one remove.[11]

In summary, then, I draw attention to these two major aspects of Bob Dylan's "poetic" style. Firstly the elaborate style, the proliferation of images, language that self-consciously draws attention to its own brilliance, with the corollary that it produces a loose, nonlinear structure which serves Dylan's avowed aim of "stopping time." And secondly a plain style, a reliance on colloquial and proverbial speech, shaped by a virtuoso use of rhyme, and leading him increasingly toward the use of modified clichés and collaged quotations from traditional sources.

These aspects of his verbal style seem to me to be properly described as "poetic." At this point, however, rather than resorting to calling Bob Dylan a poet, I would want to fold the argument back into the previous discussion, to see how these poetic devices contribute to the fuller, more complex continuum of words, music, and performance which makes up a song.

Performance

Theory

Performance rides the dividing line between sameness and difference.[12] The same song, different every night. For most concertgoers, a concert is a one-time thing: if not a once-in-a-lifetime experience, at least once in every few years.[13] The experience is unique, forceful, immediate. The audience seeks the thrill of spontaneity, the authenticity of difference, the feeling that a work is being created *here, now,* as it never has been before and never will be again.

But for the professional touring musician, it's just another night on the road, one more show, playing the same songs in the same way—and there must always be nights when they are only going through the motions, *pretending* to be inspired, *acting* spontaneity.[14] Of course, there are also nights when the performers do catch fire, when there is an electric connection to the excitement of the audience, and when they truly play the songs as if for the first time—but the operative words are still "as if." Even at its most inspired, a performance is a repetition.[15]

In other words, performance shares a good deal with the trickster motifs previously defined as *identity at one remove.* In the same way as the mask or the alias define the self in terms of the other, with a kind of sidestep motion, so too the performer always stands at one remove from any true "immediacy"—either the immediacy of the moment of original creation or the immediacy of "personal contact" with the audience.

Before developing this point, however, I should acknowledge that the word *performance* itself encompasses several overlapping but subtly different modes. The "purest" mode of performance is the concert situation, with the singer live on stage before an audience. But the word may also be applied in the sense of a recorded performance, and listening to a recording in the privacy of one's own home is obviously a very different situation from attending a concert.[16] Still, most of the ambivalence of performance applies in both situations. The recording of a singer's voice can still produce the illusion of intimacy; indeed, the illusion may be all the stronger in a private setting than in a public one. But recording also underlines the structure of absence; recording always carries with it the implication that the singer's voice (or "live presence") can be repeated, even after the singer's death.

Live performance is valued because it is seen as bringing the artist into direct personal contact, even a kind of intimacy, with his or her audience. In a literary context, this value can be seen in the popularity of "poetry readings," or indeed readings by all kinds of writers. But the notion of personal contact in the public reading situation is a tenuous one. (In Derridean terms, it depends upon the metaphysics of presence in its most traditional form: the priority of voice over writing.) The structures of writing and performance are more complex: every "reading" is a further act of (re-)writing, on the part of both the author and the listener. "Immediacy" is always already mediated. The performing self is always a text; what is at stake in performance is, as the trickster's strategies show, the very nature of the self. "Intimacy" proposes that there is a self there to be encountered; "performance" counters that that self is, necessarily, a constructed one, a textual one.

The illusion of intimacy is also held dear in popular music—though the chances of any "personal encounter" are much less in a 50,000-seat stadium than in the more cloistered confines of poetry readings, and often enough the "live" performers are reduced to gigantic figures on overhead TV screens.[17] The outrage which greeted the revelation, in late 1990, that the "singers" of Milli Vanilli had been lip-synched by other performers, both on record and on stage, testifies to the continuing importance attributed to the *presence* of the live performer.[18] Performance, in this sense, is regarded as the seal of authenticity, of sincere self-expression, of assured personal communication.

This ideal is also testified to in the work of Leonard Cohen. In 1991, in a televised speech he gave on the occasion of his induction into the Canadian

Music Hall of Fame, he spoke of "this sudden and strange and mysterious intimacy" which existed between himself and his audience. He went on to thank

> those of you who have welcomed my tunes into your lives, into your
> kitchens when you're doing the dishes, into your bedrooms when
> you are courting and conceiving, into those nights of loss and bewil-
> derment, into those aimless places of the heart which only a song
> seems to be able to enter.

This is an eloquent and moving tribute to the power of song, and to the intensity of the relationship which may develop between singers and their audience. In this case, since Cohen is referring specifically to people listening to his records in their homes, it is clear that the "intimacy" of live performance extends into the recorded medium. Indeed, recording enables an even greater intimacy (kitchens, bedrooms) than the concert stage could ever produce. In his song "Sisters of Mercy" Cohen sings that "they brought me their comfort / and later they brought me this song" (109). The comfort and the song go together. Music is redemptive. Performance heals.

Yet at the same time, and without denying any of these positive values attributed to it, I would also argue that "performance" is viewed with great suspicion. "It's a clever performance," we say, implying that somehow it is not *real*. Or more cynically, "Once you've learned to fake sincerity, you've got it made." To perform is to pretend that you are something that you are not;[19] to perform is to lie. "A singer must die," Leonard Cohen wrote (and sang), "for the lie in his voice" (208). I don't think that this line means only those singers who lie must die, as opposed to those singers who do not lie, and thus can live. I think it means that all singers lie, that performance is a lie, and that all such lying performances have death built into them as part of their structure.

The metaphysics of presence postulates a "personal encounter" as something which takes place between two independent, fully self-present individuals. It has no place for the alias, for the invented or divided self. But the activity of writing is always a doubled or divided one: the structure of writing, even at the instant of creation, inscribes a split between the I who writes and the I who is written. There is no pure, unmediated moment of "original" creation. And even if there were, *performance* is necessarily distanced from it. Performance evokes the nostalgia for such a moment of pure self-presence, but it can do so only by repeating, and emphasizing, the original division.

The activity of performance is doubled also in the sense that it is a structure of repetition. This structure is most evident in the form of recording, where the *same* performance may be played over and over again—though always in different contexts. But, just as intimacy (the characteristic of live performance) extends into recording, so also is repetition (the characteristic of recording) already implicit in live performance. I do not mean *only* that any one live performance is a repetition (or variation) of previous performances, but also that the idea of repetition is implicit even in any *one* performance.

Performance is doubled as citation and recitation, the repetition of a text that already exists prior to the moment of performance. The singer is always divided, in Dylan's words, into "I and I": the person who performs this song for you now and the person who previously wrote it. Improvisation compresses the temporality of this split but does not eliminate its structure. Any given performance of, say, "Blowin' in the Wind" is haunted by the echoes of all past performances, and by the ghost of the man who wrote it and who is *no longer there* (even if, in another incarnation, he is now on stage singing it).[20] The value of presence in performance is always shadowed by this absence; the structure of performance must always refer back to the absent origin, to the unrecoverable source of the song. A recording always implies the death of the singer. The voice will still come back, like a revenant ghost, after he is gone. But even the presence of a singer on a concert stage carries the same potentiality for haunting; a "live" performance is also a performance of death.

Practice

In 1993 I received a letter from an old friend, Oliver Botar, who told me that he had purchased tickets for a Bob Dylan concert in Toronto. It was going to be his first-ever Bob Dylan concert and he wanted to know what to expect. I reproduce here the letter that I sent him in reply.

August 2, 1993

Dear Oliver,

So you're going to a Bob Dylan concert.

Or, to be more accurate, you're going to a concert by Dylan and Santana, which is one strike against you right there. And in the CNE Grandstand, which is strike two. What can be done to save this event?

And you've never seen Dylan live before. Ulp.

But what you're probably familiar with (especially, alas, in Toronto) is the received wisdom of newspaper reviewers about Bob Dylan concerts in recent years: that they represent the pathetic attempts of a bored and aging legend to recapture a glory that is long gone; that Bob Dylan can no longer write, play, or sing; that he has not been relevant since (check one of the following, according to your ideological disposition) 1964 / 1966 / 1975 / 1980; and that only a hard core of equally aging fanatics, who have become brain-dead through repeated exposure, persist in attending the concerts and treating them as if each and every one was another step on the road to ultimate enlightenment.

Particular ingenuity is exercised on finding ways to describe Dylan's voice. Wounded animal metaphors (especially coyotes caught in barbed wire) have been worn out by long repetition. Personally I still relish the writer in the London *Daily Telegraph* who in 1989 said: "The voice—which seemed, confusingly, to be singing in Iranian—was definitely either his, or that of a very old Ayatollah who had recently sandpapered his vocal cords." So far, the best entry in the 1993 stakes is "sounding like a seal with emphysema."

So why is he even doing it? For many, that is the great mystery of the recent Dylan concerts. Why should a 52-year-old man drag himself around this horrendous schedule, playing three or four concerts a week for months on end, crossing and recrossing America, crossing and recrossing the Atlantic, playing in small halls to a couple of thousand people, playing in open-air stadiums to audiences who would rather hear rap, month after month, year after year? (The so-called Never Ending Tour has basically been running since April 1988; since then he has never been away from touring for any period longer than three months.)

He doesn't need the money; he doesn't need the fame. Does he need the adulation? There isn't even much in the way of obvious "contact" with the audience. Dylan makes none of the conventional ingratiating gestures—he doesn't tell funny stories between songs,[21] he certainly won't say "Hello, it's nice to be in Toronto." You may get one "Thank you" (pronounced "than-Kyou"); you may get a mumbled "That was a song from my latest album" after "Jim Jones" or "Tomorrow Night." Anything more than that *should be taken down verbatim and reported to the Dylan network for instant analysis.*

First bit of advice: the show will not sound like anything you expect. It will *certainly* not sound like his records. No point at all in expecting the amphetamine rush of the mid-1960s, "that high, that wild mercury sound," nor in expecting the ritual theatre of Rolling Thunder, nor the evangelical passion of 1980. Go in without preconceptions. Ignore the *Globe and Mail.* Ignore even this letter. What do I know now (August 2) about what Dylan will sound like three weeks from now? The most recent tapes I have are February and April 1993; that's not a reliable guide. Listen to what is there, not to whatever you think ought to be there.

Though of course it's not that simple. For part of what *is* there is the songs, and they carry their history with them. If he sings "Blowin' in the Wind," the performance belongs to 1963 as much as to 1993. He knows that; you know that. But the history of the songs is not some kind of yardstick by which to measure this present performance (a procedure which invites, indeed *produces,* the response that this performance is falling short). Rather, the history is an echo chamber; it adds resonance, it acknowledges your shared experience—but still, the song says *now,* this is the moment where the music is.

One thing that is clear about the 1993 concerts is that what Dylan does care about is the music. And this may be a beginning to the answer to why he keeps on doing it. More than anything else, he loves making music. This year, the songs have been stretching out in length, most of them running to seven or eight minutes, with the extension coming almost entirely in instrumentals. At times it seems as if he is singing the verses rather perfunctorily, as if to say "Let's get this verbal shit out of the way, so we can get down to the serious business."

And of course it's uneven: sometimes the instrumentals just go on for the sake of going on, and Bob and the band seem to get lost inside the repetitions. But sometimes they have the grace and complexity of good jazz solos or improvisations (the performance at New Orleans in April was especially note-worthy, inspired perhaps by the setting). Mostly what I respond to here is simply Dylan's sheer delight in making music with other people.

He first made his name as a solo performer, because that was the mode of early 1960s folk music, and I think that image misleads us still. The truth is that, ever since 1965, Bob Dylan has preferred performing with other musicians beside him. By all accounts, he is very difficult to play with (perpetually changing keys and tempos, challenging his band to follow every mercurial change in his musical direction), but he has never settled back into the role of the solo performer. He *needs* a band. He needs that sound.

"Of course it's uneven," I said—and that is also part of the conventional wisdom of critical response to the Never Ending Tour. Some nights he's on, some nights he's off. Some nights he's interested in the performance, some nights he's interested in the bottle of beaujolais in his dressing room.

Well, if you play more than a hundred concerts a year, I guess it's inevitable that some nights will be better than others. What's interesting is that in Dylan's case it *shows*. That is, for many performers there is a veneer of professionalism that they can fall back on, so that even on nights when they'd much rather be home watching baseball they still have a set pattern they can use as a kind of disguise. The songs will still come out sounding the same, even if they're bored out of their minds. Dylan has never had that. If he's off form, the audience can tell. (This has nothing to do with whether or not he talks to the audience or turns his back on them; he'll do that even, or especially, on the nights when he's really flying.)

So, to some extent, you pays your money and you takes your chances. Yes, you may get a bad night (though, to be honest, and having listened to dozens of tapes, I think that *really* bad nights are far fewer and further between than some disenchanted critics would have you believe). Or you may get a great night. Or maybe it will vary from song to song.

For that is surely one of the great and continuing glories of Dylan in performance: that he is not predictable, that he changes from night to night, that he is open to moods of improvisation, that he keeps it alive for himself by always looking for something new. Sometimes he'll pull out a song that he hasn't played for years (the advantage of having the greatest backlog repertoire in popular music) and attack it with a fresh energy as if he'd written it yesterday: he did that in '92 with "Idiot Wind," and the results were spectacular.[22] Or else a song that he sings all the time, a chestnut of five hundred concerts—the kind of title that you see on a playlist and think, "Oh no, I'll just fast-forward through this bit of the tape"—is suddenly transformed. A twist to the tune, a new instrumentation, an urgent edge to the voice, and—magic. That's what he did, in New Orleans this April, with "Mr. Tambourine Man."

Which brings me to what I think is the central problem and paradox of Bob Dylan concerts. On the one hand (as I've said), you've got to listen to what is there, to the actual inflections and grace notes of *tonight's* performance, because it's not the same as last night's, and who knows what he'll do tomorrow? But on the other hand, you're always hearing tonight's performance as, in some sense, a variation on a theme you already know. The April '93 "Mr. Tambourine Man" is a great performance in itself, but a part, a very large part of its pleasure lies in its variation from every other performance of "Mr. Tambourine Man" you've ever heard.

So what happens if you *haven't* heard a hundred other versions? What happens if you're not a Dylan tape fanatic, but simply someone who vaguely remembers what "Mr. Tambourine Man" sounded like in 1965 on your big sister's copy of *Bringing It All Back Home?* Is Dylan preaching only to the converted? Is it really only the fanatics who can appreciate what's going on in these concerts?

Let me phrase this in a very practical way: the voice. What would I say in response to "a seal with emphysema"? Well, I would say that Dylan has never (or seldom) had a conventionally "beautiful" voice, that the strength of his singing has always lain not in its tunefulness but in its expressiveness. I ask you to listen to the phrasing, to the masterful ways in which inflections and emphases change, to the strange half-pauses, to the sudden delight in pushing a line up the scale instead of letting it fall, to the moments of emphasis and attack, to the way the rhythm of the words intertwines with the rhythms of the music . . .

For, in all these ways, even if his voice is now rough and growling, even if he can no longer soar in anger or in beauty, Bob Dylan is, still, the greatest vocalist in rock and roll. But again, a lot of this response depends on my ability to compare different performances. Even more basically, it's easy for me *because I already know the words*. Dylan's articulation has never been his strong point; when he sings a song I don't already know I still have the same old problem of wondering what the hell he's saying. But with most of the songs, I know them by heart. So when someone else hears only a mumble, I hear quite clearly "The motorcycle black madonna / Two-wheeled gypsy queen," and I'm waiting to see which of the possible syllables the emphasis will fall on *this* time . . .

Take as an example Dylan's (in)famous performance at the Grammy Awards in 1991, when, at the height of the Gulf War, he went on national television and sang "Masters of War." For many people, the effectiveness of this choice as a political gesture was limited, even canceled, by the fact that they simply couldn't make out the words: they had no idea what song it was. And those who did recognize it claimed it was a poor, inexpressive performance.

As for me, I recognized it from the opening bars (no doubt because I had heard a dozen concert tapes of performances from the previous months) and I could follow every word (no doubt because I have them memorized). I thought it was a brilliant performance, the voice dripping venom, the lips sneering up over the teeth, the punk rock backing slamming every line home, the fiercest attack on an American president ever broadcast on network television.[23] But was my response made possible only by my previous and continuing knowledge of the song? Was that performance, in some fundamental sense, *incomplete in itself*? And if so, how much does that matter?

So what is my advice to you, short of saying listen to a hundred bootleg concert tapes and memorize the words of every song Bob has in his current repertoire? I think I'd ask you to listen to the music, to take the words on trust even if you can't distinguish them, and to watch this strange, shambling, uneasy figure on stage—try to get a sense, above all, of his absolute *commitment to performance*.

In some ways, even after thirty years, Dylan still looks uncomfortable on stage: the way he squints warily into the lights; the way he plants his feet wide apart as if trying to keep his balance on a boat on a stormy sea; the way he appears to ignore both the audience and his band.

But in other ways, clearly the stage is the only place he feels at home. (And that may be the personal tragedy, about which we know almost nothing, of Bob Dylan: that he has no other "home.") Dylan answers the question about why he goes on touring by saying simply "It's what I do." (Not even "what I do best"—simply "what I do.") It's like asking a carpenter why he keeps on hammering wood. These songs, this music, are what he has to give us now, and they still make every other act in popular music seem trivial by comparison.

Just go and see what it looks like, this paradox: the genius as working performer, the old man on stage who will likely go on singing until the band outnumbers the audience.

Enjoy the show, Oliver.

Stephen

Text

In April 1987 Bob Dylan joined the Irish group U2 on stage during one of their concerts and sang "Knockin' on Heaven's Door" with them. In the middle of the song, U2's lead singer, Bono, started improvising a new verse: "Well, the time has come / For this wounded world to start changing. . . ." Then he commented: "You know, I used to make up my own words to Bob Dylan songs. He says he doesn't mind." And Dylan responded: "Well, I do it too."[24]

The extent to which Bob Dylan has been willing to make up new words and new vocal arrangements to his own songs poses another set of problems for the critic. Traditional literary scholarship is always anxious to establish a definitive text, which will then provide a stable and unchanging object of study. Researchers attempt to reconstitute, from the flawed and incomplete printed versions of Shakespeare's plays, what he "actually" wrote. These arguments are usually phrased in terms of authorial intention: what did Shakespeare *mean* to write in this line? But since authors of this stature are assumed to be geniuses, there is always the temptation to argue that the "best" line (or what the editor thinks is the best line) must surely be what the author intended. Thus accidental improvements in the text, caused by misprints or obscure handwriting, may be incorporated on the grounds that the more ordinary reading was "unworthy" of this author. Editorial scholars also have to decide between early and late versions: is the first inspiration preferable to the later revision? Despite these problems, the aim remains the same: the definitive text, the stable object of study.

For Dylan there is no definitive text. There is only a shifting body of work, in which the songs change with each performance and in which the printed text has a limited authority. As Patricia Jungwirth writes:

> In Dylan's case, the "text" is not only a "composition" but a "performance"—or more commonly a series of performances, in some cases extending over many years. Each previous "performance" exists within the current performance, in the consciousness of the writer/performer, and to varying degrees within the separate consciousness of each of the audience members.
>
> The writer/performer often includes the act of composition within the "performance"—revising the "text" right before the ears/eyes of the "audience." Thus the very act of revision also becomes part of the "text"—revision may encompass lyrical, musical or vocal variations, as simple as a change of vocal inflection or emphasis, as complex as adding or subtracting words, lines or entire verses. In other words, a Dylan "text" is not usually fixed or static.[25]

Every time a critic quotes from a Dylan song, the quotation is in some way provisional, hedged around with qualifications. The purpose of this section is to set out some of these qualifications, so that they can then be understood to hover over every other set of quotation marks in this book.

It is often difficult for listeners to determine exactly what the lyrics of a Bob Dylan song are—he has never been noted for clear enunciation. I remember my amazement when I first saw a printed text of "Subterranean Homesick Blues" and compared it with my notes of what I thought he'd been singing! *All Across the Telegraph* includes an amusing section of reported mishearings or "mondegreens" (Gray and Bauldie, 268–69), which range from the comic—Rosemary "took a *cabbage* into town" (for *carriage)*—to the plausibly poetic—"She's delicate and seems like *veneer*" (for *the mirror).*[26]

One reason for these difficulties was that Dylan, like The Rolling Stones, never printed the song lyrics on the album sleeve, as if he were insisting that the words should be heard, even misheard, rather than read. It was not until *Empire Burlesque* in 1985 that printed lyrics appeared as part of an album package.[27] No major collection of Dylan lyrics was in print until Knopf brought out Dylan's *Writings and Drawings* in 1973. This edition was then updated and reissued in 1985 as *Lyrics, 1962–1985,* and it is this volume that has the best claim to be the definitive printed text of Dylan's songs.[28]

But it's a shaky claim. In several ways, *Lyrics* fails to be a definitive collection. In the first place it is drastically incomplete: not just in that it omits (obviously) anything written since 1985, but also songs from before that date. Clinton Heylin lists the titles of forty-eight songs officially copyrighted by Dylan that are not included in *Lyrics,*[29] including several of major importance: "Angelina," "Blind Willie McTell," "Foot of Pride," "Yonder Comes Sin" . . .

Secondly, *Lyrics* prints only one version of each song. Given Dylan's habit of rewriting, this practice cannot help but produce an incomplete picture. A good example is "Tangled Up In Blue," released on *Blood on the Tracks* in 1975. This song has gone through many variations in its lyrics. During the 1978 tour Dylan changed the reference to "an Italian poet," substituting a series of chapter-and-verse biblical citations, which seemed to change randomly with every performance. As previously noted, after the late 1970s "carpenters' wives" changed to "truckdrivers' wives." For the 1984 tour he revised the lyrics much more thoroughly, and this new version was released on *Real Live.* In the notes to *Biograph* Dylan commented, "On *Real Live* it's more like it should have been. . . . The imagery is better and more the way I would have liked it than on the original recording." Nevertheless, *Lyrics* prints only the original 1975 version, without including the "better" 1984 text even as a variant. In the (literally) hundreds of concert performances during the 1990s, Dylan has basically used the 1975 words—though he has recently, for some reason, changed a couple of lines to omit all mention of "Delacroix." In cases like this, *Lyrics* could make a stronger claim to be a definitive text if it printed at least the 1984 version alongside the original text. (A scholarly edition of the variorum Bob Dylan will eventually have to include all the 1978 biblical citations as well.)

It is not that *Lyrics* sticks slavishly to the text of the original recordings. Far from it. *Lyrics* is full of deviations, from the occasionally altered word to the completely rewritten song. Whether these changes are always for the better is open to debate. On "Precious Angel," for instance, Dylan sings the marvelously sensuous and erotic lines "You're the queen of my flesh, girl, you're my woman, you're my delight, / You're the lamp of my soul, girl, and you torch up the night." Both literally and metaphorically, "torch up" ignites this song. But *Lyrics* prints the much more banal "you touch up the night" (L, 426)—typo? accidental mistranscription? deliberate revision?

In other cases the rewriting is wholesale. "Goin' to Acapulco" bears little resemblance to the text sung on *The Basement Tapes,* and the jokes in "I Shall Be Free" have been extensively reworked, despite the fact that Dylan has not sung the song in public since 1963.

And there are other annoyances. The order of songs is sometimes different from the order in which they appear on the albums. *The Basement Tapes* lyrics appear, illogically, neither at the date on which they were recorded nor at the date on which they were released. And so on. *Lyrics,* in other words, bears many signs of carelessness and incompletion, as if Dylan lacked interest in publishing a complete, properly edited, and definitive text. Yet at the same time the book shows such extensive revisions that one can only conclude that it was put together with a good deal of attention and care.[30]

This divided response, that the book is both carefully considered and sloppily casual, is characteristic of the problems of Dylan's text. A similar division is apparent in many recordings, where some songs are tight, word-perfect performances and others are slipshod and hurried, with the mistakes and stumbles left in the released track rather than corrected in another take. On *Self Portrait*, for example, Dylan completely messes up one verse of "Days of '49" and audibly comments "Oh, my goodness" at the end of it. Yet this is the released version.

In contrast to singers who spend weeks in the studio honing and perfecting their material, Dylan likes to move in and out of the studio as quickly as possible. The whole of *Another Side of Bob Dylan* was recorded in a single day: June 9, 1964. Occasionally he has gone back and rerecorded songs, as he did for *Blood on the Tracks*, and recently he has allowed more elaborate studio productions, notably on the two albums produced by Daniel Lanois, *Oh Mercy* and *Time Out Of Mind.* (*"Love and Theft,"* however, seems to have been recorded, with brilliant success, on the premise "one song, one day.") But to a great extent, Dylan seems to have ignored the technical possibilities of modern recording studios and attempted instead to preserve the spontaneity and rough edges of live performance. Oh my goodness.

At the same time it must be remembered that Dylan in the mid-1960s was at the technological front line. He was one of the first performers to use the full power of electronic amplification. What many people who heard Dylan in 1965–66 reacted to most strongly, whether positively or negatively, was the sheer volume. Marlon Brando said that the fucking loudest thing he'd heard in his life was Bob Dylan and the Hawks. Dylan has never rejected the technological capacities of his music, but he has never allowed himself to be dominated by them either. He has never become a fetishist for the perfect sound system or the flawless recording.

In the same way, he has always shown disdain for the commercial and marketing aspects of his profession. He doesn't release the kind of albums his fans expect. In concert tours he ignores his most recent releases and seldom even says, "Hullo, it's nice to be here." Dylan has moved into the world of the mass media and its technological capitalism, but he continues to treat it as if it were a coffeehouse in Greenwich Village.

Which returns us to *Lyrics*. The book is presented as if it were what the fans and scholars might expect: the definitive collection, carefully edited, which would then be the reference point for all Bob Dylan studies. But this expectation is then subverted. Bob Dylan isn't interested in a definitive text any more than he is in becoming a model commercial rock star. Paul Williams describes the effect as "Dylan thumbing his nose at or trying to erase . . . his art even as he anthologizes it, still eating the document" (1990, 1:229).

The final irony is that, for all its imperfections, *Lyrics* is still the best we've got. Most quotations from Dylan songs in this book are from that source. A new, updated edition of *Lyrics* has been promised for years. At the time this book goes to press, there is still no sign of it. Would it remedy, or reproduce, the errors of previous editions? Would it give us "torch up" instead of "touch up"? Would it include an alternate text of "Tangled Up In Blue"? Who knows? (And I sincerely hope that this paragraph will be rendered obsolete as soon as it is published.)

At various stages in his career, Dylan chose to make extensive changes to the words of his songs in performance. Neil Corcoran suggests that "when Dylan revises himself in performance we may regard him as his own first critic: bringing out different nuance and emphasis, interpreting and reinterpreting in ways that serve the original text while also acting to reintroduce it to the contemporary moment" (Corcoran, 15). Such verbal revisions were especially prevalent in the mid-1970s. In the 1990s he was more conservative in preserving the words, though he still rang all sorts of changes on the musical settings and arrangements.

A good example of mid-1970s verbal revision is provided by three different versions of "Going, Going, Gone." This song first appeared on *Planet Waves* (1974), an album largely devoted to songs celebrating married love. It depicts a singer who has reached some extreme point, "the top of the end" (L, 342), which may be religious, political, psychological, or emotional. The context of the album suggests that this is a love song too, an interpretation which is reinforced by the bridge passage:

> Grandma said, "Boy, go and follow your heart
> And you'll be fine at the end of the line.
> All that's gold doesn't shine.
> Don't you and your one true love ever part."

"Grandma" implies a traditional source of proverbial wisdom, so the possible naiveté of the advice is distanced through the imputed speaker. Moreover, the proverb—"All that glisters isn't gold"—is reversed, a technique that was characteristic of Dylan's writing in this period.

Two years later Dylan returned to the song during the Rolling Thunder Revue tour. By this time the love relationships being depicted in Dylan's songs were strained and on the point of collapse. This version opens with the same verse as the original but follows it with a completely new one:

> I'm in love with you, baby,
> But you got to understand
> That you want to be free,
> So let go of my hand.

The separation is here attributed to the woman's desire "to be free," a desire that she herself still has to "understand." The onus is on her to leave him. Another new verse follows:

> I was living on the road
> With my head in the dust,
> So I've just got to go
> Before it's all diamonds and rust.

Now it is the man who feels that it's up to him to leave. If the song is to be interpreted biographically, in relation to the breakup of Dylan's marriage to Sara, the level of personal reference is complicated here by the phrase "diamonds and rust"—which is the title of a song that Joan Baez wrote about *her* relationship to Bob Dylan. At the time of this performance, both Sara Dylan and Joan Baez were on the Rolling Thunder tour and engaged in the filming of *Renaldo and Clara*.

In this version the bridge passage runs:

> Papa says, "Son, go and follow your heart
> And you'll be fine at the end of the line.
> All that's gold isn't meant to shine.
> Don't you and your life-long dream ever part."

"Grandma" has been replaced as the source of conventional wisdom by "Papa," a switch that is in keeping with Dylan's obsession at this time with the figure of the dying father. Now the gold not only "doesn't shine," it isn't even "meant to shine" (this is the version of the line printed in *Lyrics),* and the "one true love" becomes the more desperate but less specific "life-long dream."

A third version appears on the 1978 album *Bob Dylan at Budokan,* and it gives us a completely new set of words:

> Well, I just reached a place
> Where I can't stay awake.
> I've got to leave you, baby,
> Before my heart will break
>
> . . . .
>
> Now from Boston to Birmingham
> Is a two-day ride,
> But I got to be goin' now
> 'cos I'm so dissatisfied.

This version, with its long, drawn-out repetition of the final chorus, is fully committed to separation, and the wish to go is now unequivocally on the man's side. Biographical speculation would point out that this version comes after the divorce from Sara. There is also the curious point that the Baez reference has been replaced by an oblique one to Emmylou Harris, backup singer on *Desire,* and author of the song "From Boulder to Birmingham." The bridge passage finds a woman back in the advice-giving role:

> Now my Mama always said, "Go and follow your heart
> And you'll be fine to the end of the line.
> All that's gold wasn't meant to shine

—*wasn't* now, the relationship firmly relegated to the past tense—

> Just don't put your horse in front of your cart."

This brilliant last line does at least three things. It reverses a cliché, so that it now advises *against* conventional arrangements (equestrian or marital). It comments by omission on the naive expectations of the previous versions, that the singer and his one true love/life-long dream would never part. And it is a joke shared with the audience by playing its outrageousness against their memories of previous versions.

Not all of Dylan's revisions have been as drastic as those to "Going, Going, Gone." Often he will change only a single line or image. Shakespeare in the alley of "Memphis Blues Again" sometimes has "pointed shoes," sometimes a "tambourine." In one 1999 performance "Visions of Johanna" became, on two of the four choruses, "Visions of Madonna." Sometimes these changes are the accidents of a single performance, but others (like "truckdriver" for "carpenter") become permanent parts of the text. And at other times a song will be wholly and completely rewritten, as is the case with the 2002 version of the 1979 song "Gonna Change My Way of Thinking" (discussed at the end of Chapter 4).

Sometimes the rewriting is a deliberate change in direction or meaning for the song, but sometimes also it is the result of a protracted effort to get the original impulse of the song right, as Dylan shows in his comments about "Caribbean Wind" in the *Biograph* liner notes:

> Sometimes you'll write something to be very inspired, and you won't quite finish it for one reason or another. Then you'll go back and try and pick it up, and the inspiration is just gone. Either you get it all, and you can leave a few little pieces to fill in, or you're always trying to finish it off. Then it's a struggle. The inspiration's gone and you can't remember why you started it in the first place. Frustration sets in. I think there's four different sets of lyrics to this, maybe I got it right, I don't know. I had to leave it. I just dropped it.
>
> (Crowe)

While this comment simply describes the process of revision that any artist goes through, in Bob Dylan's case the process takes place at least partly in public. Two of the alternate "different sets of lyrics" to "Caribbean Wind" (one concert, one studio) are now in circulation. Again the critic faces the problem of the indeterminacy of the Dylan text. "Caribbean Wind" has no single definitive set of words. The listener has the opportunity of judging between several versions (and I personally cannot say which I prefer).

It seems safe to say that Dylan never regards a song as unalterably finished. At any time he is prepared to come back and rework the lyrics or the music— and equally he may abandon these revisions and return to the "original" text. But his continuing commitment to the performance and reinterpretation of his old songs means that the text is never definitively closed.

So what is the "text" of a Dylan song? Do we privilege the original recording, and/or the words printed in *Lyrics,* or do we look to the most recently revised concert version? I suggest that the text of a Dylan song is not any one of these choices exclusively but rather their sum. It is the accumulation of all performances, the song's total history. The text is not a fixed set of words or music but a fluid space, a performance area, which sets out a musical and thematic field within which any one version can only be provisional. Dylan minimizes the importance of a stable text as *product* and maximizes the importance of the *process* of singing and listening.

Paul Williams, the most perceptive critic of Dylan as a performer, sums up much of this argument when he writes:

> Listening to these unreleased alternate takes is a reminder that when Dylan is fully involved in the music he's making, every performance of every song is new and different and exciting. The music is so fluid, so expressive of what Dylan is feeling moment to moment, that it would be misleading to suggest that one melodic or rhythmic or lyrical variant is more true to the song's intention than another. That assumes a specific intent that precedes the writing and performing of a song, whereas all the evidence is that Dylan's songs . . . express a constantly shifting intent which is feeling-based and unconscious at least as much as it is deliberate, conscious, premeditated.
>
> (1990, 1:138)

Williams's reference to "unreleased alternate takes" brings us to another major aspect of the indeterminacy of Dylan's texts—the question of bootlegs.[31]

The first widely circulated Bob Dylan bootleg was the so-called *Great White Wonder,* which came out in 1969.[32] It was a haphazard double-album collection of recordings from the early years of Dylan's career and from The Basement Tapes. Sound quality was generally poor, and the album took its name from the complete lack of sleeve notes, illustrations, or even track listings.

In the thirty-plus years since, bootlegging has become a much more sophisticated enterprise. Sound quality has greatly improved, and the sheer amount of underground Dylan material in circulation is staggering. Bootleg Dylan falls into two major categories: studio outtakes and concert recordings. Studio outtakes consist of songs recorded in studios, usually during the sessions that produce official albums. They thus may include alternate versions of songs that do appear on the albums, with different words and/or music, and also songs that, for one reason or another, were not included on the released albums. Concert recordings are tapes made of live performances, usually by audience members carrying concealed microphones, though occasionally by direct tap out of the soundboard. The vast majority of Dylan's concerts since 1974 have been bootlegged in some form or another.

Why has Dylan been bootlegged on such a scale? The answer has to include the semimythical status that Dylan attained in the early 1960s and has never lost over the years. Consciously or unconsciously, he has cultivated an air of mystery. His most trivial statements take on an oracular status. The Great White Wonder appeared when Dylan was in seclusion; his very secretiveness fed the desire for hidden Dylan songs. Even in recent years, when he has been touring almost constantly, the fear that he might again lapse into silence has given his performances an odd kind of scarcity value.

This value is paradoxical, for Dylan bootlegs are anything but scarce. Indeed, the main reason for their persistence is simply that so much interesting material is available. Again the variability of the Dylan text comes into play. There would be little point in taping hundreds of live shows from most pop singers, because they vary their songs so little in performance: one concert is pretty much a carbon copy of any other. But no two Dylan shows, even on consecutive nights, are ever quite the same. Though there certainly is a law of diminishing returns in listening to more than a thousand performances of "All Along the Watchtower," it remains remarkable how slow that law is to set in. The range and richness of Dylan's concert performances are more than enough to sustain a steady interest in bootleg recordings of them.

With the studio outtakes there is the even more interesting problem that Dylan has chosen not to release some of his best work. Many important songs circulated widely in bootleg before they were officially released. *Biograph* (1985) made available such major titles as "Lay Down Your Weary Tune" and "Caribbean Wind." The 1991 release of *The Bootleg Series Volumes 1–3* finally added "Farewell Angelina," "Blind Willie McTell," and many more. The words for some of these songs appear in *Lyrics,* but several of them are not acknowledged even there. The very title of *The Bootleg Series* acknowledges the importance of the bootleg phenomenon in preserving (and finally forcing the release of) a very major part of Dylan's artistic legacy.33

What is the critic to do with this material? To begin with, certain legal questions arise. These are, after all, illegal recordings. Some bootleggers undoubtedly make money, though the majority do not sell tapes or CD-Rs but exchange them freely, and collectors will, in any case, buy everything that Dylan officially releases. Many such collectors object strongly to the term *bootleg,* which implies sale for profit. Rather, they take their motto from Dylan himself: "To live outside the law, you must be honest" (L, 233).

There is an ethical problem, too. One may argue that the work has a right to be heard which supersedes the author's right to control his creations—but who is to make this decision? As a critic using rejected material, I am setting myself up to second-guess Bob Dylan's editorial choices. While critics regularly do this when sifting through the manuscripts of a dead author, it is rarely that we have the chance to do so while the author is still alive. Sometimes, of course, I agree with Dylan's decisions. I would not want to see the embarrassing "Julius and Ethel" included on *Infidels,* and the 1970 recordings of "Yesterday" and "Da Doo Ron Ron" are strictly for fanatics only.

In other cases, however, I have to assert my critical judgment that Dylan has been drastically wrong in the choices he made. *Shot of Love* (1981) is often seen as one of his weakest albums, but if you add in its outtakes— "Angelina," "Caribbean Wind," and "The Groom's Still Waiting at the Altar"—the assessment is dramatically changed. These three songs present a fascinating mixture of surrealist and Christian imagery, and they show Dylan's verbal art reemerging from the straightjacket of fundamentalist rhetoric. Dylan may have felt that they were unresolved or imperfect, yet their very incompletion makes them more interesting artistic objects than the smooth banalities of "Watered-Down Love" or "In the Summertime," which did make it to the album.

The more one explores the bootleg material, the more such questions arise. By what right of authorship could one justify withholding release of "Lay Down Your Weary Tune" for twenty years? Why were we never meant to hear "She's Your Lover Now"? Whatever possessed him to suppress "Blind Willie McTell" for so long?

Such questions challenge the privileged position of the author as the ultimate source and arbiter of his work. They point to another way in which the text has escaped the author's jurisdiction and control. This excess of the text over the author, evident in its most concrete form in bootlegs, is also what I have been arguing all the way through this section: that the Dylan text is indeterminate and nondefinitive, never to be regarded as a transparent or reliable indicator of its author. In this sense "the text of Bob Dylan" rejoins "Bob Dylan as text." The songs in all their manifestations are only part of the total text, which also includes the biography, the interviews, and all the phenomena of Bob Dylan's public career—phenomena that include the assiduous wielders of concealed microphones at every concert.

"Bob Dylan" is a text that remains open: a disseminated text that gives no guarantee of any unitary self originating it, a text from which the "author" has always already disappeared. To return one last time to "Going, Going, Gone," whose variations I earlier traced, Dylan might be understood to be speaking of precisely this disappearance when he sings:

> I'm closin' the book
> On the pages and the text
> And I don't really care
> What happens next.
> I'm just going,
> I'm going,
> I'm gone.

(L, 342)

"Like a Rolling Stone"

There's never been a moment in the history of rock and roll to equal the excitement of that first sharp crack of the snare drum. Insistently, arrogantly, authoritatively, it inaugurated a new world. In Bruce Springsteen's words, from the speech he gave when Dylan was inducted into the Rock and Roll Hall of Fame in 1988: "It sounded like somebody'd kicked open the door to your mind." Then the voice snarls in: "Once upon a time. . . ." The most traditional of openings, the most revolutionary of songs.

"Like a Rolling Stone" (L, 191–92) is so foundational to Dylan that it's almost impossible to view it as an ordinary song with a specific subject, themes, and images. The lyrics present a portrait of a character who has recently experienced a drastic reversal of fortune. I will call her "Miss Lonely" (the only name the song attributes to her), but bear in mind that the "you" of a Dylan song is always a multiple other, and that in some ways the addressee is also Bob Dylan himself, the audience, or even God.

The words allow for a wide range of emotional response. Neil Corcoran sees the song as "a tale of *schadenfreude* so venomous, but also so exultant, as almost to create an entirely new emotion" (Corcoran, 161), while Mark Ford comments: "Despite its appearnng initially to be a vituperative, lower-Manhattan, score-settling song ... it seems to me inspired ... by a kind of artistic exhilaration at the possibilities suddenly discovered within a seemingly exhausted genre" (Corcoran, 133). Both the venom and the exhilaration are clearly evident in the lyrics. They express anger and a certain amount of gloating at the woman's plight. The song has often been seen as primarily, or even simply, an act of revenge. Dylan encouraged this interpretation by referring to the early draft as "a long piece of vomit." But there is also a sense that Miss Lonely has liberated herself, and that living "out on the street" is greatly to be preferred to confinement in "the finest school."

Paul Nelson saw the ending as "clearly optimistic and triumphant, a soaring of the spirit into a new and more productive present" (McGregor, 107). While there are negative connotations to being "on your own . . . without a home . . . with no direction home," there is also a sense of freedom, honesty, and self-reliance. Dylan's whole musical career up to 1965, especially his inheritance of the Woody Guthrie tradition, would suggest that to live "like a rolling stone" is a far-from-undesirable destiny. Each verse builds up to the climactic moment of release on "How does it feel?"—it is the pattern of male sexual orgasm or, more learnedly, of Aristotelian catharsis. But the question proves to have no simple answer, as is demonstrated by the song's performance history.

The original recording, of June 16, 1965, already reflects the range of possibilities. At the time it seemed like a vitriolic performance, but in retrospect Dylan's voice sounds almost mellow. He is fully involved here with the characterization: this version is *about* Miss Lonely in ways that few of the later versions would be. (Or indeed could be: inevitably, every subsequent performance is *about* "Like a Rolling Stone"; that is, about itself and the song's history.) The band drives hard and direct toward the climax of "How does it feel?", but Al Kooper's organ track—added, so legend has it, almost by accident—hints at more hymnic and celebratory moods. It remains a great rock and roll recording, and as close to a definitive performance as one can ever get with Dylan. It also remains the touchstone from which all subsequent variations derive their meaning.

Perhaps the most famous bootleg recording of Dylan, finally released officially in 1998, features "Like a Rolling Stone." It dates from Manchester Free Trade Hall, May 17, 1966. The audiences on this tour were openly hostile to Dylan's electric music, which they chose to see as a betrayal of folk music purity. Someone in the crowd yells out "Judas!" and there is a smattering of applause and embarrassed laughter. "I don't believe you," Dylan says, ironically quoting the title of one of his acoustic songs recently translated into an electric arrangement. "You're a liar!" Then he steps back from the microphone and shouts (barely audible on the tape) "Get fucking loud!"—whereupon The Hawks slam in with the opening chords of "Like a Rolling Stone."[1]

There is no doubt about the mood of this version: it's pure venom. The anger, however, is directed not at the character Miss Lonely but at the audience—and by extension at all the audiences who for the past year had been reacting with such incomprehension to the changes in Dylan's art. The vocal is pitched much higher than on the original recording, and it seems right on the edge of control. The band is dominated by pounding drums, but Robbie Robertson's guitar matches the intensity of Dylan's voice. And even in this version, the anger is modified by the fierce glee of the performance. Dylan and his band were making great music, and they knew it; even as they destroy the hecklers, there is an element of sheer joy in their energy.

Three years later, the performance at the Isle of Wight, on August 31, 1969, took place in a completely different context. It was Dylan's first major concert appearance since his withdrawal into seclusion in 1966, and it was to be his last until he resumed touring in 1974. As might be expected, he and The Band were under-rehearsed, and the version of "Like a Rolling Stone" is, to put it mildly, a mess. A genial mess, though. Dylan sings in long tumbling runs that slide down the scale like waterfalls. In the second verse he forgets the words and sings the same line three times, his mumble retreating into deeper obscurity than ever. No attempt is made to build up to a crescendo on "How does it feel?"

Two points need to be made about this performance. First, it in no way displaces or annuls the original. Indeed, it works only with reference to the original; Dylan is relying on his audience's familiarity with the song. Hey, he's saying, it's no big deal, it's just a song, not a way of life. We can have fun with it too. And second, Dylan chose to release this version officially as part of *Self Portrait*. In that context it participates in the remarkable deconstruction of his image that is that album's ironic project. No other song could have made the point quite as forcefully.

When Dylan resumed touring in 1974, his relationship with his audience was very different from what it had been eight years previously. Now the concerts were a celebration of the times he and they had been through together. The political context of Watergate gave new emphasis to lines like "even the President of the United States / Sometimes must have / To stand naked" (L, 177). As is evident in the version released on *Before the Flood*, "Like a Rolling Stone" became the climax of this celebration. The voice now stressed the liberation rather than the putdown, and the dominant instrument was Garth

Hudson's organ, whose rolling five-note phrase after each line of the chorus transformed the song into an anthem. The answer to "How does it feel?" was unequivocal: it feels great. Welcome back, Bob. It feels wonderful.

By 1980–81 the context had changed again. In his first concerts after his conversion to fundamentalist Christianity, Dylan had resolutely played only the new religious songs. When he began to reintroduce older songs into the act, one of the first was "Like a Rolling Stone." In the new context Miss Lonely became a lost soul who had missed her true "direction home" to Christ.[2] All anger had been replaced by Christian compassion and forgiveness. Dylan's voice was mournful and sympathetic, and the music had become, quite literally, more tuneful. Whereas the lines of the verse in previous versions had been sung as long runs on a single note with only a few embellishments, this version has a complex and lovely melody carefully worked out and sustained through all four verses.

In 1988, working with the trio led by G. E. Smith on guitar, Dylan attempted "Like a Rolling Stone" without keyboards for the first time. The arrangement was thoroughly reworked: there is an instrumental bridge passage before the last verse, and Smith takes long guitar solos. In many ways this rendition returned more closely to the 1965 original than to any of the intermediaries. The 1988 "Like a Rolling Stone" is a straight-ahead rock song, which once again balances between the anger of the personal attack, the liberation of the chorus, and the joy of its own music.

In general, this latter mood is the one which has been sustained throughout the 1990s. The song still appears fairly regularly in set lists, often in a crowd-pleasing spot as an encore. It functions as a celebration of the history shared by Dylan and his audience, and as such it is often very enjoyable to listen to. But at the same time, it seems that the song has become progressively drained of meaning. The performances are pleasant enough but somewhat routine, and certainly lacking in any hint of vindictiveness. It's been years since Dylan has significantly rethought or felt this song. Like Miss Lonely herself, it is badly in need of a new direction home.[3]

Genres

Muses and Minstrels: Songs about Songs

At the beginning of "You Angel You," the singer, attempting to express the happiness he feels with his "angel," declares "I feel I could almost sing" (L, 348). But he *is* singing—so the line turns on itself in a self-reflexive twist by which the ostensible content of the statement (I am not yet singing, though I feel I could) is modified to the point of reversal by the form (I am singing).

This section, "Muses and Minstrels," examines statements Bob Dylan has made about his position as a singer: about his art, its sources and inspirations, and about other artists. These statements are not those made by Dylan in interviews (seriously handled or otherwise) but those made *in the songs themselves*. As usual, Dylan is offering images of the self at one remove. The artist he addresses in these songs is a distanced version of himself—even, or especially, when that address is diverted through songs dedicated to *other* singers or artists.

These songs are all subject to the self-reflexive twist of "You Angel You." Saying "I feel I could almost sing" in an interview is very different from singing the same words in a song. The song has already, by its very existence, transcended the creative impasse that the words describe. The result is the familiar paradox of the artist's anti-art pose. If someone tells you that he can no longer write a good poem, but does so in a good poem, how is he to be believed?[1]

At the same time, the song loops round on itself. It returns the singer imaginatively to the moment of the impasse. The song reenacts the difficulty of its own creation and renews the always unfulfilled desire for its own point of origin. So another recurring motif is that of the "Eternal Circle" (L, 117). Discussing the song of that name, Aidan Day says:

> The closing of the circle of this song, its completion, does not close the larger cycle—the eternal, temporally unclosable circle of creativity—within which the work has its beginning and its end. As an object of desire, beckoning towards creation, the creative spirit is realized in this song and simultaneously . . . she always lies beyond it, like echo to a sound or shadow to the figure which casts it.
>
> (31)

This motif of the echo or the shadow ties in with such images as mask, mirror, and ghost, all of which repeat the structural relationship that the alias has to the proper name. The source of inspiration is presented as one step removed, deferred beyond the point where it can be immediately grasped, and always elusive and indefinable.

The circular motif is implicit in the very nature of song, in the repetition of the same tune in verse after verse, and in the return of a chorus after these verses.[2] The 1964 song "Lay Down Your Weary Tune" strongly thematizes this formal characteristic. The circle is a traditional emblem of unity, and the vision in this song is of a mystical or pantheistic unity between all the elements of man and nature. The verses present this unity in a series of images that unite natural phenomena (breeze, dawn) with cultural artifacts (bugle, drums)—

> The morning breeze like a bugle blew
> Against the drums of dawn

—while the chorus advises the singer to

> Lay down your weary tune, lay down,
> Lay down the song you strum,
> And rest yourself 'neath the strength of strings
> No voice can hope to hum.
>
> (L, 120)

The recurrence of the chorus is emphasized because it has the same tune as the verse. As Michael Gray comments, this device "doubles the sense of unity which covers the whole song" (197). The song moves in a circle from chorus to verse to chorus, but each element is itself a circle, the repetition of the tune.

The sense of unity is also expressed in the synesthetic nature of the images: one sense-impression is consistently conveyed in terms of another. Thus the blowing of the breeze (touch) is registered in terms of the blowing of a bugle (sound); the two different but allied senses of *blew* mediate the comparison. The "river's mirror" is "watched" (sight) as something which can be heard: a guitar's "strum." Hearing is the master term in all these analogies, and what is heard is always music.

Dylan's presentation of these movements between senses is rapid and compressed. Take the line "The cryin' rain like a trumpet sang." We begin with a familiar comparison, the visual correspondence between rain and teardrops. But the dominant aural metaphor of the song transforms *crying* into its alternate sense, so that the cry becomes a sound, calling out. The sound of the rain is then compared to the sound of a trumpet, furthering the analogical correspondence of natural phenomena and cultural artifacts. Even the sound of the trumpet is immediately modified, by another comparison, into a human voice singing. The human voice thus stands at the midpoint between rain and trumpet: natural because it is human and cultural because it is singing.

The circle is also timeless. Although the lyrics do refer to temporal progression (dawn, autumn), they present images of cyclical recurrence (hours of the day, seasons of the year). The song's dominant feeling is of a moment suspended in time, the moment of the mystic caught up in the rapture of his vision. In the face of this vastness, the individual singer seems reduced to insignificance. He is advised to lay down his weary tune and take refuge in that "strength of strings" so much greater than his own strength.

But the self-reflexive twist enters this song too, for "Lay Down Your Weary Tune" does not obey its own advice. The singer advised to stop singing does not stop singing: indeed, we only know about the advice because it is contained in the song we are hearing. To the extent that this song successfully creates the image of unity, it embodies the "strength of strings"; its voice (Dylan's) does in fact hum what "No voice can hope to hum." So the very existence of the song transcends the limitations set out in the lyrics of the song.

"Lay Down Your Weary Tune" presents a grand vision of transcendence in both man and nature, and it uses music as the mediating term of this comparison. The human creation of music, both by voice and by instruments, becomes the image for the beauty and infinity of the natural world. This metaphor also occurs in other Dylan songs. "Chimes of Freedom," for instance, replays the sense of mystic unity found in "Lay Down Your Weary Tune," but adds the experience of the social world. The chimes are heard not just by a solitary watcher on the shoreline but by a group of friends in the city, and they toll for the refugees, the rebel, the outcast: "every hung-up person in the whole wide universe" (L, 133). The metaphor of this song presents a thunderstorm as "majestic bells" playing in a "wild cathedral evening." Synesthesia is used again, since it is the flashes of lightning (visual) rather than the crashes of the thunder (aural) that are presented as "chimes."

In these songs the site and source of inspiration are located outside the singer: on the shoreline, or in the thunder. Yet that "outside" is always potentially interiorized, since the natural metaphor is a metaphor *for* the creative power of the singer himself. This paradox of inspiration, as something simultaneously coming to the artist from somewhere outside, yet also arising from within his imagination, has traditionally been presented through the figure of the Muse. As a goddess, a figure separate from the artist, the muse is the external source of inspiration, something that the artist cannot fully control. Yet she is also the projection of the artist's inner creativity; when he addresses her, he is also addressing himself.

I say *she*, for the muse is (for male artists) traditionally female. Most Dylan songs that can be interpreted as addresses to his muse recognize this tradition. But in one striking case, the muse also is male: *Mister* Tambourine Man. Perhaps because he is male and because he plays a musical instrument, he is more clearly and closely related to the singer than the female figures tend to be. Moreover, the tambourine is an instrument that cannot carry a tune by itself: it needs the cooperation of the singer if a song is to be created.

"Mr. Tambourine Man" extends the imagery of "Lay Down Your Weary Tune." Again the setting is a shoreline, the meeting of earth, sea, and sky; again the singer is alone. The song begins in the evening, but looks forward to the renewal of the cycle in the "jingle jangle morning" (L, 172). In that image the sound of the tambourine is synesthetically transferred to the natural scene. While the earlier song had at least ostensibly seen the singer's "weary tune" as futile and inadequate, "Mr. Tambourine Man" welcomes his participation in the music and the dance. The singer asks the muse to "play a song for me," and responds that he will "come followin' you" and "dance beneath the diamond sky." Most obviously, Dylan will respond with the lovely harmonica solos which have been a feature of the song from its original recording on *Bringing It All Back Home* to many subsequent concerts.

The singer's request and response bring us again to the self-reflexive twist of songs about making songs. Aidan Day points out that the repeated "play a song for me" can be read as desperate, "as much a plea as an injunction. . . . 'Mr. Tambourine Man' comprises an account of what it is to be inspired from the immediate vantage point of not being so" (20). Yet Day also acknowledges that "the work itself evidences an attainment of the creative moment which its speaker spends so much time anticipating" (24). Such an attainment is always temporary. Desire renews itself in the moment of its accomplishment, and the cycle of creation begins again.

For most of the song, the relationship between the singer and his muse is based on a clearly defined distance. The singer must appeal to the muse for inspiration, must prepare himself by stripping his senses (the "systematic derangement of the senses" called for by Rimbaud) and ridding himself of obligations ("there is no place I'm going to"), and then he must follow, be "ready to go anywhere." But in the third stanza,[3] the interaction becomes more complex:

> And if you hear vague traces of skippin' reels of rhyme
> To your tambourine in time, it's just a ragged clown behind,
> I wouldn't pay it any mind, it's just a shadow you're
> Seein' that he's chasin'.

A third figure—the "ragged clown"—enters, and then even a fourth—the "shadow" seen by the Tambourine Man and chased by the clown. Now it is the singer's turn to give advice and even comfort to his muse: "I wouldn't pay it any mind." The Tambourine Man can see only shadows and hear only "traces" of the "reels of rhyme"—rhyme being the verbal art possessed by a singer but not by a tambourine player. At the same time, the clown needs the Tambourine Man to see the shadow that he's chasing. Poetic inspiration is deferred, passed from one figure to another along a chain of substitutions, from the Tambourine

Man to the singer to the clown to the shadow. And what is the shadow a shadow *of*? Day comments, "Poetic language and poetic power chase each other in a circle of mutual implication, an incessant shadow-play" (26).

The "mutual implication" of singer and muse is also evident in "Eternal Circle." Here the muse is a woman who stands in the audience while the singer plays a song, but who disappears by the end of it. The link between them is established by the familiar I/eye pun: "She called with her eyes / To the tune I's a-playin' " (L, 117). *Eye* and *I* continue to interact throughout the song: her face reflects his words; his "eyes danced a circle / Across her clear outline"; looking at the audience he pretends that "of all the eyes out there / I could see none." But when he looks for her at the end of the song, he finds that "her shadow was missin'."

While the Tambourine Man had only seen a shadow, here the woman *is* a shadow—an absent one at that. The shadow, like the "vague traces of . . . rhyme," stands in for the full, unmediated experience that can only be posited, never realized. The work of art is always a trace. All the artist can do in his desire for the missing, deferred origin is to enter the eternal circle of creation again: "So I picked up my guitar / And began the next song."

Both "Eternal Circle" and "Mr. Tambourine Man" present the cooperative relationship, even mutual identification, of singer and muse. In other songs Dylan has stressed the distance and the demands of the muse, the degree to which he is, at times, at her mercy:

> You will start out standing
> Proud to steal her anything she sees.
> But you will wind up peeking through her keyhole
> Down upon your knees.
>
> (L, 163)

Although "She Belongs To Me" has been widely read as a love song, I agree with Bill Allison[4] that it also can be interpreted as another account of the singer and the muse. Here the muse is dominant. She has everything she needs, she's beyond the reach of the law, she should be worshipped on ritual occasions. By contrast, the singer is simply a "walking antique" in her collection. His position on his knees is not so much one of prayer as one of humiliation. The only vision she vouchsafes him is a voyeur's peek.

Yet again the ostensible meaning of the lyrics is modified by the performance—the last verse is a genuinely joyful celebration—and, interestingly, by the title. Allison points out that the first person *me* appears only in the title, not in the verses, and suggests that this unspoken *I* is to be identified with the reflexive *you* of the lyrics. So the muse, who makes these extreme demands of the singer, nevertheless belongs to him. She is the shadow that he is chasing, but she is also *his* shadow.

This muse "wears an Egyptian ring," sometimes in performance "an Egyptian red ring." The ring, a symbol of eternity, is associated with ancient goddesses of wisdom and fertility such as Isis, who was worshipped by the Egyptians as "thou lady of the red apparel" (Walker, 454). In the 1970s, songs such as "Isis," "Oh, Sister," and "Golden Loom" evoke the spiritual and creative powers of the "Sweet Goddess / Born of a blinding light and a changing wind" (L, 343) and cast her again in the role of the muse. After Dylan's conversion to Christianity, the muse figure was transformed into "Precious Angel" and "Covenant Woman." In "Caribbean Wind" she appears to him while he is "playing a show in Miami in the theater of divine comedy" (L, 466).

In all these cases the muse is an external force, a divine creature to be worshipped, Beatrice to the Dante of *The Divine Comedy*. Yet in each case she is also internalized, the partner in the dialogue of I and I. "Isis" is "a song about a marriage," and it ends with an ecstatic "Yes!" She belongs to me.

There is, however, a darker, negative characteristic of the muse. Or perhaps we should say, there is also a false muse. This anti-muse is addressed in "Dirge." "I hate myself for lovin' you" (L, 347), the song opens, and immediately we plunge into the internal debate. This "you" is no less a part of Dylan than the "you" addressed self-reflexively in "Lay Down Your Weary Tune" and "She Belongs To Me." In this song she is never identified, not even as "she." Only the conventions of address by a male singer might lead one to suppose that the "you" is a woman.

She stands in stark contrast to the beloved "you" addressed in the other songs on *Planet Waves*, yet she is as much a part of the singer as the woman to whom he sings, "You're the other half of what I am" (L, 350). "We stared into each other's eyes," Dylan sings in "Dirge," because they *are* each other's I's. Their relationship has been one of weakness and need, of simultaneous hate and love. This "you" has, like Bob Dylan, sung "songs of freedom," but also has shown him mercy beyond what he could have guessed. At the same time, she is "a painted face on a trip down Suicide Road": the false muse of fame, commercial success, "a moment's glory."

"Dirge" is a bitter and impassioned rejection of the anti-muse, but the song recognizes that the need, and the love, are real. The ending is ambiguous: "I hate myself for lovin' you, but I should get over that." Is it the love or the hate that he has to get over? Can they be distinguished from each other? This, too, is a muse who belongs to me.

So far this section has dealt with Dylan's attitudes toward his music and its sources of inspiration entirely from the perspective of Dylan as a solitary, unique figure. But the muse, in whatever aspect, "belongs to" other people as well.

The singer of "Dirge" may have "paid the price of solitude," but no singer is ever truly alone or "out of debt." Any given work is necessarily situated inter-textually within the context of other works. Any text is always part of the accumulating intertext, building and rebuilding on what is already waiting there. I take this phrasing from Dylan himself, in "11 Outlined Epitaphs":

> Yes, I am a thief of thoughts
> not, I pray, a stealer of souls
> I have built an' rebuilt
> upon what is waitin'
> . . . .
> on what has been opened
> before my time
> a word, a tune, a story, a line
> keys in the wind t' unlock my mind.

(L, 112)

It is not just that influence is inescapable; it is that *influence* is too puny and limited a word. "I can't tell you the influences," Dylan writes in "My Life in a Stolen Moment," " 'cause there's too many to mention an' I might leave one out." He lists singers like Woody Guthrie and Big Joe Williams, "records you hear but one time," the call of the coyote, the meow of the tomcat, and the "train whistle moan" (L, 72).

"Open up yer eyes an' ears an' yer influenced," the passage concludes, "there's nothing you can do about it." This is not simply a denial of the responsibility of acknowledging sources: it is recognition that the sources are everywhere, so widespread that they will never all be tracked down. It is a tribute to the whole intertext of American song which Bob Dylan had learned from midnight radios in Hibbing, from recordings like Harry Smith's *Anthology of Folk Music*, and, above all, from other singers. It is an "influence," and so much more than an influence, that continues into the saturation of intertextual quotation on *Time Out Of Mind* and *"Love and Theft."*

The rest of this section looks at three evocations in song of other artists: Woody Guthrie, Lenny Bruce, and Blind Willie McTell.5 In each case the sincerity of Dylan's tribute is not in question, but that sincerity in no way interferes with the songs' self-reflexiveness. Guthrie, Bruce, and McTell are indeed praised for their accomplishments, but they are also projections of Dylan's view of himself as an artist. They are his own images at one remove. As Ginsberg said in reference to "Lenny Bruce": "He's really talking about himself also, and all us artists" (Gray and Bauldie, 173).

"Song to Woody" was Bob Dylan's first major composition, and all the biographical accounts testify to the importance he attached to his meetings with Woody Guthrie and the song he had written for his idol. Robert Shelton quotes Dylan as having told Izzy Young, "When I wrote 'Song to Woody' in February, I gave Woody the paper I wrote the song on. Woody liked my song" (Shelton, 102). (Of course, he also told Young that he had first met Woody Guthrie when he was thirteen!)

The song works hard to establish the connection between its author and its subject. The first line of the second verse—"Hey, hey, Woody Guthrie, I wrote you a song" (L, 6)—is almost childish in its delight, which seems to arise as much from the fact that *I* wrote it as from the fact that it's *for* "you." The lyrics underline that connection in the singer's claim that *"I'm* seein' *your* world" (my emphasis), and in the even more convoluted reciprocity of "I know that you know / All the things that I'm a-sayin'." The fourth verse evokes "Cisco an' Sonny an' Leadbelly too" and enlists Bob Dylan by unspoken implication as the latest in that line.

The intimacy between author and subject is also established by the song's appropriation of Guthrie's music. The tune was one that Guthrie had used, and the words contain more than just echoes. Terry Alexander Gans comments:

Incorporated freely into the song are Guthrie lines such as: "come with the dust and are gone with the wind," from "Pastures of Plenty"; and "hittin' some hard travelin'," from "Lincoln Highway." Thus Dylan pays tribute to Guthrie by letting the man write some of the song for him.

(67–68)

By quoting Woody Guthrie as part of his own song, Dylan is projecting Guthrie as a part of himself: not just "you and I" but already, in embryonic form, "I and I."

The paradoxes and contradictions of this project of self-creation are evident in the last two lines: "The very last thing that I'd want to do / Is to say I've been hittin' some hard travelin' too." The young Dylan had, of course, been saying just that, spinning tall tales about the extent of his travels in an attempt to make himself seem more like, say, Woody Guthrie. However, the strict grammatical and idiomatic sense of the words he writes contradicts what he apparently wants to say. The "very last thing that [anyone] would want to do" is normally something that he truly does *not* wish to do. But the sense of Dylan's lines, conveyed despite the words, is that he *does* want to do some hard traveling—or at least to be able to *say* that he's done some. When he does say it, he uses, as Gans noted, a quotation from Woody Guthrie. In the ambiguities of these lines, the strain of Dylan's appropriation of Guthrie threatens to overcome the song. In performance, of course, Dylan blithely sings the lines as if there were no ambiguity there.[6]

A later poem, "Last Thoughts on Woody Guthrie," is a conscious attempt to move beyond the image of Bob Dylan as Woody Guthrie's disciple. The most important word in the title is *last*. The poem is a long, rambling piece of free-association verse. In the one recorded performance, Dylan wisely rattles through it at top speed so that its sheer energy and abundance make up for the weak lines and lame rhymes. It has strikingly little to say about Woody Guthrie, or even about music, but its extended sentence[7] eventually works round to the familiar imagistic association of religion, music, and natural grandeur:

You'll find God in the church of your choice
You'll find Woody Guthrie in Brooklyn State Hospital

> And though it's only my opinion
> I may be right or wrong
> You'll find them both
> In the Grand Canyon
> At sundown.

(L, 36)

This ending, however, feels forced and unconvincing, a rhetorical gesture rather than an achieved resolution.

There is a more telling "last thought" on Woody Guthrie in "11 Outlined Epitaphs," where Dylan writes that Guthrie was his "last idol" precisely because he "shatter[ed] even himself / as an idol" (L, 111). By the time Dylan wrote this line, he too was idolized and feeling the restrictions imposed by such a role. So his iconoclasm of Guthrie is also intended to shatter his own image, as the end of the poem makes clear:

> you ask "how does it feel t' be an idol?"
> it'd be silly of me t' answer, wouldn't it . . . ?

Like Woody Guthrie, Lenny Bruce was an outsider, an iconoclastic rebel. "He was an outlaw," Dylan sings, "that's for sure" (L, 455). Ginsberg commented on Dylan's "unexpected sympathy for Lenny Bruce at a time when he [Dylan] was supposed to be a Born Again moralist Christian, and he was coming out for the injured and the insulted and the wounded and the supposedly damned" (Gray and Bauldie, 173). One point of sympathy between the two artists may be that "Lenny Bruce," like "Bob Dylan," is an alias: the comedian was born Leonard Alfred Schneider.

As early as *Tarantula*, Dylan had written of a character called "lenny" (whom I take to be Lenny Bruce): "you know he's some kind of robber yet you trust him & you cannot ignore him" (T, 54). In Lenny Bruce, Dylan assimilates the figure of the artist to the figure of the outlaw, the trickster as thief. What Dylan values in Bruce is his clear insight, his uncompromising honesty, and the way he compelled his audiences to look at themselves with similar insight and honesty. In *Tarantula*:

> lenny can take the bad out of you & leave you all good & he can
> take the good out of you & leave you all bad / if you think youre
> smart & know things, lenny plays with your head & he contradicts
> everything youve been taught about people
>
> . . . .
>
> lenny i'm sure is already in a resentful heaven

(T, 54–57)

The first sentence is reminiscent of the muse in "She Belongs To Me": "She can take the dark out of the nighttime / And paint the daytime black" (L, 163). In the song "Lenny Bruce" the portrayal is less paradoxical. Lenny Bruce "sure was funny and he sure told the truth. . . . He just took the folks in high places and he shined a light in their beds" (L, 455).

As a result, Dylan claims, the people whom Lenny attacked "said that he was sick. . . . They stamped him and they labeled him like they do with pants and shirts." Here we begin to see the implicit identification of author and subject. Dylan too has always resisted being stamped and labeled. In "Property of Jesus," the song that immediately precedes "Lenny Bruce" on *Shot of Love,* he presents a picture of himself as similarly rejected by those who cannot bear the truth of the message he brings:

> He's the property of Jesus
> Resent him to the bone
> You got something better
> You've got a heart of stone.

(L, 456)

But Dylan's relationship with Bruce is more complex than a simple identification of two persecuted truth-tellers. The line "He was an outlaw, that's for sure" is followed by "More of an outlaw than you ever were." The *you* involves us in the familiar complexity and fluidity of Dylan's pronouns. Again the most obvious interpretation is to see it as self-addressed: the line is an acknowledgment that Lenny Bruce's alienation was more radical and fatal than anything Bob Dylan had achieved. But the implicit identification of the two nevertheless claims for the singer the outlaw status that this line qualifies.

Later in the song Dylan appears in an almost ostentatious *first* person, offering an odd biographical anecdote: "I rode with him in a taxi once, only for a mile and a half, / Seemed like it took a couple of months."[8] The meeting with Bruce is presented as a timeless moment, like the moment of the mystic's contemplation in "Lay Down Your Weary Tune," but here the object of contemplation is not a natural scene but a mundane taxi ride. The muse has become another artist, a defeated comedian laying down his weary tune. This use of the first person brings Dylan closer to Bruce by claiming firsthand knowledge, and simultaneously distances him by showing how tenuous and fleeting their contact was. It also sets up a triangular relationship between "he" (Lenny Bruce), "I" (Bob Dylan), and the "you" of "More of an outlaw than you ever were."

This "you" reappears only in the last line of the song: "Lenny Bruce was bad, he was the brother that you never had." *Bad* balances between its literal meaning (what the "Born Again moralist Christian" would see in Bruce's drug abuse) and its idiomatic use as black slang for "good." (It also recalls the line in *Tarantula* in which bad and good change places.) Bad Lenny Bruce is now "the brother that you never had."[9] Dylan's "you," who is also "I," is the brother of the "he." Dylan's appropriation of Lenny Bruce is thus much more complex than his appropriation of Woody Guthrie. Instead of a simple identification, we get a relationship deflected through a double screen of pronouns, both the "I" who "rode with him" and the "you" who was less an outlaw than he was and who never had a brother to ride with.

The brother here is similar to the shadow and trace of "Mr. Tambourine Man." A relationship at one remove is implied, a deferred identification. Lenny Bruce is also a "ghost," who "lives on and on." Like the shadow and the trace, the ghost is marginal and parasitical, absent yet present. Lenny Bruce stands in these relationships (ghost, shadow, brother) to both "you" and "I." He *is* "your" brother, and he is *not,* since "you never had" a brother. He is both close to Bob Dylan (both are scorned for the truth they tell) and distant (a casual acquaintance who once shared a brief taxi ride). Reciprocally "you" and "I" are both the brothers Lenny Bruce never had—the brothers who might have saved his life, who might have helped him to make it to Synanon. If "his ghost lives on and on," it lives on as a shadow, as a brother, as the trace of the art he once created. It lives on also in the song that Bob Dylan sings about him.

The explicit drama played out in the shifting pronouns of "Lenny Bruce" is implicit in "Blind Willie McTell." Unlike the tributes to Guthrie and Bruce, this song makes no claim for a personal relationship between the author and subject. Indeed, the whole point is McTell's *absence*. The singer remains unobtrusive, an observer only. What he sees is a "vision of desolation and expected destruction" (Bauldie, 199): a world in which "power and greed and corruptible seed / Seem to be all that there is." This world is evoked through a series of concise, imagistic tableaux, mainly relics of the Old South, the birthplace of the blues: "big plantations burning," "the ghost of slavery ships," "a chain gang on the highway." The scene is universalized in one sweeping phrase, "All the way from New Orleans to Jerusalem," which unites the Old World and the New, while implying also the "New" Jerusalem of the Apocalypse (an implication which is made explicit in recent concert performances).

In his perceptive commentary on the song, the late John Bauldie argued that its central point is not simply that the world is in this desperate state but also that no singer (no prophet) can adequately lament it:

> The problem which brought this song into being is the singer's feeling of being unable to shoulder the responsibility that he's always liked to think he inherited from those ghosts who haunt the darker side of his street—Robert Johnson, Leadbelly, Blind Lemon Jefferson, Blind Willie McTell. How can Bob Dylan offer appropriate homage, how can he address and relieve the oppression? He cannot. . . . It's that knowledge that is being bewailed—not just the fact that no-one can sing the blues like Blind Willie McTell but that Bob Dylan knows that no-one can.
>
> (200)

But here, of course, we encounter the self-reflexive twist again. To the extent that Dylan has succeeded in presenting the desperation of this vision, he *has* "shouldered the responsibility" of the blues. Bauldie concludes his article by writing:

> The irony is that in attempting to express that inadequacy, in lamenting the oppression of his knowledge, Bob Dylan sings the

blues indeed: and such a soul-rending blues as any of the old blues-men—Blind Willie McTell, Robert Johnson—might have sold their souls to be able to sing.

(202)

My argument has been that this "irony" is structurally built into this kind of song. Just like "Lay Down Your Weary Tune" and "Mr. Tambourine Man," the successful existence of "Blind Willie McTell" as a song must necessarily modify, to the point of reversal, the ostensible meaning of the lyrics.

In this sense Bob Dylan "becomes" Blind Willie McTell. The song is even more closely about himself than "Song to Woody" or "Lenny Bruce." By singing the blues *like* Blind Willie McTell, Dylan identifies the old bluesman as the "brother [he] never had." Although the word *you* is never used in this song, the relationship is as much implicit as it was with Woody Guthrie. Hey, hey, Blind Willie, I wrote you a song.

There are, however, further ironies at work here. Each verse of the song leads up to the refrain, "I know no one can sing the blues / Like Blind Willie McTell," so each verse has to provide a rhyme for "McTell." It's not a difficult word to rhyme, and Dylan runs through the obvious choices: *fell, well, bell, yell.* The one that he does *not* use is the most obvious of all: *tell.* (The closest he gets to it is as part of "St. James Hotel."[10]) What Blind Willie did in his blues was to *tell* the truth. This prophetic task is inscribed in his name; it is his signature. But the song refuses to "tell." The absence of the word is like the absence of Blind Willie: an absence at the center of the song so glaring that it draws attention to itself. At the same time, just as *blind* Willie "sees," this song tells its own refusal to tell. By singing that no can sing the blues, Dylan proves that he can.

The history of the song pushes these ironies even further, for "Blind Willie McTell" was, of course, a bootleg.[11] Recorded as an outtake for *Infidels* in 1983, the song was not released until *The Bootleg Series* in 1991; its text was not even included in *Lyrics.* It is a story that Dylan refused to tell. It is as if Dylan's suppression of this song was an attempt to act out the absence that the song inscribes. No one could sing the blues like Blind Willie McTell, and no one would hear, or sing, "Blind Willie McTell."

Among those who had heard the song, Bob Dylan appeared to be a minority of one in his opinion of it. Critic after critic acclaimed it as one of his masterpieces. The circulation of the bootleg forced the original recording into release, and eventually, in 1997, Dylan began to perform the song, magnificently, in concert. So here it was the bootleg network that made the self-reflexive twist possible and finally enabled "Blind Willie McTell" to be told.

Big Girls and Sad-Eyed Ladies: Love Songs

Love songs of one kind or another—contented love or rejected love, careless love or abandoned love—make up the great majority of popular music. Bob Dylan's songs are no exception. From the lovely "Girl of the North Country" to the haunting "Most of the Time," Dylan has produced a memorable array of images of love.

In the section "Biography" in Chapter 3, I tried to indicate some of the dangers and limitations of interpreting Dylan's songs as directly or unproblematically autobiographical. But I also concluded that the biographical element could not be entirely excluded, and that often I still have to respond to the love songs at least partly in terms of their possible references to women in Dylan's life, if only because those are the terms the songs themselves invite, and even stage. This section surveys some of Dylan's most memorable love songs and attempts to trace in them the delicate and elusive dance between confession and dramatization, between biographical reference and lyrical creation.

The degree to which Dylan's early love songs were based on his affair with Suze Rotolo was widely acknowledged around Greenwich Village. Bob Spitz records that "friends familiar with his domestic situation felt embarrassed by such a public disclosure"; one unnamed friend "found it difficult to sit through [Dylan's] performances 'because the stuff he was doing was so transparent and Suze wasn't around to defend herself'" (200). This point is not unreasonable: it has always been true that poets get the unfair advantage of being able to tell their side of the story, while the subjects of their poems are denied a voice. For a popular singer, this imbalance may be repeated night after night in front of large audiences, which may even include the person being addressed. What could Sara Dylan have thought, listening to the agonized Rolling Thunder performances of "You're a Big Girl Now"?

For an audience wider than the immediate circles of 1962 Greenwich Village folkies, the biographical reference would have been unidentifiable, and in many songs there is no direct reference to Suze Rotolo. It is widely assumed that

"Don't Think Twice" is about her, but nothing in the song's text openly acknowledges that connection. The song is so generalized that it could be about any relationship on the verge of breaking down. In "Down the Highway," on the other hand, when Dylan sings:

> Yes, the ocean took my baby,
> My baby took my heart from me.
> She packed it all up in a suitcase,
> Lord, she took it away to Italy, Italy

(L, 55)

The specificity of *Italy* points directly to the circumstances of Suze Rotolo's departure for Perugia. For a brief moment it stages the real; it brings into the song the intertext of Dylan's life.[12]

The most direct and undisguised of the songs about Suze (so much so that Dylan later expressed regret for ever having made it public) is "Ballad in Plain D." Despite the title, this song fails to achieve any of the fictional distance of a true ballad. The "Plain D" is plain Dylan, naked and exposed. The first word of the song is *I*, and in performance this word is held like a long, drawn-out cry: I-I-I-I-I.

The almost painful directness of the song is evident in the clumsiness of some of the writing. "Ballad in Plain D" contains what is arguably the worst line Dylan ever wrote: the description of Suze as "a magnificent mantel-piece, though its heart being chipped" (L, 142). Other lines, however, give a precise rendering of the language of bitter, repetitive arguments. The bitterness is reserved mainly for "her parasite sister," who lives on Suze's creativity like a parasite or a false mirror image. Part of the song's weakness is that it seems too obviously an act of revenge against this overdrawn character. When the singer describes himself as "nailing her [the sister] to the ruins of her pettiness," the pettiness is just as much his own.

Suze is presented as a passive victim, compared to a lamb or a child. This idealization of the woman is two-edged. It deprives her of both adult status and the responsibility for her actions. The singer is not so much her lover as her guardian. This tendency to see women as childlike, and thus to condescend to them, shows up in several Dylan songs: think of "she breaks just like a little girl" (L, 231) and "You're a big girl now" (L, 356).

"I" is the most complex character of the three. While "Ballad in Plain D" is clearly an attempt at self-justification, it also admits his share of the blame. This ambivalence shows in the lines "Myself, for what I did, I cannot be excused, / The changes I was going through can't even be used," in which, of course, the changes *are* used, simply by being mentioned, even though the ostensible meaning is to refuse the mitigation they offer.

To the extent that he blames himself, he also recognizes the degree to which he reflects the "parasite sister." They are, in effect, parasites on each other, and the song is as much about his relationship to her as about his love for Suze. This alignment is presented in the tableau of "Her sister and I in a screaming battleground. / And she in between, the victim of sound." It is even more evident in a revision Dylan made in the text printed in *Lyrics*. On the record he sings, "I gagged in contradiction, tears blinding my sight"; in *Lyrics* this line appears as "I gagged twice, doubled, tears blinding my sight" (L, 143). The revised form emphasizes the doubling of the "I," but the doubling is with *the sister*, not with "the victim of sound": Carla, not Suze.

Even for a listener unaware of any biographical details, "Ballad in Plain D" is plainly a highly personal song. It attempts to stage the breakup of Dylan's relationship with Suze Rotolo, but too many elements remain unresolved for the staging to succeed. Only in the last stanza does Dylan attempt to achieve some degree of distance from the events, by reverting to a traditional ballad formula. On the one occasion when the song recurs in Dylan's work, as part of the soundtrack for *Renaldo and Clara*, the distance is achieved by using not Dylan's own recording but a performance by another singer, Gordon Lightfoot. In that context, doubled as quotation, "Ballad in Plain D" is more effective.

In none of these songs, however explicit, does Suze Rotolo's name appear in the text (though her photograph is featured on the cover of *The Freewheelin' Bob Dylan*).[13] The name is included, however, in "11 Outlined Epitaphs" as "beautiful Sue," who is "the true fortuneteller of my soul" (L, 114). She is compared to a frightened fawn (an echo of the lamb in "Ballad in Plain D") and she is also associated with silence: "there is no love / except in silence." This association is interesting, since it recurs in other songs that are clearly *not* about Suze. "Queen Jane Approximately" posits as the ideal lover "somebody you don't have to speak to" (L, 201). In "Love Minus Zero / No Limit"—which most commentators take as an early song for Sara, because of its Zen-like qualities—"My love she speaks like silence" (L, 167).

Silence is always the condition of the "you" in love songs: by definition, the addressee cannot speak. In *Tarantula* Dylan wrote that "there is no Second Person" (T, 134). The mode of address elides the 'other' while invoking her. For example, the question that closes "Sad-Eyed Lady of the Lowlands"—"Should I leave them by your gate, / Or, sad-eyed lady, should I wait?" (L, 239)—can never be answered. It does not close the song but rather leaves it open to a choice without resolution.

"Sad-Eyed Lady of the Lowlands" has sometimes been dismissed as gorgeous but meaningless, the final excess and decadence of Dylan's self-indulgent piling up of psychedelic images. Michael Gray, for example, calls it "sexy, furlined wallpaper."[14] But in the context of my argument here, the song is very interesting: not so much for the vexed question of who it was written for[15] as for its dramatic play of "I" and "you" triangulated with a pervasive "they."

The verses contrast the mystical sad-eyed lady—who almost disappears in the haze of images that surround her—and a hostile third party, variously identified as kings of Tyrus, farmers, businessmen, or simply a generalized "they." As if reacting against the lady's lack of definition, "they" repeatedly try to pin her down, to define and possess her: in the words of the recurring lines of the song, to bury, carry, outguess, impress, kiss, mistake, persuade, employ, and destroy her. But the lines' very repetition and their obsessive refrain—"who among them? . . . how could they?"—begin to imply subversively that the singer, too, is obsessed by these same desires. What "they" want is the dark suppressed side of what the "I" wants.

The song's triangular structure is repeated and compressed in the chorus:

> Sad-eyed lady of the lowlands,
> Where the sad-eyed prophet says that no man comes,
> My warehouse eyes, my Arabian drums,
> Should I leave them by your gate,
> Or, sad-eyed lady, should I wait?

Here the "prophet" mediates as a third party between the lady and "I," but all three are connected in terms of eyes. The lady and the prophet are assigned the same adjective, *sad-eyed* (sad-I'd), while "I" offers as his tribute a whole warehouse full of eyes/I's.[16] All three thus can be seen as aspects of the same sad-eyed I.

In Dylan's singing of the choruses, the singular *prophet* sometimes becomes the plural *prophets*. Similarly, there is more than one possible biblical source for this line. Of the Hebrew prophets, the one who most extensively preached against Tyrus was Ezekiel:

> The word of the Lord came again unto me, saying,
> Son of man, say unto the prince of Tyrus,
> . . . .
> I will bring strangers upon thee, the terrible of the nations: and
> they shall draw their swords against the beauty of thy wisdom, and
> they shall defile thy brightness.
> They shall bring thee down to the pit, and thou shalt die the
> deaths of them that are slain in the midst of the seas.
> (Ezekiel 28:1–2, 7–8)

After its destruction, Ezekiel prophesies, Tyrus will become "a place for the spreading of nets in the midst of the sea" (26:5). The "terrible of the nations" that God brought upon Tyrus was Babylon, and Babylon in turn was denounced by the most "sad-eyed" of all the Hebrew prophets, the lamenting Jeremiah:

> The sea is come up upon Babylon: she is covered with the multitude
> of the waves thereof.
> Her cities are a desolation, a dry land, and a wilderness, a land
> wherein no man dwelleth, neither doth any son of man pass thereby.
> (Jeremiah 51:42–43)

The "lowlands," where the sad-eyed lady remains inaccessible, are, then, a place where "no man comes" / "wherein no man dwelleth"; they are a "desolation," the result of destruction by the sea. "The sea is come up upon Babylon," and Tyrus is "a place for the spreading of nets in the midst of the sea." These biblical associations further echo the traditional British folk song "Lowlands," in which "the lowlands of Holland" refers, paradoxically, to the sea, to the treacherous sandbanks on which fishermen foundered their boats. In the folk song it is the ghost of a dead sailor who returns from the sea—like the ghost in

"House Carpenter"—to inform his loved one of his death: "The cold sea weed was in his hair, / Lowlands, Lowlands away, my jo."[17]

Another verbal echo in the chorus evokes a different long-lost sailor, Odysseus. When Odysseus blinds the Cyclops, he escapes by giving a false name: No Man. Under this evasion he conceals his identity, in the same way as Robert Zimmerman is concealed by the alias Bob Dylan. As No Man, then, Bob Dylan can come where no man comes, into "a land where no man dwelleth"; as Odysseus, he can reach his sad-eyed lady, offer her his warehouse I's, and wait by her gate for the answer that the song cannot give him. My love, she speaks like silence . . . and the track fades out on a harmonica solo.

However one resolves the question of biographical reference in these early songs, there can be little doubt that the love songs Dylan wrote in the 1970s take as their major focus his relationship with Sara. What one can read in these songs, looking back at them over the retrospective sweep of a decade, is the narrative (mediated, indirect) of that relationship: in Ingmar Bergman's phrase, "scenes from a marriage." The songs move from the idyllic presentations of mutual love on *New Morning* and *Planet Waves,* through the increasing stress of *Blood on the Tracks* and *Desire,* to the breakup of the marriage on *Street Legal.* Of course, this narrative is partly fictionalized, and cannot be read *simply* as autobiography; and of course it is a one-sided picture. We hear only the man's version of what was going on, and the songs are not always free of self-pity and special pleading. But at their best they are strikingly intense and vivid portraits of the singer's emotional state, and of a fragmenting relationship.

The critical interest of these songs, however, does not lie in any attempt to piece together a biographical account of what "really" happened between Bob and Sara. The question is not so much how close Dylan is to the protagonist of these songs as how much distance he can achieve. For example, in the first phase of this narrative, he had to tackle the problem of writing straightforwardly happy love songs in a nonclichéd manner about a stable and reciprocal relationship. It's all too easy to write about unhappy love—*My baby left me and I'm standing here alone on the corner in the rain*—or to write songs that take revenge on abandoned lovers. One great cliché of Dylan criticism has been that he only writes well when he's angry—which is why most listeners find it easier to respond to the familiar venom of *Blood on the Tracks* than to the daring simplicities of *Planet Waves.*

In writing this kind of happy love song, Dylan was continually on the edge of cliché. At his best he would use a conventional phrase but somehow hit it slightly off-center, so that it's not quite the way a listener would expect. For example, in "You Angel You," the opening phrase—"You got me under your wing" (L, 348)—echoes "I got you under my skin" at the same time as it literalizes the "angel" cliché by insisting on the physical reality of the "wing." As Dylan sings the song on *Planet Waves* (the lines are revised in *Lyrics),* he continues: "I just walk and watch you talk / With your memory of my mind." The *walk/talk* rhyme is sheer cliché, but this version twists it around so that the lines collapse all the categories of separation. Talking is watched, not listened to; *her* memory is of *his* mind. Then comes "You know I can't sleep at night for trying," where *trying* substitutes a realistic observation (there are times when you can't get to sleep for thinking about it) for the expected, and half-heard, *crying*.

The next line—"Never did feel this way before"—insists on the uniqueness of the experience even as it leads into a phrase that is anything but unique: "If this is love then gimme more." Again the cliché is literalized, as the line continues "and more and more and more and more," embodying the sentiment in the very repetition of the phrase which articulates it. The statement in "You Angel You" is not at all complex, but the verbal wit is very precise. It may lack the flamboyance of, say, "The motorcycle black madonna / Two-wheeled gypsy queen" (L, 175), but it certainly lacks nothing in subtlety.

Not all the songs on *Planet Waves* manage to maintain this distance. Large parts of "Wedding Song" remain, verbally, utterly banal, though the beauty of the tune and the urgency of the performance redeem it.[18] In retrospect one can sense a desperation in this song; the singer protests too much, and the overstatement of his case betrays some uneasiness about its validity. While much of *Planet Waves* is devoted to the celebration of this "wedding," the album is shot through with flashes of doubt and uncertainty. "Something There Is About You" stages a vivid autobiographical image—"Rainy days on the Great Lakes, walkin' the hills of old Duluth" (L, 345)[19]—and attempts to associate the present love with the past. But at the same time, the singer insists: "I could say that I'd be faithful, I could say it in one sweet, easy breath / But to you that would be cruelty and to me it surely would be death." Scarcely a reassuring statement of marital stability.

Such premonitions take center stage on *Blood on the Tracks*, in which almost all the love songs are full of anxiety, jealousy, and the fear and sorrow of separation. Even the most carefree and cheerful of them, "You're Gonna Make Me Lonesome When You Go," says *when*, not *if*. Most of these songs project this emotional turmoil into a quasi-fictional setting, as in "Idiot Wind," in which a highly personal statement is prefaced by a piece of blatant fiction: "They say I shot a man named Gray and took his wife to Italy, / She inherited a million bucks and when she died it came to me. / I can't help it if I'm lucky" (L, 367). Both "Tangled Up In Blue" and "Simple Twist of Fate" also weave autobiographical elements into fictional structures.[20] "If You See Her, Say Hello" assumes that the separation has already occurred and projects a future attitude of rueful acceptance and quiet sorrow. When the singer says (in one of Dylan's most brilliantly concise lines), "Sundown, yellow moon, I replay the past" (L, 369), he is already "replaying" the future. But *all* these scenes are "replayed": staged and projected as if they were on film, and thus distanced from the singer's immediate and painful experience.

After the melodramatic flourish of its opening, "Idiot Wind" becomes an increasingly bitter and recriminatory portrayal of separation. The "you" of the song is blamed for not knowing the singer better and for the "corrupt ways" that have "finally made you blind." But again the separation is not absolute, and the song carries a subtext of hints at the merging of this "you" and "I." The final verse states: "I kissed goodbye the howling beast on the borderline which separated you from me." Once the beast is kissed goodbye, it no longer guards this border, so the "you" and "me" can merge into the "we" of the final chorus. The vicious invective of "You're an idiot, babe. / It's a wonder that you still know how to breathe" is modified to "We're idiots, babe. / It's a wonder we can even feed ourselves." Nothing is forgiven, but the singer is prepared to accept a share of the guilt and responsibility.

"Idiot Wind" became progressively fiercer as it went through its various versions. By the time of the Rolling Thunder recording preserved on *Hard Rain*, it had become a triumphalist rant, with little room for this acknowledgment of complicity. But its earliest form, from the New York sessions,[21] is much softer, more forgiving and sympathetic, not so much in the words as in the performance. When Dylan sings, in lines deleted in the released version, "You close your eyes and part your lips, and slip your fingers from your glove, / You can have the best there is, but it's going to cost you all your love, / You won't get it for money," the words may be sardonic and angry, but the voice is almost unbearably tender. The singer offers freely all the love it's going to cost.

The *Blood on the Tracks* song that least depends on any fictional distancing is "You're a Big Girl Now," which—like "Ballad in Plain D" or "Wedding Song"—seems to have slipped past all alias disguises to an almost embarrassing directness. All three songs appear at times to reveal more than the singer intends or is aware of—though one should bear in mind that this disingenuousness may, in fact, be a calculated effect. Take, for instance, these lines, which show the singer desperately trying to come to terms with his lover's newly asserted independence:

> Time is a jet plane, it moves too fast
> Oh, but what a shame if all we've shared can't last.
> I can change, I swear, oh, oh,
> See what you can do.
> I can make it through,
> You can make it too.

> (L, 356)

The singer appears to accept his share of the responsibility for what has gone wrong, and promises to change. At the same time he hints that "time" is really to blame, and he shifts the burden of responsibility quickly back onto the woman by demanding that she match his offer. But if he was wrong in the first place, why should she have to change as well? Nor can the song resist gestures of self-pity:

> Oh, I know where I can find you, oh, oh,
> In somebody's room.
> It's a price I have to pay
> You're a big girl all the way.

The title phrase itself betrays, perhaps unconsciously, the singer's paternalistic condescension. How many women of the mid-1970s would have taken kindly to being congratulated on their maturity in the phrase "You're a big girl now"?

These problems are especially evident in the performances of the song during the Rolling Thunder tour. The version on *Hard Rain* is extremely long: seven minutes, as opposed to the four and a half on the *Blood on the Tracks* recording, though no words have been added. Dylan sings with excruciating slowness, dragging out the pauses, wringing every drop of emphasis from the words. It's like witnessing a confessional psychodrama played out onstage in front of an audience—an audience which on many occasions included Sara.

"You're a Big Girl Now" reveals a deep division in the singer's attitude. On the one hand, he is trying to come to terms with the changes in his relationship; on the other hand, his language remains within the patterns of paternalistic condescension and sexism which, we may speculate, caused the problems in the first place. This "big girl" is no more real, no more human, than the "sadeyed lady."

And indeed the sad-eyed lady reappears, on *Desire*, in "Sara," the most undisguised of Dylan's love songs, which openly flaunts the autobiographical references that he had so often kept oblique or hidden. This tactic is not an innocent one: the factual references are used to establish the singer's credentials and build up sympathy for his position. We get intimate glimpses of Bob, Sara, and the kids at play, on a beach, on holiday in Portugal. And we get Dylan writing his image of this family into his own songwriting history:

> I can still hear the sounds of those Methodist bells,
> I'd taken the cure and had just gotten through,
> Stayin' up for days in the Chelsea Hotel,
> Writin' "Sad-Eyed Lady of the Lowlands" for you.

(L, 390)

The autobiographical accuracy of this statement is open to some question (was this song written for Sara, or for Joan? — see note 15); but what is important here is that the life is *staged*, presented in dramatic terms as part of a performance.

From one point of view, the performance is simple and predictable: the oldest trick in the patriarchal book, emotional blackmail by way of the kids.[22] In the late 1970s such an approach was likely as anachronistic and counterproductive as saying "you're a big girl now" or "our Father would not like the way that you act"—but does the singer of this song realize that? Between the verses, the chorus's repeated appeals to Sara surround her with a strange array of epithets: "Sweet virgin angel, sweet love of my life . . . Radiant jewel, mystical wife . . . Scorpio Sphinx in a calico dress . . . Glamorous nymph with an arrow and bow."

In phrases like these, one sees again the inability to come to grips with the woman as a real, other person. In the verses she is trapped in the traditional role of motherhood; in the choruses she is lost in a haze of romantic abstractions.

From another point of view, "Sara" repeats the mythological drama staged in the other songs on *Desire*. The references to the children stress Dylan's position as a father whose authority has failed; his voice too "trembles" as he calls out to his errant wife. And Sara, as the "mystical" wife, takes on the characteristics of Isis, who could be both virgin and mother, with her saintlike face and ghostlike soul.[23]

The problem presented *in the songs*—we have no way of knowing how close that was to the problems that existed in real life—is that the singer has no way of reconciling these divisions. Whether Sara is portrayed as a mother or a mother-goddess, she does not appear in the songs as a human being met as an equal. Like the addressee of any song, "Sara" is denied speech—she has to speak like silence. This imbalance is always present in love songs, but in Dylan's songs it is accentuated by the consistent idealization of the woman. Only in *Renaldo and Clara* does Sara Dylan have a chance to appear in her own right, but even there she is hedged around by the fictional structures of the film. Ultimately her response could only be made outside the songs, though the songs anticipate it. It is clearly feared and foreseen even in the lines which plead against it: "Sara, oh Sara, / Don't ever leave me, don't ever go."

But she did leave, and on *Street Legal*, which Christopher Butler describes as "the album as confessional poetry" (Corcoran 63), Dylan provides a concise summary of the separation. The last three songs on the album act as a mini-trilogy replaying the past. "True Love Tends to Forget" is a tender, rueful, slightly ironic look at the fading away of the love once so joyfully celebrated:

> I'm getting weary looking in my baby's eyes
> When she's near me she's so hard to recognize.
> I finally realize there's no room for regret,
> True love, true love, true love tends to forget.

> (L, 411)

The old motif of looking in the lover's eyes/I's is repeated here to stress the extent of the separation. If she is "hard to recognize," then so is what he must see in her eyes: his reflection. The chorus holds onto the phrase "true love" for as long as it can, repeating it three times and stretching out the long vowel of *true,* in an exact formal expression of the way the singer also has held onto true love for as long as he can, but now recognizes, in the last few quick, clipped, short syllables, that true love "tends to forget."

The second song in the sequence, "We Better Talk This Over," takes the separation a stage further. It replays some final discussions, but from the resigned acceptance that the affair is over. Some lines are still bitter and angry: "I feel displaced, I got a low-down feeling / You been two-faced, you been double-dealing" (L, 412). There is perhaps a hint of reciprocity in these lines, with the singer "displaced" into the position of the other; there is even a distant pun between *dealing* and *Dylan.* Sara and Bob were, as a couple, "double-Dylan"— but then Bob, as the ghost of Robert Zimmerman, was a "double-Dylan" all by himself. At another point in this song, the unlikelihood of the lovers getting together again is compared to "the sound of one hand clappin'." The image not only recalls Sara's interest in Zen but also reinforces, in the very absence of the second hand, the lost ideal of reciprocity.

Much of the bitterness is modified, however, by two factors. First, the tune is jaunty and cheerful, seemingly in opposition to the mood of the words. Secondly the writing is witty, twisting colloquial phrases to new uses and making full use of Dylan's virtuoso rhyming:

> Why should we go on watching each other through a telescope?
> Eventually we'll hang ourselves on all this tangled rope.
> Oh, babe, time for a new transition
> I wish I was a magician
> I would wave a wand and tie back the bond
> That we've both gone beyond.

The artist's delight in the creation of this intricate, witty song has already taken him some way beyond its pain.

Some way: for the pain returns in the final song, the epic "Where Are You Tonight? (Journey Through Dark Heat)." The singer is now definitively alone: "There's a woman I long to touch and I miss her so much but she's drifting like a satellite." A satellite does not normally "drift," but moves in a regular orbit round a fixed center. Drifting, this woman has strayed from her appointed course around the central position traditionally occupied by the man. At other points the singer recognizes that this conflict is also, as always, an internal one: "I fought with my twin, that enemy within, 'til both of us fell by the way." Here the twin (alias, ghost, shadow) is seen as an "enemy," and the result of divided identity is mutual destruction.

The language of "Where Are You Tonight?" is more generalized and symbolic than in most of Dylan's love songs of the 1970s; the internal conflict again takes on a social dimension. The "long-distance train" of the first line already looks forward to the "slow train coming" of the following album.

But it *is* also a farewell to Sara, and the song rises to a great emotional climax of cathartic release. The final chorus sums up and puts an end to the narrative that all the love songs of the 1970s had told:

> There's a new day at dawn and I've finally arrived.
> If I'm there in the morning, baby, you'll know I've survived.
> I can't believe it, I can't believe I'm alive,
> But without you it just doesn't seem right.
> Oh, where are you tonight?

In the twenty-five years that have passed since this farewell, there has, of course, been a temptation to read every Dylan love song as being, in some sense, a return to Sara. When, on *Time Out Of Mind,* he sings "After all these years you're still the one," it is almost impossible *not* to hear the hopeless echo of a great love that has never fully been forgotten, nor abandoned.

Among such songs, perhaps the purest, and one of the most moving Bob Dylan has ever written, is "Most of the Time," from *Oh Mercy.* (There is a magnificent cover version by Sophie Zelmani.) The song operates by a simple ironic reversal. The singer declares that he is all right, in control ("I can deal with the situation . . . I can survive and I can endure"), and that he no longer thinks of his lost love ("Don't even remember what her lips felt like on mine"). But each declaration is undercut by the repeated phrase "most of the time." What he feels like the *rest* of the time (even if it is a minority) is never directly described, but as the protestations of his imperviousness multiply, and grow more and more desperate, the simple understatement of the song accumulates into a massive overstatement:

Most of the time she ain't even in my mind
Wouldn't know her if I saw her, she's that far behind
Most of the time I can't even be sure
If she was ever with me, or if I was ever with her . . .
I don't compromise and I don't pretend
I don't even care if I ever see her again
Most of the time.

Dylan's voice is quiet and restrained, but its denial is belied by the surging emotion of the musical backing. It's a love song of such intensity and purity that the listener is totally swept up into its tenderness and its pain. Quite simply, it breaks your heart.

Outside The Law: Narrative Songs

"To live outside the law, you must be honest," Bob Dylan wrote in 1966, and it has become one of his most widely quoted maxims.[24] This section, "Outside the Law," looks at some of the characters in Dylan songs, especially in his narrative songs, who live outside or on the margins of the law. The greater part of it concentrates on a close reading of "Lily, Rosemary and the Jack of Hearts," perhaps Dylan's most enigmatic narrative. But I want to begin with another outlaw, John Wesley Harding, not least because the initials of his proper name, JWH, may also be read as Jaweh, the unspoken name of God the Father (see p. 86). This conjunction of motifs—the outlaw, the name, the father—runs throughout this discussion, and it is picked up again later, in Chapter 7's section on "Brownsville Girl."

In a 1969 interview, in a typically casual and self-deprecatory manner, Dylan commented:

I had the song "John Wesley Harding," which started out to be a long ballad. I was gonna write a ballad on . . . like maybe one of those old cowboy . . . you know, a real long ballad. But in the middle of the second verse, I got tired. I had a tune, and I didn't want to waste the tune, it was a nice little melody, so I just wrote a quick third verse, and I recorded that.

But it was a silly little song.

(Miles 1978, 85)

However accidentally the effect may have been produced, the impression, as Dylan acknowledges, is one of reduction. "John Wesley Harding" sounds like the remains of a longer song, or like an exercise in structuralist narratology, such as Joseph Campbell analyzing the components of myth or Vladimir Propp reducing Russian folktales to a sequence of thirty-one narrative "functions": hero meets obstacle, hero finds helper, hero overcomes obstacle, and so on. We are given not so much a fully developed outlaw ballad as a selective invocation of the semiotic codes of outlaw ballads, a skeletal series of the basic narrative gestures of the genre.

Stanza 2, for example, offers several such gestures toward narrative, but each one immediately withdraws into equivocation and incomplete specification:

'Twas down in Chaynee County,
A time they talk about,
With his lady by his side
He took a stand.
And soon the situation there
Was all but straightened out,
For he was always known
To lend a helping hand.

(L, 249)

The name "Chaynee County" appears to promise a documentable historical incident, but the biographies of the nineteenth-century outlaw John Wesley Hardin do not mention it.[25] The "situation" remains undefined and unexplained; the song merely asserts that it is well known, "a time they talk about." Repeatedly Dylan evades responsibility for his narrative by attributing it to rumor and general report—an evasion we also see in "Lily, Rosemary and the Jack of Hearts." The effect is to cast some doubt on Harding's character. We are not told unequivocally that he never hurt an honest man but only that "he was never *known* / To hurt an honest man" (my emphasis).

Similarly "took a stand" seems decisive and courageous until one examines the implications of its juxtaposition with "his lady by his side." As Michael Gray comments, "Within the cowboy ethic, the hero should neither have needed his lady by his side to give him his courage nor have placed her inside the danger zone" (35). What the song grants to its hero with one hand, it takes away with the other. The situation is "straightened out," as it should be by a hero, but then the equivocation "all but" cancels this accomplishment. The song raises several questions—what is the situation? what part of it is *not* straightened out?—but rather than answer them, it takes refuge in cliché: "To lend a helping hand."

Such ambiguities are common in Dylan's narrative songwriting. It is notoriously difficult to make out exactly what goes on in songs like "Black Diamond Bay" or "Tweeter and the Monkeyman." At times, as in "John Wesley Harding," the difficulty is due to the gaps and ellipses in the story. At other times the narrative is buried or implicit, as happens in "Señor (Tales of Yankee Power)."

Much critical attention to "Señor" has focused on whether it should be read as a religious or a political allegory. In view of its 1978 composition date, immediately before Dylan's religious conversion, John Herdman writes that "It seems reasonable to assume that the Lord is being addressed here" (109). This view has found strong support in several extended internet debates.[26] Alternatively, in view of the subtitle, "Tales of Yankee Power," a political reading seems more likely: the song is about American imperialism in Central America. The song invites such allegorical interpretations, whether religious or political, with its overtly symbolic language, but there is also a straightforward narrative level to the action.

I infer from Dylan's use of "Señor" that the speaker of the song is Central American, possibly Mexican, employed to accompany a "Yankee" as a guide or hired gun on some unspecified mission. The line "do you know where she is hidin'?" suggests that they are looking for a woman, possibly the Yankee's wife or daughter, while the line "their hearts is as hard as leather" suggests that the two of them face the prospect of tough adversaries, possibly kidnappers holding the woman. The narrative is so sketchy that most of these problems cannot be solved, but enough of a narrative exists that they can be posed. At first the speaker is merely puzzled and ignorant: he does not know where they are going or how long they will be riding. As the song proceeds, however, he becomes more committed and even eager for the fight to begin:

> Señor, señor, let's disconnect these cables,
> Overturn these tables.
> This place don't make sense to me no more.
> Can you tell me what we're waiting for, señor?

> (L, 410)

This suggested narrative makes grim sense as a political allegory. American imperialism imposes itself through hired surrogates like the Nicaraguan Contras, who eventually become more eager and more bloodthirsty than their sponsors, and who adopt the cause of "Yankee power" as their own.

"Señor" is the most oblique of Dylan's narrative songs, conveying its story line through hints and implications. More often the ambiguity of Dylan's narratives depends on the technique noted above, the omission of causal connectives. John Herdman bases a fascinating analysis of "Tangled Up In Blue" on the proposition that Dylan deliberately intends to mislead his audience. Herdman argues that various stanzas of this song refer to different women, whereas the listener is led to suppose, by the undifferentiated use of the simple pronoun *she*, that the references are all to the same character (55–58). It is true that Dylan's use of pronouns is always tricky, but for me the song continues to make more sense if the women *are* all the same character. Nevertheless, the mere possibility of Herdman's argument points to the indeterminacy of Dylan's narrative (or anti-narrative) techniques.

His narratives frequently make abrupt transitions from one scene into the middle of the next, eliding causal connections. In "Tweeter and the Monkeyman," the fourth stanza begins with the title characters "cornered" by the "undercover cop," cuts to Jan taking a gun and leaving her husband, and then cuts back without explanation to "The undercover cop was found face-down in a field / The Monkeyman was on the river bridge using Tweeter as a shield." Did Jan kill the cop or had the Monkeyman already killed him and escaped before she got there? Against whom is Tweeter being used as a shield—other cops? Jan? The song doesn't say.

The whole point *is* that the song doesn't say. There are clear dangers in attempting any definitive statements of what "actually" goes on. It is not as if the events of these narratives have ever existed in any form outside the songs, as if there is any other source of information to be appealed to. The "story" exists *only* in the words and performances of the songs, and these words include elements that resist clear reconstruction. Indeterminacy remains the basic characteristic of all Dylan's major narratives, and there is no appeal beyond it.

Many of these narrative songs, as I have suggested, focus on outlaws. The outlaw figure's attraction is that he stands for the romantic outsider, the ultimate individualist, one who stakes his destiny against the forces of society and conformity. When Dylan sings that "to live outside the law, you must be honest," he reflects what David Pichaske calls "the myth of the moral outlaw":

> The outlaw springs from and champions the huddled masses, living among them, protected by them from pursuing agents of the law, somehow more moral in his excommunication (and more admirable by virtue of his relative cunning and leanness) than the forces of "justice" which hound and, invariably, kill him.
>
> (43)

A good example is Woody Guthrie's "Pretty Boy Floyd," of which Dylan made a splendid recording in 1988.[27] But while the traditional American outlaw ballad celebrates the outlaw's clever evasion of justice, Dylan concentrates more on *un*successful outlaws: those who are caught and condemned by the law, or betrayed and killed by their "friends." John Wesley Harding "was never known / To make a foolish move," but again this invulnerability is a matter of report to which Dylan is unwilling to commit himself. Almost all his other outlaws *do* make foolish moves, and many of them die for it.

In the 1965 "Outlaw Blues" Dylan sings:

> Ain't gonna hang no picture,
> Ain't gonna hang no picture frame.
> Well, I might look like Robert Ford
> But I feel just like Jesse James.
>
> (L, 168)

The singer identifies with Jesse James, not as the successful bank robber, but with Jesse James at the moment he is shot in the back by Robert Ford while hanging a picture on the wall of his room. It is interesting to note, however, that the song hints at a double identification, not only with the dead outlaw but also with the universally despised figure of the traitor who killed him.[28] On the other hand, the music he wrote for Sam Peckinpah's *Pat Garrett & Billy the Kid* is almost completely devoted to Billy, not Pat. Again, it is the hunted, dying outlaw that Dylan chooses to identify with: "Billy, don't it make ya feel so lowdown / To be shot down by the man who was your friend?" (L, 335).

Many of these features of the outlaw narrative—the indeterminate narration, the equivocal "hero"—find their fullest expression in "Lily, Rosemary and the Jack of Hearts" (L, 364–66). The events of this song go by in a rapid succession of cinematic cuts, omitting sections of the narrative, which the listener must attempt to reconstruct in retrospect.[29] The song begins by suggesting that one story is already finished: an unspecified festival is over, and "anyone with any sense had already left town." The characters who are left, about whom this story will be told, are those without sense, those whose actions are driven more by their passions than by reason.

We are then given the strange detail of "the drillin' in the wall."[30] Not until the song's end can this line be retrospectively identified as a clue pointing to a bank robbery. The robbery is always in the background, like a sound at the edge of consciousness. The Jack of Hearts takes no part in the actual robbery, though he has presumably planned it. Indeed, the Jack of Hearts is always defined in this song by a curious mixture of presence and absence: "The only person on the scene missin' was the Jack of Hearts." On the scene and simultaneously missing: the Jack of Hearts is always there but not there, leader of the gang but not participating in the looting of the bank, present but absent from the scene of the murder. He is, indeed, a figure of the trickster, and, precisely *because of* his elusiveness, perhaps the most fully realized trickster in any of Dylan's songs.

Even his introduction into the song is shadowy and uncertain. When he first appears we are told not that he *is* the Jack of Hearts but only that he *looks like* the Jack of Hearts. This equivocation is repeated in the next stanza, when "he moved into the corner, face down like the Jack of Hearts." The character's similarity to the Jack is defined in terms of disguise or absence. He is *like* the Jack of Hearts *because* his face cannot be seen. He fully enters into the song only after the third stanza, in which Lily's drawing of the card in the poker game evokes him, creates his presence, draws him into the textual reality.

The same three stanzas concisely introduce the other leading characters. Lily performs in the saloon and loses at poker. Big Jim is the local mine-owner, a figure of wealth and power, complete with bodyguards (who mysteriously vanish for the rest of the song).[31] Rosemary lives outside of town, presumably at Big Jim's mansion, and she is initially subservient to him, whispering apologies for being late. It seems probable that Rosemary is married to Big Jim and that Lily is his mistress.

The elusive nature of the Jack of Hearts is stressed as Big Jim stares at him:

> "I know I've seen that face before," Big Jim was thinkin' to himself,
> "Maybe down in Mexico or a picture up on somebody's shelf."

Again the Jack of Hearts is defined by his likeness, which can never quite be pinned down. In narrative terms it is most likely that the "somebody" who keeps the Jack's picture is Lily, who has definitely known the Jack of Hearts in the past, but nothing excludes the possibility that it might instead be Rosemary.

Lily's cabaret performance is not directly described. Instead, it is replaced by a series of foreboding images: the arrival of the hanging judge, the continuation of the drilling in the wall, Rosemary staring at her face reflected in a knife. These images come together at the climax of the song, so it is interesting that they stand in for *Lily's* performance. Although she seems the most innocent of the characters, it is Lily who first conjures up the Jack of Hearts, and it is Lily's song or dance that prefigures the tragic conclusion.

When Lily talks to the Jack, in her dressing room after her performance, her tone is friendly but not passionate. She assumes that he has come to see her because he is down on his luck, and she warns him not to touch a freshly painted wall. Her most emotional comment, "I'm glad to see you're still alive," is not exactly a declaration of love.[32] She tells him that he looks like a saint: in what sense? that he looks dead, emaciated, ascetic, beatific? As always, the Jack of Hearts is not quite there; he is present in the room, but he doesn't say anything.

The next stanza tells us that "the leading actor hurried by in the costume of a monk." Who exactly *is* "the leading actor"? It might be Rosemary, though it is more likely that she would be called an "actress," or it might be Big Jim on his way to Lily's dressing room to confront her and the man he suspects is visiting her. But neither Rosemary nor Big Jim has any reason to wear a disguise; the only person who consistently appears in disguise is the Jack of Hearts. But here a further question arises: *in which direction* is this character "hurrying by"? Toward Lily's dressing room or away from it? The answer must surely be away from it: where else would the Jack have had the opportunity to put on the costume of a monk? He could scarcely have done so sitting at a table in the saloon. But if this is the case, then the Jack of Hearts has *already left* Lily's dressing room before Big Jim arrives. What, then, would be the reason for the murder? What would there be for Big Jim to see when he bursts in?

There is a narrative impasse here that the song never resolves. The identity of "the leading actor" and the direction in which he hurries must remain unknown. The succeeding events make sense only if we can assume that the Jack of Hearts is still in Lily's dressing room. This is certainly what stanza 12 tells us: the Jack of Hearts is there, with Lily's arms around him. (Stanza 12, however, has a very equivocal status: Dylan omitted it from the revised take of the song which was released on *Blood on the Tracks*, but included it in the published *Lyrics*.)

It is important to note here that if the Jack of Hearts is still in Lily's dressing room, in her arms, when Big Jim bursts in, then he has been, despite his apparent cleverness and invincibility, caught. Despite the song's assertions of the power, resourcefulness, and trickery of the Jack of Hearts, he has been trapped in the most elementary way, through his weakness for a woman. Unlike John Wesley Harding, he has made a foolish move. He escapes Big Jim, not through his own skill, but through a woman's intervention. On the other hand, if he is "the leading actor" and was leaving Lily's dressing room, then he has done what the trickster always seems to do: slip away just in time, leaving his absence behind, both on the scene and missing.

No wonder then that Dylan as narrator also steps back from the action and draws attention to the indeterminacy of the narrative: "No one knew the circumstance but they say that it happened pretty quick." The climactic events are presented in such spare terms that several interpretations are possible:

1) The dressing room door bursts open and "Big Jim was standin' there, ya couldn't say surprised." He is unsurprised because what he sees is, as he suspected, Lily in the arms of this strange man whom he dimly recognizes, the Jack of Hearts. Big Jim attempts to shoot the Jack of Hearts, but his "cold revolver clicked"—presumably because it is empty. And the only person who could have emptied it would be Rosemary. Rosemary, standing beside Big Jim, is the only person in position to stab him in the back. Thus the Jack of Hearts escapes from the situation entirely by virtue of Rosemary's efforts. This remains the standard and the most likely interpretation.

2) The dressing room door bursts open and "Big Jim was standin' there," but the Jack of Hearts has already gone, "in the costume of a monk." But in this case surely Big Jim *would* be surprised, since he expected to find Lily with another man. So why would Rosemary have to kill him?

3) The door bursts open and Big Jim is standing there, *already dead,* already stabbed in the back by Rosemary. The gun clicks because he doesn't have time to fire it, only to pull back the hammer. In this case it doesn't matter whether or not the Jack of Hearts is still in the room.

4) The above all assume that Big Jim bursts open the door, but the song does not actually say this: "The door to the dressing room burst open and a cold revolver clicked. / And Big Jim was standin' there, ya couldn't say suprised. . . ." Big Jim is standing *where?* If he is already inside the dressing room, then perhaps the Jack of Hearts bursts open the door, having returned after his previous visit. In this case the person in the best position to stab Big Jim in the back would be Lily.

The second, third, and fourth interpretations are all farfetched and require massive assumptions about what has been left out of the narrative. The point is that the song is so elliptical that nothing in the text excludes any of these interpretations. At the central point of his story, Dylan is deliberately vague: "No one knew the circumstance," and Dylan accepts that limited viewpoint. He refuses the stance of the omniscient narrator.

Instead we jump ahead to the robbery and then, even more drastically, to the hanging. The circumstances of the murder may be obscure, but that does not prevent arrest, trial, sentence, and execution following within a matter of hours. Rosemary is "on the gallows," probably for a crime she did commit, to save the Jack's life, but just possibly for a crime that he, or even Lily, actually committed. In either case Rosemary acts as a sacrificial substitute. The Jack of Hearts is now most crucially "the only person on the scene missin'." Whatever Rosemary covers up for him, the Jack of Hearts makes no move to save her from the gallows. Lily may be thinking about him, but he is gone.

Lily's reflections in the final stanza move beyond the particular characters and events of the drama to include more general topics:

She was thinkin' 'bout her father, who she very rarely saw,
Thinkin' 'bout Rosemary and thinkin' about the law.[33]
But most of all she was thinkin' 'bout the Jack of Hearts.

The figure of the father is closely associated with the idea of law in both religion and psychoanalysis. God the Father—Jaweh, JWH—decrees the Law to Moses on Mount Sinai. According to Freud, the father institutes the law by laying down the prohibition against incest. Jacques Lacan uses the French phrase *le nom du Père* to refer not only to the Name of the Father, which vests the law in the property rights of the proper name, but also to the prohibition *(Nom/Non)* which the father proclaims. For Lacan, the Name of the Father also institutes the symbolic realm of language.

The figure of the father is particularly important to Bob Dylan in the songs of the 1970s. As the bearer of an assumed name himself, he would be very conscious of the problematic nature of the proper name, the patronymic (discussed in Chapter 2, "Signature"). There are, of course, biographical reasons for the increasing prominence of the father image—his own father's death in 1968, the birth and rearing of his children, the instability of his marriage—but it also coheres with the deepest continuing obsessions of his writing. In the 1970s the image of the unsuccessful or dying outlaw fuses with that of the helpless, missing, or dead father.

As early as 1967, "Tears of Rage" evoked the figure of the impotent father in its echo of *King Lear*—

Oh what dear daughter 'neath the sun
Would treat a father so,
To wait upon him hand and foot
And always tell him, "No"?

—and immediately associated it with the outlaw—

Tears of rage, tears of grief,
Why must I always be the thief?

(L, 312)

Of the songs Dylan wrote for *Pat Garrett & Billy the Kid*, the one he has returned to again and again in concert is "Knockin' on Heaven's Door." In the film it accompanies the scene of Sheriff Baker's death; but Baker's role as a sheriff rather than an outlaw is less important than his role as a dying *father*. The second verse makes the phallic implications unmistakable:

> Mama, put my guns in the ground
> I can't shoot them anymore.
> That long black cloud is comin' down
> I feel like I'm knockin' on heaven's door.

(L, 337)

The killing of Sheriff Baker is a primal scene, the father's death, and it counterpoints the killing of Billy, the "Kid," by *his* surrogate father, Pat Garrett. The father's killing (or castration) of the son is the feared event that the Oedipal scenario is intended to ward off. Oedipus meets his father, Laius, at the crossroads, and their fight is always to the death. In *Tarantula* "boy dylan" is "killed by a discarded Oedipus" (T, 120). In "Highway 61 Revisited" God the Father demands of Abraham (the name of Robert Zimmerman's father), "Kill me a son" (L, 202). This is the primal scene of psychology, myth, and narrative, which has to be staged and restaged—in words Dylan later added to "Knockin' on Heaven's Door"—"just like so many times before." Or, as the Mexican hired gun says to *his* surrogate father in "Señor": "Seems like I been down this way before" (L, 410).

On the album *Desire* (1975), the theme of the dying outlaw or father is omnipresent. Rubin "Hurricane" Carter, accused of murder and "falsely tried," now "sits like Buddha in a ten-foot cell," the innocent outlaw, who "could-a been" but now never will be "champion of the world" (L, 377), rendered impotent by a corrupt justice system. Joey Gallo, somewhat unconvincingly portrayed as a humane mobster, dies because he refuses to carry a gun in the presence of children. The idea of helplessness is extended to Joey's father, who "had to say one last goodbye to the son that he could not save" (L, 384). The unnamed protagonist of "Romance in Durango" is shot down from ambush, leaving his beloved Magdalena unprotected. In "One More Cup of Coffee" Dylan sings, "Your daddy he's an outlaw / And a wanderer by trade," but the father's trembling voice undermines his patriarchal authority (L, 381). Similarly "Oh, Sister" presents a rebellion against patriarchal authority: "Our Father would not like the way that you act" (L, 382). Everywhere, the father's authority is challenged, ignored, or overthrown; the fathers themselves are helpless, wounded, or dead.

In "Lily, Rosemary and the Jack of Hearts," these obsessive images are again present, but given the ambiguities of the narrative, they are dispersed among the various characters in inconsistent and indeterminate combinations. Who *is* Lily's father? Stanza 7 tells us that Lily comes from a broken home, but there is no other direct clue. It is possible that her father is the Jack of Hearts, an interpretation quite consistent with what she says to him in her dressing room and with her "very rarely" seeing him. It is even barely possible that her father is Big Jim.

The most obvious interpretation of the relationships between Big Jim and the two women is that Rosemary is his wife and Lily his mistress. But, again, the song does not actually say this. Rosemary, we are told, was "tired of *playin' the role* of Big Jim's wife" (my emphasis), a phrase that suggests equally the possibilities that she is or is not legally married to him. We are not told simply that Lily "had Jim's ring" but that "it was *known all around* that Lily had Jim's ring" (my emphasis). Again Dylan refuses the stance of the omniscient narrator, reporting only the general opinion or gossip, which may or may not be true.

On a symbolic level, Big Jim certainly appears as Lily's father. He is a "king" while Rosemary first appears "looking like a queen without a crown." Lily, on the other hand, "was a princess, she was fair-skinned and precious as a child." King, queen, princess: in this triangle, Lily is indeed "precious as a child," a daughter.

The imagery of kings and queens also leads in the direction of playing cards. In the nursery rhyme the Jack of Hearts is a thief, as he is in the song; more generally, jacks or knaves are the villains of the deck—the trickster again. The Jack of Hearts is one of two jacks (the other one is the Jack of Spades) presented in profile so that only one eye shows. One of Dylan's earliest songs, written in 1960, was called "One-Eyed Jacks"; the singer appeals to a Queen and a Jack to "forget my name" (quoted in Shelton 1986, 54). Already, the Jack is associated with the forgetting or disowning of the father's name. In *Tarantula* "boy dylan" is killed by a *discarded* Oedipus.

"One-Eyed Jacks," besides being a slang term for masturbators, is the title of a 1961 movie in which a traveling outlaw (Marlon Brando) falls in love with a young woman and must fight and eventually kill her father (Karl Malden), who is an outlaw turned sheriff. *One-Eyed Jacks* was based on a novel about Billy the Kid. One of its scriptwriters was Sam Peckinpah, who had directed Dylan in *Pat Garrett & Billy the Kid* just a year or so before Dylan wrote "Lily, Rosemary and the Jack of Hearts" (Tatum, 133, 159). The major song that Dylan composed for the film, "Knockin' on Heaven's Door," was written for a scene in which a sheriff who is also a father is dying. The line of association—Jack of Hearts, one-eyed jacks, Billy the Kid, dying fathers—is unbroken.[34]

Each of the other characters is also associated with cards. We first see Lily engaged in a game of poker; she "had two queens, she was hopin' for a third to match her pair." What Lily gets, however, is not a third queen but the Jack of Hearts, which disrupts her hand just as the arrival of the real Jack of Hearts disrupts the "pair" of Rosemary and Big Jim. But in poker, one-eyed jacks are sometimes wild cards. Being a wild card certainly suits the trickster nature of the Jack of Hearts: both present and absent, both himself and something else. If Lily plays one-eyed jacks as wild, then the card she draws can indeed count as a third queen and give her a winning hand.

Rosemary also has her associations with cards: she is "a queen without a crown." No queen in the standard deck wears a crown; all have embroidered shawls over their heads. More significantly, almost every mention of Rosemary in the song draws attention to her eyes. On her first appearance she wears false eyelashes, but as she asserts her independence from Big Jim her sight becomes clearer and she loses her association with falseness. On her second appearance she looks at her image reflected in the knife which she later uses to kill Big Jim. When she appears beside Big Jim in the dressing room at the moment of the murder, she is "steady in her eyes," and on the gallows "she didn't even blink." In contrast to the shiftiness of a one-eyed jack, Rosemary sees herself and her actions directly and honestly.

Big Jim is described as a king, and he owns a diamond mine. Of the four kings in the standard deck, only the King of Diamonds is one-eyed. Separated in suit from the Jack of Hearts, Big Jim is nevertheless linked to him by their one-eyed nature, so in a curious sense, Big Jim could be the father not only to Lily but even to the Jack of Hearts. As a one-eyed king he is associated mythologically with one-eyed Odin, father of the Norse gods, who sacrifices his eye to gain wisdom and power. The dying father-gods of myth are all sacrificial figures, often killed by their successors, whose deaths recur in cyclical patterns.

The central Dylan motifs of the outlaw and the dying father are thus dispersed throughout the ambiguous narrative of "Lily, Rosemary and the Jack of Hearts." Big Jim, although not a particularly sympathetic character, nevertheless figures in the imagery as dead father and sacrificial victim. The idea of sacrifice is even clearer in Rosemary, whose death on the gallows allows Lily and the Jack of Hearts to go free. Rosemary, like Christ, "died a criminal's death" (L, 426). But the main outlaw of the song, the Jack of Hearts, escapes.

Depending on how you interpret the ambiguities of the relationships, the Jack of Hearts could be both a father (to Lily or to the members of his gang) or a would-be son who kills the father of the woman he loves. Whoever "the leading actor" of this drama is, he appears "in the costume of a monk": that is, of a holy father whose law prevents him from ever becoming a real father. Fathers, sons, and sacrificed daughters are bound together by the social and psychological structures of "the law."

In the end, of course, the Jack of Hearts stands for the trickster mode of Dylan himself. The Jack evades the Name of the Father by using an alias: we never know his "real" name. He is constantly in motion and hard to pin down. Like John Wesley Harding, he is "never known / To make a foolish move." Yet he also is ambiguous: it can be argued that he does "make a foolish move" when Big Jim traps him, and that he escapes only because of Rosemary's courage and self-sacrifice. He may live outside the law, but it is not clear that he is entirely honest. At the end of the story, instead of riding in heroically to the rescue, he simply disappears. He is absence.

In the same way, Dylan is absent from the story he stages for us. The narrative preserves a strict impersonality, and at several key points it pulls back from omniscience, choosing to report only what "was known all around" or what "they say" but "no one knew." The elisions and ambiguities of the narrative create unsettling gaps in the familiar patterns of the conventional story and ultimately deny the listener any secure position *vis-à-vis* the fictional world. Unknown and undefinable, the Jack of Hearts constantly disappears into these gaps, and so does Bob Dylan.

Shouting God's Name: Religious Songs

Bob Dylan's conversion to Christianity took place late in 1978, as a result of a personal visionary experience in which he felt "a presence in the room that couldn't have been anything but Jesus."[35] Early in 1979, he "made a formal declaration of faith before ministers of the Vineyard [Christian Fellowship]. He [was then] baptized and [took] a three and one-half month 'School of Discipleship' under the auspices of that church," led by Pastors Kenn Gulliksen and Larry Myers (Ricketts, 35). News of the conversion circulated as rumors among startled Dylan fans and was confirmed by the release, in August 1979, of the album *Slow Train Coming*.

Reactions to the conversion, and to the album, varied from shocked disbelief in Dylan's belief to perverse delight that he had again succeeded in doing the utterly unexpected. This was the trickster's move all right—a drastic reshaping and renewing of the self—but its effect was to return Dylan more explicitly than ever before to the complementary role of the prophet. As argued in Chapter 1, the stances of prophet and trickster have been in dynamic tension with each other throughout Dylan's career. In 1979 the trickster surprised everyone by putting on the mask of the prophet and wearing it, apparently, without even a touch of irony.

What was surprising was not so much the commitment to a religious worldview (the prophetic element had always been present in Dylan's work) as the rigid, dogmatically based form in which that view had been adopted. Almost immediately, followers of Dylan began to question how long he could remain content within the bounds, not so much of his new faith as of the rhetoric that it employed and enforced.

Certainly that rhetoric was for many the most distressing feature of the religious albums.[36] While Dylan was able to adopt the conventions of gospel *music* and to shape them into an idiom that remained recognizably his own,[37] he was less successful at manipulating the words, verbal formulas, and clichés of fundamentalism. The results show in some very slack writing. Compare, for instance, the brilliance of his juxtaposition of "Lincoln County Road or Armageddon" (L, 420) in "Señor," with the lame and predictable "Are you ready for Armageddon?" (L, 450) on *Saved*. Or take a line like "He unleashed His power at an unknown hour that no one knew" (L, 437), where the last phrase is a redundant repetition included only to fill out the rhyme. Or consider the tortured, clumsy syntax of the chorus to "Covenant Woman":

I just got to thank you
Once again
For making your prayers known
Unto heaven for me
And to you, always, so grateful
I will forever be.

(L, 444)

Dylan was always capable of letting the occasional weak or awkward phrase slip by: he has never been a perfectionist in his lyrics. But in these songs, especially on *Saved*, the proportion of poor writing is so great that it can only be attributed to the constraints of a religious orthodoxy with a strongly formative rhetorical code. For the first time in his career, Dylan seemed prepared to accept, without questioning, not just an established view of the world but also the verbal forms in which that view had to be expressed.

It could of course be argued that Dylan's extensive use of biblical language at this period is another example of what I described, in Chapter 2, as his practice of quotation, citation, and re-citation. Just as scholars like Greil Marcus have tracked down the multiple quotations from folksong, blues, or bluegrass which inform almost every line of albums such as *Time Out Of Mind* or *"Love and Theft,"* so too have scholars like the late Bert Cartwright documented the intricate weave of biblical references in *Slow Train Coming* and *Saved*. There is a definite degree of continuity here, and the citationality of Dylan's gospel lyrics does link them to his other works.

But at the same time, I think there are decisive differences. At its best (as on *"Love and Theft"*) Dylan's citational practice depends on deriving quotations from many different and diverse sources — as when, for example, in "High Water (for Charley Patton)," Charles Darwin is abruptly located on a Southern highway, being chased by the High Sheriff out of the traditional song "Po' Lazarus." Here, the various references (including the sly joke of a convict called Lazarus being wanted "dead or alive") work together and play off each other to create a rich intertextual web of meanings. By contrast, in Dylan's early gospel lyrics, all the quotations come from the same source (the Bible), and are uniform in tone; there is no opportunity for imaginative collage or ironic distance. These qualities do return in songs later in the gospel period, such as "Caribbean

Wind" or "Foot of Pride," where Dylan again seems to be working the language, rather than letting it work him.

In 1979, however, Dylan was less concerned with linguistic subtlety than he was with the urgency of his new message. Apart from confounding his fans with the radical nature of his conversion, the trickster was content, for a while, to take back seat to the prophet.

One of the most striking aspects of *Slow Train Coming* was its return to the themes of social critique so prominent in the early 1960s. This prophetic view has always been a fundamental aspect of Dylan's work, and at various times it has been inflected through different idioms. In the sixties the conventions of folk music provided the stance of the "protest singer," in the tradition of Woody Guthrie and Pete Seeger, rooted in the Labor movement and continuing in the civil rights and anti-war movements. That tradition lent moral authority to Dylan's early songs. The songs did not represent merely the dissatisfaction of an isolated individual; they were based on a cohesive social and political position, held by a community.

When Dylan stepped away from what he saw—rightly—as the coercive demands of folk-protest purity, he moved to a different political and moral stance, which was individualistic to the point of anarchism. Songs such as "Desolation Row" seek their moral authority not in any communal vision but in the uniqueness of the writer's perceptions. Their moral guarantee is found at the limit of the singer's nerve, and nerves. With *Slow Train Coming*, Dylan returned to a communally based position, one considerably older than the protest singer's but not entirely dissimilar to it: that of, quite literally, the prophet. In the biblical tones of Jeremiah, Dylan spoke out against a "world gone wrong."

The songs on *Slow Train Coming* offer acerbic comment and satirical criticism of rock 'n' roll stars and scientists; Karl Marx and Henry Kissinger; "adulterers in churches and pornography in the schools"; American dependence on "foreign oil" and "counterfeit philosophies"; "woman haters" and "spiritual advisors"; the obscenity of "grain elevators . . . bursting" in the midst of starvation; "unrighteous doctors dealing drugs"; and all those who "talk about a life of brotherly love" without knowing "how to live it" (L, 423, 431, 432, 436). These topics are generally consistent with the kinds of social positions and causes that Dylan had previously championed.

But their association with the language of born-again Christianity gave them, in the American context, a more right-wing inflection than many of

Dylan's old supporters were entirely comfortable with. There is an unpleasant element of jingoism or even racism—see the reference to the "sheiks" with their "nose rings" (L, 436). On the whole, however, Dylan's position might be described more accurately as populist than as reactionary.

These topics are also fairly general targets, and their generality shields them from much potential dispute. (We might all agree that pornography should not be taught in schools; the difficulty arises when we try to specify which particular texts are pornographic.) The religious albums offer no individual portraits or case histories as vivid or compelling as "Ballad of Hollis Brown" or "The Lonesome Death of Hattie Carroll." Rather, they use the generalized rhetoric of "Blowin' in the Wind" or "The Times They Are A-Changin'."

Precisely because it appeals to the authority of religious truth, the prophetic stance must also be deeply concerned about false prophets. One common target of the religious songs is the "preacher with . . . spiritual pride" (L, 423). "Man of Peace" warns that Satan in disguise "Could be the Führer / Could be the local priest" (L, 482). Dylan echoes here his earlier distrust of "corpse evangelists"— a phrase that occurs in the same song as his self-criticism "Fearing not that I'd become my enemy / In the instant that I preach" (L, 139). The irony is that the Dylan of 1979 *is* preaching. He may at times be preaching against preachers, but he is preaching.

The dogmatism of this preaching is most evident in the absolute judgments that it delivers: "Ya either got faith or ya got unbelief and there ain't no neutral ground" (L, 426). This is a world governed by absolute moral imperatives: "You're gonna have to serve somebody, / Well, it may be the devil or it may be the Lord / But you're gonna have to serve somebody" (L, 423). The choice is a clear-cut binary opposition in which the opposed terms, Lord and devil, are predefined. So it is really no choice at all. "Gotta Serve Somebody" may appear to be a disturbing song, challenging its listeners to examine and renew their beliefs and commitments, but at another level it does not challenge at all. It offers the security of a moral world in which decisions have already been made for you.

This absoluteness also derives from the context of the Apocalypse. Moral judgments are absolute because they are all potentially the Last Judgment. Apocalyptic visions have been pervasive in Dylan's work, from "I'd Hate to Be You on That Dreadful Day" (1962) to "When the Night Comes Falling from the Sky" (1984) and "Shooting Star" (1989):

> It's the last temptation, the last account,
>
> Last time you might hear the Sermon on the Mount,
>
> Last radio's playin' . . .

In the 1960s this urgency could be attributed to the immediate possibility of apocalypse in the secular form of nuclear war. While clearly haunted by this prospect, like so many of his generation, Dylan responded in a positive fashion, refusing to accept its inevitability passively. In "Let Me Die in My Footsteps" he rejects the fall-out shelter—"I will not carry myself down to die"—and somehow transforms the specter of obliteration into a celebration of "every state in this union" (L, 21–22). Similarly, the singer in "A Hard Rain's A-Gonna Fall" is not silenced by imminent destruction but proclaims his resolve to "stand on the ocean until I start sinkin' " (L, 60). In "Talkin' World War III Blues" Dylan even exorcises the specter of nuclear war with cheerful black comedy.

On *Slow Train Coming,* Apocalypse in its biblical sense takes the center stage of Dylan's imagination. The title itself is a powerfully suggestive image of a doom that is both inevitable and unpredictable: the train is definitely coming, but (since it's not on time) when? But Apocalypse still is not to be feared. As in the songs of the 1960s, the album challenges listeners to declare their allegiance (to the devil or the Lord) and take action: "When you gonna wake up and strengthen the things that remain?" (L, 432).[38] The singer and his "precious angel" are called "to the judgment hall of Christ" (L, 426), and the record closes by triumphantly anticipating the time "When He Returns" (L, 439). One could see all these songs as fulfilling the prophetic imperative of "Hard Rain": the singer should bear witness in the final days, and know his song well before he starts singing.

Absolutism of judgment, however, has a less positive side. There is often an unpleasant sense that Dylan is gloating over the fall and punishment of the unbelievers. The singer who proclaims "I'd hate to be you on that dreadful day" must be self-righteously sure of where he will stand, and the song seems to take an almost sadistic delight in the other's doom. Vengefulness is again evident on *Slow Train Coming,* especially in lines like the horrific "Can they imagine the darkness that will fall from on high / When men will beg God to kill them and they won't be able to die?" (L, 426). As Aidan Day comments, "the blackest feature of the imagining here is that it attributes to the highest light a power of the abysmal dark" (107). There is great relish in this black imagining: listen to how

Dylan emphasizes the word *able*. Several critics of Dylan's religious albums have pointed out that their theology is notably lacking in Christian compassion and forgiveness.[39] The unregenerate are consigned to hell with gleeful abandon.

However, not all aspects of the lyrics from these songs are quite so absolutist. Even in the most dogmatic inflection of his prophet stance, Dylan is unable entirely to banish the indeterminacies of the trickster—and even these songs reveal traces of ambiguity, of familiar splits and hesitations in the singer's presentation of himself.

Consider, for example, the pronouns. As always, Dylan's use of them is shifting and unstable in reference; his use of *you* is especially problematic. The least ambiguous prophetic denunciations occur in the third person, referring to generalized classes of sinners or unbelievers: "gangsters in power" or "masters of the bluff and masters of the proposition" (L, 432, 436). The use of *you* is more various. It is striking, for instance, how seldom *you* addresses God directly. Only "I Believe in You" and "What Can I Do for You?" maintain a dialogue with the divinity for the whole song. It is as if Dylan feels too humble or unworthy to talk to God directly; the songs never adopt the mode of prayer. Even "I Believe in You" is ambiguous, since much of it uses language that might just as well be addressed to a secular lover—and *you* in "Precious Angel," "Covenant Woman," and "In the Summertime" clearly refers to a woman whom Dylan regards as his spiritual guide.

At times the *you* does designate the targets of the prophet's denunciation, the unregenerate others. Often, however, closer examination suggests that this *you* also refers self-reflexively to Dylan himself, in the familiar mask of the divided self. When Dylan sings "take off your mask" (L, 437), he clearly addresses himself, attempting to present himself in a unified form, without disguise, before the throne of Judgment. But the internal division continues, and the mask remains in place.

This point has been most strongly argued by Day, who contends that the religious songs reflect a split "within the lyric-speaker's own identity. Time and again it is a conviction of his own depravity which traumatizes the speaker of these lyrics" (99–100). This interpretation is most plausible in songs in which the *you* conflicts with an *I:* that is, when the speaker is still struggling with those aspects of himself that cling to the old ways and are reluctant to accept the submission of the new faith. The old ways are often those of riches and fame, "The glamour and the bright lights and the politics of sin" (L, 459). The song from which this line is taken, "Dead Man, Dead Man," is a particularly good example. The *you* is not only a generalized sinner—"Uttering idle words from a reprobate mind"—but also, more immediately, someone who has power over the *I*, someone who can "take me down to hell." This *you* is thus interchangeable with the *I*—"The ghetto that you build for me is the one you end up in"— or more accurately, with the *I*'s dark, unregenerate side. This self-identification is further suggested by the chorus: the phrase "dead man," with the accent always on the first word, distantly echoes the name "Dylan," and the last line provides again the central pun of identity: "Dust upon your eyes"—your *I*'s.

At other times, the ambiguous reference of *you* hints at a different self-identification, namely, that of Dylan with Christ himself. In "Gonna Change My Way of Thinking" he sings:

> Stripes on your shoulders,
> Stripes on your back and on your hands,
> Swords piercing your side,
> Blood and water flowing through the land.
>
> (L, 428)

In biblical terms, the "stripes" of the whip, and the piercing of the side, out of which blood and water flow, refer to the passion of Christ (John 19:34). The redemptive quality of the suffering comes from Jesus, but if the *you* were to be understood as self-directed, then the singer takes that redemptive quality on himself. This would not be the only time that Dylan, even before his born-again incarnation, had hinted at an identification with Jesus. (As Robert *Zimmerman*, after all, he was already a carpenter and the son of a carpenter.) Michael Gray writes:

> From *Blood on the Tracks* onwards, we are given parallel after parallel between Dylan and Christ: both charismatic leaders, both message-bringers to their people, both martyrs because both get *betrayed*. In retrospect, it is as if Dylan eventually converts to Christianity because of the way he has identified with Christ and understood His struggles through his own.
>
> (210–11)

The Christ with whom Dylan most often identifies is the suffering Christ: Christ on the cross, Christ "in the garden" of Gethsemane (L, 448). In *Renaldo and Clara* Dylan is told: "Stand and bear yourself like the cross"; in "Shelter from the Storm," he presents himself as a sacrificial victim who wears a "crown of thorns" and says, "In a little hilltop village, they gambled for my clothes" (L, 360–61). There are no Dylan Christmas songs,[40] and references to healing and miracles are scarce. Dylan's Christ is overwhelmingly the dying and resurrected Lord.[41]

In passages like those cited above, it seems that Dylan is appropriating Christ's image in much the same way as he did the image of Lenny Bruce or Blind Willie McTell. Jesus is another mask of the self, one of many possible models for the trickster's continuously shifting sense of identity. Before 1979, this mask was primarily an aesthetic gesture, a way of incorporating a complex and culturally overdetermined reference—Christ—into the play of masks and mirrors that made up Dylan's multiple self-portraits. After 1979, the gesture of identification could not be made in such explicit terms, since it would be, for a true believer, blasphemous. With the possible exception of the lines from "Gonna Change My Way of Thinking," Dylan in the religious albums never directly refers to himself as Christ—but the shadow of Christ's image hangs over them, and there is always this potential identification to be made.[42]

It is not until *Oh Mercy* (1989) that Dylan again presents a direct allusion to himself as Christ, and when it occurs the allusion is as much to Judas as it is to Jesus. These two characters are so closely linked in Dylan's imagination that they seem like twins, each other's mirrors or ghosts: I and I. When the 1966 heckler yelled "Judas!" at a Dylan whom he had presumably seen previously as Jesus, he showed how easy it is for the two figures to be conflated in one person.

Judas and Jesus appear together in "Masters of War" and also in "With God on Our Side," which notes that "Jesus Christ / Was betrayed by a kiss" and poses the question of "Whether Judas Iscariot / Had God on his side" (L, 93). This is a difficult theological point. In some sense Judas is carrying out God's will by making the Crucifixion possible. Many modern presentations of Judas, such as Martin Scorsese's controversial film *The Last Temptation of Christ*, see him not as pure evil but as an idealist trying to force Jesus' hand, to make him declare his divinity.

The identification of the two figures finds literal expression in the oath "Judas Priest," which is in origin a euphemism for "Jesus Christ."[43] In Dylan's "Ballad of Frankie Lee and Judas Priest" (L, 252–54), the two characters are intricately implicated with each other. Some commentators have suggested that Frankie Lee, since he clearly opposes Judas, should be seen as a Christ-figure. The grounds for this identification are slight: an ambiguous reference to Frankie's "deceased" father (God is dead?) and his dying "of thirst" (echoing Christ's words on the cross). Frankie Lee would be a very secular Christ: he borrows money, he confesses to "foolish pride," he is a gambler, he dies raving, and there is no suggestion of salvation or resurrection.

Conversely, several of Judas Priest's actions are Christ-like: he lends money generously, he lives in Paradise, he holds his dying friend in his arms. The reversal is incomplete, however. Frankie Lee is still innocent, and Judas and the house he inhabits are still very sinister. The song's only conclusion is that "nothing is revealed," so the two characters' links to each other remain as mysterious as they are profound. Like Pat Garrett and Billy the Kid, "they were the best of friends," and Judas Priest carries in the euphemistic echo of his name the ghostly alias of Jesus Christ.

Judas reappears on *Oh Mercy* in "What Was It You Wanted?" In this song the speaker is the object of multiple and unreasonable demands from an unspecified *you*, who may be a fan, a lover, God, or perhaps Dylan addressing himself. But at one point the *you* is unmistakably Judas: "What was it you wanted / When you were kissing my cheek?" We are again in Gethsemane. This is the same kiss (Matthew 26:48–49) with which Judas betrayed Christ in "With God on Our Side." The watchers in the shadows are the waiting soldiers whom Peter attacks in "In the Garden." And Dylan, the recipient of the kiss, is Christ.

"What Was It You Wanted?" is followed immediately by "Shooting Star," with its line about "the last temptation," which may well be a reference to Scorsese's film. At one point in this film, Judas angrily demands of Christ, "What good are you?" Again, *Oh Mercy* has a direct echo: in "What Good Am I?" Dylan presents a searching self-examination of his effectiveness as a Christian. But if the title phrase is indeed a direct quotation from the film, then the song is not so humble, for it again casts Dylan in the role of the Savior.

Between "What Good Am I?" and "What Was It You Wanted?" the perhaps timely warning of "Disease of Conceit" intervenes. The split within the self is here clearly identified and denounced: "seein' double" is a symptom of the disease, one which "gives you delusions of grandeur, and an evil eye." If identifying with Christ is a delusion of grandeur, then the evil eye/I again evokes Christ's doubled counterpart, Judas, who waits, with his kiss, in the following song.

Thus, to summarize, the general themes of Dylan's religious work lead into one another. His prophetic social critiques lead to the absolute judgments of Apocalypse. Judgment of others leads to judgment of the self and the self-directed *you* of some lyrics; the *you* in turn takes on the characteristics of both Jesus Christ and his linguistic shadow, Judas Priest. Far from being a monolithic mass of dogmatic certainties, the songs reveal much ambiguity, internal division, and complexity. Nevertheless, I still argue that the lyrics of *Slow Train Coming* and *Saved* are inhibited by the clichés of a rhetoric that is fundamentally opposed to ambiguity, division, and complexity. If you are a Christian believer, the lyrics of these songs may well be eloquent proclamations of the Truth; if you are not, they may remain as occasions of skepticism and debate.

So, for those listeners and critics who value lyrical complexity more than doctrinal purity, the most interesting of Dylan's "religious" songs tend to be those which occur at the end of this period, as Dylan begins to reintroduce a more symbolic or even surrealist vocabulary.

In "Every Grain of Sand," for instance, there is still a strong reliance on divine power and mercy, but that providential presence figures less in images of a conventional God than in a generalized, almost pantheistic vision. The mood is even reminiscent of "Lay Down Your Weary Tune": the singer is aware of "every leaf that trembles . . . every sparrow falling . . . every grain of sand" (L, 462). The biblical source (Matthew 10:29–31) stresses God's presence—a sparrow "shall not fall on the ground without your Father"—but the song's context is more secular—"I am hanging in the balance of the reality of man."[44] These images point to a universal sense of unity, in which even the scattered grains of sand are gathered up in the singular act of counting.

By contrast, the protagonist of the song, whose sense of his sinfulness excludes him from this unity, is presented in images of fracturing and internal division. The singer is separated not only from the divine unity but also from himself. In the first stanza he hears "a dyin' voice inside me," and in the second he compares himself to Cain, his brother's murderer. He seeks for a "mirror of innocence on each forgotten face." The mirror might declare his wholeness and self-knowledge, but this insight would have to come, not from within himself, but from his reflection in another person's face acting as a mirror. These doubled images are themselves divided: the mirror is "broken" and the face is "forgotten."

Another traditional image of self-possession, the proper name, also comes to him from the outside, and its site is the "doorway of temptation." In the last stanza, "I hear the ancient footsteps like the motion of the sea / Sometimes I turn, there's someone there, other times it's only me." Like the "shadow" in "Mr. Tambourine Man," this "someone" is and is not the singer himself. It is the doubled projection of his self-division—the Abel to his Cain or the Jesus to his Judas—which separates him from the innocent self-possession that exists "in every leaf that trembles, in every grain of sand" and which thus leaves him, uncertain and sinful, "hanging in the balance."

"Every Grain of Sand" uses looser, more imagistic language than most of the other religious songs, but it remains quite straightforwardly comprehensible. The same cannot entirely be said for an extraordinary trio of songs recorded for *Shot of Love* but not included on the released album: "Angelina," "The Groom's Still Waiting at the Altar," and "Caribbean Wind."[45] Here the language becomes frankly surrealistic—though still with a solid grounding in biblical quotation and allusion—and none of the three songs has any clearly demarcated line of argument or narrative. Characters and pronouns come and go with bewildering nonspecificity, and they move in a landscape of unexplained symbols and bizarre juxtapositions.

All three songs are set in an atmosphere of violence, which mixes contemporary political references—especially to Central and South America—with the language of apocalypse. "Angelina" contains the remarkable couplet "Tell me, tall men, where would you like to be overthrown / In Jerusalem or Argentina?" While "Argentina" might be simply a convenient rhyme for "Angelina," the geographical-political reference recurs in "The Groom's Still Waiting at the Altar" as part of an even more remarkable rhyme: "What can I say about Claudette? Ain't seen her since January, / She could be respectably married or running a whorehouse in Buenos Aires" (L, 464). (Dylan has always been a virtuoso rhymster, but this couplet is arguably his finest and most outrageous accomplishment.)

South America is obliquely evoked in another song of this period, "Trouble," whose reference to "stadiums of the damned" (L, 461) recalls the murderous events of Salvador Allende's overthrow in Chile. The reference to "killing nuns and soldiers . . . fighting on the border" (L, 464) points to the death of American nuns in El Salvador in 1980. "Caribbean Wind" is more general in its pictures of violence—"famines and earthquakes and train wrecks and the tearin' down of the walls" (L, 466)—but its title returns us to the Central American region and to the "Tales of Yankee Power" Dylan had previously attacked on *Street Legal*.

In the released version, the wind is strictly Caribbean, blowing between Nassau and Mexico. In the earlier concert version, it also "blows hard / From the Valley Coast to my back yard" and "howls / From Tokyo to the British Isles." Specific areas of political tension, like Central America, are broadened out to the universal violence of Apocalypse. The geographical setting, "West of the Jordan, East of the Rock of Gibraltar," is the traditional site of the final battles of Armageddon, which are witnessed by the singer in "Angelina"—"I see pieces of men marching, trying to take heaven by force, / I can see the unknown rider, I can see the pale white horse."[46] "Caribbean Wind" warns that all things are being brought "nearer to the fire." The end of history is prophesied in "The Groom's Still Waiting at the Altar"—"I see the turning of the page, / Curtain risin' on a new age."

But although the end is announced, it is also delayed. Apocalypse is at hand but not yet here; the groom is at the altar but still waiting. Almost ten years later, in "Ring Them Bells," Dylan announced that the wait would be extended further: "time is running backwards, and so is the Bride." These references to the groom and the bride are based on the Song of Solomon, which is alluded to in the opening lines of "Caribbean Wind"—lines that also contrive to unite Rome and Jerusalem, Milton and Dante, with a virtuosity of intertextual reference that Dylan had not shown since "Desolation Row":

> She was the rose of Sharon from paradise lost
> From the city of seven hills near the place of the cross.
> I was playing a show in Miami in the theater of divine comedy.
>
> (L, 466)

The rose of Sharon appears in the Song of Solomon (2:1), which has been the subject of a long tradition of allegorical interpretation as an account of "the

'mystical union' between Bridegroom and bride, between Christ and the soul"
(Pelikan, 128). This union culminates in the celebration after the defeat of
Satan: "Let us be glad and rejoice . . . for the marriage of the Lamb is come, and
his wife hath made herself ready" (Revelation 19:7). If, however, the groom is
still *waiting* at the altar, then the final battle of Armageddon has not yet been
won; if time and the bride are running *backwards*, then the world is moving cat-
astrophically further away from victory.

Traditional Christians have always recognized that this interpretation presents the "danger" of "eroticism": "The Song is after all still a love poem and a
very explicit love poem at that, even if one reads it as an allegory; and the allegory can easily revert to the very eroticism it is intended to transcend" (Pelikan,
130). But Dylan seems unconcerned about such danger: all three songs openly
court the erotic. Each centers on a particular woman, though the shifting of
names and pronouns keeps her identity indeterminate. The violence of the
songs' political landscape extends into their view of sexual relations. "Angelina"
evokes a "combat zone," not only in the military sense but also in reference to
the notorious red-light district of Boston. The combat zone is dominated by the
"furnace of desire," whose flames are fanned by the Caribbean winds. Just as the
"ships of liberty" must remain "distant," so this desire must remain unfulfilled.
Lovers are always at cross-purposes: "Don't know what I can say about
Claudette that wouldn't come back to haunt me, / Finally had to give her up
'bout the time she began to want me." Claudette may end up as a bride or a
whore; the singer has no way of knowing her, and his futile words are the ghosts
of their relationship.

This composite but unknowable woman, like the woman in "Precious
Angel," is a religious messenger, who "told about Jesus, told about the rain," but
she also unites this evangelical mission with the political one: "She told me
about the jungle where her brothers were slain." The songs are full of messengers, both good and evil. In "Caribbean Wind," "every new messenger brings
evil report" while the singer in "The Groom's Still Waiting at the Altar" "got the
message this morning, the one that was sent to me." The noun *angel* etymolog-
ically means "messenger," so this motif links "Precious Angel" to the longing
expressed in the name's repetition in the chorus: "Angelina—Oh, Angelina."

These shifting images of the women are matched by a familiar indeterminacy in the identity of the singer. "Angelina" presents him as characteristically

divided within himself ("My right hand drawing back while my left hand advances") or possibly divided among several separate characters ("Your best friend and my worst enemy is one and the same"—that is, me).

The most drastic internal split comes in the concert version of "Caribbean Wind": "Stars on my balcony, buzz in my head, slayin' Bob Dylan in my bed, / Street band playin' 'Nearer My God to Thee'." Here the singer, Bob Dylan, witnesses his death—or more precisely, the death of his name—and hears the hymn played at his funeral. The hymn's title is echoed in the chorus, "Bringing everything that's near to me nearer to the fire." *Near to me,* then, is also nearer to Thee, suggesting again the implicit identification of Dylan with Christ. The fire is the fire of hell, "the flames in the furnace of desire," but also perhaps the refining and purifying fire of God's love. "In God's truth," Dylan promises the woman in "Angelina," "tell me what you want and you'll have it of course." The satisfaction of desire is possible, then, but only when the request is made "In God's truth."

This reintroduction of a symbolic vocabulary in the *Shot of Love* outtakes paved the way for the more controlled use of imagery on *Infidels*, especially in "I and I," a very complex song, which may stand as the summation of this period of Dylan's work. The song has a double focus, enunciated by its title and its chorus. In the secular context "I and I" is the definitive image of the mask of the divided self: the double, ghost, alias, or shadow that always intervenes in the supposedly unified human subject. In a theological context, however, the chorus speaks, as we shall see, of the unspeakable Name of God.

The song begins with an intimate confession: "Been so long since a strange woman has slept in my bed" (L, 480). The woman is idealized and thus, rather like the sad-eyed lady, denied individuality in human frailty: "In another lifetime she must have owned the world, or been faithfully wed / To some righteous king who wrote psalms beside moonlit streams." The biblical allusions suggest both David, composer of the Psalms, and Solomon, author of the song of the bridegroom and the bride.[47] As her lover, Dylan would then be associated with these two divinely inspired singers.

But the song also disclaims this identification. The singer is not, after all, "faithfully wed" to this strange woman, and in the second verse he tries to avoid her rather than face the challenge she might pose by waking up and wanting him to talk. He says he has nothing to say: a disclaimer that goes all the way back to "I know I ain't no prophet / An' I ain't no prophet's son" (L, 27). The paradox of anti-art persists, however, for the whole song indicates by its very existence that he *does* have something to say.

The third stanza (which Dylan omits in performance) invokes "the worthy [who can] divide the word of truth." This phrase comes from Paul's second Epistle to Timothy (2:15), which the King James Version gives as "rightly dividing the word of truth." The New English Bible gives a simpler translation, "be straightforward in your proclamation of the truth," but the older wording is intriguing in its suggestion that truth *can* be divided, and that the Word of God is *not* indivisible. The idea of division is certainly central to the song. In the next line Dylan tells how he has learned "to see an eye for an eye and a tooth for a tooth." His phrasing again plays variations on the commonly accepted sense. Instead of demanding punishment by *taking* an eye for an eye, "to [see] an eye for an eye" means accepting the other for what or who it is. And, especially in the context of the chorus, the pun is unavoidable: to see an I for an I.

The fourth stanza provides a wonderful imagistic vignette of two men in a railway station "waiting for spring to come, smoking down the track." Note how *smoking* could apply grammatically either to the men or, more ominously, to spring. The slight echo of "slow train coming" is picked up in a remarkably mild and even friendly invocation of Apocalypse: "The world could come to an end tonight, but that's all right." The source of this acceptance is in the singer's confidence that the woman will still be waiting for him when he returns.

He does not rest, however, in that security. The last verse finds him again on the road, traveling through darkness even at noon. The division of the self is asserted at the level of language—"Someone else is speakin' with my mouth"—and countered at the level of faith—"but I'm listening only to my heart." The singer presents himself as a humble Christian servant, who has "made shoes for everyone . . . while I still go barefoot." But this humility is tempered by the sudden intrusion of the phrase "even you," which introduces into the song an unidentified second person addressee. "Even you" seems to imply an enemy, someone for whom he might not be expected to make shoes; but the *you* is also an enemy who has been forgiven, who has been seen as an I for an I rather than having an eye extracted for an eye. (*Barefoot* also disturbingly echoes the "barefoot servants" who observed the onset of Apocalypse in "All Along the Watchtower.")

The verses present, then, a drama typical of the religious songs: a protagonist who feels a double division, split within himself and separated from God, but who yet struggles toward a higher unity. The chorus evokes this absent God in terms that paradoxically combine division and unity.

The term "I and I," as I have said, may be taken in a secular context, referring to the essential alienation within every human consciousness. In a religious context the immediate source of the phrase is in the Jamaican cult of Rastafari. As Tracy Nicholas explains:

> For the Rastafarians, the most powerful and significant letter of the alphabet is also a word and a number: "I." I is part of His Imperial Majesty's title—Haile Selassie I. It is the last letter in Rastafari. "I" is so important that a Rasta will never say "I went home," but would say instead "I and I went home," to include the presence and divinity of the Almighty with himself every time he speaks. "I and I" also includes bredren, who also say "I and I." In this simple way, through language, Rastafari is a community of people all the time. . . . "I and I," then, reminds the Rastafarian of his own obligation to live right and at the same time, it praises the Almighty.
>
> (38–39)

"I and I" is thus a way of naming God while naming one's self. It asserts the immanence of the divinity, His presence in every moment of self-awareness and speech. These secular and religious senses may then be ironically juxtaposed: "I and I" testifies simultaneously to unity and separation.

Dylan takes irony a step further by the additional juxtaposition of the Rasta term with the line "One says to the other, no man sees my face and lives." The biblical source is Exodus 33:20, in which God says to Moses, "Thou canst not see my face: for there shall no man see me, and live." In contrast to Rastafari, this view of God is one of absolute separation: far from including Him in every utterance of "I," it asserts that man can *never* see God, never draw close to Him. The implied but unspoken reconciliation of these two views would come in Christianity, in the incarnation of the absolutely 'other' as human.

Dylan's line, however, contains an element not present in Exodus: the phrase "One said to the other." An orthodox reading would see this as God (the

One) speaking to man (the other), but there is also a strong suggestion, given the divided name of the divinity as "I and I," that "One" and "the other" are both aspects of God and that God, like man, suffers a divided identity.

What is going on here is a very complex collage of the names of God. "I and I" is the Rasta way of naming God as both unity and division. In the Old Testament, the only name that God gives Himself is "I AM THAT I AM" (Exodus 3:14), a formulation which declares the indivisibility of God but can do so only by again simultaneously doubling the *I*. It is "I AM THAT I AM" that transliterates roughly as Jehovah, or Jaweh, or JWH, as in "John Wesley Harding." God's name is unknowable and unutterable. An orthodox Jew will not even write out the word *God* but spell it *G–d*. "I and I Am That I and I Am" is thus a name for the unnamable. In "Political World" Dylan sings, "You climb into the frame / And shout God's name / But you're not even sure what it is." "I and I" is his most serious and complex attempt to be sure of that name, and to name it in song.

Postscript 1

The above discussion of Dylan's religious songs focuses almost exclusively on the period from 1979 to 1983, the years during which his commitment to an explicitly Christian theology was most public and sustained. In subsequent years he has become more reticent about his private views and more ambiguous in the ways he expresses them. Indeed, internet discussion groups, such as rec.music.dylan, often feature protracted debates on what he believes now and whether or not he is still a Christian.

Undeniably there is still a strong religious dimension to Dylan's work, though it no longer seems to be channeled through any theology as strict or exclusive as that of the Vineyard Christian Fellowship. He does seem to have made deliberate attempts to reconcile his Christian faith with his Jewish heritage. His writing in recent years has seemed to me ambiguous (as argued later, in relation to *Time Out Of Mind*; see Chapter 7). Rather, the religious focus has shifted away from his own writing to his choice and performance of other people's songs. In his concert repertoire he has shown a marked fondness for gospel songs from the bluegrass tradition, such as "Hallelujah, I'm Ready To Go," "Somebody Touched Me," or the suitably apocalyptic "This World Can't Stand Long."[48]

And, of course, the phrase used repeatedly throughout this book to characterize Dylan's prophetic stance—his view of a "world gone wrong"—comes from a song by the Mississippi Sheiks which was the title track of his 1993 album. (This album concludes with a quite gorgeous performance of "Lone Pilgrim," perhaps the finest moment in all of Dylan's "religious" music.)

So the question of Dylan's private beliefs may well be set aside as not strictly relevant to a critical approach. What matters are the songs: from the impassioned evangelical deliveries of 1980, to the convolutions of "Caribbean Wind" or "I and I," through to the elegant and uplifting bluegrass gospel of recent years. If Bob Dylan has a true abiding religion, it is to be found in his commitment, as a performer, to these songs. And indeed, he has said as much himself. As close to a definitive statement as we are ever likely to find is the following, from a 1997 interview with David Gates:

> Here's the thing with me and the religious thing. This is the flat-out truth: I find the religiosity and philosophy in the music. I don't find it anywhere else. Songs like "Let Me Rest on a Peaceful Mountain" or "I Saw the Light"—that's my religion. I don't adhere to rabbis, preachers, evangelists, all of that. I've learned more from the songs than I've learned from any of this kind of entity. The songs are my lexicon. I believe the songs.

> (64)

Postscript 2

Just when I thought that I'd arrived at "as close to a definitive statement as we are ever likely to find" on Dylan the prophet, along comes Dylan the trickster to mess things up again.

Spring 2003 saw the release of a CD called *Gotta Serve Somebody: The Gospel Songs of Bob Dylan*. It's an album of cover versions of Dylan gospel songs, performed by some major names in contemporary gospel music: Shirley Caesar, Dottie Peoples, Aaron Neville, Mavis Staples. It is an altogether *serious* album: the singers and producers are all devoted to the Christian message. The song selection is drawn entirely from the first two gospel albums, *Slow Train Coming* and *Saved:* nothing as problematic as "Caribbean Wind," or even "Every Grain of Sand." Even within these two albums, the selection omits anything as edgy as "Precious Angel" or as whimsical as "Man Gave Names To All the Animals."

The performances are vivid, intense, and committed, especially Helen Baylor's wonderful reading of "What Can I Do For You?" Only Rance Allen's hyperbolic rhetoric on "When He Returns" seems overdone. Several performers do make changes or additions to Dylan's lyrics, none of them for the better. A few feel compelled to interject "Jesus" at points where Dylan had discreetly left the name implicit.

In many ways, Dylan seems to have willingly collaborated in this project. The liner notes thank him and his manager, Jeff Rosen, as "men of word and deed." And he did agree to contribute one original recording to the album, a new version of *Slow Train Coming*'s "Gonna Change My Way Of Thinking," sung as a duet with Mavis Staples. So the appearance was that Dylan was reaffirming his commitment to these songs, to their message, and to his own prophetic stance.

But then you listen to the track itself, which is utterly bizarre, Dylan in full trickster mode. (There is no doubt that the effect is fully intentional. The track was cut in April 2002, and is credited as a Jack Frost production, recorded and mixed by Chris Shaw — the same production team responsible for *"Love and Theft"* the year before.)

"Gonna Change My Way Of Thinking" (L, 428-9) was a regular feature of the 1979 and 1980 tours, but has not been played in concert since. The track begins with Dylan and his road band launching into the first verse ("Gonna change my way of thinking / Make myself a different set of rules") as a hard-driving, raunchy blues, sounding every bit as serious and committed as the other singers on the album. But after just one verse, the song suddenly breaks off, and Dylan announces, in a self-consciously theatrical voice, "Why look, someone's coming up the road, boys." There follows a comic dialogue between Bob and Mavis Staples, in which Mavis comments on the view from Bob's house (Bob responds "You can sit on this porch and look right straight into Hawaii") and says she's hungry (Bob says he will "knock off" a few backyard chickens and "fry 'em up"). This dialogue is actually taken, almost word for word, from a novelty record by Jimmie Rodgers and the Carter Family. It's pure country-and-western hokum; so what on earth is it doing on an intensely devout gospel album?

Eventually Bob and Mavis get round to restarting "Gonna Change My Way of Thinking ," but when they do, the lyrics bear scarcely any relation at all to the original. Whereas the original was a heavy, rather grim set of theological admonitions ("Jesus said, 'Be ready / For you know not the hour in which I come'"), the new words are largely secular and often whimsical. The original laments that "You forget all about the golden rule"; the new version cheerfully admits "we live by the golden rule / Whoever got the gold, rules." Some of the new writing is very sharp:

> The sun is shining
> Ain't but one train on this track
> I'm stepping out of the dark woods
> Trying to jump on a monkey's back

The second line gracefully alludes to both *Slow Train Coming* and *Blood on the Tracks;* the third line concisely evokes both the sinister "dark woods" (echo of Robert Frost?) and an escape from them; and the fourth line brilliantly reverses the cliché "Get this monkey off my back," while at the same time gesturing ambiguously towards the evolutionary theories of Charles Darwin (last seen out on Highway 5).

The whole effect is to deflate the stern orthodoxy of the album's other tracks, and to provide instead a playful pastiche, or even parody, of Dylan's own gospel mode. The track is so utterly different in tone from the rest of the album that it once again calls into question the nature of Dylan's position on the Gospel, or at least on the gospel songs.

This effect reaches its climax in the last lines of the song (which are also the last lines of the record):

> I'll tell you something
> Things you never had you'll never miss
> Tell you something else, a brave man will kill you with a sword
> A coward with a kiss

In that last line you can see, one more time, Judas "in the garden" with his kiss. But there is also another, even more direct quotation, from the famous lines of "The Ballad of Reading Gaol":

Yet each man kills the thing he loves,
By each let this be heard,
Some do it with a bitter look,
Some with a flattering word,
The coward does it with a kiss,
The brave man with a sword!

(170)

Only Bob Dylan the trickster could bring a whole album of gospel music to a close with a quotation from Oscar Wilde.

"All Along the Watchtower"

In Chapter 1, "Prophet and Trickster: An Overview," I argued that Dylan's continuing stance might be defined as an interaction between the figures of the prophet and the trickster. One of the most interesting instances of this interaction is to be found in "All Along the Watchtower."

The song begins with an enigmatic and aphoristic dialogue between two figures, the Joker and the Thief: both of them aspects of the trickster, both of them recurring motifs in Dylan's work—"Jokerman . . . why must I always be the thief?" Normally, both of these figures stand on, or beyond, the margins of society. The Joker refuses to take things seriously; the Thief just takes things.

But in this song, their dialogue is, in fact, quite unthieflike and unjokerly. The Joker complains to the Thief about, precisely, theft: that the commercial interests of business and agriculture are illegitimately appropriating personal property. And the Thief enjoins the Joker not to joke: to remain calm in the face of crisis and to bear true witness in the face of impending apocalypse. In other words, the trickster, both as joker and as thief, talks in a rhetorical style more appropriate to the prophet.

Conversely, the prophet talks in the elusive, incomplete manner of the trickster. The third stanza derives from the Book of the Prophet Isaiah (21:8–9): "My lord, I stand continually upon the watchtower. . . . And behold, here cometh a chariot of men, with a couple of horsemen" (plus, perhaps, a memory of the "barefoot" captives in Isaiah 20:4). But Dylan pointedly omits the point of Isaiah's prophecy: "Babylon is fallen, is fallen; and all the graven images of her gods he hath broken unto the ground" (Isaiah 21:9). Instead, he leaves the approach of the "two riders" as an open ending: a trickster's puzzle, ominously unanswered.

One way of reading the puzzle, of course, is to argue that the two riders *are* the Joker and the Thief. The song is circular in form, and the open ending of stanza 3 loops back into the dialogue of stanzas 1 and 2. (In recent concert performances, Dylan has indeed repeated the first verse as an "ending" to the song.) Throughout the song, then, the prophet and the trickster are implicated in each other. They use each other's language, they change places in the narrative. If the song is a loop, with the ending tied back into the beginning like a serpent's tail into its mouth, then it is also a closed circuit, which begins with the assertion: "There must be some way out of here. . . ."

It ends with a beginning: "the wind began to howl." Dylan always seems to reserve a special place for the word *howl* in his songs: "I kissed goodbye, the howling beast, on the borderline that separated you from me"; "The ghost of electricity howls in the bones of her face" (L, 368, 223). *Howl* is, of course, for Dylan, and for anyone else of his generation, Allen Ginsberg's word.

"What I'm trying to do now," Dylan told Ginsberg, "is not [use] too many words. There's no line that you can stick your finger through, there's no hole in any of the stanzas. There's no blank filler. Each line has something" (Miles 1989, 392). What he's describing is his new style—post-psychedelic, post-*Blonde on Blonde,* post–motorcycle accident—the style of writing which produced the Basement Tapes and *John Wesley Harding.* Ginsberg is certainly not far from his mind when he writes that final line of "All Along the Watchtower."

So perhaps the "two riders . . . approaching" are Allen Ginsberg and Jack Kerouac?

Any song-lyric-text which ends with the word *howl* is also an open invitation to the vocalist, and to the musicians, to do just that: *Howl!* The verbal text exhausts itself and is caught up in the nonverbal signification of music. The instruments now become an extension of the voice; in another medium, they replicate, transmute, and transcend the vocal gesture of the howl.

Dylan's harmonica does this on the original recording, but the definitive "Watchtower" howl remains Jimi Hendrix's distorted, multitracked, virtuoso guitar. Hendrix's version remains the greatest of all Dylan covers—even, perhaps, the only one to successfully reimagine a Dylan song. Every one of Dylan's concert performances—and this is the song he has performed more often in concert than any other title in his catalog—pays tribute to Hendrix: from the soaring melodies of The Band in 1974, to the grinding guitar assaults of the early 1990s, to the introspective hesitations of the sublime version performed in Rostock in 1998.

From one point of view, what Hendrix was doing was responding to a response. At the time that Dylan's original version was released (December 1967), it stood in a peculiar relation to musical history. In late 1965 to early 1966, Dylan had dominated the musical world with his combination of hard-driving rock music and long, expansive, surrealistically image-drenched lyrics. Then, for over a year, he dropped right out of the public eye. Though we can now, with the benefit of retrospect and our knowledge of the Basement Tapes, see the logical progression to *John Wesley Harding*, at the time that album came as a complete surprise. The period of Dylan's silence had been marked by the triumph of "psychedelic" rock: The Beatles' *Sergeant Pepper*, the San Francisco hippie Summer of Love, Jefferson Airplane, early Jimi Hendrix, the excessive over-reaching of The Rolling Stones' *Their Satanic Majesties Request*. How could the author of *Blonde on Blonde* respond to what he had started? How could he top them all?

He "topped" them, of course, by ignoring them completely, by taking a trickster's end run round the problem. Instead of the growing volume of electric rock, *John Wesley Harding* relied on a muted acoustic guitar, drums, bass, and harmonica. Instead of psychedelic excess, he offered concise country and western—as far as it was conceivable to go, both musically and politically, from Haight-Ashbury hipness. Instead of proliferating surrealist images, he offered short enigmatic lyrics in regularly rhyming stanzas.

So, one way of seeing Hendrix's "Watchtower" is to understand it as the response to the response: the reclaiming of Dylan for psychedelic electric rock. This is how ploughmen *ought* to "dig" my earth! This is the Dylan that the end of the hippie summer of 1967 *ought* to have delivered.

Dylan, of course, like a good trickster, has the last laugh. After all, the Hendrix version was perhaps what he always had intended in the first place. The tracks recorded in Nashville in November 1967 were supposed to have been overdubbed by The Band, adding in a full electric instrumentation. The story is that Robbie Robertson, listening to the tapes, realized that they were already perfect, and he persuaded Dylan to issue them as they were, with no overdubs. If The Band *had* added an extra layer to the song, would Hendrix have felt the same necessity for his own supplement?

But what Hendrix really saw was that, whatever its instrumentation on *John Wesley Harding,* "All Along The Watchtower" was, in fact, a great, an ulti- mate rock and roll song. And that is an intuition which Bob Dylan has endorsed in concert ever since—so far (at the time of this writing) at least twelve hundred times.

chapter 5

Intertexts

Intertext: Allen Ginsberg

At one point in the Basement Tapes, we hear Dylan and The Band enjoying themselves with a delightfully silly song called "Every Time I Go To Town." On the tape, this performance flows directly into the corniest of rock and roll classics, "See Ya Later, Alligator (In a While, Crocodile)." They begin playing around with the words, and Rick Danko improvises the line "See ya later, Allen Ginsberg." Dylan almost breaks up laughing, but he manages to keep singing. Together, he and Danko weave Ginsberg's name into an increasingly fractured set of transformations on the song's wording.

Danko	Dylan
See you later, Allen Ginsberg	
See you later, crocogator	See you later, alligator
In a while, Allen Ginsberg	After a while, crocodile
. . . .	
See you later, Allen Ginsberg	Allen Ginsberg, later gator
In a while, allocrile	Later, later, Allen Ginsberg
Little later on the Nile	Allen Ginsberg, later, later
See you later if you're mile	Allen Ginsberg after a while
See you later, crocogator	Allen Ginsberg, Allen Ginsberg
	Allen Ginsberg after a while . . .

The good humor of the tape is infectious. Dylan clearly enjoys the pun, but there is no malice in it. The song is in no way laughing *at* Allen Ginsberg. Rather, it's a friendly joke at the expense of someone the singer knows and likes.

At the time of the Basement Tapes, Dylan's most recent contacts with Ginsberg had been the previous year. Ginsberg had visited Woodstock on August 19, 1966, just three weeks after Dylan's motorcycle accident, and had brought him a poetic gift:

> When he was ill in the sixties—when he had his crash—I brought him a box full of books of all kinds. All the modern poets I knew. Some ancient poets like Sir Thomas Wyatt, Campion. Dickinson, Rimbaud, Lorca, Apollinaire, Blake, Whitman and so forth.
>
> (Gray and Bauldie, 171)

(If it really did contain "all the modern poets [Ginsberg] knew," it must have been a *very* large box!) Barry Miles reports that Dylan then

> telephoned [Ginsberg] from his bed in Woodstock and asked, "What's [your] poetry like now?" As for himself, he told Allen, "What I'm trying to do now is not too many words. There's no line that you can stick your finger through, there's no hole in any of the stanzas. There's no blank filler. Each line has something."
>
> (1989, 392)[1]

At the time Ginsberg was unaware of the playful homage paid him by Danko's doodling. Indeed, Dylan and The Band may well have forgotten about it themselves. The fragment of tape on which the song appears was not circulated, even on bootleg, until 1992. In the summer of 1993, at his office in New York City, I finally played it to Allen Ginsberg, who asked for a copy.

The relationship between Allen Ginsberg and Bob Dylan was often portrayed, not least by Ginsberg and Dylan themselves, as a father-and-son relationship. Most notably, in *Renaldo and Clara* Ginsberg appears as a fictional character called The Father, and several scenes show him offering religious instruction to Dylan as his son, Renaldo. Of course, these scenes are ironic in many ways:

two Jewish poets playing out motifs from Christian theology; the whole joke (a friendly and entirely non-homophobic joke) of the notoriously gay Ginsberg being portrayed as a progenitor. But beneath the irony there is an entirely serious tribute to the depth and commitment of the friendship between the two.

Chronologically they are in fact somewhat closer than "father and son" would suggest. Ginsberg, born in 1926, was only fifteen years older than Dylan, born in 1941. Moreover, Ginsberg was a slow starter in publishing his work; his first book, *Howl and Other Poems,* appeared in 1956, a mere five years before Dylan's first record. As far as the dates are concerned, it might be more sensible to see Ginsberg not as a father but as an elder brother. And as the two got older, the distance between them must have shrunk even further.

Even so, Ginsberg was clearly a predecessor. It is hard to overestimate the importance and impact of *Howl* as the book which really jolted America out of the somnolence of the 1950s and declared the possibility of a vital, colloquial, contemporary poetry. Ginsberg, always the selfless promoter of other people's works, insisted that the really important influence on Dylan was Jack Kerouac's *Mexico City Blues* (1959). Maybe so, but *Howl* came first, and it's hard to conceive how the cultural climate which surrounded Dylan in the early 1960s could ever have been possible without the impetus of Allen Ginsberg.

Dylan's first reading of Ginsberg dates, in all probability, from his brief university career in Minneapolis in 1959–60; Ginsberg had certainly listened to the early Dylan recordings. They met for the first time in New York in late 1963. In one interview (otherwise unsubstantiated),[2] Ginsberg claimed that they actually met on the same evening as Dylan's disastrous appearance at the Tom Paine award dinner of the Emergency Civil Liberties Committee, when he made his stumbling confession of identity with Lee Harvey Oswald. If so, it was a traumatic evening, and the circumstances might well have sealed the friendship as a special emotional bond.

Whatever the date, it is clear that there was an immediate rapport between the two, and that they remained close friends for the following thirty-four years. Of course, Ginsberg was sexually attracted to Dylan, and made no secret of the fact; equally clearly, the attraction was never reciprocated. But what is most important, and most admirable, is that neither one of them let these facts interfere with their friendship. Ginsberg could accept Dylan's lack of interest without rancor; even more remarkably, Dylan could live with Ginsberg's attraction without feeling threatened or defensive.

Throughout the mid-1960s, there were a series of contacts between Ginsberg and Dylan, too many to detail more than the highlights. For example, on one of his early visits to England, probably in 1964,[3] Dylan came into possession of a typescript copy—the only copy in fact—of a collection of early Ginsberg poems entitled "The Gates of Wrath." Ginsberg had mislaid his own copy some ten years earlier. Someone in Britain obviously saw enough of a connection between the two to entrust Dylan with the task of returning it to Ginsberg. The title of the manuscript is a quote from William Blake, and may in its turn have served as a source for Dylan's "Gates of Eden"—which, in a further turn, is cited in Ginsberg's jubilant poem "Who Be Kind To" (June 1965):

> the boom bom that bounces in the joyful
> > bowels as the Liverpool Minstrels of
> > Cavernsink
> raise up their joyful voices and guitars
> > in electric Afric hurrah
> > for Jerusalem—
> The saints come marching in, Twist &
> > Shout, and Gates of Eden are named
> > in Albion again

(1984, 360)

At some uncertain date in 1964, Ginsberg attended a Dylan concert. Afterward, backstage, several of the Daniel Kramer photographs that later appeared on the cover of Dylan's album *Bringing It All Back Home* were taken[4]—including the unusual photograph of a clean-shaven Allen Ginsberg, wearing a top hat then worn, in another photo, by Bob Dylan.[5]

In February 1965 Dylan appeared on the Les Crane TV talk show:

> Les Crane: Have you ever given any thought to acting; think you might enjoy acting?
> Bob Dylan: Well, I'm gonna try to make a movie this summer. Which Allen Ginsberg is writing. I'm rewriting.

LC: Allen Ginsberg the poet?

BD: Yeah. Yeah.

LC: He was on this program, you know.

BD: Yeah.

LC: Extolling the virtues of marijuana one night.

BD: Really? Allen? *[Surprised. Audience laughs.]* Sounds like a lie to me. *[Audience laughter.]*

LC: That's really—you think I'm lying?

BD: No, I didn't mean that.

LC: Allen Ginsberg was sitting in that chair where Caterina Valente is sitting right now and he said that he thought we ought to legalize pot.

BD: He said that?

LC: Right on television!

BD: Phhewwww!

LC: Can you imagine that?

BD: Nah. Allen is a little funny sometimes. *[Audience roars with laughter.]*

LC: Allen's a little funny sometimes, huh? Yes. What's this movie going to be about?

BD: Oh it's a, sort of a horror cowboy movie. *[Audience laughs.]* Takes place on the New York Thruway. I play my mother.

(Miles 1989, 380)

Bringing It All Back Home, complete with the Ginsberg photograph, was released in March 1965. Dylan's liner notes include the comment: "why allen ginsberg was not chosen t read poetry at the inauguration boggles my mind" (L, 180). (Given that the president in question was Lyndon Johnson, perhaps the mind boggles a little less.)[6]

Later that summer, they met by chance in England (Ginsberg having just been expelled from Czechoslovakia), and Ginsberg famously appears in the background of the card-flipping rendition of "Subterranean Homesick Blues" in D. A. Pennebaker's *Dont* [sic] *Look Back.* At the same time, Ginsberg's manifold skills in negotiating personal relationships were apparently called upon to mediate a frosty encounter between Dylan and The Beatles—which he accomplished partly by falling onto John Lennon's lap and asking him whether he'd read William Blake![7]

Late in the year, the two met again in San Francisco. On December 5, Lawrence Ferlinghetti gathered together a large number of writers at his City Lights Bookstore for what was, in effect, the last "group photograph" of the Beat Generation. The photograph includes Ginsberg, Ferlinghetti, Peter Orlovsky, Michael McLure, Richard Brautigan, and many others. Bob Dylan was present, but he preferred not to be included in the photograph. Typically, he was unwilling to intrude into a scene which he knew was not his, however much he had inherited from it. Dylan was, however, photographed separately with Ginsberg and McClure.[8]

Two days earlier, on December 3, Ginsberg had taken part in a Dylan press conference conducted and filmed at KQED, an educational TV station in the Bay area. Since the videotape of this occasion survives, it affords a remarkable document of Bob Dylan's public stance at this crucial juncture of his career—and of Allen Ginsberg's relation to Dylan at this time. Dylan's mood throughout this press conference is mercurial. Sometimes he answers questions with a monosyllabic shrug, seeming to be more interested in lighting one of his multiple cigarettes; some questions he answers with brilliant, playful flights of fancy; some questions he takes perfectly seriously and gives intelligent, interesting answers. Asked at the outset what kind of music he writes (folk music? popular music?), he answers "vision music . . . mathematical music"—which may not have been very enlightening for the San Francisco press corps, but which must surely have struck Ginsberg as a very precise description of their joint heritage from William Blake.

Another question asks Dylan to name his favorite poets. He replies with a list that includes Rimbaud, W. C. Fields, "the trapeze family," Smokey Robinson, Charlie Rich . . . and Allen Ginsberg. At which point the camera dutifully cuts to a shot of Ginsberg in the audience. Ginsberg was there, obviously, as a "plant," to feed Dylan predetermined questions. When Ginsberg asks, "Have you found that the texts of the interviews with you which have been published are accurate to the actual conversations?", Dylan produces a reply so impassioned and articulate that one of the other reporters calls attention to its difference from his mumbled, improvisational responses to so many other questions. The obvious implication is that Dylan knew the question was coming and had his answer prepared.

What is most interesting, however, is that no attempt is made to disguise the fact that Ginsberg is a plant in the audience. Rather, their exchanges draw public attention to the fact of their private friendship. Early on, after Dylan has been asked a rather obvious question about whether he will ever try other art forms such as painting, Ginsberg interjects: "Will there ever be a time when you'll be hung as a thief?" The audience laughs, and Dylan says, "You weren't supposed to say that."

Later, Ginsberg feeds him the straight line: "Are there any young folksingers or rock groups that you would recommend for us to hear?"

"I'm glad you asked that!" Dylan responds, in a way that makes perfectly clear that the question was preplanned.

Still later, Ginsberg interjects another unplanned question: "What is the strangest thing that ever happened to you?"

"You're gonna get it, man!" Dylan splutters.

"But what is the weirdest thing that ever happened to you?" Ginsberg persists.

"I had you here as a friend!" Dylan protests.

Again the audience laughs. A small, private smile passes over Dylan's face as he looks up at Ginsberg.

"I'll talk to you about it later," he says.

All these exchanges, planned or unplanned, serious or playful, underline Ginsberg's difference from the other questioners, and dramatize the offstage friendship between Ginsberg and Dylan. Lines like "You weren't supposed to say that" openly admit the collusion between them; lines like "I'll talk to you about it later" promise that that collusion will continue in a privacy, even an intimacy, which the press-conference audience will not be permitted to share. In a remarkable display, Ginsberg and Dylan put their friendship on stage for the whole world, briefly, to witness.

In March 1966, on a plane en route to Denver, Dylan gave an interview to his old friend Robert Shelton. Shelton's extended—but still highly edited—transcript of this interview is one of the highlights of his Dylan biography, *No Direction Home*. Thus, Dylan to Shelton, March 1966:

> I know two saintly people. I know just two holy people. Allen Ginsberg is one. The other, for lack of a better term I just want to call "this person named Sara." What I mean by "holy" is crossing all

> borders of time and usefulness. . . . If we are talking now in terms
> of writers I think can be called poets, then Allen must be the best.
> I mean Allen's "Kaddish," not "Howl." Allen doesn't have to sing
> "Kaddish," man. You understand what I mean? He just has to lay it
> down. He's the only poet that I know of. He's the only person I
> respect who writes, that just totally writes. He don't have to do
> nothing, man. Allen Ginsberg, he's just holy.
>
> (353)

Around the same time, in San Francisco at the end of 1965, Dylan gave
Ginsberg a gift of money ($600), which Ginsberg used to purchase a portable
tape recorder. Ginsberg used the machine to tape a Dylan concert (thus becoming one of the pioneer bootleggers), but primarily to record his own stream-of-
consciousness observations as he and Peter Orlovsky traveled across America in
their Volkswagen van. These tapes became the basis of "The Fall of America,"
Ginsberg's definitive poetic chronicling of the Vietnam years.[9]

"The Fall of America" is a loose, open-form, open-ended epic. As such, it
takes its place in a modern tradition of long poems—stretching from Whitman,
through Pound and Williams, to Zukofsky and Olson—which are no longer
reliant on narrative. Rather, they rely simply on their *length*, on their capacity to
encompass ever more diverse materials within their accretionary growth. Pound
said of the all-inclusive nature of his *Cantos* that "the modern world / needs
such a rag-bag to stuff all its thoughts in," and he explained in a 1962 interview:
"The problem was to get a form—something elastic enough to take the necessary material. It had to be a form that wouldn't exclude something merely
because it didn't fit."[10]

Ginsberg's personal variation relies on the central metaphor or structuring
device of *travel*. The poet is almost constantly in motion, traveling (by road, rail,
and plane) back and forth across the United States. This image of restlessness,
of constant change, of a lack of any stable base, is picked up from Kerouac's *On
the Road* to act as a metaphor for the sense of displacement felt, not only by
Ginsberg, but by the whole nation during these unsettled years. It also serves as
a non-narrative, open-ended structure for the sequence.

Many of the poems in Ginsberg's sequence are specifically set "on the road,"
and they record the passing perceptions of what the poet sees as he looks out

the windows of his Volkswagen camper van, driving through America. Even the length of the line, echoing Whitman and responding to the space and extent of the country, promises a *long* poem. Each extended line is, after the manner of Charles Olson, a single moment of perception, caught and recorded as the Volkswagen rolls past. Ginsberg called this method of composition "auto poesy" (the *auto* punning on "automatic writing," since the lines were jotted down spontaneously and left largely unrevised); it is the dominant, though not exclusive, format for the poems included in *The Fall of America*.

The sequence evokes Dylan at several key points, including its opening: the very first page hails "Bob Dylan's voice on airways, mass machine-made folk song of one soul" (1984, 369). He appears again in "Wichita Vortex Sutra," the astonishing rhetorical climax of Ginsberg's work, in which the poet fully assumes the mantle of the prophet and takes it upon himself, on the authority of his own inspired consciousness, to declare the end of the war.

> I lift my voice aloud,
>> make Mantra of American language now,
>>> I here declare the end of the War!
>>>> Ancient days' illusion!—
> and pronounce words beginning my own millennium.
> Let the States tremble,
>> let the Nation weep,
>>> let Congress legislate its own delight
>>> let the President execute his own desire—
> this Act done by my own voice,
>>> nameless Mystery—
> published to my own senses,
>> blissfully received by my own form
> approved with pleasure by my sensations
>> manifestation of my very thought
>> accomplished in my own imagination
>>> all realms within my consciousness fulfilled
>> 60 miles from Wichita . . .

(1984, 407)

All right, so the Vietnam War did not end in February 1966, "60 miles from Wichita"—but Ginsberg's proclamation of its end was, nevertheless, the supreme act of the political imagination in America during the 1960s. It set the nation free, in spirit, years before that liberation could be realized in the realm of cold historical fact. It assumes and defines the stance of the poet as prophet, the stance which, I have argued, Bob Dylan also took as his own. In 1966, Ginsberg claims to imagine America as "this nation one body of Prophecy" (1984, 406); a year later, Dylan lifts this body into his embrace: "We carried you in our arms / On Independence Day" (L, 312).

And at this point of "Wichita Vortex Sutra," at this ecstatic height of Ginsberg's prophetic reach, Bob Dylan enters the poem:

> The war was over several hours ago!
> Oh at last again the radio opens
> blue Invitations!
> Angelic Dylan singing across the nation
> "When all your children start to resent you
> Won't you come see me, Queen Jane?"
> His youthful voice making glad
> the brown endless meadows
> His tenderness penetrating aether,
> soft prayer on the airwaves
>
> (409)

Ginsberg later commented on these lines to Paul Carroll:

> I think Dylan's "Queen Jane" is a great lyric poem, done as it is in blues style, an invitation to return to relationship. . . . Angelic because he looks like an angel & has spiritual or transcendental instinct & manifests them in music and poetry. . . . Dylan is as literally angelic type as anything in history or literature.
>
> (Carroll, 107)

Contacts between Ginsberg and Dylan continued throughout the early 1970s, with Ginsberg addressing to Dylan—at a decidedly low point in the latter's career—a number of sympathetic and understanding poems, especially "Blue Gossip" (1972). But their most important and productive collaboration came in November 1971, as Ginsberg made his most serious attempt to translate the achievements of his poetry into the medium of popular song. In this attempt he was deeply indebted to Bob Dylan, and indeed, in this respect the two men exchanged roles. Ginsberg, who as the elder poet had been Dylan's inspiration, became for a while, as a musician, Dylan's pupil. But although Dylan was, in one sense, Ginsberg's "guru" in the field of popular music, he continued to play a carefully subsidiary role in the actual recordings.

The man who was instrumental in bringing them together was David Amram. Amram, who is a fine and incredibly eclectic musician, as adept in jazz or folk idioms as he is in classical traditions, had written the score for *Pull My Daisy*, the 1959 film by Robert Frank and Alfred Leslie which featured Ginsberg, Gregory Corso, and a brilliant, improvised narration by Jack Kerouac. In October 1971 Dylan attended one of Ginsberg's readings in New York, and later, at Amram's apartment, they decided to try recording together. Over the next few weeks, there were three recording sessions: two at the Record Plant studio and one for the PBS television program "Free Time." A wide variety of musicians, poets, and "friends" played at these sessions. *Holy Soul Jelly Roll* (the definitive collection of Ginsberg recordings) gives the following lineup for the recording of "Vomit Express" at the Record Plant:

> Allen Ginsberg: vocal, finger cymbals
> Bob Dylan: guitar, vocal
> Peter Orlovsky: vocal
> Anne Waldman: vocal
> David Amram: French horn, recorder, piano
> Perry Robinson: clarinet
> Jon Sholle: guitar
> Happy Traum: banjo[11]
> Surya: zither
> Moruga: drums

Anne Waldman recalls these sessions:

> Allen the verbal wiz always asking questions. Dylan mysterious,
> cryptic, harder to read. Who was the older brother? Allen wanting
> eagerly to learn from Dylan tricks of the music trade and in partic-
> ular whispered secrets of recording studio praxis, concerned about
> spontaneity, & wanting us to *hear all the words.* How do you do it,
> Bob? Attention to the finest particulars of speech! Of course Allen
> was master in his own vocalization of text and shapely, too, on the
> page, but how do it with the music? . . . Dylan was master of this
> vocal gift, intelligence with terrific enunciation, his passionate bite
> on the words. Hissing the consonants, stretching the vowels. No
> naive sloppiness here. . . . So there was humor in Dylan's playing the
> master, kind of laid back, accommodating, giving Allen uncondi-
> tional loving space (he loves Allen), Allen being eager to please
> Dylan and fluttery. And the poems/text were never compromised.[12]

The songs vary from Buddhist chants to Blake poems. The most upbeat
rocker is Ginsberg's cheerful "Vomit Express." But perhaps the most significant
piece is "September on Jessore Road," based on Ginsberg's personal observation, a month before, of the "millions of Hindu refugees from East Pakistan
communal strife [who] crowded starving in floods on this main road between
Bangladesh and Calcutta" (Ginsberg 1984, 788). The poem was written explicitly to be sung and recorded at these sessions, and it was intended to impress,
especially, Bob Dylan. The recording was, however, a complete mess, with
musicians playing in different rhythms and keys, and with nobody, least of all
Ginsberg, able to pull it together.

But almost two decades later, Hal Willner, the producer of Ginsberg's boxed
CD set *Holy Soul Jelly Roll,* remixed the original tapes, combined them with
later recordings, and came up with a definitive, and stunning, version of
"September on Jessore Road." In large stretches of this new version, which lasts
over ten minutes, Willner has eliminated everything except Ginsberg's
(redubbed) voice and Dylan's keyboards (piano or organ). These keyboard
phrases, originally intended as fills to a much fuller instrumentation, now stand
on their own as counterpoint to Ginsberg's vocal.

In the *Holy Soul Jelly Roll* booklet, Ginsberg describes them as "dropping piano bombs, percussive punctuations underlining different phrases. That was the high point of the recording—Dylan coming down with all ten genius fingers intermittently at the right places" (1994, 35). It may well be Dylan's finest keyboard performance on record.

Ginsberg continued to produce and record songs, many of which are very interesting—especially the superb and deeply moving "Father Death Blues." He did record with Dylan one more time, in 1982, at the Rundown Studios near Dylan's house in Santa Monica, California. They recorded a lively version of "Do the Meditation Rock" and two takes of "Airplane Blues." Dylan, with typical reticence, played bass.

Ginsberg greeted the 1975 release of *Blood on the Tracks* with elation, writing in his journal a long, rapturous, and extremely perceptive analysis of "Idiot Wind." Later that year, he joined Dylan as part of the Rolling Thunder Revue.

The Revue was, right from the start, highly self-conscious of its relation to American culture and history—as witness the decision to tour in the northeastern states, starting at Plymouth, in the last months of 1975, on the eve of the American Bicentennial. In one of the scenes planned for *Renaldo and Clara* (but not used in the final edit), Dylan was to play a Pilgrim Father coming ashore at Plymouth Rock—where he would be greeted by a character played by Allen Ginsberg, always already America. And one of the most moving occasions on the tour was the visit paid by Dylan and Ginsberg to the grave of Jack Kerouac.

Talking to Larry Sloman, Mel Howard recalled the reasons for inviting Ginsberg:

> The thing about Allen is he's a wonderful historian, he tends to see things, everything has a historical significance. So Allen saw Dylan rightly connected to the whole tradition of the Beat generation and through that to the earlier poets, Poe, the whole sense of the American vagabond. So Allen was keen to add that element to it, and of course, Dylan is mindful of that, that's why he invited Allen, so that there'd be input from people in the whole area of poetry and Kerouac and what the country was about.
>
> (299)

Ginsberg's role on the 1975 tour, then, was as a direct link to the American poetic tradition: to "Kerouac and what the country was about." Left unresolved was the question of what Ginsberg might actually do on stage. In his journal Ginsberg records a conversation he had with Dylan in New York, before the tour began.[13]

"Bob," he asks, "what do you want of me—what's your fantasy, yr. idea—"

"Well it's up to you to decide, you're the king, whatever you want to do, get it together—I'm presenting you, it's about time, this country has been asleep, it's time it woke up," Dylan replies.

On the basis of this conversation, Ginsberg at first believed that he would take part in all the concerts, either singing or chanting mantras. As the tour developed, however, his onstage participation was severely limited.[14] Usually he appeared only as part of the final chorus, joining in the singing of Woody Guthrie's "This Land Is Your Land." (Ironically, this limitation may have worked to Ginsberg's advantage, as it directed his attention to ideas for *Renaldo and Clara.*) He did appear at Trenton State Prison during the special performance put on for Rubin Carter and his fellow inmates. Sloman describes the occasion:

> Then a surprise, as Dylan yields the stage to "Mr. Allen Ginsberg,
> an American poet from Paterson, New Jersey."[15] And Ginsberg is
> great here, sing-screaming his poems of rebellion, getting a huge
> rise out of the convict section with a line about butt-fucking.
>
> (356)

And he appeared also at Falmouth, Massachusetts, reading "Kaddish" to a surprised audience of middle-aged female mah-jongg players![16]

But for Ginsberg, perhaps the most important feature of Rolling Thunder was the opportunity it gave him to study Dylan in performance, closely, night after night. He wrote a great deal of commentary, some of which was published in the tour's newsletter, in the liner notes for *Desire,* and in the poems "Rolling Thunder Stones" (1984, 642–44), but a great deal of which, recorded in his private journals, has never been published.

Much of this commentary focused on the precision of Dylan's articulation and breath, an area which for Ginsberg, with his background in Buddhist meditation, combined aesthetic, moral, and social values. "His diction is real clear," Ginsberg told Larry Sloman. "I'm impressed by the way he lifts his lip in what seems to be a sneer but is really an attempt to pronounce the consonants clearly. He's showing an elastic, rhythmic precision, singing much more like he speaks" (65). And in Ginsberg's liner notes to *Desire:*

> Dylan's Redemption Songs! If he can do it we can do it. America can do it. . . . Drunken aggressive beer bottles'll never redeem anybody— But clear conscious song can, every syllable pronounced, every con- sonant sneered out with lips risen over teeth to pronounce them exactly to a T in microphone. snarled out NOT for bummer ego put-down but instead for egoless enunciation of exact phrasings so everyone can hear intelligence—which is only your own heart Dear.
> . . . .
> Song become conscious poetry, the best you can say in total rhythm, allowing for your speech to fall like your mother's radiotalk, allow- ing for the singer to open his whole body for Inspiration to breathe out a long mad vowel to nail down the word into everyone's heart.
> . . . .
> How far has he gone? All the way from scared solitude inner prophetics—building on that mind-honesty strangeness—to open- hearted personal historical confession. . . . Who woulda thought he'd say it, so everybody'd finally know him, same soul crying vul- nerable caught in a body we all are?—enough Person revealed to make Whitman's whole nation weep.

One of the journals was written in a small pocket notebook which Ginsberg scribbled in during the actual concerts. Doubtless it was the page size which enforced a very short line, but many of the passages emerge as precisely anno- tated poetry. Ginsberg observes Dylan:

> Leaning into the
> microphone in
> time for first syllable
> breath, then at end

of phrase stepping back
uplifting guitar one
knee bent—turn
face in spotlite
red spray feather
in hat, long scarf
hanging to waist, rested,
mouth to microphone
"Any day now"

Or this precise observation of a concert in Rochester, November 17:

O Sister, stomping
left to right &
leaning tilting body
left & right with
each stomp—
    deserving of
      "Affect—shoon"
      "Direc—shooon"
Grave
    Saved!
and a long Space—
darting piercing
glances—head
shifted suddenly
left, right—
red fern
darting up from
hat—
Hurricane—
lips lifted over
teeth—*ever*
*l*ying, *says*
and between words

cops, and next line
begun—Iodine
lips, hoarse solid
head-dead
rhymes exact on bongo
shock percussion—
"He ain't the *guuy*"
and one
    Time
lips lifted up for
long black tie hanging
wrapped double below
throat—

Perhaps the most ecstatic passage in the journals was prompted by a performance in Quebec City:

29 Nov 75
 —"I shall be
released"—Death
Cry—
    The suffering
of Dylan singing
giving his whole body
to Isis—
    Any Day Now—
Despair uttered,
prayers signified over
heads of audience.
Pedal walking
feet, one toe
lifting as another
goes to ground, like
pantomiming motion-
less footsteps—

Sing Dylan

        Sing

outsing the
centuries
in a single
hour—
sing in present
time & fill
this space
with tears,
with vowels
with mother
moons & howls
from the back
of the heart's
abdomen
Sing the Dominion
of suffering
Sing thyself
into Death
past Heavens
& Hells—

Or finally, a single phrase, all by itself on a page, which may stand as an emblematic summary of everything Ginsberg was trying to record in these journals:

Dylan overtaken
by his songs.

Both Allen Ginsberg and Bob Dylan had to cope, from very early in their careers, with the demands of fame, with being seen as the poetic spokesmen of their generations. In his biography of Ginsberg, *Dharma Lion*, Michael Schumacher suggests that the two of them were fascinated by each other's very different responses to these demands.

Ginsberg was almost compulsively open, laying himself bare—sometimes quite literally—making himself vulnerable to all sorts of attacks, allowing himself to appear foolish or naive, but always, with heroic honesty, bearing witness to his beliefs and convictions. Dylan has tended to protect himself more, taking refuge in secrecy, isolation, and disguise: preserving within himself a private place which none of his fans has been allowed to enter. Like Schumacher, I believe that their friendship was, to a large measure, based on their respect for each other's positions. I'm sure that Ginsberg often wished he were Dylan; I'm not so sure that the converse is true.

What they ultimately did share was a conception of the poet as prophet. Both of them saw the poet's role as far more than the expression of purely personal feelings, but rather as a public statement of a morally responsible position. Ginsberg's three greatest poems are all elegies; an elegy is, by definition, the public statement of a private grief. "Howl" was an elegy for his friends, the pioneers of the Beat Generation; "Kaddish" (which the very private Dylan saw as Ginsberg's greatest poem) was an elegy for his mother, and for his own childhood; "The Fall of America" was an elegy for his nation. Put them all together, and what you have is what Bob Dylan has been singing about throughout his career, from "Hard Rain" to "Highlands": a world gone wrong. Within such a world, the only voice that is possible is the voice of the prophet: Jeremiah or Blind Willie McTell, Allen Ginsberg or Bob Dylan.

On April 5, 1997, Bob Dylan gave a concert in Moncton, New Brunswick. It included a beautiful, slow, heartfelt rendition of "Desolation Row." At the end of the song, Dylan addressed the audience:

"A friend of mine passed away, I guess this morning, that was one of his favorite songs: the poet Allen Ginsberg. Allen, that was for you."

Intertext: Greil Marcus (The Basement Tapes Revisited)

Greil Marcus has always been one of the most controversial figures in Dylan criticism.[17] He is responsible for some of the most brilliant critical writing on Dylan and on rock music generally, in books like *Mystery Train*, in his liner notes to the official release of *The Basement Tapes*,[18] and in his extraordinary essay on "Blind Willie McTell" (included in his collection *The Dustbin of History*).

But his enthusiasm for Dylan has wavered—he was one of the authors (with the magazine's editors) of the infamous *Rolling Stone* dismissal of *Self Portrait,* "What is this shit?"—and he is frequently attacked, on internet newsgroups, for intellectual obscurantism and self indulgence. The focus for many of these attacks is his 1997 book *Invisible Republic: Bob Dylan's Basement Tapes.*

My copy of *Invisible Republic* arrived shortly after the book's release, only a couple of days before I was due to leave for Europe. So I took it along with me, and read it in disjointed snatches: on planes, in Parisian cafés, and in the splendid surroundings of Castle Plankenstein, site of the annual Austrian Bob Dylan convention. I had thought that this would be a rather masochistic exercise, reading about the Basement Tapes when I had no access to the recordings, and indeed there were times when it was furiously frustrating to read one of Marcus's ecstatic, over-the-top evocations of a song without being able to have it playing in the background as I read. But in the end it wasn't too bad, since all these songs are so deep inside my head that I could hear them anyway, even in the middle of Saint Germain des Prés.

Another reason not to suffer too much from being without the original recordings was that, as I read, I discovered that surprisingly little of the book seemed to be about Bob Dylan. Digressions abounded—or at least, what appeared at first sight to be digressions: a detailed history of the West Virginia Mine War; biographies of old-time musicians like Clarence Ashley and Dock Boggs; long excerpts from Puritan sermons; and Marcus's increasingly elaborate and fanciful creations of two mythical towns he called Smithville and Kill Devil Hills. I began to conclude that the real subject of the book was not Bob Dylan but Greil Marcus.

Not that I particularly minded this personal focus—indeed, I rather like overtly subjective criticism, the kind of book in which the ostensible subject gets cheerfully lost inside the maze of interlocking connections which make up the critic's sensibility. Other readers, I found out later, minded a whole lot more.

About three weeks later, when I finally got home not only to my tapes but to my computer, and logged on to rec.music.dylan, I was surprised and somewhat shocked by the vitriolic nature of the abuse that was being heaped upon Marcus. The book was described, in some of the kinder postings, as pretentious, self-indulgent garbage. Marcus was criticized quite disproportionately for some minor factual errors. A lot of the postings were deeply anti-intellectual in tone: "I don't understand words like 'anagogic,' therefore this book is trash." I was sympathetic to some of the accusations of overwriting (Marcus can at times be too clever for his own good) and to the charge of false advertising (that the book had far less to do with Bob Dylan than its presentation might lead you to expect). Even so, the attacks seemed far in excess of anything I remembered the book as warranting.

So I sat down to read it again. And, of course, to listen to the Basement Tapes again.

What is the abiding fascination of the Basement Tapes? For people of the 1960s generation, a lot of it inheres in the simple fact that these were the first "bootlegs" we ever heard. Nowadays, when there are so many bootlegs so readily available that the only surprise is the existence of any Dylan performance not out on CDR a week after it happens, it may be hard to appreciate the thrill of those first scratchy, hard-to-come-by recordings. (I still keep on my shelf a copy of *The Great White Wonder*, even though there is nothing on it that I do not now possess in far higher sound quality: nostalgia is laid into the grooves of the vinyl.) There was that initial allure of the forbidden: that these were songs we weren't supposed to hear; that we were penetrating secrets; that we were eating Eve's apple, the fruit of an esoteric Tree of Knowledge.

Some of that allure survives, even for later generations. There is still something very private about the Basement Tapes, and listening to them sometimes seems, uneasily, like an invasion of that privacy. "We were playing with absolute freedom," says Robbie Robertson (Marcus 1997, xiv), "we weren't doing anything we thought anybody else would ever hear, as long as we lived." And that is what makes the Basement Tapes unique, still, even among the whole mass of Bob Dylan bootlegs. Unlike any concert recording or studio outtake, these are recordings made *without any audience in mind*.

Theoretically, of course, *any* performance presupposes some form of audience—even the singer in the bathroom shower fantasizes applause. And the Basement Tapes acetate did become a demo recording for other artists. Even so, these songs were performed in a situation as free from any expectation of an audience as it is possible to conceive. The assumed stance of the Basement Tapes, the position that Dylan and The Band implicitly claim to be occupying, is one without an audience. They are playing *for themselves*. And we get to hear them. It's a voyeur's dream.

So one of the truest pleasures of the Basement Tapes is your sense of the enjoyment the musicians are taking in their own work. They are playing these songs because they want to, because they like them—not because they're trying to please or impress an audience. At times they are frankly fooling around, as in the open parodies of "I Am a Teenage Prayer" or "See You Later, Allen Ginsberg." At times the music is relaxed, at times it's frenzied, at times it's deeply serious. But every mood is underlined by the carefree sense that this is not music they *have to* play for anybody. As a result, there is a tremendous unity to the Basement Tapes, an absence of any imposed aesthetic or commercial hierarchy. "I'm in the Mood" is just as important to them as "I'm Not There." From this perspective, "Teenage Prayer" means as much as "Tears of Rage."

There are, of course, other perspectives, in which "I'm Not There" and "Tears of Rage" will emerge as supreme masterpieces. But these are the perspectives of time and retrospect. In the basement, everything is equal. Which means also that Bob Dylan is just another songwriter, part of a broad and eclectic tradition, and Bob Dylan the singer would lay no greater stress on his own work than on John Lee Hooker's or Ian and Sylvia's.[19] So from this point of view it makes no sense to say that some of the Basement Tapes songs are trivial, not to be taken seriously. And it makes no sense to criticize Marcus for "reading too much into" songs like "Lo and Behold." It is impossible to read too much into the songs of the Basement Tapes, because the songs are all one song, part of the one great song that is the total tradition of American music.

At one point in *Invisible Republic* (102), Marcus refers almost in passing to Walter Benjamin's *Passagen-Werk,* known in English as *The Arcades Project.*[20] One of the most important documents in twentieth-century social thought, *The Arcades Project* was a vast and ultimately unfinished enterprise in which Benjamin used the shopping arcades of nineteenth-century Paris as a key image around which to arrange a comprehensive study of capitalist economics and bourgeois culture.

For years and years, Benjamin assembled notes and observations on anything even remotely connected to the topic: it became his obsession, and even if he had not died, it seems unlikely that he would ever have been able to bring it to a conventionally finished state. It was a typical modernist structure, like Ezra Pound's *Cantos:* a "capacious rag-bag" into which the most miscellaneous material could be stuffed, incapable of ever arriving at anything like traditional completion, held together only by the personality of the assembler. Much of the manuscript consisted of quotations transcribed from other sources. Benjamin was the "author" of less than half the text.

Marcus alludes to Benjamin in the course of his discussion of Harry Smith, and it's clear that he sees Smith's *Anthology of American Folk Music*[21] as analogous to *The Arcades Project*. The *Anthology* is likewise a miscellaneous collection, drawn together from a wide variety of sources yet united by a single image—the tradition of American music—and by the personality of its assembler. Harry Smith did not write or perform a single line from any of the songs in his anthology, though he did compose for it a set of notes as idiosyncratic as those that Bob Dylan provided for *World Gone Wrong*. Yet Marcus is surely justified in treating Smith as the *Anthology*'s "author." The conceit of viewing it as an imaginary town called Smithville may be a little too cute, but the sense that these songs make up a coherent world, and that Harry Smith is in some way responsible for that creation, seems undeniable. As was the case with Benjamin, the truest index to Harry Smith's consciousness and sensibility is to be found not in what he wrote but in the traces of what he assembled.

Almost unspoken here is the further analogy to the Basement Tapes themselves. Like the *Anthology*, like *The Arcades Project*, the montage of songs on these tapes is an apparently miscellaneous collection of utterly diverse material: folk songs, country classics, blues, contemporary pop schlock, original Dylan compositions, parodies, riffs, fragments, tentative improvisations, accomplished masterpieces. Harry Smith could well be a character in "Tiny Montgomery" or "Million Dollar Bash"; Walter Benjamin could be the grave speaker of "Tears of Rage" or "Nothing Was Delivered."

Like Benjamin, Dylan is the author of less than half the material he gathers together here, and yet we can legitimately read, in the traces of the choices he makes, a map of his own sensibility. "He would pull these songs out of nowhere," Robertson recalls. "We didn't know if he wrote them or if he remembered them. When he sang them, you couldn't tell" (xvi). Everything on the Basement Tapes is "by" Bob Dylan. And like *The Arcades Project*, it is essentially, inevitably, uncompleted. The Basement Tapes never attain a perfect form. They just stop for a while, and then they go on—in albums from *Down in the Groove* to *World Gone Wrong*. Dylan's most serious attempt to re-create the Walter Benjamin/Harry

Smith self portrait through miscellaneous aggregation is, of course, the album which he would entitle, ironically yet also sincerely, *Self Portrait*.

Equally unspoken is Marcus's most ambitious (or, if you like, pretentious) analogy of all: for this form—the form of *The Arcades Project*, of the *Anthology of American Folk Music*, of the Basement Tapes—is also the form that Marcus himself approximates in *Invisible Republic*. Again, it's a miscellaneous collection, bringing in bits and pieces from all over the place: Dock Boggs, John Winthrop, Sharyn McCrumb, Herman Melville, Johnny Cash, Walter Benjamin.

Just as somewhat less than half the songs on the Basement Tapes are Dylan originals, so somewhat less than half of Marcus's book is directly about Bob Dylan. A passage on the West Virginia Mine War strays no further from the center of Marcus's book than a performance of "Rock Salt and Nails" strays from the center of the Basement Tapes. And again, *Invisible Republic* is essentially a self portrait, as much about Greil Marcus as it is about Bob Dylan—but if one reads "Greil Marcus" in the traces of Bob Dylan, that's only because one has previously read "Bob Dylan" in the traces of Blind Willie McTell.

> Gonna build me
> Log cabin
> On a mountain
> So high
> So I can
> See Willie
> When he goes
> On by

Thus Greil Marcus writes out the first verse of Clarence Ashley's 1929 recording of "The Coo Coo Bird," attempting to reproduce in his line division the hesitant rhythms of Ashley's singing. Marcus goes on to comment:

> It sounds like a children's ditty only until you begin to realize the verse is made to refuse any of the questions it makes you ask. Who is Willie? Why does the singer want to watch him? Why must he put aside his life and embark on a grand endeavor . . . just to

accomplish this ordinary act? The verse can communicate only as a secret everybody already knows or as an allusion to a body of knowledge the singer knows can never be recovered, and Ashley only makes things worse by singing as if whatever he's singing about is the most obvious thing in the world.

(117–18)[22]

The quality which Marcus identifies in this song, that it is "made to refuse any of the questions it makes you ask," is the quality which Dylan has defined simply as "mystery." Marcus quotes repeatedly from statements Dylan made in 1965 and 1966. Folk songs, Dylan said, "are nothing but mystery," and he wonders why "the traditional-music people" (those who most attacked his new style) could not "gather from their songs that mystery is a fact, a traditional fact" (113).

The mystery about Willie arises from the "traditional fact" that "The Coo Coo Bird," like so many other folk songs, draws on an eclectic repertory of formulaic verses, and that the connections between verses are long forgotten, omitted, and thus obscured. Any given verbal formula acts, then, as "a secret everybody already knows," as "an allusion to a body of knowledge the singer knows *[pause]* can never be recovered." In such songs the gaps or dislocations are introduced *between* verses; each verse makes sense in itself, but cannot readily be connected to the verses before or after it. It's a technique which Bob Dylan was fully familiar with: consider the gap between the first two verses and the third verse of "All Along the Watchtower." But in some of the songs of the Basement Tapes, the gaps and dislocations are even more radical. They seem to enter at the level of the individual words, or of the syntax joining them.

One of Marcus's early chapters contains a bravura reading of the song "Lo and Behold." I agree with almost all of his interpretation, especially his singling out of the incident in which the train conductor asks the singer's name and "I gave it to him right away / Then I hung my head in shame" (L, 308)—though I am surprised that Marcus doesn't push this point even further, to focus on the whole importance of the assumed and/or proper name in the work of Robert Zimmerman/Bob Dylan. But Marcus's analysis stops short of the weird verbal peculiarities of this song's chorus:

> Lo and behold! Lo and behold!
> Lookin' for my lo and behold,
> Get me outa here, my dear man!

These lines certainly rival "The Coo Coo Bird" for sheer mystery. Who is the "dear man" addressed? Why should he have the ability, or the desire, to extricate the singer from his situation? Why is he "dear"—is this simply a parodic use of English upper-class diction (and if so why, in a song with an exclusively American setting?) or is there a serious hint of homosexual attraction? Why does Dylan, on every singing of the title phrase, place the stress on the wrong syllable, singing BEhold instead of the normal beHOLD? How many puns are implied here (lo/low; b/be/bee; *hold* as a noun, *hold* as a verb; behold/beholden)? And why is the phrase "lo and behold" treated as a noun, as a thing that can be possessed, as "my" lo and behold?

These questions (none of which I have answers for) progress from the thematic to the grammatical, from simple puzzles of the story line to fundamental dislocations of the very conditions of utterance. A "verse . . . made to refuse any of the questions it makes you ask" indeed! But the Basement Tapes go even further.[23] In "I'm Not There (1956)"[24] mystery and indeterminacy do not merely dislocate the utterance, they undermine it utterly.

Part of the indeterminacy of "I'm Not There" derives from the circumstances of its recording. Dylan was (presumably) working from a half-completed text and improvising words, or "dummy lyrics," as he went along. And alas, he never went back to it: the song exists *only* in this single, half-incomprehensible performance. (Marcus quotes a description of "I'm Not There" as "the greatest song ever written" [199]; it would be more accurate to call it the greatest song *never* written.)

The slurs and mumbles as the vocal slides over unwritten patches provide an irresistible challenge to transcribers: a single line can produce readings as diverse as "She's my Christ-forsaken angel," "She's my prize-forsaken angel," and "She's my price for Lake and Angel"! Marcus confidently quotes "She knows that the kingdom weighs so high above her" when almost every other transcription gives "waits." There is no way to resolve these differences. There is no definitive text against which variants could be measured. The method of composition creates mystery as the condition of the utterance.[25]

Similarly, even when individual words are more or less clear, the syntax keeps breaking down into incoherent fragments: "She's the way, for sale and beautiful, she's mine for the one"; "It don't have approximation, she's my own fare-thee-well"; "I've been told, like I said, when I before, carry on the grind." In another acute comment Marcus says of this syntax that "a sentence is an opportunity to find a word" (199): one key word that will carry the emotional weight, even if the syntax surrounding it is totally indeterminate.

For mystery does not mean complete incomprehension. For all the difficulty of figuring out what individual words or lines mean, the listener never has any doubt about the emotional resonance of "I'm Not There." As a song of loss, separation, guilt, and abandonment, its impact is clear and overwhelming. (In the same way, you can attribute a meaning to "The Coo Coo Bird" without ever having to explain who Willie actually is.) Marshall McLuhan's slogan "the medium is the message" might here be translated as "the mystery is the meaning." Obviously a great deal of this emotional meaning is conveyed by the music, and especially by the intonations of Dylan's voice. ("I'm Not There," mumbles and all, is one of his greatest ever vocal performances.) Like Clarence Ashley, Dylan performs even the most fragmented lyrics "as if whatever he's singing about is the most obvious thing in the world"—as if mystery is simply a fact, a traditional fact.

This rooting of the songs in mystery is clear enough in those Basement Tapes compositions which are self-evidently "serious" (grave, portentous, tragic, elegiac): songs like "Tears of Rage," "This Wheel's On Fire," or "Nothing Was Delivered." But what is truly remarkable about the Basement Tapes is that the same sense of mystery is equally present in songs which announce themselves as comic, trivial, or downright foolery: "Tiny Montgomery," "Million Dollar Bash," or "Please, Mrs. Henry." Here one finds the same gaps and dislocations in the utterance. How is one to recuperate any sense of conventional meaning from lines like "Don't ya tell Henry / Apple's got your fly" or "the comic book and me, just us, we caught the bus" or "Pick up your nose, you canary"? These lines go much further than the simple surrealism of "The motorcycle black Madonna / Two-wheeled gypsy queen." They are fundamentally indecipherable within the normal rules of linguistic communication. Like the experimental writing of Gertrude Stein, they demand new rules.

It would be too much to claim that "mystery" can also be found in all the Basement Tapes tracks which are not Dylan compositions, or to see it in everything from "Wildwood Flower" to "Waltzing With Sin," from "I Don't Hurt Anymore" to "I'm In the Mood." But what is consistent is the seriousness with which Dylan approaches the singing. Very rarely—and then only when the song is an overt parody—does his voice betray any sense of condescension to his material. The schlockiest pop song gets the same grave considered performance as "Young But Daily Growing" or "Too Much of Nothing." Again, I think this characteristic derives from the situation of having no audience. There is no one here to impress or to pose for, so the singer's ego is not involved. He can, in the words of Leonard Cohen, "speak the words, convey the data, step aside" (1993, 287). He can respect the material and deliver the song in its integrity. It's this quality which Marcus hears (I think quite rightly) in artists like Clarence Ashley and Dock Boggs, and it's this quality which Dylan rediscovered so spectacularly on *Good As I Been To You* and *World Gone Wrong*.

In all these performances it seems as if he has built himself a log cabin, or a basement, in which he can calmly sit to watch Willie, whoever the hell he is, pass by.

Facing the hostile European crowds of 1966, Bob Dylan defiantly draped the back of his stage with a gigantic Stars and Stripes and told his audience: "This is not English music you're listening to. You haven't actually heard American music before." It was a bold statement, conflating aesthetic concerns (acoustic versus electric, folk versus pop) with the political (the association of "purist" folk music with left-wing political causes, as against the association of "commercial" pop music with American capitalism and imperialism). A year or so later, the Basement Tapes constituted Dylan's most serious attempt—all the more serious for being completely informal—to define "American music."

Greil Marcus describes Harry Smith's *Anthology of American Folk Music* as mystery, in the senses I've tried to define above, but also as "mystery . . . disguised as a textbook" (96). The academic discipline of this textbook might be history, or, more precisely, cultural studies. The musical tradition that Smith defined by anthologizing it, and that Dylan continued in the Basement Tapes, constitutes an image of American history: not the officially proclaimed public history of American triumphalism, but rather the "invisible republic," an alternate reality to the rhetoric of the political elites. It's America seen from the viewpoint of that log cabin, America (just like Willie) passing by.

Two specific lines of song echo back and forth from each other all the way through Marcus's *Invisible Republic:*

And she never hollers cuckoo till the fourth day of July.
>   (Clarence Ashley, "The Coo Coo Bird")
We carried you in our arms on Independence Day.
>   (Bob Dylan, "Tears of Rage")

The double reference evokes a mythic history of America. Its truth is to be found more in the structures of myth than in the factual records of political or military history, more in the images Americans have chosen to define themselves by than in the manifold ways in which they fall short of these images. Marcus quotes John Winthrop's 1630 image of the Puritan settlement of America as "a city on a hill" and notes that, whereas Ronald Reagan had used it as "a sign of American triumphalism," the phrase was, in its original context, "a prophecy of self-betrayal" (209). For Marcus, the mythic image of America is paradise lost, utopia betrayed. "What Winthrop's speech did do," he writes, "was lay the wish and the need for utopia in the American story; without it there is no American history." But the result has been "the inevitable betrayals that stem from the infinite idealism of American democracy" (89).

Such a view of American history seems to strike deep chords in Bob Dylan's work, nowhere more so than in the Basement Tapes, and in the songs he wrote a couple of months later for *John Wesley Harding*. In the first chapter I described Dylan as combining the roles of the trickster and the prophet—and certainly there is a good deal of the trickster in the playfulness of many Basement Tapes songs. I also described one inflection of the prophet as being related to the American tradition outlined by Sacvan Bercovitch in *The American Jeremiad* (1978), a book which draws on many of the same historical sources as does Greil Marcus. The key example of Dylan as American prophet, I suggested then, was "Tears of Rage."

"Tears of Rage" is a definitive statement of the "inevitable betrayal" of "infinite idealism." It is a song with an aching sense of loss, defined by its amazing identification of American history—"Independence Day"—with the ultimate Western tragedy, Shakespeare's *King Lear*—"Oh what dear daughter, beneath the sun, could treat a father so . . . ?" But the same sense comes back time and time again—"time out of mind"—in all the Basement songs: "Too Much of Nothing," "Nothing Was Delivered," "This Wheel's On Fire." And even more clearly in "As I Went Out One Morning" on *John Wesley Harding:*

> As I went out one morning
> To breathe the air around Tom Paine's,
> I spied the fairest damsel
> That ever did walk in chains.
>
> (L, 250)

This "damsel," I would argue, is the same child that "we carried . . . in our arms on Independence Day"—America itself, necessarily betraying its own ideals, Liberty in chains, the failed realization of Tom Paine's dreams.[26]

The same sense of betrayal permeates the folk song selections from the Basement Tapes: the cynical drover who betrays his employees in "Hills of Mexico," or the abandoned girl who sings "You've gone and neglected your frail wildwood flower." It permeates even the non-American folk song selections: the convict languishing in his cell in "The Royal Canal," the bride whose marriage is so cruelly blighted in "Young But Daily Growing." Or consider the extraordinary thirty-second fragment of "900 Miles." Where other performers, like Peter Paul and Mary, had sung it slow and mournful, like a gentle lament, Dylan screams it out as a Ginsbergian *howl!*—never, never in American history, has nine hundred miles been such a long, long way.

All of which brings us back, one more time, to "I'm Not There." Marcus describes this song as one of ultimate betrayal: *"No one,* you say to the singer, can be left as alone as you have left this woman, can be as abandoned as finally as you have abandoned her—because it is plain that this is no mere love affair that has dissolved" (201). The implication is that the song is, again, about the mutual betrayal of America and her people, each abandoning the other. But while "Tears of Rage" still has the space to wonder, in frustrated bafflement, *why* the singer "must be the thief," "I'm Not There" clearly accepts the responsibility, and the guilt.

Absence, then, is at the heart of the Basement Tapes. In "I'm Not There," at its simplest level, it is the absence of a lover who might have stood with his loved one to give her basic human comfort. It is also the absence, politically and morally, of a certain ideal which founded American democracy as a city on a hill but now finds itself exposed as another instance of a world gone wrong. It is the absence even of God—if one were to accept the reading of the line as "Christ-forsaken angel," what could be more utterly devastating than the plight of an angel abandoned even by the Son of God? More abstractly, it is the absence of conventional systems of signification, as the language of the songs retreats into fragmentation and incoherence: the absence, in post-structuralist terms, of any transcendental signified. It is also the absence of "Bob Dylan," 1966 rock star, from these 1967 performances-without-an-audience. And it is the absence which constitutes mystery, or mystery disguised as a textbook. It is the final, most resonant words which The Basement Tapes leave us:

> I wish I was there to help her
> But I'm not there, I'm gone.

"New Pony"

"New Pony" (L, 405) is one of Dylan's neglected masterpieces—neglected above all by himself. After the initial recording on *Street Legal,* he has never performed it in concert. Yet it is a fascinating song, featuring a complex interaction between several different modes of discourse.

At one level, it is a mean and dirty blues, sung in Dylan's best vindictive snarl. The image of the woman as a horse needing to be tamed and broken, while undoubtedly problematic from any contemporary feminist view, is a traditional image, from a long line of blues songs up to (most recently, in 1978, for Dylan) the Roger McGuinn–Jacques Levy collaboration "Chestnut Mare."[1] The "pony" of Dylan's song appears in three contexts: as victim, as aesthetic display, and as the object of sexual desire. She first appears as a horse which has broken its leg and "needed shooting": the hapless victim of an ostensibly humanitarian kindness/violence. She next appears as a virtuoso of aesthetic spectacle: "she knows how to fox-trot, lope and pace." But finally she appears as "bad and nasty," which seems to be (in the politics of sexual hypocrisy) the reason that the singer wants to "climb up one time on you." In all these contexts the woman-as-pony is severely subjected to the domination of the man: as rider, as mounter, and ultimately as executioner.

But these verses (woman as victim) alternate with verses in which the woman exercises an eerie kind of independence. The singer wonders "what's going on in [her] mind," and confesses that "I never know what the poor girl's gonna do to me next." In this mode the woman is "Miss X": an emblem of the unknown and unknowable, but also "Miss Ex," the free woman, the ex-wife.[2] This woman is portrayed as having an ambivalent kind of freedom. Her actions are unpredictable not only to the singer but also, it seems, to herself.

She functions as an automaton, a voodoo doll whose "feet walk by themselves." She isn't fully herself, but rather a "shadow" of herself : "it was early in the mornin', I seen your shadow in the door" (L, 405). (This line occurs in a verse which, intriguingly, Dylan does not sing on the released version but which is included in *Lyrics*). This shadow—like so many of Dylan's displaced images: ghost, alias, mirror, echo—occupies a liminal position: "in the door," neither inside nor outside. (This image is most fully developed by Dylan in the superb song from *Time Out Of Mind*, "Standing in the Doorway.") As "Miss X," the woman maintains a position of distance and mystery; as "Miss Ex," she is still subject to definition in relation to the male.

So these two modes—the dirty blues, in which the woman-as-pony is the object of male desire; and the equivocal independence of the woman who stands apart from him as a "shadow in the door"—interact with each other, and are in turn further modified by a third mode, that of (incipient) gospel. The whole of *Street Legal* hovers on the edge of the fully religious mode which was to declare itself unambiguously on the following year's *Slow Train Coming*.

Here, the woman-as-pony is named "Lucifer": Star of the Morning, the fallen angel, Satan. On one level, this naming simply reflects a traditionally misogynist view of woman-as-devil, the fallen Eve as the mother of all evil. But Dylan complicates this simplistic response by his assertion that the destruction of evil (the shooting of the pony) would "hurt me more than it could ever have hurted her." This phrase is certainly ambivalent—it is often used entirely insincerely—yet if we take it seriously, it expresses a kind of sorrow at the self-destructive fate of Lucifer—or, in the words of Mick Jagger ten years earlier, "sympathy for the devil."

The gospel tone is asserted most forcefully in the interventions of the chorus of female backup singers: "How much longer? How much longer?" In a gospel context these lines clearly express the impatience of the believer for the advent of apocalypse, the Second Coming of Christ. In the words of "Señor," from the same album, "Can you tell me what we're waiting for?" This apocalypse will mark the ultimate defeat of Lucifer, so that the doubts and hesitations of this song will be resolved, seemingly, in the finality of Revelation.

But the singer of the song is not yet ready for that finality. The question "How much longer?" remains an open one, not yet answered. And in the meantime, in the secular interval of waiting for apocalypse, he can still confess that the woman remains for him an object, not only of domination and desire, but also of love. The song closes on the statement of this unresolved paradox:

> Well, you're so bad and nasty
> But I love you, yes I do.

chapter 6
Movies

Pat Garrett & Billy the Kid

Bob Dylan's participation in Sam Peckinpah's film *Pat Garrett & Billy the Kid* seems to have come about largely by accident.

The best historical account is given in an article by Chris Whithouse, "Alias, Pat Garrett and Billy the Kid" (1987). Whithouse relates how the idea of Dylan taking part in the movie was first suggested by Bert Block, Kris Kristofferson's manager, and was then promoted by the scriptwriter, Rudy Wurlitzer. In 1972 Dylan was at a low ebb of his creativity and appeared to be drifting without much sense of direction, so the suggestion may have been a welcome one to him. He had, after all, a long-standing love for movies, especially for westerns; one can find in his lyrics direct quotes from classic 1950s westerns such as *The Gunfighter* and *Shane*.[1] He embraced the idea enthusiastically, attended a special screening of Peckinpah's most famous film, *The Wild Bunch*, and wrote a few verses of a song about Billy which he took with him when he first went to meet the director. Peckinpah knew very little about the legendary "Bob Dylan," but was immediately taken both by Dylan himself and by the as-yet-fragmentary song. More or less on the spot, Dylan was signed up both to compose the music for the film and to take part in it as an actor.

It seems likely that Peckinpah came to regret the impulsiveness of these decisions. Bob Dylan has many great talents, but they do not include those, in the conventional sense, of composing a film soundtrack or being a dramatic screen actor. Indeed, his efforts in both of these directions were extremely awkward, and seemingly unassimilable to the traditional concepts of a "well-made" Hollywood movie. What is remarkable about the finished product is the extent to which Peckinpah was able to *use* that very awkwardness and turn it to the film's advantage. Bob Dylan makes a major contribution to the aesthetic success of *Pat Garrett & Billy the Kid,* not in spite of but precisely because of the fact that he was so ill-suited to the roles he was expected to play.

Peckinpah, of course, was not entirely assimilable either. Throughout his career, he fought with the studios for control of his projects, and often lost. What might have been his most important film, *Major Dundee,* survives only in a butchered form, with studio-imposed cuts which render its later stages well-nigh incomprehensible.[2] And MGM eventually took away from him the final cut for *Pat Garrett & Billy the Kid,* releasing a shortened version which drastically alters the intentions and effects of the original. Fortunately, Peckinpah's original director's cut has subsequently been released on video, and there is now no need for anyone to look at the studio version except for reasons of perverse masochism.

So there is a strange parallel between Peckinpah's difficulties in accommodating Dylan and MGM's difficulties in accommodating Peckinpah. Perhaps Peckinpah recognized this similarity and tried to make more allowances for Dylan's maverick talents than the studio was making for his. Peckinpah did, however, begin to have his doubts about whether Dylan's music was going to be sufficient to sustain an entire movie, and he called on his regular composer, Jerry Fielding, for advice. Fielding was an old pro at the business of composing film soundtracks, and he had a professional contempt for amateurs in his own area of expertise. Fielding was full of disdain for Dylan; the feeling was reciprocal.

Some of Fielding's comments are, within their own terms of reference, entirely reasonable. "Just because you play a guitar and sing doesn't qualify you for scoring a picture," he said. "Considering the complexities of scoring a picture, Bobby Dylan has no more business attempting it than Sam Peckinpah has selling popcorn in the lobby of the theater" (Whithouse, 118).

Film music has to be flexible, adjusting itself to the rhythms of the visual scenes, and much of the time it should be unobtrusive, perceptible only in the background of the listener's consciousness. If a film audience *notices* the music, then the music has in some sense failed. Dylan's music was wrong on both counts. Most of the pieces he wrote consisted of a few simple, repetitive chord sequences and guitar riffs. There wasn't much variation in them; they couldn't be faded in and out of the background of scenes; they insisted on being rather prominently *heard.*

Fielding was especially offended by the song "Knockin' on Heaven's Door." "Everybody loved it," he said. "It was shit." And in more detail: "It was infantile. It was sophomoric. It was stuff you learn not to do the second year you score a piece of film. . . . It's wrong that he's singing 'Knock-knock-knockin' on Heaven's Door' with a rock drummer in a scene where a guy is dying and the emotion speaks for itself" (Whithouse, 119). Fielding's specific objection here is to the vocals, to the use of *words* in a scene where "the emotion speaks for itself." Peckinpah evidently agreed with him; in the director's cut, this scene uses an instrumental version of the song, but not the vocal track. MGM, which had paid good money to get a Bob Dylan soundtrack, put the words back into their version.

Fielding and Peckinpah were probably right in this instance. The scene of Sheriff Baker's death by the river *is* fully realized visually, and the words of the song would be an intrusion. However, the ultimate irony is that the song has subsequently become so well known that many viewers now supply the words, silently, in their heads. A similar case arises with the song "Ride, Billy, Ride," which Dylan wrote for the ending of the movie and which does not appear in either version of the film. It's a gorgeous piece of music, but it would have been all wrong for that place in the film.[3] The mood of the music is perfect, but the words enforce an exclusive concentration on Billy, while the film's focus in its final scene is on Pat. Indeed, it is notable that all of Dylan's music focuses on Billy, while the film is more interested in setting up a complex balance between Billy and Pat.

A more interesting instance is "Billy Surrenders," the musical accompaniment to the early scene in which Billy is captured by Pat Garrett. The surviving studio outtakes include two fascinating comments by Dylan as he prepares to record a rough take of this music. The first is Dylan's only documented response to the professional composer: "This guy Jerry Fielding's going to go nuts, man, when he hears this!" As no doubt he did, for "Billy Surrenders" is a strikingly static, repetitive piece of music, the same phrase played over and over with no development or variation. As it turns out, however, that's exactly what the scene needs. In the movie it's a point of suspended time. Billy stands in a hieratic crucifixion pose, Pat and the rest of the posse descend from the hills, and nothing happens. There is no dramatic development in the scene: it's a tableau, a frozen, static image of one point of equilibrium in the Pat–Billy relationship. And Dylan's music gives it exactly the right formalizing touch, emphasizing its ritual aspect—the way in which (in a phrase Dylan was to use repeatedly a few years later in relation to his own filmmaking ambitions) it "stops time."

But which came first, the scene or the music? Did Peckinpah edit this scene in the only way he could to fit Dylan's music, or was Dylan responding to something he had already sensed in the filming of the scene? The latter actually seems more likely.

The second comment I want to quote from the studio outtakes comes when Dylan is describing the scene for his musicians. He narrates how Billy comes out of the cabin and how Pat and the posse come down the hill toward him, and then Dylan says: "There's like a big pause. They stop, and there's silence." This comment indicates that Peckinpah had already conceived of the scene as a point of suspended time, and that Dylan's music responds to the scene consciously and brilliantly (even if it did make Jerry Fielding go nuts).

Similar considerations apply to the one more or less finished song that does appear in the movie, "Billy" itself. In some sense, Dylan never finished it. It never became more complete than it was on that first evening when he sang some verses for Peckinpah. There are multiple studio takes of it, but no definitive version; nor, alas, has Dylan ever gone back to it in concert.[4] Jerry Fielding complained that it had "a limitless number of verses that he would sing in a random order." Fielding's idea was that "by having Dylan sing a relevant verse as it fit the story at roughly nine separate points throughout the picture, it might be coherent. Dylan never understood what I wanted" (118).

I think it's more likely that Dylan clearly understood what Fielding wanted and just wasn't interested—either in completion or in coherence. The song evokes episodes in Billy's story, but it is determinedly nonlinear, non-narrative. The order of the verses *has to be* random. Again Dylan's interest is in "stopping time"; again he is trying to achieve the effect of stasis, trying to turn an art of time into an art of space. "Billy" can never be completed, since its ending, more than anything on the screen, would signify Billy's death. Dylan's own "ending" for his music was more radically open-ended:

Ride, Billy, ride ride ride
Ride, Billy, ride ride ride
Ride until you can't ride no more . . .

Dylan's music, then, may not have fit the conventional expectations for "scoring a picture," but there are at least some occasions when it perfectly fits the action and mood. At the same time, there are many moments in the music that are too fully and idiosyncratically "Bob Dylan" to be subordinated to the collaborative process of making a Sam Peckinpah movie. These moments are better appreciated on their own, as independent creations, either on the official soundtrack album or on *Peco's Blues*, the bootleg CD of studio outtakes.5

Peckinpah's problem of what to do with Dylan the musician was repeated when it came to Dylan the actor. Accounts from the set claim that Dylan impressed everyone with his ease and naturalness, even performing tricky feats like knife throwing or riding a horse over difficult terrain.

"You see him on screen and all eyes are on him," Kris Kristofferson said. "There's something about him that's magnetic. . . . He's a natural . . . *fantastic* on film" (114). By no means all viewers would agree with this assessment. In many scenes Dylan's acting seems wooden and awkward—in at least one scene, his dialogue has clearly had to be overdubbed. Dylan has never been totally at ease in front of a camera (as several disastrous music videos attest). Peckinpah must very quickly have seen what the limitations were—but again, he was able to work around them, and in many ways to turn them to the film's advantage. Dylan as Alias makes a major contribution to the film's thematic richness and density.

In the first place, the film is *about* celebrity and reputation. "At least I'll be remembered," says Alamosa Bill, dying from Billy's gunshot, and Kip McKinney, heading into the final confrontation, mutters, "I hope they spell my name right in the papers." All the characters are intensely conscious of their place in history, of what people think about them, of how they'll "be remembered." And all these remembrances revolve around the two most famous reputations of all: in the nineteenth-century context, Billy the Kid, and in the twentieth-century context, Bob Dylan.

Peckinpah plays with the notion of celebrity by the very self-conscious casting of the film. The small parts are inhabited by a veritable roll call of famous actors: Slim Pickens, Katy Jurado, Chill Wills, Harry Dean Stanton, Elisha

Cook, and others. A whole history of the Hollywood western could be written on the basis of this film's cast list. Many of them were, by 1972, getting on in years, and on screen they portray characters who are also aging and dying. It's the end of the West, and also, to a great extent, the end of the western. This elegiac note—the idea that a whole generation, a whole way of life, is on the verge of extinction—is thematically central to the film, but what I want to emphasize is the effect on the audience of a kind of *double recognition:* "Hey, that's Elisha Cook; I remember him from *Shane* twenty years ago. God, he's looking old!" The actors are recognized both as they once were and as they appear now, both within this fiction and in terms of their lives and reputations external to it. A few years later, Dylan used precisely the same effect in his casting of *Renaldo and Clara.*

The same double recognition underlies the self-conscious casting of Peckinpah himself (as the old man in the final scene building coffins) and of the screenwriter, Rudy Wurlitzer (as Tom O'Folliard, getting shot down in a characteristic burst of Sam Peckinpah bloody special effects). It extends to the casting of Rita Coolidge as Billy's shy girlfriend, which plays on the audience's knowledge that Coolidge was also Kristofferson's partner in "real life." And of course it includes Kristofferson, and Dylan.

The film always assumes that its audience is aware that the actor playing Alias *is* Bob Dylan. Wurlitzer's script deliberately evokes classic Dylan lines in the dialogue of the opening scene. "How does it feel?" Billy asks, and Pat replies, "It feels like times have changed." This is the paradoxical effect of double recognition: the audience hears Billy the Kid and Pat Garrett, sharing a drink in a bar in Fort Sumner, New Mexico, in 1881, sitting around swapping Bob Dylan quotations.

Such a recognition also produces an important doubling effect between nineteenth-century outlaw celebrity and twentieth-century rock star celebrity: Coolidge, Kristofferson, Dylan. Best known as singers, none of the three actually sings on camera. The closest we come is when Kristofferson, in the scene after Billy breaks out of jail, half-speaks and half-sings his farewell to Lincoln— "I've never seen no town so lowdown as Lincoln." The scene is, at every level, a *performance.* Within the fiction, Billy is parading his invulnerability, taunting the citizens of Lincoln for their unwillingness to stop his escape. He puts himself on stage for them, and the power of his reputation ensures that they remain a passive audience. Outside the fiction, what we see and hear, from our audience position, is a performance by Kris Kristofferson.

This equation between the roles of outlaw and rock star had been intriguingly made by Sam Shepard in his play *The Tooth of Crime*, which was produced in 1972, the same year as *Pat Garrett & Billy the Kid*. Shepard's play portrays an aging protagonist, Hoss, a famous man waiting for some ambitious young kid, Crow, to come along and challenge his position. The fame and the position are presented in terms which apply equally well to rock stars and gunfighters. The play contains explicit references to Bob Dylan, while its plot is based on the archetypal western movie *The Gunfighter*, which twelve years later would become the basis for Shepard's major collaboration with Dylan, "Brownsville Girl." It seems unlikely that anyone involved with *Pat Garrett & Billy the Kid*—Peckinpah, Wurlitzer, or Dylan—had already seen *The Tooth of Crime*, but in view of Shepard's later connections with Dylan, the coincidence of date is certainly intriguing.[6]

This theme of celebrity is closely connected to the themes of identity and naming, and it is here that Dylan's character, Alias, is most obviously relevant. "Who are you?" Garrett demands the first time they meet, and the answer is pure Bob Dylan trickster equivocation: "That's a good question."

The question is repeated later in the film by Billy and his gang, and produces the following exchange:

–What's your name, boy?

–Alias.

–Alias what?

–Alias anything you please.

–What do we call you?

–Alias.

–Hell, just call him Alias.

–That's what I'd do.

–Alias it is.

Remarkably—given the appositeness of the whole notion of the alias to the career of Bob Dylan—there is some historical justification for the presence in Billy's gang of a character who called himself simply Alias. In *The Authentic Life of Billy, the Kid,* the book attributed to Pat Garrett and ghostwritten by Ash Upson, published in 1882 within a year of Billy's death, Garrett writes: "Billy's partner doubtless had a name which was his legal property, but he was so given to changing it that it is impossible to fix on the right one. Billy always called him 'Alias'" (Whithouse, 126).7 Like the name "Bob Dylan," "Billy the Kid" was an alias, for the character who was called, at various times and with various degrees of accuracy, William H. Bonney, Henry McCarty, or Austin Antrim.

Peckinpah's film surrounds Alias with suggestions of deliberate myth making. He is first seen working in a newspaper office,8 and thus carries echoes of the journalists and dime-novelists who had begun, even within Billy the Kid's lifetime, to transform him into myth. (Similar characters—newspapermen and novelists—are given more prominence in Arthur Penn's version of Billy's story, *The Left-Handed Gun,* and also, more recently, in Clint Eastwood's *Unforgiven.)* At other times, Alias seems to function as a kind of Greek chorus or an embodiment of fate. Kristofferson said that he thought of Alias as "the Fool in [Lear.] He sees it all, he knows the legend and can see where it's all going . . ." (120).

Alias is the witness to all the key scenes in the film; as the witness, he is the voice which will preserve Billy's story, recast it as legend, and project it into perpetuity. In this sense the nineteenth-century character Alias has already been displaced by the twentieth-century musician Bob Dylan, who will write, knowing exactly where the legend is going: "There's guns across the river aimin' at you. . . ."

But in his most memorable scene, Alias is displaced from himself and reduced to the voice of the other, even within the fiction. During a lethal confrontation with two of Billy's gang, Garrett uses Alias as his instrument, forcing him to knock out one of the men with a rifle butt, and then keeping him in the background, out of the action but still audible (so Garrett knows where he is), by requiring him to read aloud the labels from a shelf of canned food. Part of the joke is that Bob Dylan, the "poet," is here reciting lines like "Beans. Canned Beans. Succotash. Tobacco. Beans." Dylan had his revenge during the studio sessions recording the soundtrack, when he laid down a "wild track" (preserved on *Peco's Blues)* which embellishes the line with the invented tradenames "Second Coming Coffee" and "Climax Tobacco."

More important is the idea that Garrett has here taken away from him his voice, his identity, his capacity to take action. In the same way as the name Alias always points somewhere *else,* always locates identity in the name of the other, in this scene Dylan's voice becomes the voice of the other. He is set at one remove from himself; the name which is his "legal property" is no longer proper, no longer his own. This self-displacement is always, fundamentally, the effect of the alias.

The proper name—our society's traditional guarantee of authenticity and self-identity—becomes improper: it is a construct, a disguise, a mask. Usually an alias substitutes one name for another: for example, "Bob Dylan" for "Robert Allen Zimmerman." But in this case the alias is doubled, because the name "Alias" refers to itself as the process of renaming, the gesture of displaced and disguised identity.

The theme of the alias as a mask of identity is central to this whole book, but here I want to note how ideally it fits into the themes of *Pat Garrett & Billy the Kid*—especially in relation to the two central characters. Throughout the film, Pat and Billy are paralleled to each other, even equated with each other. The opening sequence (in Peckinpah's original version) intercuts scenes of Garrett's eventual death by assassination with scenes of Billy shooting at chickens, and the editing presents the illusion of Billy's shot actually killing Pat, across a time-gap of twenty-five years. Similarly, at the end, after shooting Billy, Pat turns and fires at his own reflection in a mirror, shattering it—and in that shattered mirror reflection, the right-handed Pat Garrett has, of course, become the left-handed Billy the Kid.

Billy's left-handedness actually belongs more to legend than to history; none of the contemporary accounts describe him as left-handed. The image became part of the mythical depiction of Billy as, both literally and figuratively, "sinister." For most of the film, Kristofferson portrays Billy as right-handed, but toward the end there is a scene of him practising target shooting with his left hand, as if already rehearsing for his legendary role. His efforts are applauded by the watcher who sees what is to come: Alias, played by Bob Dylan.[9]

Identity and celebrity are presented in *Pat Garrett & Billy the Kid* as fluid, indeterminate entities. The characters cross and blend with each other, the actors blend and cross between their fictional roles and their "real life" celebrities. In all of this interplay Bob Dylan, both as musician and as actor, takes a central part. If the film is, as I believe, one of the most successful westerns in the dying phase of that genre, then it is to no small extent due to the peculiar and idiosyncratic presence of Bob Dylan.

Renaldo and Clara

What came is gone forever every time

Allen Ginsberg, "Kaddish" (1984, 210)

The image on screen is a face in white makeup, leaning into the microphone with the tense urgency of a steel spring. The lips are drawn back almost in a snarl. The eyes move in and out of the shadow of a wide-brimmed hat; they gaze searchingly into the darkness, and into the light.

Who is this singer? What is his alias this time? One answer would be that it's Bob Dylan, filmed in documentary style during a 1975 concert of the Rolling Thunder Revue. Another answer would be that it's the fictional character Renaldo, the central figure in the long, complex, and multilayered movie *Renaldo and Clara*. Renaldo, of course, is played by an actor called Bob Dylan—and the film is directed by someone who is also called Bob Dylan. I and I, and I.

Not many people, unfortunately, have had the opportunity to see *Renaldo and Clara*. Although Dylan clearly regarded the film as a major part of his work—he spent more than a year editing it—it remains the most inaccessible of his texts. Unlike the record albums, it is not in public circulation. Since its critical and commercial failure, prints are scarce, and most viewers have access only to poor-quality videotape copies on which the rich color patterns can only be guessed at. Moreover, its four-hour length makes even a single complete viewing a daunting prospect. Most film audiences are not trained in maintaining such a long attention span, especially for a film that offers little in the way of linear plot and continuity but relies instead on a nonlinear pattern of associations in which connections must often be made between scenes widely separated in time.

Moreover, *Renaldo and Clara* is full of allusions and connections that often depend upon information not made explicit in the film itself. Much of the effort of explication was undertaken by one of the film's stars, Allen Ginsberg, who conducted a long interview with Dylan in 1977.[10] To some extent it is a weakness of the film that some of the points Dylan makes in this interview, points that are crucial to a viewer's understanding, could not be gathered from the film itself by even the most perceptive audience. Repeated viewings elucidate the symbolic meanings of most characters, but when Dylan says that Ramon, who appears with "Mrs. Dylan," is the ghost of her dead lover, nothing in the scene as filmed gives the slightest hint that Ramon is supposed to be dead. Yet the idea of dead lovers and ghosts is thematically important.

"You wanna stop time," Dylan told Ginsberg, "that's what you wanna do. . . . We have literally stopped time in this movie" (1989, 10). The major way in which Dylan attempts to stop time in *Renaldo and Clara* is by abandoning the linear progression of plot and narrative, a technique relatively common in twentieth-century literature: Ginsberg cites the "cut-up" novels of William Burroughs and the collage method of Ezra Pound's *Cantos* as analogues. Nonlinear narrative is also present in much avant-garde cinema and in the work of such directors as Jean-Luc Godard, but it is foreign to mainstream American cinema.

The many narrative elements within the film are rarely presented in logical sequence. Instead, fragments of the different possible "plot lines" appear in shuffled order, juxtaposed with other narrative sequences, as well as with documentary or concert footage. A repeated conceit of the film is to show an emcee introducing a performer, or a performer introducing a song, only to cut away to a different sequence at the moment when the performance is about to start.

On one such occasion, the emcee at the Seacrest Hotel in Falmouth introduces "without doubt a very interesting and clever personality," Allen Ginsberg, and we see Ginsberg sit on a stool and prepare to begin his reading of "Kaddish." But the film cuts away—to a scene in which David Blue talks about the presence of Ginsberg and Kerouac in Greenwich Village—and it is an hour or longer before the film returns to the Falmouth reading.

Consistently, Dylan works to disrupt and deny the linear expectations of the film audience. The various scenes of *Renaldo and Clara* do not "follow on" from each other; they exist side by side, held in the same timeless moment. One shot at the end of the film, in which the camera circles around Renaldo lying on the floor, suggests that the timeless moment is the moment of Renaldo's dream.

The effect is that the scenes are laid out spatially rather than temporally. The viewer is invited, eventually, after several viewings, to make connections between them, not in terms of their chronological sequence, but in terms of imagistic associations which crisscross the temporal divisions. Ginsberg describes the film's method:

It's like a tapestry. What he did was, he shot about 110 hours of film, and he looked at it all. Then he put it all on index cards, according to some preconceptions he had when he was directing the shooting; namely themes; God, rock 'n' roll, art, poetry, marriage, women, sex, Bob Dylan, poets, death, maybe 18 or 20 thematic preoccupations. Then he also put on index cards all the different characters, all the scenes, the dominant colors blue or red, and certain other images that go through the movie, like the rose and the hat and American Indians, so that finally he had an index of all of that. And then he went through it all again and began composing it thematically, weaving in and out of these specific compositional references. So it's compositional, and the idea was not to have a plot but to have a composition of those themes.

(Bicker, 8)

One brief series of edits illustrates the kinds of transitions that Dylan arranges out of his index cards. In a major sequence late in the film, Renaldo (played by Bob Dylan) is confronted by two women, Clara (Sara Dylan) and the Woman in White (Joan Baez). The sequence plays back and forth between the real identities and histories of the actors and the fictional roles of the characters.

At one point we see the Woman in White looking at Clara and demanding, "Who is she?" Whereupon we cut directly into a shot of Bob Dylan on stage singing, "Sara, oh Sara / Sweet virgin angel, sweet love of my life." The biographical reference could scarcely be more blatant, but as the scene ends the camera pans to the character called "Mrs. Dylan" (played by Ronee Blakley), who is standing onstage, wearing a large red hat that recalls the hat Renaldo wears throughout the movie. A cut then returns us to a different sequence, introduced much earlier, in which a CBC reporter, told that "You'll recognize Bob, he's got a hat on," mistakes Ronnie Hawkins for Bob Dylan. Hawkins and Blakley now reappear, playing the roles of Mr. and Mrs. Dylan. So, in quick succession, "Bob Dylan" has been split into the character of Renaldo, the man onstage who sings of Sara, and a fictional character played by Ronnie Hawkins.

The next edit returns to the shots of David Blue playing pinball, which have been regularly interspersed ever since the beginning of the film. Here, Blue first tells us that Bob Dylan is a myth—"You know what a myth is? It's a myth!"—

and then that Bob Dylan is not a myth—"He lives like a human being. He [has] a wife and family, you know what I mean, it's ridiculous." With the mention of wife and family, the film cuts back into the scene of Renaldo and Clara (Bob and Sara Dylan) making love on a bed. So in this sequence, four totally different times and narrative lines have been woven together into a continuous collage on the myth and reality of Bob Dylan's marriage.

This sequence also shows the importance of the soundtrack as part of the collage. Music is pervasive throughout the film—fifty-five musical selections are listed in the closing credits, twenty-two by Bob Dylan. To extend Ginsberg's tapestry metaphor, the music, with all its manifold associations *outside* the film, provides the warp through which the weft of Dylan's index-card composition is drawn.

The soundtrack includes not only music, but also poetry, by Allen Ginsberg and Anne Waldman. One of the few performances that Ginsberg actually gave on the Rolling Thunder tour, as I noted in the earlier section on Ginsberg in Chapter 5, was his reading of "Kaddish" at Falmouth. Extracts from this reading appear at several points in *Renaldo and Clara* and are woven into complex collages. Most of the time, the reading is presented as voiceover for scenes with different visuals; only once do we actually *see* Ginsberg reading.

One scene, in which Clara is walking through the streets of Montreal (the beginning of the sequence depicting the jailbreak of the convict Lafkezio), features a complex soundtrack, mixing and overlaying Ginsberg's poem with Dylan's song "She Belongs To Me." It begins with lines from "Kaddish" clear on the soundtrack: "with your eyes of Russia / with your eyes of no money." Then we begin to hear Dylan's song in the background: "She's got everything she needs, / She's an artist, she don't look back" (L, 163). Dylan's song advances to the foreground on the soundtrack, but Ginsberg's reading persists in the background: "with your eyes of shock / with your eyes of lobotomy" (1984, 226–27).

The assertion of female independence in Dylan's song is thus ironically juxtaposed with Ginsberg's images of his mother's helplessness and confinement—while both elements of the soundtrack are in turn set against the visual image of the free woman, Clara, helping a convict escape from prison.[11]

Close to the end of the film, there is a scene in which Ginsberg and Blakley and several other women dance to piano music in an empty room. The dance begins as slow and stately, but becomes quite animated, with Ginsberg jitterbugging around the room. And on the soundtrack, "Kaddish" again: "What came is gone forever every time"—a line which Dylan has called "the key line of the movie" (1984, 210). This final quotation breaks off at precisely the point in the poem where the film's *first* quotation from "Kaddish," three hours of screen time earlier, had started—thus forming an endless loop. Dylan has, in effect, performed a "cut-up" collage, Burroughs-style, on Ginsberg's text.[12] In *Renaldo and Clara* "Kaddish" has no beginning and no end, it circles upon itself, it stops time.

Another technique for breaking up linearity is the repeated presentation of parallel images that reflect and double each other. Indeed, doubling or duality is the central obsessive gesture of the film. Everything in *Renaldo and Clara* happens at least twice: every reference, gesture, and name finds its double at another point in the structure. For example, there are two scenes that deal with palm reading: Scarlet Rivera reads Renaldo's hand, and a couple of scenes later, Mama Frasca reads the palm of The Father (played by Allen Ginsberg). Each scene in turn contains doubles: "You have a duality in your life," Scarlet tells Renaldo—one of the film's great understatements—while Mama Frasca tells The Father, "You have been married twice."

"Well, sort of," responds Allen Ginsberg!

Doubles also appear within individual scenes. Two street preachers harangue the crowds on Wall Street. The two preachers not only double each other's gestures, one of them also repeats exactly the arm gesture of George Washington's statue behind him. The preachers reappear in a later scene, in which intercutting makes it appear as if Renaldo in Toronto can see them in New York—thus doubling the United States and Canada. (The film moves freely back and forth between these two countries, and between two languages, as in the wonderful bilingual line "Not *pour moi, monsieur; c'est un* mistake.")

The scene concerning Hurricane Carter insists repeatedly on the *two* witnesses who have contradicted their testimony against him. Prominent in the background of this scene is a cinema, Harlem's Apollo, which is showing *Earthquake*, thus implicitly echoing two natural disasters.[13]

Doubling within single scenes is also accomplished by using mirror images. In the angry dialogue between Ramon and Mrs. Dylan, the camera begins by shooting through the bathroom mirror, pulls back, and follows the couple into the bedroom, where a second mirror is prominent on the wall. In one bordello scene The Father is offered "a mirrored room" from which he can watch the proceedings. Other forms of mirroring are more indirect. In two scenes we catch glimpses of a second camera crew filming and being filmed. A shot of Dylan and Baez onstage singing together is followed in the next shot by Renaldo and Clara looking at a newspaper photograph of Dylan and Baez onstage singing together.

Characters' names are also doubled. David Blue, for instance, appears as a kind of chorus throughout the film. In his interview with Ginsberg, Dylan said: "You know in the old Greek play, the Chorus? David [Blue] seems to know what's going on. . . . He's the narrator who links the movie to generational history" (1989, 25). Blue's witty, articulate reminiscences of Greenwich Village in the early 1960s are among its most enjoyable scenes. But "Blue" also keys the color coding of the film: the concert sequences are all shot with a strong visual emphasis on red and blue. These colors combine patriotically with Renaldo's whiteface stage makeup in the tight close-up of him singing "Tangled Up In Blue."

"Blue," like "Dylan," is an assumed name: David Blue was originally David Cohen. David Cohen is then doubled by *Leonard* Cohen, who makes several phantom appearances in the film. The women in the bordello (Anne Waldman, Denise Mercedes, and Linda Thomases) are referred to collectively as the "Sisters of Mercy," the title of a Cohen song. It is one of these women who offers Allen Ginsberg "a mirrored room," recalling the line "Suzanne holds the mirror" from Cohen's "Suzanne," which is sung in the film by Joan Baez.[14]

At the center of these doublings stands the multiply doubled figure of Bob Dylan. He is both *outside* the film, as its director-editor, and *inside* it, as an actor. As actor he is both the character Renaldo and the man who sings Bob Dylan's songs onstage. As Renaldo he has to confront Bob Dylan's history, in the shape of characters played by Joan Baez and Sara Dylan; as Renaldo he also dreams the whole film, as if he were Bob Dylan, its director-editor. Doubling is thus the technique by which *Renaldo and Clara* stages Bob Dylan, enabling him to tell the story of himself—the story that begins, as always, "I is another."

It begins onstage. In the film's first shot we see the cast of the Rolling Thunder Revue singing "When I Paint My Masterpiece." The choice of song already points both to the visual nature of the film (a song about painting opens a film about singing) and to its ambition. *Renaldo and Clara* advertises itself as Bob Dylan's masterpiece. The song's third line—"You can almost think that you're seein' double" (L, 300)—introduces the motif of doubling.

In fact, what Dylan sings in this performance is "You can almost think that you're seein' *your* double" (my emphasis), placing the audience squarely in front of the film's mirror. The screen in *Renaldo and Clara* always acts as a mirror. Dylan says that Renaldo "looks right at you through the mirror" (Ginsberg 1989, 23).

This first scene also introduces the theme of the mask or disguise, since it is here that Dylan/Renaldo wears the semi-transparent mask as described by Sam Shepard, in the passage I quoted earlier in Chapter 2, "Mask." For most of *Renaldo and Clara*, however, the characters don't wear actual masks, but rather white facepaint. The effect recalls the *commedia dell'arte* tradition and more specifically, Marcel Carné's film *Les Enfants du Paradis*. Dylan frequently talked about this film on the Rolling Thunder tour, and he cited it to Ginsberg as a successful example of a film which had "stopped time" (10). There are several significant parallels between *Renaldo and Clara* and *Les Enfants du Paradis*. Some are incidental details, such as characters carrying a red flower. More importantly, both films feature climactic scenes in which the central male character (Baptiste, Renaldo) is confronted by two women, his wife and his former lover (Nathalie and Garance; Clara and the Woman in White). In both cases the central question is the ambiguity of the word *love*, its inadequacy to cover, as a single word, the range of emotions experienced between the characters. Baptiste repeatedly demands of Garance, "Do you love me as I love you?"; Renaldo says to both Clara and the Woman in White, "Do I love you like I love her? No." But the most essential point of similarity between the two films lies in their deliberate confusion of identities, between "real life" and stage personae. The characters of *Les Enfants du Paradis*, whether they are literally actors or not, are all theatrical; their identities are roles which they play, in every scene. The same is true in *Renaldo and Clara*.

"Bob Dylan," for instance, is not only the singer/actor/director, but also a fictional character, played by Ronnie Hawkins. We see him mainly in two contexts: one of mistaken identity and one of seduction. In two scenes a CBC reporter in Toronto naively mistakes Ronnie Hawkins for Bob Dylan, and the Hawk plays the scenes to the hilt. Asked what he thinks of Bob Dylan, he replies, "A hero of the highest order," to which the reporter can only respond, "Why do you say that about yourself?" A more subtle variation on mistaken identity occurs in the scene in which Dylan/Hawkins finds his way barred by a security guard played by Mick Ronson in a thick Yorkshire accent. The guard refuses to believe that Ronnie Hawkins is Bob Dylan and tells him, "I don't know you from Adam, so off you pop." The colloquial English phrase echoes, as a distant double, the American *pop* as father, while *Adam* recalls the *first* father.

In the other scene involving Hawkins as "Bob Dylan," the unseen father plays a major role. The scene—which begins, typically, inside a mirror reflection—depicts "Bob Dylan" attempting to persuade a young woman to accompany him on the upcoming Rolling Thunder Revue tour. "You're a lovely young lady," he tells her. "We'll do things that kings and queens have never tried." But she resists him, insisting that "I have to get my father's approval."

There are several ways of extrapolating the significance of this scene. One is to follow the appearances of the woman whom "Bob Dylan" is trying to seduce.[15] The credits refer to her simply as "The Girlfriend," and Dylan says, "she's the one figure of real Truth in the movie. . . . She's actually the one person in the movie thinking more of Renaldo than of herself" (24). As such she continually challenges Renaldo, as when she tells him, "Looks like every time you look at me, you turn away"—a comment on Renaldo's shifty gaze, which never directly faces the camera.

The Girlfriend is also connected with the film's religious imagery. In one early scene she spreads her arms in a crucifix and says to Renaldo, "Stand and bear yourself like the cross and I'll receive you." This statement is followed by a shot of a crucifix. The Girlfriend's obedience to her absent father may thus be seen as religious obedience to the divine Father. By contrast, the fictional figure of the Father (played by Allen Ginsberg) is fully involved in the sexual scenes in the bordello. Several scenes amount to a full-scale erotic parody of Christian iconography. Mama Frasca (herself a parody of the Mother) sings a song called "God and Mama," which invites the listener: "Why don't you kneel / Pray Jesus / And you'll cry." While she sings, Joan Baez is trying on Mama's wedding dress. The white dress prefigures Baez's later appearance as the ghostly Woman in White and, of course, suggests virginity. A shot of a marble statue of the Virgin Mary[16] is immediately followed by a scene in the brothel, where the Father (Ginsberg) jovially oversees preparations for the deflowering of the Son (David Mansfield), who wears only a ludicrous pair of angel's wings. Father, Son, and Virgin thus form a parodic trinity—further emphasized by Ginsberg's publicly avowed homosexuality.

In other scenes religious imagery is more seriously presented. Ginsberg the Father instructs Renaldo the Son, by translating for him the Stations of the Cross. Renaldo lights a candle for the Virgin and stands beside the crucifix. The identification of Renaldo/Dylan as a Christ-figure is strongly suggested. At the beginning of the film, Renaldo responds to the question, "You running from the law?" by claiming, "I am the Law."

This discussion of religious imagery began by looking at the line "I have to get my father's approval," spoken by the Girlfriend to the fictional "Bob Dylan." I now return to this character and his fictional wife, "Mrs. Dylan," played by Ronee Blakley. In the same way as the lead singer in the concert footage is both Renaldo and Bob Dylan, Ronee Blakley appears onstage both as Mrs. Dylan and as herself. She is shown in concert, delivering a strong performance of (Ronee Blakley's) "Need a New Sun Rising." The title evokes not only the traditional "House of the Rising Sun" (performed in the film by Dylan/Renaldo) and the rising of the Son (Christ), but also the ending of Dylan's song "Romance in Durango," in which the dying hero, who has killed a man called Ramon, tells his doomed lover, "We may not make it through the night" (L, 386). The point of this reference is that Blakley has just appeared as Mrs. Dylan in the prior scene with a character also called Ramon, whom Dylan describes as the ghost of her dead lover.

This ghostly appearance links the fictional Mrs. Dylan to the Sara Dylan for whom Dylan claims he wrote "Sad-Eyed Lady of the Lowlands," whose title in turn evokes the traditional British ballad, "The Lowlands of Holland," in which the ghost of a dead lover appears to a woman. "Sad-Eyed Lady" appears on the soundtrack of *Renaldo and Clara* in ambiguous reference to both Joan Baez and Sara Dylan. It begins as accompaniment to the last exit of the Woman in White (Baez) and continues in the background of a conversation between Renaldo and Clara (during which, incidentally, Renaldo is standing in front of a mirror).

In *Tarantula* the ghost is described as "more than one person" (T, 120). In the film, too, the appearance of a ghost sets up multiple echoes. "We've all had a lot of friends who died," says Mrs. Dylan to Renaldo, and *Renaldo and Clara* is full of their ghosts.[17] The Woman in White herself is described as a ghost. When Ginsberg asked about her, Dylan responded that she was "the ghost of Death—Death's ghost. Renaldo rids himself of death when she leaves"; she is "the Supreme Ego, White Death" (1989, 18). But if Death is to have a ghost, then Death itself must be dead. In that sense the Woman in White represents that which survives beyond death, the woman who lives on. And she too is "more than one person."

There are several scenes in which the Woman in White is clearly played not by Joan but by Sara. During the sequence in which she rides in an open, horse-drawn carriage through snow-covered streets, there is a deliberate confusion of roles. In the first few shots she is clearly Sara/Clara, but when she arrives at her destination she is Baez. The ghost then, returned from the lowlands of death, is both Joan Baez and Sara Dylan—as well as Ramon, the lover of "Mrs. Dylan."

These equivocal references point to the central obsession emerging in the second half of *Renaldo and Clara:* the staging of Dylan's private life as public spectacle. Casting Joan and Sara in fictional roles provides a certain distancing effect, which enables Dylan to talk openly about the parts these two women have played in his life. If pressed too far he can always retreat into the assertion that they are only fictional characters. But the audience knows (and Dylan knows that the audience knows) that these actresses *are* Joan Baez and Sara Dylan, and the audience inevitably has a certain voyeuristic curiosity in watching them enact in public their private claims on Bob Dylan. *Renaldo and Clara* exploits this voyeurism in much the same way as Hitchcock often relied on the baser instincts of his audience; we should rightly feel uncomfortable with our own fascination.

We also may feel uncomfortable with some things that Dylan, as director of the film, does to the women. Several long sequences take place in a "sporting house," a bordello which Dylan refers to as "Diamond Hell." Despite this title, it is presented in the rosily idealized manner of cinematic fantasies about whorehouses. The provocatively undressed women displayed for the camera, including Joan Baez and Sara Dylan, are referred to as the Sisters of Mercy: an allusion not just to the Leonard Cohen song but also to that song's use on the soundtrack of Robert Altman's *McCabe and Mrs. Miller,* which features a similarly romanticized brothel. Both Sara and Joan have since commented rather bitterly on the reductiveness of these scenes. "After all the talk about goddesses," said Sara, "we wound up being whores." Similarly Baez complained, "We looked around for these mystical, powerful, life force scenes, we ended up playing a bunch of whores" (both comments cited in Bicker, 51).[18]

The women, however, take their revenge in several unscripted, improvised scenes in which they confront Renaldo, and it is to Dylan's credit (as director and editor) that these scenes, in which he generally comes off rather poorly, were retained in the movie. In the first of these scenes Joan Baez, possibly in character as the Woman in White, confronts Renaldo in a bar. Larry Sloman contends that Baez had planned this confrontation without Dylan's knowledge: "There was so much she wanted to say and ask him but . . . she was afraid and he was so elusive. . . . And we talked about the fact that maybe the way to get him pinned was to do it on camera where he wouldn't back down" (300). Sloman characterizes Dylan's response as "stunned but . . . brilliant. . . . Dylan is funny and turns what could have been maudlin into something really inspired" (301). Describing the same scene, Sam Shepard is only slightly more cautious:

> This is turning into either the worst melodrama on earth or the best head-to-head confessional ever put on film. Dylan is dancing around, soaked in brandy, doing his best to dodge the Baez kidney punches. She just stands there, planted, hoisting one-liners at him like cherry bombs. Producers are wincing in the background. Musicians are tittering. Cameras are doing double time.
>
> (1977, 68)

Well, maybe you had to be there. On film the impact is considerably muted, partly because the cameras are *not* "doing double time"; that is, the scene is shown from only one camera viewpoint, focused on Baez, so Renaldo/Dylan's face is never clear. There is no cutting back and forth to articulate a full interaction between the two characters.

The main question that Baez poses in this scene—"What do you think it would have been like if we'd got married?"—brings the staging of Dylan's private life clearly to the center of the film. It makes sense only in reference to the close relationship Dylan and Baez had shared ten years before, the relationship broken by Dylan's marriage to Sara. Dylan simply evades the question—"I don't know"—and turns it back against her—"I haven't changed much, have you?" Baez has nowhere to go; she gives a sick grin and answers, "Maybe." But while she answers, her hands are switching their brandy glasses on the bar. Perhaps

Dylan gave his definite answer much later, in the editing process, in which this scene is intercut with Baez singing "Diamonds and Rust," and is then immediately followed by a scene in which Renaldo trades the Woman in White (Baez) to an escaped convict in exchange for a horse.

This confrontation may have been unplanned, but the other major scene between Renaldo, Clara, and the Woman in White is very elaborately set up. It is prepared for by a long series of intercut shots in which the Woman in White, played by both women in turn, drives through a snow-covered city and eventually enters a room where Renaldo and Clara are together. The scenes that follow unite many disparate themes of the movie.

We first see Renaldo and Clara talking to each other in the privacy of their bedroom. It is the first time that their names have actually been spoken in the film, and no sooner are the names mentioned than the possibility of *changing them* comes up. "We'll be famous," says Clara. "Renaldo and Clara. Maybe I should change my name, huh?" The immediate allusion may be to Robert Zimmerman adopting an alias in order to become famous, but the comment also points to the whole web of doubled names throughout the movie. This scene cuts back to the brothel, where Baez and Sara appear in their other roles as Sisters of Mercy, but again the fictional stages the biographical when Baez, as if picking up Clara's comment from the previous scene, asks Sara, "Did you ever have another name? One time I was involved with somebody, I think there is a possibility he was involved with you"!

An edit returns us to the bedroom and to the entry of the Woman in White, who looks at Clara and demands of Renaldo, "Who is she?" I have already outlined the quick sequence of cuts that follow from this question: Dylan/Renaldo onstage singing "Sara"; Ronee Blakley as "Mrs. Dylan"; David Blue saying, "He [has] a wife and family, you know what I mean, it's ridiculous"; and back to the bedroom. In the ensuing scene the two women openly compete for Renaldo's affection, or even attention. Clara offers to take off his vest and scratch his back; the Woman in White writes him love letters. (On the soundtrack Bob Dylan and Joan Baez are singing a duet of "The Water Is Wide," a traditional song about the separation of two lovers.) Clara appears to win this round: "She can't give you what I can give you, Renaldo," she says, and the Woman in White departs, announcing that she is going to Honduras. As she leaves, Clara fires a sweetly innocent parting shot: "Are you sure you've got the right room?"

But a couple of edits later, the Woman in White returns, and now the two women begin to join forces against Renaldo, if only to force his decision. "I can't share any longer," the Woman in White declares. Trying to pacify her, Renaldo finds himself quoting Bob Dylan: "No reason to get excited" (L, 252). "You have to tell me something," says the Woman in White, and Clara modifies this to "You have to tell us *both* something." Renaldo promises to tell the truth, and the Woman in White asks, "Do you love her?" Pinned, Renaldo gives an answer that is either simply evasion, or a quotation from *Les Enfants du Paradis,* or the closest thing to "the truth" that Renaldo (or Bob) could ever come up with: "Do I love her like I love you? No. Do I love you like I love her? No."

After a brief cutaway to the band onstage, the sequence resumes with Clara and the Woman in White comparing notes.

"He never gives straight answers," says Clara, accurately enough.

"Evasiveness is all in the mind," protests Renaldo. "Truth is on many levels."

"Horseshit," both women reply in unison.

"Has he always been like that?" Clara asks.

"For the ten years I've known him," the Woman in White replies.

"Has he ever given you a straight answer?"

"Not to my recollection."

The dynamics of the scene have now shifted completely. The two women are no longer in competition with each other but have joined in a tacit exclusion of Renaldo. Trying to get back in, Renaldo declares, "I'm a brother to you both"—thus recalling "Oh, Sister" and its invocation of patriarchal authority. But Clara defuses the threat by remarking simply, "Then we'll be a family."

Again the mood of the scene changes. It is as if the players, juggling their private and fictional worlds, are trying out various modes and resolutions. After a few interpolated scenes, the film returns to the bedroom, where Clara poses the same question to the Woman in White: "Are you in love with him?" Her answer seems direct enough—"Yes, I was in love with him"—but the past tense makes it just as evasive as Renaldo's. Clara now returns to the offensive: "She's cold, Renaldo, you don't want a cold woman." She mocks the Woman in White for being a virgin. But one of the interpolated scenes had shown Sara Dylan, playing a Sister of Mercy, telling Allen Ginsberg, "You all want the virgin."

The Woman in White finally leaves, and Renaldo and Clara embrace. But Clara can't let go: "She's cold, Renaldo . . . she's probably barren."

"You don't even know her," Renaldo protests.

"I know her. We're like sisters," Clara answers.

Thus the evocation of "Oh, Sister" is repeated, this time by Clara, to a purpose very different from Renaldo's previous allusion. The shot of the Woman in White leaving the house is accompanied on the soundtrack by the beginning of "Sad-Eyed Lady of the Lowlands."

By the end of the sequence, then, the status quo has been restored: Renaldo is again with Clara, and the Woman in White (Death's ghost) has been banished. Renaldo has won the whole confrontation, and he has done so by doing nothing. As John Herdman comments:

> Renaldo . . . controls situations through his very passivity. He seems to be played upon, tugged emotionally from Sara by the Woman in White . . . and then tugged, physically, back again; he appears like a little child, smothered and overwhelmed by the attentions of his rival lovers, yet in the end it is they who are manipulated by him, who ask him questions which he will not answer, who seek from him what he withholds. Clara may have his body, but neither of them has his soul.
>
> (141)

There is no resolution to this sequence, nor obviously can there be any conventional closure to a film as diffuse and wide-ranging as *Renaldo and Clara.* The staging of Bob Dylan's private life as public psychodrama is only one aspect of the film, albeit the most important one, but in this analysis I have scarcely touched on the political aspects of *Renaldo and Clara,* such as its concern for the American Indian, the campaign for Hurricane Carter, or the evocation of the Puritan history of New England.

Closure, in the conventional sense, requires a more traditional structure, with a central character to hold the film together. Renaldo, however, is too vague and undefined as a fictional character to achieve this closure. "Renaldo is everybody," Dylan told Ginsberg. "Don't you identify with Renaldo?" (1989, 11). But it is hard to identify with "everybody." What does hold the film together is not Renaldo but Bob Dylan, not the actor but the singer. Dylan's music, recorded in the intense and passionate performances of the Rolling Thunder Revue, continually grounds *Renaldo and Clara* in emotional reality. That reality is both *inside* the movie (in the songs we see performed on stage) and *outside* it (in the songs' independent existence). So *Renaldo and Clara* cannot have a center in the traditional manner. Any center is immediately split and doubled, consigned to the play of doubles that forms the movie's texture. The center is both inside the film and outside it; it is both Renaldo and Bob, I and I.

"Female Rambling Sailor"

In 1992, in a rare response to shouted requests from the crowd, Bob Dylan told an audience: "This one's got all that stuff in it. You'll see—all that and more!" But what "this one" turned out to be was not one of his own songs, but a traditional ballad called "Golden Vanity." And "all that stuff" was pure emotion—love, death, betrayal, sacrifice—and pure poetry.

From the early 1990s on, Dylan has sprinkled his concerts with other people's songs—ballads, blues, gospel, bluegrass—providing his fans with a veritable history of musical tradition. Back in the sixties he had done more than any other performer to change the image of the "folksinger" from someone who performed traditional songs to someone who felt obliged to write his own compositions: the "singer-songwriter." In the nineties Dylan seemed intent on righting that balance.

Among the traditional broadside ballads, Dylan in the early 1990s showed a small but marked interest in the sub-genre often referred to as "trouser songs": that is, ballads about women who dress up as men and go off to sea, often to follow their lovers.[1] Songs of this type show up on both the albums of traditional songs which Dylan issued at this time: "Canadee-i-o" on *Good As I Been To You* (1992) and "Jack-A-Roe" on *World Gone Wrong* (1993). But perhaps the most interesting of these songs is "Female Rambling Sailor," which Dylan performed six times in concert in 1992, but has never recorded.

"Female Rambling Sailor" is of British origin. The place names—Gravesend, the River Thames—seem to be English, though Dianne Dugaw speculates that the song may in fact come from Ireland. A surviving broadside text from the 1820s features a "before-and-after" illustration of the female rambling sailor. The song has also been collected in Australia, and it may well be there that Dylan learned it.[2]

Most trouser songs work toward a happy ending. In "Jack-A-Roe" the young woman successfully disguises herself, follows her departed lover, finds him wounded in a battle, heals him, and marries him. In "Canadee-i-o" the woman is abandoned by her faithless lover, but ends up married to the ship's captain instead. "Female Rambling Sailor," however, briskly dismisses any such possibility:

> Her true love he was pressed away
> And drownded in some foreign sea
> Which caused this fair maid to say
> I'll be a rambling sailor

The lover is killed off at the beginning of the song; there is never any question of her finding him and bringing him back. Indeed, it is the knowledge of his death which *causes* this woman to go to sea. It is the sea itself, the life of a sailor, which becomes her "heart's delight" (as opposed to the lover who was "pressed away": that is, he was an involuntary conscript, not someone who chose to be a sailor). The song repeatedly stresses her courage, and her competence: "No sailor there could her excel." The romantic plot, which normally works to recuperate the protagonist back into a conventional woman's role, is here very firmly refused.

She does die, however. The song can't quite let such a drastic transgression of gender propriety go unpunished. She dies by accident, in a fall, and we are then given a nicely comic recognition scene:

> When her lily white breast in sight it came
> It appeared to be a female's frame
> Rebecca Young it was the name
> Of the female rambling sailor

Given this book's whole emphasis on the proper name and the alias, it will come as no surprise when I say that "Rebecca Young" interests me greatly, and that I suspect that at some level Dylan also was taken by this detail (as well as by the song's lovely and intricate tune).

Most obviously, what is going on here is the recuperation of the heroine into a properly female role. The "lily white breast" and the name go together; both are signals of traditional gender. In death the woman is returned to her female body and to her "proper" name. The name is the grounding of the woman's reality, which she had attempted to escape but by which she is now reclaimed.

But the song continues to subvert this recuperation. For one thing, the name itself, in its *im*proper sense, restores her to life and vigor: young. Perhaps even "forever young." And having given us the proper name, just this once, the song proceeds to ignore it: in all the succeeding verses, up to and including the last line of the song, the protagonist is again referred to only as "female rambling sailor." This is, after all, the name she has *chosen* for herself. Her identity. Her alias.

chapter 7
Summations

Summation 1: The Years of Creation—"Visions of Johanna"

If there is one song which acts as a summation of what I called in Chapter 1 Dylan's Years of Creation, it would be "Visions of Johanna." Indeed, if you shoved me up against a wall, put a gun to my head, and asked me what single song was Bob Dylan's best, I would swallow hard, silently ask pardon from the ghost of Blind Willie McTell, and answer "Visions of Johanna" (L, 223–24).

The song was written in late 1965, and in its earliest version it was known by the title "Freeze Out."[1] The first known concert performance was on December 4. Several studio versions were recorded between November 1965 and (the definitive version, as released on *Blonde on Blonde)* February 1966.[2] (One of these versions is known as "Nightingale's Code," because of an extra line in the final verse: "He examines the nightingale's code.") The song remained in Dylan's repertoire throughout 1966, and has made regular though not frequent appearances ever since.[3] While all these versions differ in terms of musical style, the words have remained, for Dylan, remarkably constant, though in recent years he tends to omit the third verse, "Little boy lost. . . ." (For those interested in biographical details: Dylan's affair with Joan Baez had effectively ended by May 1965, six months before the song was written. He married Sara Lowndes on November 22, about a week before the song was first performed in public.)

"Visions of Johanna" is structured around two fundamental oppositions: the opposition of presence to absence, especially in relation to the absence of Johanna; and that of enclosure to expansion, the song's spatial movement back and forth between physical enclosure and mental or psychic opening out. I see these oppositions as pairs of binary opposites: terms which are apparently opposed to each other, but which may paradoxically conceal an underlying unity. If I were to privilege any of these terms, it would be *absence*. Dylan seems to me a great poet of absence, from the unsupplied "answer" blowing in the wind all the way through to the fatal destiny which is "not dark yet—but it's getting there." As suggested in the section on the Basement Tapes, one of Dylan's greatest songs is a statement of absence: "I'm Not There." Just like Johanna.

The song begins in an enclosed space (a room, *ein Zimmer),* but it immediately suggests expansion: "Ain't it just like the night to play tricks when you're tryin' to be so quiet?" That is, the night is a trickster; the enclosed space of the room is immediately exploded into the multiple possibilities of trickster indeterminacy.

What is the effect of this line being posed as a *question?* It does not seem to be a question posed *to* anyone within the song; rather, it seems addressed to the listeners, and as such, it is purely rhetorical. The listeners, by definition, cannot respond; even if they could, the form of the question clearly expects a positive answer. It would scarcely be appropriate for anyone to reply: "Well, no, actually, a propensity to play tricks has never struck me as being especially characteristic of the night." And yet it *is* an odd, idiosyncratic observation. It suggests a fundamental disharmony between human emotions and the natural environment: what is "just like the night" is that it is alien, opposed to the singer's wishes and expectations. This conclusion may strike us as having undoubted emotional truth for an individual (the singer) in a particular situation (this song), but it can't really be supported as a general proposition about the nature of nights. What the form of the question does, then, is to pull the listeners into complicity with the singer. Answering "Yes," we are solicited to accept his point of view, to give him our tacit agreement. The simple formula "Ain't it?" has already positioned us in the song, and preconditioned us to accept whatever the singer has to tell us.

"We sit here stranded," the song continues, "though we're all doin' our best to deny it." How many people are included in this "we"? If the line continues the generalizing mode of the opening, then *we* could again equal *everyone.* Being "stranded" (and attempting to deny being stranded) is the general condition of humanity, just as playing tricks is the general condition of the night.

Alternatively the *we* could be another gesture, like the rhetorical question of the first line, to implicate the listeners, to pull them into the same position as the singer.

Another possibility is that this line could introduce us to the specific narrative situation in the song, the characters "in this room." How many are there? The lowest possible number is two—the singer and Louise. The problem is the word *all,* which is not usually applied to two people: *both* would be a more normal usage. When I first began listening to the song, back in 1966, I always envisioned a small group of people, about five or six, gathered in a dark room.[4] It is possible that the *all* includes not just those who are physically present (the singer and Louise) but also all those who are spiritually present: Johanna, and all the other characters who progressively appear as the song widens its scope beyond the enclosed room—the all-night girls, the night watchman, the "little boy lost," the women in the museum, the peddler, the fiddler, and so on.

The question of who is included in *we* is the first pointer to the insistent *absence* of Johanna, a physical absence which is always also a spiritual presence. The song begins in a room, in a confined setting with a limited cast of characters, but from that point it steadily expands, until reaching the ultimate explosion of the singer's consciousness.

Louise, meanwhile, "holds a handful of rain." *Rain* can be seen as a drug reference, like so many of Dylan's uses of the word in the mid-1960s—"lost in the rain in Juarez," "the rainman gave me two cures" (L, 207, 229). Dylan denied that "Visions of Johanna" was "a drug song." As he told an audience in England in May 1966, "it's just vulgar to think so." The irony is that, at the moment he said this, he sounded very much as if he was stoned out of his mind. Even so, the word *vulgar* was exquisitely chosen for an English audience. It's not a question of morals, but one of taste. "Visions of Johanna" may or may not be about drugs, but it's not good manners to say so in public. (In the same vein, in 1991 Dylan introduced "Rainy Day Women" as "one of my early anti-drug songs"!)

The trouble with "drug songs" is that the interpretation tends to be reductive: once you've said a song is about drugs, that absolves you from having to say anything else about it. All meanings become reduced to the one meaning. Drugs are undoubtedly part of "Visions of Johanna." The whole song can be read as the gradual onrush of a psychedelic hallucination, starting within the realistic confines of the one room and moving out to the surrealist action of the final verse, in which "my conscience explodes." But drugs are scarcely the whole story—it's just vulgar to think so.

Rain has other resonances within Dylan's work. In "The night blows cold and rainy," it is associated with the loneliness and fragility of his lover, who is outside in the rain, "At my window with a broken wing" (L, 167). In "Chimes of Freedom" it is a force of liberation and the proclamation of truth, as "the rain unraveled tales / For the disrobed faceless forms of no position" (L, 132). In "Lay Down Your Weary Tune" it is part of the triumphant celebration of pantheistic unity through all nature: "The cryin' rain like a trumpet sang / And asked for no applause" (L, 120). In "Percy's Song" the repeated chorus, "Turn, turn to the rain / And the wind" (L, 121) suggests that the rain is an emblem of fate or destiny. Most memorably of all, that destiny becomes the apocalyptic fate of all humanity in "A Hard Rain's A-Gonna Fall" (L, 59–60).

All of these associations could be read into Louise's "handful of rain." Certainly the song is about loneliness and vulnerability, and there is a strong sense of overshadowing destiny, imminent death. At the same time, *rain* can be an image of life, of fecundity and growth, of the returning spring—"Western wind, when wilt thou blow, / The small rain down can rain?" If Johanna's visions are deeply ambiguous and often associated with death, then perhaps what Louise offers here is an alternative vision, a handful of life.

Finally, quite simply, why not take the line literally? Louise holds, cupped in her hand, a handful of rain. Perhaps she has just reached out a window and gathered it in. It will not stay there long: cupped hands are not a stable or permanent container. Very soon, the rain will trickle through her fingers and be lost.

But Louise is also "tempting you to defy it." How do you "defy" rain, in all the various senses outlined above? If *rain* is a drug, then to defy it is presumably to refuse to use it. If rain has some more general, emotional meaning, such as loneliness or destiny, then to defy it is to refuse to submit, but rather to assert your own worth and survival against the "cruel" rain, the "hard" rain. However one reads it, the action of defiance seems to be a praiseworthy one. The odd word then is *tempting*. A temptation is usually an inducement to do something that you should *not* do. Can you be "tempted" to do good? Louise is pictured here in one of the stereotypical female roles, that of temptress. But she is not tempting you to join her in her addiction (if that's what it is); she is tempting you to *defy* it. Louise is always an ambivalent character. It is typical that her gesture should be one both of positive action and of temptation.

The following lines—"Lights flicker from the opposite loft . . ."—set a scene: not just the physical location but a mood, an emotional ambience. "This room" is an enclosed space, but the idea of enclosure is evoked by words which simultaneously open that space out. The "opposite" loft suggests that "this room" too is a loft, that is, an unusually *large* room; and "opposite" already takes us out of this room, across the street, beginning the song's outward momentum.

In 1965, the reference to country music might well have been understood as condescending, especially for the hip urban circles that Bob Dylan was moving in. But Dylan's later move to country music—and the very fact that the definitive track of this song was recorded in Nashville—should prevent us from seeing too much disparagement in "nothing, really nothing to turn off." Dylan's knowledge and respect for all forms of American popular music can never be underestimated.

What the lines mostly convey is a feeling of weariness, of things running down: images of energy failing or muted, lights that "flicker," heat pipes malfunctioning, the radio turned down. "Nothing, really nothing to turn off" conveys weariness on the edge of total apathy. Nothing of any importance or vitality is happening in this room . . .

"Just Louise and her lover so entwined"—a partial exception, perhaps, to that lack of energy? But *entwined* suggests a motionless embrace rather than active lovemaking; the aura of passivity is reinforced if we take "her lover" to be a reference to the singer himself, distanced in the third person. Is this lover to be equated with the singer, or is this lover a third character, as yet unnamed, male or even female? Either way, the mood of passivity is enhanced: whether seeing himself from a distance, or watching other people make love, the singer is uninvolved in the dramatic situation. His attention, his thoughts, and his emotions are engaged elsewhere—focused, as always, on the absent Johanna.

"And these visions of Johanna that conquer my mind." *Conquer* is by far the most active verb of this first stanza. After a whole string of images that suggest lassitude and passivity—stranded, deny, flicker, cough, play soft, turn off—comes the sudden, active incursion of *conquer*. Johanna does not sidle into the singer's mind; she takes it over by force, like an invading army.

Although physically absent from the room, she dominates the scene. The first-person pronoun *my* appears in the song for the first time, only to surrender its territory.

What significance can be attached to the name "Johanna"? There are two major possibilities.

The first is the biographical interpretation, that "Johanna" is intended to recall Joan Baez. Johanna's insistent *absence* in the song could be related to the ending of Dylan's affair with Baez earlier that year: Johanna, indeed, is "not here." Well, maybe so—though to argue that Dylan was writing and first performing a song dominated by Joan Baez during the week of his marriage to Sara seems a bit much to me. But even if it's true, this interpretation adds nothing to the song. The character of Johanna and the nature of her visions are in no way illuminated or expanded by an identification with Joan Baez. For this reason alone, I would set the biographical reading aside, as being, at best, irrelevant.[5]

The second reading of "Johanna" does seem to add meaning and richness to the song. I first heard "Visions of Johanna" when Dylan sang it in concert in Vancouver in March 1966, and, until *Blonde on Blonde* came out several months later, I was quite convinced that I had heard a great Dylan song called "Visions of Gehenna."

> Gehenna: 1. The place of future torment, hell. 2. A place of torture; a prison.
>
> *(Oxford English Dictionary)*

Gehenna is the word for "hell" in the Greek and Latin New Testaments. In medieval Latin it also referred to the process of judicial torture.

I have no way of knowing whether Bob Dylan intended this association to be made (though in performance he has always emphasized the aspiration of the *h*: Jo-*H*anna). In the text as we experience it, irrespective of authorial intention, these sinister connotations of *Gehenna* always shadow the image of Johanna. The two definitions in the *Oxford English Dictionary* correspond to the two major themes I am proposing. As hell, the place of *future* torment, *Gehenna* speaks to absence: it is not yet here, and paradoxically, when it *is* here, it will be the greatest absence of all, the absence of heaven. And as a prison, as the place of judicial torture, it is an ultimate image of enclosure.

As for the visions, there is a grammatical ambiguity built into the preposition *of.* These are visions *of* Johanna in the sense that Johanna herself is what is seen, is the subject matter of the visions. So if you ask, what does the singer actually *see* in these visions, one answer is quite simply: Johanna herself. At the same time, the phrase can mean visions *belonging to* or *originating from* Johanna. In this case the singer's mind has been "conquered" even more thoroughly: he sees what Johanna sees; her perceptions have become his. Note also that the word *visions* is in the plural—not *a* vision, not one fixed way of looking at the world, but several visions, a multiplicity of viewpoints.

Visions are notoriously difficult to describe. Almost by definition, they are beyond definition. Often what a poet or mystic does is not so much try to describe the actual content of the vision as to re-create the conditions in which the vision took place. But the poem will do so from within the transformed consciousness of the vision itself, so the poem becomes circular, self-reflexive, self-referential. "These visions of Johanna"—five times repeated, *these* visions. The visions are the song itself. The visions describe the conditions of their own taking place. What is it that the visions of Johanna tell you? They tell you that Johanna's not here.

Johanna's absence is the whole point of the song. Its ramifications are endless, but let me here state three possible inflections.

1) Absence is death. It is possible that Johanna is dead. Whether or not that is true, the imagery that surrounds her is full of intimations of death: ghost, skeleton, Gehenna.

2) In linguistics, *absence* is the condition of the sign. A sign always points to something that is not there; meaning is always deferred somewhere else. (This is the main line of linguistic theory, from Saussure to Derrida.)

3) As in any binary pair, one term implies and underwrites the other. The image of Johanna's absence is shot through with the image of her presence. Her "visions" have more immediacy and reality for the singer than does the actual presence of Louise. Johanna's absence *fills* the song.

In the second stanza the song begins its process of opening out from the enclosed room and the confined cast of characters. We move quickly from the room to the neighboring lot to the suburban train. In addition to the singer and Louise, we have an unspecified number of "ladies" and "all-night girls." But the emotional mood hasn't changed. The lot is "empty," with the same vacancy, the same lack of energy as the flickering lights. There is an implied moral vacancy as well: "all-night girls" and "escapades" suggest a kind of desperate, forced gaiety as a cover for the reality of prostitution.

At the same time, the "key chain" restates the image of imprisonment. The sexual "freedom" they appear to be enjoying (swapping partners via their keychains) is itself another form of enslavement. When "the all-night girls . . . whisper of escapades," surely the word *escape* is itself imprisoned inside *escapade.* The song sees these women as sad and empty, trapped inside a bleak and meaningless charade of freedom.

Louise reenters, with the description that "She's delicate and seems like the mirror"—a phrase which has been the source for repeated and creative mishearings, from "veneer" to "Vermeer." But it's just Bob Dylan's odd way of pronouncing *mirror.*

The mirror is a complex image, with multiple cultural connotations. Like the ghost, the double, the alias, it is one of Dylan's repeated images of deferred identity, the self at one remove. It can be used to suggest a view of the self which is variously accurate, idealized, or distorted:

> • A mirror gives you an accurate picture of yourself, as you really are, without flattering disguises or self-deceptions.
>
> • Especially in Renaissance times, the mirror presented an idealized image, you as you ought to be, a model to aspire to. (See various books of advice and moral precepts with titles like *A Mirror for Princes.)* In psychoanalysis "the mirror stage" describes the way in which the human infant forms an idealized self-image.
>
> • More frequently in modern times, the emphasis has been on distortion: the fact that a mirror provides a *reversed* image, in which all values are also reversed.

So the mirror is, broadly speaking, an image of truth or self-knowledge, but it does come in these three different, and indeed contradictory, inflections. What kind of mirror is Louise? What, or who, is she a mirror *of?*

On the one hand, Louise may be the mirror reflection *of Johanna*. In this case it seems that distortion or reversal is the primary inflection. Louise is everything that Johanna is not. She is physical while Johanna is spiritual; she is very much *here*, while Johanna is absent—is, indeed, absence itself. As a mirror image, Louise "makes it all too concise and too clear." What her mirror shows, in all its concision and clarity, is that "Johanna's not here."

On the other hand, Louise could be the mirror image in which the singer sees *himself*. He and Louise are very much alike—perhaps even "entwined"— and both of them feel acutely their separation from Johanna. The visions that conquer *his* mind in the first verse are now about to occupy *her* face. Within the surrealist landscape of the song, all the other characters act as his reflections, or projections; all of them "seem like the mirror." But if Louise, in this sense, presents the singer with an accurate reflection of himself, there is no guarantee that he sees or understands it—"like Louise always says / 'Ya can't look at much, can ya man?' " This line recalls T. S. Eliot: "human kind / Cannot bear very much reality" (1963, 190). The mirror tells a truth which is not always palatable.[6]

So consider, finally, the curious equivocation of "seems like the mirror." How do you *seem* like a mirror? A mirror is itself a visual illusion. Another association of mirrors is with trickery—"they do it with mirrors"—with making things *seem* to be what they're not. Louise is the semblance of a semblance, the illusion of an illusion. The phrase "seems like" sets up a dizzying recession of images, like an array of facing mirrors which multiply reflections into infinity. But perhaps the equivocation protects Louise herself. As a mirror, whether of Johanna or for the singer, she exists only in relation to other people, in a subsidiary role. What she is as herself, the part of her that is not dependent on either Johanna or the singer, is held back, guarded behind the deferral of *seems*.

Louise "makes it all too concise and too clear. . . ." *Too* implies a criticism. The singer doesn't want things to be concise and clear; he prefers expansiveness and vagueness. Louise, with her down-to-earth realism, cuts straight to the point—"Johanna's not here." The singer wants to work around that point, as if to disguise the brute fact of her absence. So the song becomes ever less concise and clear. As its verses progress, it moves out into an ever wider, more surrealistic landscape. Louise's vision—clear, concise, realistic—is seen as too restricted, too reductive, in comparison with the vision(s) of the absent Johanna.

Then: "The ghost of 'lectricity howls in the bones of her face." Well, what can you say? If "Visions of Johanna" is ultimately my favorite Dylan song, then this is my favorite Dylan line. John Herdman refers it to French Symbolist poetry: it "finely exemplifies Baudelaire's theory of [correspondences] and might well have been envied by . . . Rimbaud" (29). It might well have been envied by any poet who has ever written.

It is a beautiful line; it is a terrifying line. Perhaps it speaks of a kind of ravaged, hollowed-out beauty in Louise's face, but it also speaks of death and imprisonment. The ghost howls in the Gehenna of its bones. As with the lights flickering in the first verse, the energy of electricity has died, has become a ghost of itself. Over and over, the song returns to *remains,* to what's left: the flickering lights, the useless memories, the paintings in museums, the corroding empty cage. The visions of Johanna are "all that remain," all those remains. They *are* the ghost that howls, imprisoned, in Louise's face.

In the third stanza the song continues to broaden out. From the enclosed room of verse 1, and the "empty lot" of verse 2, we are now out "in the hall"—of the same building? of another building?

The cast of characters has expanded too. At a literal level, the "little boy" is a new character (unless he is to be identified with Louise's "lover" in verse 1). He and the singer are both portrayed in relation to an unnamed "her," who could be Louise, or Johanna, or yet another new character. This lack of specific reference is a common feature of Dylan's pronouns. At a more symbolic level, the "little boy lost" can be read as a projection of the singer himself, dividing and objectifying an aspect of his own personality. (Certainly it is biographically true of Dylan at this time that he was not immune to the charges that "He brags of his misery, he likes to live dangerously.")

The little boy is the target of a criticism which may well be all the more scathing for being self-criticism. Aidan Day speaks of "the little boy's embarrassing self-parade and the speaker's disdain for that parade of self" (120). John Herdman writes of how "the blatancy of those piled-up internal rhymes—gall, all, small talk, wall, hall—[embodies] the effrontery of the little boy's hypocrisy" (29). There is a juvenile posturing here which seems far removed from either the world-weary realism of Louise or the visionary insubstantiality of Johanna. The portrait is brilliantly done, but the little boy is just too easy a target for Dylan's sarcasm—which may be why this verse seems the thinnest in texture, the least interesting section of "Visions of Johanna" (and, thus, the verse which Dylan has most often omitted in concert).

Even the chorus lines of this verse are much thinner than those that have gone before. After "The ghost of 'lectricity howls in the bones of her face," I suppose anything would be a comedown, but "How can I explain? / Oh, it's so hard to get on" seems to take anticlimax a little *too* far. Perhaps it is the "little boy lost" who speaks these lines: they have a whining, self-pitying quality found nowhere else in the song.

By contrast, the fourth stanza opens with the most daring leap in the song: "Inside the museums, Infinity goes up on trial." The previous transitions—from the room to the empty lot outside; from Louise and Johanna to the "little boy lost"—could at least be located within a continuing dramatic situation. But the fourth verse affords no direct connections to the previous three. None of the same characters appear, and the setting—even the time of day—shifts totally. It is only by virtue of thematic links and parallels that this verse maintains the continuity of "Visions of Johanna."

The first thematic link is the continued outward movement. From room to empty lot to hall, all more or less private places, we are now in a public location, a museum. It is still a real place—the next verse takes us to an entirely imaginary setting—but it is a place far removed from the intense privacy and self-enclosure of the original room.

A museum is a paradoxical space. In terms of public or private spaces, works of art offer a wide range. Some were designed to be seen in public places, on a large scale—murals, altarpieces. Some were designed for more private situations—the easel-painting, whose dominance in the history of Western art stems from its amenability to being possessed, placed in a room in its proud purchaser's home. The museum puts them all into a public space, open at certain hours each day, within which each viewer is invited, as it were, to re-create a private space. How often have you stood in a museum waiting until someone moves out of the way so that you can have an uninterrupted view, so that you can commune in peace with your favorite Cézanne? How often have you left the room in which the tour guide is talking? It is difficult to create a private space for yourself in a museum—you could never do it, for instance, in front of the *Mona Lisa* in the Louvre, with its constant hordes of tourists, with its shield of bulletproof glass—yet that privacy seems a condition which the works of art themselves demand.

Paintings are uneasy in museums. There is something about the museum setting that works against the ideal conditions—privacy, peace, prolonged exposure—in which paintings should be viewed. In the museum, the painting "goes up on trial." It is there to be ranked, cataloged, criticized, used as an object in art history. The work of art is often seen as an emblem of freedom—of the creator's free imagination, of the liberating influence it may have on its viewers—but in the museum this freedom is enclosed, put on trial. (One meaning of *Gehenna* is "judicial torture.")

In Dylan's line this tension is expressed by the paradox of "Infinity" being put "on trial." By definition, infinity is beyond all restrictions: it *cannot* be put on trial. What the museum does—what all structures of cultural institutionalization do—is to *attempt* to confine, measure, categorize, and contain objects which are, in fact, beyond confinement, measurement, category, or containment. We are back at the theme of expansion and restriction, here stated in its most acute form. The song has expanded its view, beyond the private room and into the social world, but what it meets in that social world is another, stronger image of confinement. Inside the museum, we will find the forces of freedom—infinity, salvation, the *Mona Lisa*, Johanna—surrounded by, and fighting against, the forces of imprisonment.

"Voices echo this is what salvation must be like after a while." What voices? Whose voices? This judgment is delivered anonymously by an impersonal and deferred authority. Perhaps the echoing voices are the "voices" of the paintings themselves. Perhaps they "echo" down the museum's long, empty halls and galleries. Again, the singer subtly avoids his own responsibility for the opinions expressed. Just as in the first verse he had enlisted the listener's agreement by the form of the question "Ain't it just like the night," so here the source of the judgment is deflected onto these anonymous "voices" and, even further, onto the *echoes* of these voices.

The voices do not say what salvation *is* like, only what it *must be* like. The museum, or the work of art, provides a glimpse of something you cannot fully know, an intuition rather than a certainty. The paradox is that within "Infinity," which is timeless, the words "after a while" would have no meaning. But we are not yet truly in "Infinity": we are, instead, stuck "inside the museums." This line expresses a weary cynicism in keeping with the mood of the song. Even salvation, it suggests, must get boring. Even the ideal state becomes a prison. The paintings in the museum long for change, for movement, for anything. Almost twenty years later, in "Don't Fall Apart on Me Tonight" (1983), Dylan returned to the same image, in the same setting:

> But it's like I'm stuck inside a painting
> That's hanging in the Louvre,
> My throat start to tickle and my nose itches
> But I know that I can't move.

> (L, 483)

As a supreme example of art trapped in the museum, Dylan offers the *Mona Lisa* and famously speculates that she "musta had the highway blues / You can tell by the way she smiles."[7] The *Mona Lisa* has long been the object of this kind of speculation: endless attempts to *say*, in words, what her famous smile "means."[8] The *Mona Lisa* is notoriously self-sufficient; that smile seems to suggest a secret which can never be told. The visual can do without the verbal. But at the same time, the smile cries out for interpretation; it wants stories to be told about it, it wants words. The painting demands that some irreverent young hipster come along and say, "Mona Lisa musta had the highway blues / You can tell by the way she smiles."

"Highway blues" is an image of endemic restlessness, a longing to be somewhere else, a desire to be (in the Dylan/Kerouac phrase) "on the road again." So one reference point for Mona Lisa is Johanna. Like Mona Lisa, Johanna is presented in the song as an emblem of feminine mystery: elusive, never quite definable, absent. What that smile says is that Mona Lisa is always *somewhere else*. However present she may be to the painter's vision and brush, the smile guards a secret place that Leonardo will never penetrate. Like Johanna, she has her own visions, private and unknowable, and they make her smile.

The images in the first half of this verse sum up the two structuring binary pairs: presence/absence and enclosure/expansion. Inside the museum, the image of Mona Lisa is present and enclosed, but it contains within itself the possibility of being absent (on the highway) and of breaking away entirely from the "trial" to which the institution of the museum subjects it. If Mona Lisa stands most obviously for Johanna, she also stands for Louise (there are faint echoes of both names: Mona / Johanna; Lisa / Louise). Louise, much more than Johanna, feels the restriction and imprisonment of being on display. And Mona Lisa, behind her screen of bulletproof glass in the Louvre, might very well look out at the constant crowds of tourists watching her, and say, like Louise always does, "Ya can't look at much, can ya man?"

The second half of the verse turns from the paintings in the museum toward the spectators. "See the primitive wallflower freeze," it begins. Again the listener is addressed directly, but this time without the appeal for agreement and complicity implied by the rhetorical question "Ain't it . . .?" This time the address is in the imperative mood: *see*. An apposite word, one might think, since we're in a museum. But of course, the listener to a song can never truly "see," only hear. And what follows is, in fact, something to listen to: a complex series of puns and wordplay.

The word *freeze* is printed in the *Lyrics* as *f-r-e-e-z-e*; that is, as a verb, to be very cold, or metaphorically, to become motionless. That reading encourages us to understand *wallflower* in its sense as a person who has not been asked to dance, a neglected outsider. (A few years later, Dylan did in fact write: "Wallflower, wallflower / Won't you dance with me? / I'm sad and lonely too" (L, 301). His son Jakob would adopt this usage as the name of his band, The Wallflowers.) So the "wallflower" would "freeze" in the sense that the person excluded from the celebration would be left, alone and motionless, on the outside. The line would, then, relate to other images of loneliness and exclusion, such as the "little boy lost," last seen "muttering small talk at the wall." The working title of this song was "Freeze Out."

But *freeze* can also be spelled *f-r-i-e-z-e*, in which case it means a horizontal band of painting or decoration on a wall. This sense works much better in the museum setting, and provides a possible application for "primitive." What we are being asked to "see" is another museum image: a frieze, or mural painting, in a so-called primitive style, of flowers painted on a wall.

These two senses coexist in the line, neither one canceling out the other. What we are asked to "see" is something we can only *hear*: the indeterminacy of the freeze/frieze pun. Both senses convey an image of delicacy and fragility—the wallflower frozen out at the dance, the frieze preserved in the museum—which stands in stark contrast to the grossness of the image which immediately follows—the "jelly-faced women," one of them with a mustache, who "can't find their knees."

These women are gross caricatures of uncultured museum visitors who cannot appreciate the artistic images in front of them. In these lines we can hear the sneering, put-down tone of Dylan at his least sympathetic: the kind of vicious but easy vituperation in which (so all the biographies inform us) Dylan and his circle tended to indulge themselves. As with the sarcasm directed, in the previous verse, at the "little boy lost," the target is just too obvious, and the lines are too mean-spirited to be truly effective.

But another curious echo lurks in these lines: the infamous painting by Marcel Duchamp entitled *LHOOQ* (1919). What Duchamp did was to take a reproduction of the *Mona Lisa* (in which the subject, being three-quarter length, has no knees) and draw a mustache and beard on it. Then he added the title, which reads in French as an obscene pun. The two gestures—mustache and pun—are both adolescent nose-thumbing at the seriousness of "high art," and at the institutionalization of the museum which places the *Mona Lisa* behind bulletproof glass. Duchamp's gestures are performed with a cool, detached irony. While puncturing the pretension which surrounds the adulation of the *Mona Lisa,* he also proposes that his own piece, which is deliberately devoid of conventional artistic "craft," is just as worthy of a place "inside the museums" as Leonardo's masterpiece.[9]

If Duchamp's image is an irreverent parody of the *Mona Lisa,* then Dylan's line can also be read as an equally irreverent—indeed, savage—parody of Johanna. The singer, perhaps, is beginning to resent the saintlike image he has himself created. Having given us Johanna as Mona Lisa, perfect image of ethereal enigma, he now gives us the exact opposite, the grossly physical "jelly-faced women," of whom the little boy lost sniggers, in Duchamp's French letter pun, "Elle a chaud au cul."

Marcel Duchamp has taken us from the classical painting of Leonardo to the modern art of Surrealism. Much of Dylan's poetry in the mid-1960s was indebted to his reading of the French Symbolist poets, especially Rimbaud, who were also influential in the development of French Surrealist painting in the 1920s. A central technique of Surrealism, the sudden juxtaposition of bizarrely unrelated objects, was derived from a line by Lautréamont: "the chance meeting, on a dissection table, of an umbrella and a sewing-machine." Dylan's songs in the mid-1960s are full of such meetings (which could also, of course, be seen as the results of drug-induced hallucinations), and here he produces one of his finest: "jewels and binoculars hang from the head of the mule." Poetically the danger is that the technique becomes just too easy, too predictable: *any* juxtaposition of unrelated objects serves the purpose, and the novelty fades very quickly.

I think this line works better than most—partly because of its internal patterns of rhyme and alliteration (jewel/mule; hang/head), but mainly because of the subtle variations it plays on the themes of the preceding stanza. We have been concerned with painting, and with vision: the painter's vision that creates the *Mona Lisa,* the spectator's vision that reads her smile, the scornful vision that ridicules the "jelly-faced women," the ironic vision that draws a mustache on the *Mona Lisa.* "Jewels" and "binoculars" are both concerned with vision. Jewels are objects of vision, beautiful things to look at. They are also supplementary, added to the beauty of a woman—is it relevant here that Mona Lisa wears no jewels? Binoculars are an instrument of vision, improving it in some cases, but singularly ineffective and inapposite for looking at paintings. Both in turn are irrelevant to the mule that wears them, or is forced to wear them.

The whole stanza, then, may be read as dealing with the distortion of vision: infinity put up on trial, salvation turning against itself, paintings stifled in the museums, Mona Lisa longing for the highway, Leonardo's painting defaced by Duchamp—all culminating in this dumb, patient beast who bears the instruments of a vision which is totally alien to him. The "visions of Johanna" are becoming progressively darker.

The final stanza of the song completes its outward journey, from the private room to the social world of the museum to a frankly imaginary landscape of surreal or "psychedelic" images. Instead of named characters (Louise, Johanna), we now have symbolic characters, named by their function—peddler, countess, fiddler. These may be seen as entirely new figures, appearing and disappearing as they flash briefly across this fast succession of images, but it is more interesting to see them as continuations of the same characters in new guises. Thus, I see both the "peddler" and the "fiddler" as further projections of the singer himself. "Madonna" is clearly Johanna, and the "countess" is probably Louise.

In terms of the binary opposition of enclosure and expansion, this shift in tone can be seen either way. As a movement outward, it represents the final liberation of the singer's mind and imagination. Unrestricted by the confines of the room in which the song started, he now moves freely into a world where his own imagination is the only law. But the recurrence there of the same obsessive figures—Johanna, Louise—suggests that this freedom is largely illusory. The movement outward is also a movement inward, into the enclosure of his own psyche.

The exchange of dialogue in the opening lines is described by John Herdman as "a tit-for-tat in terms of cynicism" (30), each stage marked by an increasing bitterness and callousness. "Peddler" suggests a vagabond, someone out on the road with something to sell, whereas "countess" suggests a social rank more exalted than anything previously associated with Louise—though the word is delivered with considerable irony and is undercut by the context. The major point is the incompatibility of the two figures, coming from opposite ends of the social spectrum. The countess may be engaged in social work, doing good deeds for the poor, "caring" for the peddler, but she is only "pretending to care." Any gesture of care or affection is quickly canceled out in the bleak world of this song.

The peddler responds to this hypocrisy, suggesting that everyone is a parasite, living on other people's needs or fears or troubles. Even the countess is a parasite on the peddler as she makes a show of her charity. It would indeed be difficult, if not impossible, to name someone who is *not* a parasite. Such a person, if he existed, would be a worthy object of prayer, in two senses.

- Such a person would be so rare that he would be the object of veneration and gratitude. You could say of prayer of thanks "for" his existence.
- You would say a prayer "for" him because he would *need* your prayers. Someone who managed to exist in the social world without being a parasite would be an innocent abroad, helpless, the prey of all those who *are* parasites. You would have to say a prayer "for" his simple survival.

Louise responds with her dismissive put-down: "Ya can't look at much, can ya man?" The emphasis on what can be *looked at* picks up not only the mirror references but also the whole problematic of vision in the previous verse. Louise stresses the limitation of the singer's vision—by contrast, presumably, to the vision of Johanna. But ironically the line also rebounds on Louise herself. She uses it to dismiss whatever insight, however pessimistic, might have been contained in the line about the parasite;[10] she refuses to acknowledge its possible truth. That is, *she herself* "can't look at much"; she uses the line to avoid dealing with the peddler's argument. Moreover, this evasion is a habitual gesture; the line is what Louise "always says." It is her stock response to anything that challenges her view of the world. Accusing other people of avoiding the truth, she avoids it herself.

Finally, Louise's words are undercut by her action. Whatever she thinks about the singer/peddler, nevertheless she "prepares for him." I take it that this line means that she prepares for a sexual encounter which both of them know will take place, despite all the rhetorical slanging matches they have been engaged in against each other. The countess and the peddler acknowledge that they are, sexually, parasites on each other. This remnant state is what remains for them, whatever they may say, in the continuing absence of Johanna.

That absence is restated by the reference to "Madonna" and her failure to appear. "Madonna" is the obvious, ultimate image for Johanna—so obvious, in fact, that one can detect a distinct air of sarcasm. The singer, frankly, is getting a little pissed off with Johanna. This disillusionment comes across partly in the vocal delivery, partly in the contrast between the dignity of "Madonna" and the colloquial *showed*. Her absence is beginning to irritate him; the line comes as a caustic commentary on the contrast between Johanna's reticent purity and the cynical realism of Louise's sexual "preparations." The whole song has been spent "waiting for Johanna," but, like Beckett's Godot, she shows no signs of showing up.

Instead, we see a cage, another image of enclosure, like the room, like the key chain, like the museum, like Gehenna. But this cage is already "empty"— Johanna is absent from all enclosing structures—and, moreover, it has lost its power to imprison. Its bars are corroded, rusted away. The corroded cage might be an image of liberation, but "there's nothing, really nothing" to set free. Johanna is freedom, but what use is freedom if it simply translates as absence? More positively, one might argue that the cage corrodes *because* it is empty, because it has lost its function and is no longer needed.

The following line indicates that the site of the cage is a stage (the identification being reinforced by the rhyme). The blue gown traditionally associated with the Virgin Mary now becomes a stage cape, flourished before an audience. Like a magician's cape, it enables Johanna to disappear. Johanna's absence seems like an *es-cape* from an imposed role: leaving the stage/cage behind, she moves into the invisibility of her visions.

Similarly the fiddler/peddler now "steps to the road." "The road" is a traditional site of freedom. Stepping there, he is going out on his own, or perhaps in search of Johanna. But "the road" is also, for a touring musician, the workplace. By 1966, it may be argued, Dylan was beginning to see "the road" as a prison, and the previous two rhymes have identified "stage" and "cage."

Next, the fiddler "writes ev'rything's been returned which was owed." Given the general cynicism and disillusion of the song, one might find this rather an unexpected line. It would seem more in keeping if *nothing* had been returned—as, for instance, in the 1967 song "Nothing Was Delivered." The "Nightingale's Code" recording gives a slightly different version; there, Dylan sings "Knowing everything's gone which was owed." But this whole section of the song—the rapid succession of short lines rhyming with *showed,* all leading up to the explosion of *explode*—is building a sense of finality. By the end of the song, after the explosion of the singer's conscience, nothing remains except the visions. The cage is empty, the truck is loaded, all debts have been settled. Nothing is left to get in the way of the final encounter with Johanna.

At this point the variant recording inserts the extra line: "He examines the nightingale's code / Still left on the fish-truck that loads."[11] The nightingale is noted for the beauty of its song, so to examine its code is, perhaps, to seek for the secret of that beauty. The peddler/fiddler (Dylan himself?) is searching for the source of artistic inspiration. At the same time, the nightingale is associated with death. Listening to the song of the nightingale, John Keats felt himself "half in love with easeful death," and wishing to "cease upon the midnight with no pain." Both associations—beauty and death—meet in the figure of Johanna. The nightingale is yet one more vision of Johanna. And, as always, she is absent. The code is her trace, her signature, left behind on the fish-truck; the nightingale itself, like the bird in Keats's poem, has flown on, out of sight.

And so, at the climax of the song, the singer's "conscience explodes." *Conscience* is used here, surely, as in Hamlet's soliloquy, in its sense as "consciousness," rather than as "moral guide." This line clinches one aspect of the "drug" interpretation: the hallucinogenic experience has been getting steadily weirder, more and more surrealist in tone, and at this point the drug finally takes over. Any remaining semblance of rational thought or communication vanishes, and the song can do nothing but end. *Ex*-plode continues to insist on the movement out, the expansion of consciousness, rather than *im*-plode, the collapse of the mind into itself, into its own visions. Still, it is a violent image, with the threat of destruction. What guarantee is there that an exploded conscience can ever put itself back together again?

"The harmonicas play," the singer sings. Well, *a* harmonica plays, at any rate; it is Bob Dylan's most characteristic instrument. But although Dylan carries with him a selection of harmonicas in different keys, it always appears as a solo instrument: I am unaware of any recording, at any point in Dylan's career, which features more than one harmonica at a time. Why the plural? Perhaps, with the explosion of his conscience, Dylan sees himself scattered and split: the elusive "I," the little boy lost, the peddler, the fiddler, all playing their various harmonicas?

None of the available recordings of "Visions of Johanna" features any extended harmonica solo by Dylan. The most usual pattern (in the *Blonde on Blonde* recording, and in the acoustic performances from 1966) is as follows: a brief harmonica introduction; harmonica "fills," about one line each, between each verse; and a harmonica closing, about two lines. The "Nightingale's Code" recording adds an extra harmonica fill before the second last line of each verse; that is, there is a brief harmonica phrase immediately before "The harmonicas play. . . ." For the most part, then, the harmonica is used for punctuation and for laconic commentary, rather than being allowed to extend into a full solo.

What the harmonicas play is "the skeleton keys and the rain." This line is a brilliant pulling together of the major themes and images of the whole song. *Skeleton*, on its own, suggests death. It takes us back to the various associations of Johanna with death: her absence, her ghost, Gehenna as the future state beyond death, even the missing nightingale. The image of an actual skeleton appears for a moment, and then (absence/presence) disappears into the phrase "skeleton keys." The double meaning of *keys* picks up on all the earlier references to enclosed spaces: to the "key chain," to the museum where "Infinity goes up on trial," and to the "empty cage" which rhymes with *stage*. A curious association here is that a *skeleton key* is usually thought of as a key which can *open* any lock: it is an image of liberation, of expansion. But logically a skeleton key can also *close* any lock; there is no reason why it should not also be an image of imprisonment.

Key is, as it were, the key word of the line. Besides its association with *skeleton,* it also works backward, to "harmonicas," and forward, to "rain." The harmonicas play in a certain musical key, a key here defined as "skeleton." That is, the harmonicas play in the key of death. Or, the harmonicas play in a key which will open every door, every possibility within the music. But *key* is also slang for a kilogram of heroin. The juxtaposition of *keys* and *rain* takes us back, one last time, to Louise and her "handful of rain." For a moment, Louise appears in the skeleton keys of the harmonica's music, before she too is swept away into the dissolution of the final line.

The whole line—"The harmonicas play the skeleton keys and the rain"—is a final assertion of the writer's mastery before the song vanishes into the silence of the visions. It stands alongside "The ghost of 'lectricity howls in the bones of her face" as one of those moments when the sheer brilliance of the imagery transfixes the listener. Long before you have any idea what the line "means," it embeds itself in your memory. These are the moments of poetry which remind us that behind and beyond all these characters—Johanna, Louise, the singer/peddler/fiddler—stands the figure of Bob Dylan, creator of this song. And for all its bleakness, cynicism, world-weariness, and despair, "Visions of Johanna" remains a work of art, something created, an assertion—no matter how dark its vision—of the poet's power.

Yet, in the last line—"these visions of Johanna are now all that remain"—he appears to stand aside from that power. The surrounding world that he has so brilliantly portrayed is now allowed to vanish. The singer moves entirely inside, into his visions; the visions have become his only reality—except insofar as the visions *are* the song. Given this circular self-referentiality, the outside world is not abandoned but re-created. The song describes the process by which the singer arrives at the point where the visions are all that remain, but the visions are, in turn, the condition for creating the song.

"All that remain"—what remains? What remains may be the remainder: what is left over, unneeded, a useless residue. *Remains,* in the plural, is a word for relics: bones, ghosts, skeletons. The skeleton keys and the r[em]ain. But what remains is also what survives, what refuses to die, what goes on stubbornly living.

The visions of Johanna remain paradoxical to the end. One can see this conclusion as utter defeat: the singer allowing his own mind to be occupied (conquered) by another person's vision. The singer loses all touch with the external, social world and moves into his own private Gehenna: a place of torment and trial. Equally, one can see the conclusion as victory: his conscience, exploded, is finally free from all restraints, and it can now move into the visionary reality in which creation is possible—the creation, for instance, of this song.

What happens after the voice has stopped singing? In most of the 1965–66 recordings, the harmonica comes in for one or two lines, then brings the song to a close. On the "Nightingale's Code" recording, however, Dylan adds, in the middle of the harmonica ending, a couple of vocal phrases. They sound like a wordless moan on the vowels *o* and *a*—the sounds of Johanna's name. They could be moans of pain or of pleasure, of grief or of sexual climax. They could be the voice signing off from the burden of words altogether, signaling the final takeover of the visions as an escape from language. I have no idea what they mean, really, but this is my favorite ending to the song. That wordless cry seems right to me. To quote Eliot again: "Words, beyond speech, reach into the silence" (1963, 194).

Summation 2: The Years of Commitment—"Brownsville Girl"

If there is one song which acts as a summation for Bob Dylan's career during what I call in Chapter 1 the Years of Commitment, it is "Brownsville Girl."[12] Like many major works in this phase, the song is a collaboration, between Dylan and Sam Shepard, and not the least intriguing thing about it is trying to figure out just who wrote what. The long, rambling lines have a kind of colloquial poetry that recalls Shepard's plays, but Dylan's half-spoken, half-sung delivery makes them entirely his.

Shepard recalls that he and Dylan "wrote [the song] together in the spring of 1985. . . . We spent two days writing the lyrics—Bob had previously composed the melody line, which was already down on tape."[13] Shepard's memory may be slightly at fault though, for the earliest version of the song—at this stage called "Danville Girl" or "New Danville Girl"—was recorded in December 1984. Reemerging as "Brownsville Girl," it was partially rerecorded in May 1986 and issued in July of that year on *Knocked Out Loaded*.

One previous attempt at a collaboration between the two had not worked out. Shepard was hired as a writer for the Rolling Thunder tour, to provide

dialogue for the film Dylan was making on that self-consciously mythic journey. But Shepard soon found it absurd to think of creating a fixed script for such
a wild, free-form improvisation as *Renaldo and Clara* was becoming. He left the
tour, though he later produced one of the best written accounts of it in his
Rolling Thunder Logbook.[14]

Other affinities between Sam Shepard and Bob Dylan exist.[15] Both came
from the Midwest and arrived in New York at age nineteen (Dylan in 1961,
Shepard in 1963). Both had assumed new names: Shepard's was adapted from
his given name, Samuel Shepard Rogers V—the disavowal being as much of the
number as of the patriarchal name. Dylan's productivity in the mid-1960s was
matched by Shepard's (sixteen plays staged in six years). A large photograph of
an iconic Bob Dylan is a major prop in Shepard's *Melodrama Play* (1967), and
Dylan is evoked in *The Tooth of Crime* (1972): "The big ones. Dylan, Jagger,
Townsend. All them cats broke codes. Time can't change that" (1981, 209).
Several of Shepard's early New York productions were directed by Jacques Levy,
who worked as stage director on the Rolling Thunder tour[16] and cowrote with
Dylan most of the songs on *Desire*.

More recently, after the "Brownsville Girl" collaboration, Shepard wrote a
play about himself and Dylan. The title, *True Dylan*, is an ironic twist on
Shepard's own *True West*, and it further questions the possible "truth" of an
assumed name. The subtitle—*A one-act play, as it really happened one afternoon
in California*—plays between the rival claims of journalism and fiction. Much
material appears to be biographical, with Dylan reminiscing about his motorcycle accident and about James Dean, but strange, surrealist touches—mysterious music, an unseen car crash—give it, even in its most "accurate" moments,
the feel of a Sam Shepard creation.[17]

However, the aspects of the Dylan/Shepard affinity with the most relevance
for "Brownsville Girl" are found in the film that constitutes the song's intertext.
"Well, there was this movie I seen one time," the first verse begins, "about a man
riding across the desert and it starred Gregory Peck" (BG). Shepard recalls:
"The film the song was about was a Gregory Peck western that Bob had once
seen, but he couldn't remember the title. We decided that the title didn't matter." "Danville Girl" begins "I wish I could remember that movie just a little bit
better" (DG). Before making the revisions that led to "Brownsville Girl," however, it is likely that Dylan *did* remember the movie, and he may even have seen

it again to refresh his memory. The film in question is *The Gunfighter* (1950), directed by Henry King.[18]

Movie references occur repeatedly in the works of both Dylan and Shepard. "I keep praying," Shepard wrote, "for a double bill / of / *BAD DAY AT BLACK ROCK* / and / *VERA CRUZ*" (1982, 86)—two films that must have shown in 1954 at the Lybba Theater in Hibbing, owned by Bobby Zimmerman's great-grand-father and his brother, and named for Bobby's great-grandmother. Sam Shepard has become a highly successful movie actor, in *Days of Heaven, The Right Stuff,* and his own *Fool for Love.* His screen image, sometimes treated straight, sometimes ironically,[19] is very much that of the cowboy: the kind of part that, say, Gregory Peck played. Shepard is even the same physical type as Peck: long, lean, and hard. When the protagonist of "Danville Girl" says that all he remembers of *The Gunfighter* is Gregory Peck and that "everything he did in it reminded me of me," one might hear Sam Shepard talking.

But one might equally hear Bob Dylan. During a 1971 visit to Israel, a reporter asked Dylan how he had spent his thirtieth birthday. He replied, "We went to see a Gregory Peck movie—I'm quite a fan of his" (Shelton 1986, 414). In 1997 Peck delivered the laudatory speech for Dylan at the Kennedy Center Honors awards ceremony:

> I thought of him as . . . a kind of nineteenth-century troubadour, a maverick American spirit. . . . Sometime ago I bought a new Dylan album and I was listening to a song called "Brownsville Girl." . . . Dylan was singing about a picture that I made called *The Gunfighter,* about the lone man in town and people are comin' to kill him and everybody wants him to get out of town before the shootin' starts. When I met Bob, years later, I told him that meant a lot to me, and I guess the best way I could sum him up is to say Bob Dylan's never been about to get outta town before the shootin' starts![20]

The Gunfighter begins with a shot of "a man riding across the desert." He is Jimmy Ringo (Gregory Peck), a notorious gunfighter pursued by his fame. In every town is a brash young kid eager to make a name for himself as the man who shot Jimmy Ringo. In the first sequence we see such a challenge and its fatal result. Followed by the dead kid's brothers, Ringo moves on to the next town, where he meets an old friend, now the town marshall, and where he hopes to reunite with Peggy, the local schoolteacher, his old sweetheart and the mother of his child.[21] Threatened by the avenging brothers and by *this* town's dumb kid, Hunt Bromley, Ringo delays his getaway until he can talk to his son and to Peggy, from whom he exacts a vague promise to see him next year. The marshall disposes of the brothers, but as Ringo is riding out of town he is shot in the back by Hunt Bromley. In the climactic scene, which is described graphically and accurately in the song by Dylan and Shepard, the townspeople begin to lynch the killer but are stopped by the dying gunfighter, who says:

> "Turn him loose, let him go, let him say he outdrew me fair and
>   square.
> I want him to feel what it's like to every moment face his death."
>
> (BG)

The memory of the film persists throughout the song. By the end of the second stanza, Dylan remembers the movie less as one that he has seen than as one that he has taken part in: "I can't remember why I was in it or what part I was supposed to play" (BG). In the third stanza the protagonist is

> standing in line in the rain to see a movie starring Gregory Peck
> . . . .
> He's got a new one out now, I don't even know what it's about.
> But I'll see him in anything, so I'll stand in line.
>
> (BG)

The last verse, like the second and third, returns to *The Gunfighter* in its closing lines, and offers a briefer plot summary:

> All I remember about it was it starred Gregory Peck,
> He wore a gun and he was shot in the back
> Seems like a long time ago, long before the stars were torn down.
>
> (BG)

The final phrase has obvious apocalyptic overtones, but it also may refer, more simply, to the decline of the Hollywood "star system." *The Gunfighter* was the product of the Hollywood studios (Twentieth Century Fox in this case) in the 1950s, when stars like Gregory Peck were assigned to scripts as automatically as their fans concluded, "He's got a new one out now, I don't even know what it's about / But I'll see him in anything, so I'll stand in line." In the "new" and very different Hollywood, Sam Shepard writes a screenplay for the German director Wim Wenders *(Paris, Texas,* 1984) or appears as an actor in a production of his play *Fool for Love,* directed by Robert Altman. One kind of star has indeed been torn down, but others have been erected in its place. The fans' worship is just as intense, if no longer as unquestioning.

Shepard deals with the question of fame, of stars and their audiences, in *The Tooth of Crime.* Its futuristic setting fuses the roles of pop star and gunfighter: the central character, Hoss, worries about his position on the charts and about the young "gypsies" who, like Hunt Bromley, are out to get him. "Look at me now," he says. "Impotent . . . . Stuck in my image. Stuck in a mansion. Waiting. Waiting for a kid who's probably just like me. Just like I was then. A young blood. And I gotta off him. I gotta roll him or he'll roll me" (1981, 226). That could be Jimmy Ringo talking—or, indeed, any of the dying, powerless fathers of Bob Dylan's outlaw songs.

The potentially lethal nature of the rock star's audience is also a prominent topic in *Rolling Thunder Logbook.* Shepard relates in vivid detail Roger McGuinn's "profound fear of being assassinated on stage . . . imagining the hands of the gunman as they polished the barrel with a chamois skin and then the black barrel of the rifle sweeping the width of the stage trying to find the correct angle" (1977, 60). Later, Shepard writes: "Strange fear comes over me that the audience might actually devour Dylan and the band. It seems that close. I'm afraid for them" (119). And in a short section simply entitled "Fans," he writes: "Fans are more dangerous than a man with a weapon because they're after something invisible. Some imagined 'something.' At least with a gun you know what you're facing" (89). In the 1986–87 *Rolling Stone* interview, Shepard is asked, "How do you avoid the so-called powers of relentless and overintrusive fans?" He answers, "Carry a gun!" and then laughs. The laughter is surely uneasy.

The first function of *The Gunfighter* as intertext in "Brownsville Girl" is thus to point to the theme of fame, to the ambivalence of audiences, and to the vulnerability of the "star." *The Gunfighter* finds echoes in Shepard's *The Tooth of Crime* and in his *Rolling Thunder Logbook*, which in turn bears witness to the intensity of these pressures on Bob Dylan. In "Brownsville Girl" the stars do not just fall, they are torn down.

Other elements of the Jimmy Ringo character are just as important for Dylan and Shepard: Ringo is a father, and as a father he is absent. *The Gunfighter* is understandably reticent about plot details, since it wishes to establish both that Ringo has been an outlaw and that Peggy is a virtuous 1950s heroine. But somehow they have gotten married and had a son. She is now living under an assumed name, working as a schoolteacher, and bringing up her son in ignorance of his father's identity— so much so that in playground gossip the boy prefers Wyatt Earp to the legendary Jimmy Ringo. Only after his death does she identify herself as "Mrs. Ringo," with little Jimmy adding, "And his boy!" The final shot of the film shows a horseman riding back into the desert: Jimmy Ringo's ghost, like Lenny Bruce's, lives on and on. The final situation (mother and son reunited, father returning to the desert) is also identical to the ending of Sam Shepard's *Paris, Texas*.

The theme of the absent father is found in several Shepard works, notably in *True West*, where the two brothers on stage refer continually to "the old man" living as a recluse in the Mojave Desert.[22] In *Fool for Love* "The Old Man" is also the stage direction's designation for the father, who is both present and absent throughout: "He exists only in the minds of May and Eddie, even though they might talk to him directly and acknowledge his physical presence. The Old Man treats them as though they all existed in the same time and place" (1983, 15). *Fool for Love* sets up a complicated story in which the father is absent from two families in turn, keeping each in ignorance of the other. Presence in one necessarily implies absence in the other: "I was gone," he protests, "But I wasn't disconnected" (74).[23]

In Shepard's plays, the essence of the father's role is not just that he is absent but that his very absence has to be "staged," imagined, projected as a presence underlying the action. Similarly, *True Dylan* returns obsessively to the empty sites of death—the curve of the road where James Dean was killed, the back seat of the Cadillac where Hank Williams died—as places haunted by the felt presence of the absent dead: their ghosts.

Throughout this book, I have outlined the conjunction of these motifs—the ghost, the outlaw, the dying father—in Bob Dylan's songs, especially on *Desire*.

Shepard's Rolling Thunder association with Dylan did not begin until shortly after *Desire* had been recorded (July 1975), but at the time of the tour these were the most urgent Dylan compositions of which Shepard would have been aware. The central songs on *Desire*—"Isis," "Oh, Sister," "Sara"—depend on themes and images which recur both in Shepard's plays and in "Brownsville Girl."

Most discussions of "Sara" (including mine) focus on its autobiographical nature and see the name Sara as referring unproblematically to Dylan's wife. However, Robert Shelton reports that "Dylan joked on his Rolling Thunder tour . . . that 'Sara' was not necessarily about his wife, [but] perhaps about the biblical Sarah" (464). As "joked" indicates, this suggestion has been treated with general incredulity, but I suggest that it is worth a closer look. Given the Oedipal play around the proper name, the patronymic, and the adoption of a pseudonym, it is intriguing that the son of Abraham Zimmerman should have married a woman called Sara.

In Genesis, Sara is the wife of the patriarch Abraham. She bears him a son "in his old age" (21:2) when he might have been considered incapable of fatherhood. On two separate occasions, however, she is described not as his wife but as his sister, or rather, she is asked to take on the *alias* of his sister. In Genesis 12:

> It came to pass, when [Abram] was come near to enter into Egypt, that he said unto Sarai his wife, Behold now, I know that thou art a fair woman to look upon: Therefore it shall come to pass, when the Egyptians shall see thee, that they shall say, This is his wife: and they will kill me, but they will save thee alive.
>
> Say, I pray thee, thou art my sister: that it may be well with me for thy sake; and my soul shall live because of thee. (12:11–13)

The deception is undertaken for self-protection in a foreign land. As one commentator points out,

> Abram appears in the story in a very unfavorable light. In order to save his own skin, he tells Sarai to pass herself off as his sister. A marriage contract with a beautiful woman could always be arranged through her brother; a husband might have to be liquidated. The lie pays dividends. As a result of Sarai's presence "in Pharaoh's house-

hold" [Abram] receives "sheep and cattle and asses, male and female slaves, she-asses and camels." (Davidson, 25)

Abraham, that is, has saved himself and made a profit by placing his wife in a dangerous position, in much the same way as John Wesley Harding placed "his lady by his side" when he "took a stand." A later chapter of Genesis repeats the story in another setting, but this time attempts to rehabilitate Abraham's reputation by claiming that his story is true, that Sara really *is* his sister: "And yet indeed she is my sister; she is the daughter of my father, but not the daughter of my mother; and she became my wife" (20:12).

Davidson's commentary is again illuminating:

> Some modern scholars believe that behind the present form of the story lies the memory of a type of marriage involving a wife-sister relationship. . . . Such a marriage in which the wife has the legal status of sister is said to be a particularly solemn and binding relationship.
>
> (25–26)

The curious situation described in the Genesis stories about Sara finds echoes in both Bob Dylan and Sam Shepard. In Shepard's *Fool for Love,* for instance, the two central characters, Eddie and May, are lovers who are also brother and half-sister, in the same relationship as that claimed by Abraham: they have the same father but different mothers. Their situation on stage, under the eyes of their ghostly and disapproving father, The Old Man, reflects the lines of Dylan's "Oh, Sister":

> Oh, sister, when I come to lie in your arms
> You should not treat me like a stranger.
> Our Father would not like the way that you act
> And you must realize the danger.
>
> (L, 382)

The theme of filial disobedience reaches back to "Tears of Rage," in which another daughter says no to her father. That daughter is described as "[be]neath the sun," with the inevitable pun on *son* (L, 312). The appeal to the authority of "Our Father" desperately reasserts patriarchal privilege. But why should Dylan have addressed this appeal to Sara as *sister*, unless he was already thinking of the Genesis story in which the wife and the sister are one?[24]

There are other possible mythological sources for the image of the wife as sister, the most important of which is the story of Isis. In Egyptian mythology Isis is the sister and wife of Osiris, who is the father of their child Horus. After Set murders Osiris, Isis recovers his body from a tamarisk tree; later, when Set has dismembered the corpse,

> Isis patiently began another search for her husband's body and, finding the parts one by one, preserved them carefully. . . . She found them all except the phallus, which Set had cast into the Nile. . . . But Isis modeled another and reconstituted the body of her husband, anointing it with precious oils. She thus . . . restored Osiris to eternal life.
>
> (Ions, 59)

Isis can restore Osiris, the dead father of her child, not only to life but also to potency. Her female power encompasses the male; it is she who creates the phallus. Isis is the Great Mother Goddess, the primordial female figure whose worship, many mythographers believe, preceded that of any male deity. "The worship of Isis," writes Richard Cavendish in his book on the Tarot,

> spread beyond Egypt to become one of the major mystery religions of the Roman world. She was a great mother goddess, who had many aspects, forms and symbols. . . . She was the ideal and complete woman and the prototype of the human woman. . . . Just as Isis had brought Osiris back to life, so her mysteries promised immortal life after death to those initiated into them. The ceremonies of initiation included a mock death and resurrection. . . . There was probably also a "sacred marriage" or sexual union of the initiate with a woman representing the goddess.
>
> (74)

The Christian worship of Mary arose in part as a response to, or co-option of, the cult of Isis. The Egyptian Isis was closely associated with the River Nile, whose annual flood, on which Egypt's agricultural and economic survival depended, was mythologically represented as caused by the tears of Isis weeping for her brother/husband, Osiris (Witt, 14–15). One legend of the Tarot pack is that the cards were used to divine the date for the Nile flood. In the Tarot Isis is represented by The Empress, whose image appears on the back cover of Dylan's album *Desire* (Cavendish, 76–78; Shelton, 463).

Dylan approaches this powerful body of mythological material in the song "Isis." In the midst of his songs on dying fathers, he attempts to evoke the Mother (like a rolling *Beatty* Stone). But he does so with hesitation. Isis is not the protagonist of the song that bears her name; the focus is Osiris. And Dylan stops short of the full implications of the Isis cult, preferring to deal with her in safer terms as the goddess who was "chiefly revered as the faithful wife and mourner" (Ions, 62).

"This song is about marriage," Bob Dylan told a Rolling Thunder audience in Montreal, on the live recording of "Isis" issued on *Biograph*.[25] Ostensibly the song is about a man who marries Isis "on the fifth day of May" (L, 378) and who then departs on a strange journey with another man, attempting to recover bodies from a pyramid. When the other man dies, the protagonist buries him in the empty tomb and returns "by the fourth [of the following May]" to renew his relationship with Isis. Dylan's awareness of the Isis myth is clearly documented. Shepard's *Rolling Thunder Logbook* contains a page of "Isis Notes," referring to the "voyage of soul after death" and "trials by fire, water, sex" (1977, 140). Ginsberg's liner notes for *Desire* invoke "Isis Moon Lady Language Creator Birth Goddess . . . Divine Mother," while Dylan's own notes pray "Isis and the moon shine on me" (L, 392).

The key reference to the Isis myth in Dylan's song is the line "She was there in the meadow where the creek used to rise." Given the transposition of the myth into humbler terms, the Nile becomes a "creek." Its failure to rise invokes the failure of fertility, a crisis which, as in the Osiris myth or the Grail legends, calls for a sacrificial death and rebirth. In the song this ritual is accomplished by the protagonist and the stranger whom he meets. Indeed, the two characters may be two aspects of the same role, a doubling of the self as the dying father (sacrificial victim) and the reborn son (bridegroom of Isis). The protagonist heads out to "a high place of darkness and light [where] the dividing line ran through the center of town." Here he undergoes a ritual purification ("wash my clothes down") and encounters his double as the "man in the corner [who] approached me for a match" (an obvious double-meaning on *match).* The would-be grave robber then dies, and the protagonist substitutes his body for the missing one which he had hoped to steal. Reborn, "different," the son returns, completing the ritual cycle of the seasons and the year (from the fifth to the fourth of May) to reconsecrate his mystic marriage with Isis.

When he does, he might well address her "Oh, sister," like Eddie to May in *Fool for Love,* like Abraham to Sara, like Osiris to Isis. There is even a further possibility of bridging these different mythologies. If Dylan had been reading Robert Graves's *The White Goddess,*[26] he would have seen that Osiris is some-times identified with the Greek god Proteus, and further that Proteus also may have been the mythological "priest-king of Pharos [who] married Sarah, the god-dess mother of the 'Abraham' tribe" (276–77). Proteus, the shape-shifter, is cer-tainly a god who suits Dylan's trickster persona. The link through Proteus may be tenuous, but "Oh, sister" clearly identifies Isis with Sara, and Osiris with both Abraham and his protean son. The clearest connection is simply in the tight sound pattern that unites the names: Isis, Osiris, Oh sister, Oh Sara, Desire.

In "Isis," then, the theme of the dying father is explicitly mythological. Just as the worship of Isis was subsumed by the cult of the Virgin Mary, just as the legends of the dying god (Atthis, Osiris) were gathered up into the Christian doctrine of the Resurrection, so too Dylan moved into his Christian phase, in which all the references to outlaws and dying fathers could be summed up in "the Man who came and died a criminal's death" (L, 426). The role of dying, sacrificial father thus mutates through Abraham and Osiris to Christ. In Dylan's songs it moves from Sheriff Baker putting his guns in the ground to the dying gunfighter of "Danville Girl," of whom Dylan remarks, "everything he did . . . reminded me of me" (DG).

So now it is time to return to "Brownsville Girl" and the question of what actually happens at the narrative level. In a 1986–87 *Rolling Stone* interview, Sam Shepard offers the following account:

It has to do with a guy standing on line and waiting to see an old Gregory Peck movie that he can't quite remember—only pieces of it, and then this whole memory thing happens, unfolding before his very eyes. He starts speaking internally to a woman he'd been hanging out with, recalling their meetings and reliving the whole journey they'd gone on—and then it returns to the guy, who's still standing on line in the rain.

This is a plot summary considerably more coherent than any that can with any confidence be drawn from the text itself. "Brownsville Girl" never develops a single, coherent narrative: rather, it presents the fragments of several possible narratives, sometimes evoked and discarded within a line, whose relationship to each other remains unspecified.[27] Dylan, Shepard continues, is "a lot of fun to work with, because he's so off the wall sometimes. We'd come up with a line, and I'd think that we were heading down one trail over here, and then suddenly he'd just throw in this other line, and we'd wind up following it off in some different direction." This fragmentation and indeterminacy are present even in "Danville Girl," but most of the revisions Dylan made before "Brownsville Girl" increase them (the exceptions being the references to *The Gunfighter,* which are clearer in the later version).

The continuing protagonist is referred to only as "I." In the first stanza he recalls a relationship with a woman specified only as "you." Together they travel to San Anton' and the Alamo, and then cross the border into Mexico, where "you went out to find a doctor and you never came back" (BG). It is never specified whether she went to find a doctor for herself or the protagonist, nor is any reason given for her failure to return.[28] (The possible suggestion that the "doctor" is an abortionist reinforces the idea of the father's failed authority.) The protagonist's response, more cautious than the average macho cowboy hero's, is "I would have gone out after you but I didn't feel like letting my head get blown off" (BG), but he gives no reason why he might anticipate such a fate. This story line is then dropped, and the final lines of the first stanza present the protagonist riding in a car with a second woman ("she ain't you") while remembering the first.

This distinction between "you" and "she" is clear in the first stanza, but the rest of the song falls back into the indeterminate pronoun reference characteristic of Dylan. In the second stanza the protagonist again travels in a car with a woman, but whether she is "you," "she," or even a third character, is unspecified, as is the sequence of events. "We" visit Henry Porter, or to be more precise, "we pulled up where Henry Porter used to live" (BG). Henry is absent, though Ruby (possibly Henry's wife) says that he will be back soon. In Henry's absence the song focuses briefly on Ruby, her sense of despair and isolation, her wish to return home, yet also her world-weary realization that escape is impossible. The protagonist proclaims that he and his woman are "going all the way, 'til the wheels fall off and burn," but Ruby "just smiled and said, 'Ah, you know some babies never learn' " (BG). The song then shifts back to memories of *The Gunfighter,* and we never do find out whether Henry shows up.

Stanza 3 is set in Corpus Christi, whose name echoes the sacrificial theme of the dying god. It opens with another compressed melodrama, in which the protagonist is caught in a crossfire and mistakenly arrested. He is rescued from his predicament by the perjury of yet another unnamed woman. Again she is referred to only as "you," but whether she is the same "you" as in the first and/or second stanza is unspecified. By the end of the stanza, he is separated from her and "standin' in line in the rain to see a movie starring Gregory Peck" (BG).

Stanza 4 has very little narrative content. A few general remarks are addressed to "you," and Henry Porter makes a brief reappearance, only to be further consigned to the indeterminacy of the song: "the only thing we knew for sure about Henry Porter is that his name wasn't Henry Porter" (BG). The line vaguely suggests criminality in that "Henry Porter" might be, like the "part I was supposed to play" in *Pat Garrett & Billy the Kid,* an alias.[29] Again the later version increases the indeterminacy of the narrative; this disclaimer of Henry Porter's name and identity is not present in "Danville Girl."

Between each stanza, a chorus addresses a "Brownsville girl" or a "Danville girl," also designated as "you."[30] The name Brownsville unifies the geographical references—San Antonio, the Alamo, Amarillo, Corpus Christi—along the border area between Texas and Mexico that has fascinated Dylan from "Just Like Tom Thumb's Blues" (1965) to "Señor (Tales of Yankee Power)" (1978). As a border town it stands between the various realms of history, fiction, and myth;[31] its identity is marginal and indeterminate, like that of Bob Dylan, or the narrator of the song.

It is possible that most of the women in the song—the *you*'s of stanzas 1 through 4, the companion in stanza 2, and the "Brownsville girl" of the chorus—are the same person, and that a chronology might be reconstructed to account for the events. This is evidently the way Sam Shepard sees the song. But it is equally possible that the song refers to four or five different women (in the same way that "Tangled Up In Blue" does) and that the scattered events cannot be convincingly arranged into a logically sequential plot. The best response to the song is to leave the indeterminacy open and to accept that the construction of a conventional story is not one of its purposes.

However, while the various narrative fragments may not comprise a coherent plot, they are thematically congruent with each other, and with the overriding intertext of *The Gunfighter*. While none of the male characters in the song is explicitly identified as a father, all share a sense of failure and helplessness. The image of the western protagonist as a capable, independent cowboy hero is continually undermined, as it is in so many of Sam Shepard's plays. In the stereotyped western thriller, the male hero is supposed to rescue the damsel in distress, but in "Brownsville Girl," the protagonist of stanza 3, who "didn't know whether to duck or run, so I ran," has to be rescued from jail by a woman perjuring herself. Conversely in stanza 1 *he* fails to rescue *her* (or her counterpart), abandoning her to an unknown fate. A similar willingness of ostensible heroes to allow women to suffer for them has already been noted in "John Wesley Harding," "Lily, Rosemary and the Jack of Hearts," and even in the biblical Abraham. The grand project of stanza 2—"going all the way, 'til the wheels fall off and burn" (BG)—seems to fizzle out and be forgotten. By stanza 4 the protagonist is reduced to saying, "Hang onto me, baby, and let's hope that the roof stays on" (BG). At the equivalent spot in "Danville Girl," he says, "Tell me about all the things I couldn't do nothing about." Henry Porter is identified by where he "used to live," by his absence, and by the falseness of his name.

The song is thus concerned with a failure of patriarchal authority, grounded in the death of the Gregory Peck character in *The Gunfighter*. The father's death returns us once more to the Oedipus myth and the place it holds in contemporary theories of narrative. The pleasure of narrative, Roland Barthes speculates, is an Oedipal one: the drive "to denude, to know, to learn the origin and the end"; so "every narrative (every unveiling of the truth) is a staging of the (absent, hidden, or hypostatized) father" (1976, 10). The staging of the absent father is a central project of Dylan's work. *Tarantula's* story of "a discarded Oedipus" (T, 120) becomes the model for all stories, for the act and impulse of story telling itself. The participant in narrative—the protagonist, the hero with whom the reader is invited to identify—moves toward a disclosure which is also a closure: the revelation of a truth that was there from the start, an ending that was in place before the beginning. "All narrative," writes Teresa de Lauretis, "in its movement forward toward resolution and backward to an initial moment, a paradise lost, is overlaid with . . . an Oedipal logic" (125). Oedipus desires the ending of his story, but simultaneously fears it, not only because the ending is intolerable—the father, unhidden, turns out to be the man he killed at the crossroads[32]—but also because he suspects that there is no ending, only another beginning.

The movement of narrative is the movement of desire, and desire always reconstitutes itself in the very moment that any apparent or temporary goal is fulfilled. The ending of one story is always the beginning of another—even, in the case of Oedipus, the beginning of itself. Desire depends upon a lack, upon the felt or staged absence of its object. In language, meaning itself is absent: a sign constitutes itself by the absence of the thing signified, which is always deferred, usually to another sign, where it is deferred in turn. Desire seeks the foundation of meaning, the origin, "the father," even while knowing that the only constant is the search itself. Narrative stages the simultaneous presence and absence of that goal. The goal's absence is required for desire to be able to move toward it, but equally its presence is required, if only as image, as re-presentation, to place it onstage in front of the viewer's eyes, as a story.

The Oedipus myth deals also with the role of the father in the incest prohibition—specifically in mother-son relations. The father's death in *The Gunfighter* and his abdication in *Paris, Texas* leave the mother-son pairing intact—yet with the implication in both cases that the son is left positioned to take over the role of the father, to act out the Oedipal fantasy of being both husband and son to his mother (in relation to Sara, to be both Abraham and the son of Abraham). Elsewhere the theme of incest is deflected to the brother-sister relationship, as with Eddie and May in *Fool for Love* or Isis and Osiris in "Isis." The erotic implications of "Oh, sister, when I come to lie in your arms" are immediately countered by the *Nom/Non du Père:* "Our Father would not like the way that you act." These lines come, after all, from an album called *Desire*.

Much of Dylan's work in this middle period is overshadowed by the figure of the failed, absent, or dying father. Even the invocation of Isis serves less to worship the Goddess than to reinscribe the theme of the father. In the unfolding drama of Dylan's lifework, the Christianity which he would adopt a few years after *Desire* may be seen to function not only to replace the core of conviction in love, in himself as a father, which he lost in the breakup with Sara, but precisely to replace that image of the father with another that is simultaneously authoritative (the patriarchal God of the Old Testament, the lawgiver) and sacrificial ("the Man who came and died a criminal's death").

As lawgiver or prophet, as Abraham, the father is in patriarchal mythology the source, the point of origin. In *Paris, Texas,* Travis buys himself a plot of land in Paris, Texas, because he believes it is where his parents first made love: it is mythically the site of his origin. But what he actually buys is a vacant lot. The place of origin has been vacated, emptied of both presence and meaning. Nor does he truly possess or inhabit even this wasteland: he only carries its photograph, which is nothing more than a sign, a reference to something not present, something which itself is absent and vacant. The meaning, the origin, is somewhere else, like the wandering father in *Fool for Love,* whose presence in one family necessarily entails his absence in the other. The sanction of the sign, its guarantee of meaningfulness, lies not in presence but in absence, in deferral, in difference.

Travis has wandered in the desert, "somewhere without language," and his reintroduction to the Symbolic order is gradual and difficult—he does not speak for the first half-hour of the movie. Yet "every man has your voice," Jane tells him, gazing at the two-way mirror in which he is both present and hidden. Behind that mirror, he is the ultimate sanction and authority of the male patriarchal order, for whom the woman, even the mother, is objectified spectacle, fantasized pornography. The mirror/screen, in which the child begins the process of ego-identification, deflects and displaces all communication between Travis and Jane. In the film they never meet face to face.

Traditionally the face of God is also hidden. "No man sees my face and lives," as Dylan quotes Exodus in "I and I." The doubling that is present throughout Dylan's work splits the self as it splits the sign. The "I" that writes and the "I" that is written, presence and absence, signifier and signified, are all divided by the gap that is the action of desire. The "dividing line" of "Isis" runs through not just "the center of town" but through the center of the Author, between "I and I"—"Everything he did in it reminded me of me" (DG). Alias: the name as other.

In *Renaldo and Clara* Ronnie Hawkins plays "Bob Dylan" while Dylan himself appears wearing a mask. "The audience is totally bewildered," Sam Shepard records in *Rolling Thunder Logbook*, "still wondering if this is actually him or not" (1977, 114). In Shepard's *True Dylan* the Dylan character claims that "You always know who you are," but immediately undercuts that certainty by adding, "I just don't know who I'm gonna become" (64). In "Things Have Changed" (2000), he proclaims: "I'm trying to get as far away from myself as I can." On *"Love and Theft"* he admits: "I'm not even acquainted with my own desires." And again, ultimately: "I don't think of myself as Bob Dylan," Bob Dylan says on the liner notes to *Biograph*. "It's like Rimbaud said, 'I is another.'"

Rimbaud's *autre* is also an *auteur,* the figure of the Author whose Death was proclaimed by Roland Barthes. "The Author," Barthes writes, "is thought to nourish the book, which is to say that he exists before it, thinks, suffers, lives for it, is in the same relation of antecedence to his work as a father to his child" (1977, 145). What dies in the text is the figure of the father (the Author) as the transcendental Signified. But, as Barthes remarks, our narratives continually restage that death, oedipally killing the father all over again, just like so many times before. The absent father in Dylan and Shepard can never be entirely disposed of. Like The Old Man in *Fool for Love,* he is gone but not disconnected. His absent presence must always be re-presented, as it is in "Brownsville Girl."

"Brownsville Girl" longs toward a point of mythical origin, which "seems like a long time ago, long before the stars were torn down" (BG). Yet the ideal of paradise—before the apocalypse, before the fall—is itself an image (like Travis's photo of a vacant lot in *Paris, Texas*) and so is always already betrayed, infected by semiotic deferral. What happened "a long time ago"—the originary myth of "Brownsville Girl"—is, after all, *The Gunfighter,* a movie that already enacts the drama of the dying father. The song too begins with this image, begins with the end of the film, and returns to it at *its* end, just as the end of Oedipus's story is the dis-closure of its beginning. The song's fragmented and indeterminate narrative breaks up the linear drive of story toward its ending, only to reinstate that drive, dispersed and disseminated across half a dozen subplots, whose incompletions try repeatedly to evade the Oedipal ending, the impossible closure of desire. There is no paradise, prelinguistic or prenarrative. The serpent is always already in Eden; the story has always already begun.

All of the characters in "Brownsville Girl," including Jimmy Ringo and Gregory Peck, live in the time *after* the stars have been torn down. It is a time of failure and betrayal—"Way down in Mexico you went out to find a doctor and you never came back / I would have gone out after you but I didn't feel like letting my head get blown off." It is a time of separation—"I can't believe we've lived so long and are still so far apart"—and a time of absence—"Henry ain't here"; "she ain't you" (BG). It is a time when the sign is irrevocably divided from its meaning—"when I saw you break down in front of the judge and cry real tears / It was the best acting I saw anybody do" (BG). It is a time of desire — but the constitutive element of that desire is that no one (author, singer, protagonist, audience) is acquainted with it.

In "Brownsville Girl" the figure of God the Father as ultimate source and authority of meaning has been replaced by the figure of Henry Porter. About Henry Porter, we know where he "used to live" but not where he is now. He is present in the song only as an absence and a promise of return, a Second Coming, which is never fulfilled. Like the Jack of Hearts, he is both "on the scene" and "missing"; like Proteus/Osiris/Bob Dylan, he is a trickster, a shape-shifter, elusive and invisible. He is the absent father whose presence is necessarily staged; he is the God who has vanished from His creation, returned like Travis to the desert; he is the author who has become *un autre*. He bears the authority of the Name, but it is a *Nom* which is also *Non:* "the only thing we knew for sure about Henry Porter is that his name wasn't Henry Porter" (BG).

Named and unnamed, present and absent, central and marginal, he stands in the place of the impossible origin as a stand-in for the other absent presence in the song, the kid from Hibbing, Minnesota, the son of Abraham Zimmerman, who on his thirtieth birthday went to see a movie starring Gregory Peck and found that "everything he did in it reminded me of me"(DG). I and I.

After all, the only thing we know for sure about Bob Dylan is that his name isn't Bob Dylan. It's Alias.

Summation 3: *The Years of Performance*—Time Out Of Mind
In the summer of 1997, Bob Dylan suffered an attack of histoplasmosis pericarditis, "an inflammation of the sac around the heart, preventing the heart from expanding and filling correctly," complicated by a fungal infection "that

grows in soil enriched with bird droppings in certain parts of the Midwestern and southeastern states" (Sounes, 420). In other words, birdshit almost killed him. The disease is only theoretically fatal; if diagnosed early, it is easily treatable. Nevertheless, it was serious enough that Dylan himself said "I really thought I'd be seeing Elvis soon" (an interesting glimpse of his priorities for the afterlife), and internet fans worldwide became urgent and instant experts on the intricacies of histoplasmosis pericarditis. The general public stirred enough to realise that, if he was in danger of dying, that must mean that he wasn't yet dead; and a small shudder of mortality passed through the survivors of the 60s.

Later that year, when his new album *Time Out Of Mind* came out, its rather dark and gloomy tone was ascribed to his brush with death—totally erroneously, since the album had already been completed well before his illness. It was also hailed as a masterpiece (eventually winning a Grammy), and as Dylan's "return" or "comeback" album. True Dylan fans, of course, smugly contended that it was no such thing. How could it be a comeback if he'd never been away? And anyway, wasn't *Time Out Of Mind* in effect the third album in a trilogy, beginning with his two albums of solo recordings of traditional material, *Good As I Been To You* and *World Gone Wrong*? Wasn't *Time Out Of Mind* the culmination and summation of what I have called in this book The Years of Performance?

Well, yes, it was, at least at the time (and so it certainly seemed when I wrote the first draft of what follows in this section). Since then, of course, the 2001 appearance of *"Love and Theft"* has thrown all these categories into doubt. Despite its initial critical and popular success, *Time Out Of Mind* runs some risk of being totally eclipsed by its more spontaneous and spectacular successor. Nevertheless, I believe it is an album which stands up to repeated listening, both in the original Daniel Lanois studio production, and in Dylan's on-stage reworkings, at least two of which ("Cold Irons Bound" and "Not Dark Yet") have established themselves as classic pieces in his repertoire.

Time Out Of Mind was at the time the most suggestive and rewarding title of any Dylan album since *Desire* (though again, it could well be argued that *"Love and Theft"* has since surpassed it). The phrase "time out of mind" is most often used to describe a tradition or custom which is so ancient that its origins are beyond specific memory: "We've always done it this way, time out of mind," or "It's been like this since time immemorial."[33] The first insistence of the phrase is on continuity: traditions that have been passed down through the generations, preserved in unbroken succession. But at the same time, paradoxically, the phrase also inserts a break, or disjunction, into that continuity. The origin cannot be remembered. The unbroken succession *is* broken, at that point where it can no longer be grounded in its founding instance. This double nature of "time out of mind"—both continuity and disjunction, a tradition separated from its own foundation—is the controlling idea, both formal and thematic, of *Time Out Of Mind*.

Of course, the phrase invites other readings as well. The words *time out*, taken by themselves, are used in sports to describe a moment when the clock is stopped. "You wanna stop time," Bob Dylan told Allen Ginsberg. "In order to stop time you have to exist in the moment, so strong as to stop time and prove your point" (1989, 10). Dylan has always believed that one of the main functions of art is to "stop time"; all of his work has been an attempt to call "time out." At the same time, *out of mind* suggests the shadow implication of insanity, which is indeed not far away from some of the extreme statements of despair, disillusion, and abandonment in the lyrics of *Time Out Of Mind*.

Consider the implications of these ideas for the verbal style of the album. Some critics complained that the lyrics are simple to the point of being simplistic: "brain-dead" was one description used on the internet.[34] Certainly there are no lines in these lyrics that call attention to themselves in the self-consciously brilliant manner of "The ghost of electricity howls in the bones of her face" or "Hunger pays a heavy price to the falling gods of speed and steel" (L, 223, 500). Occasionally you do get a twist on an expected cliché: instead of burning to the ground, a house burns "to the sky" (TIF).[35] But for the most part, the language is kept simple, and even the rhymes—which have often in Dylan been occasions for startling virtuosity—are largely predictable. So where's the poetry?

It comes, in the first place, in Dylan's vocal delivery: in the tiny moments of hesitation which suspend the listener's expectations, in the ways the voice extends, growls, or breaks on certain syllables. When he sings, "I'm thinking of that girl who won't be back no more" (TIF), listen to the sudden hollow break in the voice on the word *more*. Listen to the pause in the middle of "You can say I was on anything . . . but a roll" (H). Or listen to a line like "It's not dark yet, but it's getting there" (NDY): the words are absolutely simple, without any "poetic" ornamentation or device, yet the vocal delivery renders them devastating. There is poetry to be found, too, in the artful juxtapositions of apparently artless phrases: when, for example, the self-consciously "smart" line about "finding a janitor to sweep me off my feet" is met with the cool response, "That's all right mama, you do what you gotta do" (MM). Neither line is particularly striking in itself, but in combination their effect is much more complex and ironic—especially when you factor in the echo of Elvis Presley singing Arthur Crudup's "That's All Right, Mama."

Indeed, the most fundamental level of the album's poetry derives from such echoes, from what might be called the "time out of mind" effect; that is, almost every line on this album *sounds* traditional, sounds as if it came from another place, another time. Quotations, echoes, allusions—everywhere the album sets up a rich weave of intertextuality. Thus Dylan inserts into his own writing the disjunction of "immemorial" tradition. The lines are his and yet not his, traditional and yet not traditional, based on an origin that has been occluded, asserting their continuity with generations of experience and yet unable to name the source of their authenticity.

The album is replete with echoes and quotations; indeed, it is not difficult to research a potential source for every single line. Quite literally, as he told David Gates, "The songs are my lexicon" (64). That statement is a key to any appreciation of *Time Out Of Mind.* Traditional songs form its lexicon, its dictionary, the data base for its vocabulary. There are obvious quotations from traditional material—"You took the silver, you took the gold" (MM), "I'll eat when I'm hungry, drink when I'm dry" (SD)—and even negative quotations—*no* gamblers, *no* midnight ramblers like there were before (TGH). Jimmie Rodgers is there, "waiting for a train" (TGH), and even Leonard Cohen proclaiming, "I'm your man" (CW). There is an abundance of lonesome roads, country shacks, and deep muddy water. The singer has "been all around the world" (TGH), and the river runs, where else, to the sea. Clouds are compared to "chariots that swing down low" (H).

Some of the older songs being echoed are songs that Dylan has performed, so they amount to a kind of self-quotation. "Make You Feel My Love" is written more or less exactly to the tune of "You Belong To Me," the 1950s pop tune sung by Dylan on the *Natural Born Killers* soundtrack. The line "I've been to Sugartown, I've shook the sugar down" (TGH) evokes Elizabeth Cotten's "Shake Sugaree," so memorably performed by Dylan in concert in 1996. The line "until my eyes begin to bleed" (DRB) recalls the Mississippi Sheiks' "Blood In My Eyes," recorded by Dylan on *World Gone Wrong.*

Other self-quotations and allusions to previous Dylan songs are more direct. In "Can't Wait" the repeated "how much longer" echoes "New Pony." "Million Miles" is almost an anthology of Dylan quotations. "The last thing you said before you hit the street" echoes "the last thing I remember before I stripped and kneeled" from "Señor." The rhyme of *once* with *couple of months* is repeated from "Lenny Bruce"; and "Rock me baby" recalls the *Pat Garrett & Billy the Kid* outtakes. Heaven's door, once being knocked on, is now in danger of being closed. Them bells are still ringing. And most obviously of all, "Highlands," in its length and climactic position, responds to "Sad-Eyed Lady of the Lowlands."

The effect of this tissue of intertextuality is to problematize the position of the "author" within these songs and in relation to his audience. Dylan's previous album was *World Gone Wrong*—and it's not too fanciful to describe *Time Out Of Mind* as *World Gone Wrong* "written by" Bob Dylan. It's as if Dylan is saying to his audience: Okay, so you want an album of "original" songs—but what is original? Who is the author of a line like "I've been riding the midnight train" (SD)? When a song has existed "time out of mind," its origin becomes forgotten. Scholars may tell you who actually wrote "Cocaine" or "Stone Walls and Steel Bars," but in a very real sense songs like these have become "trad." or "anon."

Again, the paradoxical effect of a song's existing "time out of mind" is to introduce a point of discontinuity into continuity: the loss of origin, the occluding of source, the becoming-anonymous of the author. And that's what Dylan is playing with all through *Time Out Of Mind*—working on the edge of making himself anonymous. Yet, even as he does that, he also reinscribes his own identity and originality. There simply aren't many singers around who can inhabit the full range of the tradition as knowledgeably or as convincingly as can Bob Dylan. These are other people's songs, the quotations tell us; these are my songs, insists the voice. Or to put it another way, Dylan's identity *is* this equivocal relation to tradition. His originality lies in his quotations. The songs are his lexicon, and, like them, his own existence stretches back "time out of mind."

(What is the origin of "Bob Dylan"? May 1941, the birth of Robert Allen Zimmerman? Fall 1959, the adoption of a self-given name? The emigrant journeys of the Edelstein, Solemovitz, Zimmerman ancestors? The anonymous sources of the great folk ballads, or the 1920s recordings of Dock Boggs? The first time he listened to Elvis, or read Rimbaud? How far back, "time out of mind," can you trace the sources of "Dirt Road Blues" or "Cold Irons Bound"? Where in history could you call "time out"? Even to try it, you must be out of your mind.)

This sense of a disjunction within continuity is, I am suggesting, the key to understanding the apparent "lack of originality" in the lyrics. But the same sense of disjunction is also the central *thematic* concern of the album. Repeatedly the singer presents himself as divided within his own consciousness, separated from any assurance of authority, reaching toward a salvation which can only be posited in terms which repeat and reinscribe the very disjunction which it is supposed to heal.

From the songs of *Time Out Of Mind* there emerges, with great depth and consistency, a figure of the singer, characterized, in the first place, by extreme uncertainty and self-doubt. The most-often repeated phrase on the album is *I don't know*—"Just don't know what to do" (LS); "Feel like talking to somebody but I just don't know who" (MM); "I don't know what 'all right' even means" (TGH); "I just don't know what I'm going to do" (TIF); "If I ever saw you coming I don't know what I might do" (CW). Similar phrases repeat the uncertainty: *I wonder, I wish I knew, I can't even remember.* . . . In "Highlands," faced with a decision as simple as what to order in a restaurant, the singer retreats into a maze of indecision: "I got no idea what I want / Maybe I do but I'm just really not sure." It's a startling contrast to the confident, and sometimes dogmatic, tone of the prophetic voice Dylan has used on other albums.

This self-undermining of the singer's authority extends to repeated statements about the inefficacy of words, of the very act of speaking. "There are things I could say," he tells us, "but I don't" (SD). And later in the same song: "I see nothing to be gained by any explanation / There's no words that need to be said." The singer is "tired of talking, tired of trying to explain" (TIF). And climactically in "Highlands": "The party's over and there's less and less to say."

Of course, there is always the paradoxical point that all such statements are, to some degree, self-defeating, since it is only within language that the supposed inefficacy of language can be proclaimed. The more successfully the singer expresses the proposition that he has nothing left to say, the less valid the proposition becomes. But the important point here is not so much logical as emotional. What these lines express is a profound sense of despair on the part of the singer. It is his vocation, and his very existence as an artist, that is being called into doubt. When he tells his lover to "seal up the book and not write any more" (TGH), it might as well be himself that he is addressing.

Just as the phrase "time out of mind" introduces a disjunction into the continuity of tradition, so the lyrics present a disjunction within the consciousness of the singer. He is presented to us as a figure profoundly divided from himself. The old familiar Dylan images for self-division recur: the shadow, the ghost, the proper name. "I'm hanging on," he sings, offering a momentary image of survival and persistence, and inviting us to complete the phrase, as it had been completed seventeen years earlier, "to a solid rock" (L, 446). But now, after a second's pause to allow for that memory, the line inexorably continues, "to shadows" (LS). "The ghost of our old love has not gone away," he tells us (SD); and even more directly, "I left my life with you somewhere back along the line" (CW). Sometimes the images of self-division are startlingly physical. The idea in "You took a part of me that I really miss" (MM) is realized quite literally in "the flesh falls off my face" (SD) and "My eyes feel like they're falling off my face" (TIF).

As always in Dylan, the ultimate image here is the name, the alias. "When I'm gone you will remember my name," he sings (TIF), as if the integrity of the name can only be achieved in his absence, as if only in death will he become identical with the deferred memory of his name. The name is what (he) lives on; the name is what survives. In "Dirt Road Blues" he says that he will continue his rootless wandering until two conditions are fulfilled: " 'til everything becomes the same" and until his absent lover "hollers out my name." In a world characterized by self-division, a world gone wrong, nothing can ever be the same as its name. It is the world of what Derrida calls "différance"; that is, both difference and deferral, the constitutive disjunction from source or origin, the condition of being an alias, "time out of mind."

At times this sense of self-division borders on insanity, on the singer being "out of [his] mind." The absence of light is "making me sick in the head" (SD); or "I'm beginning to hear voices when there's no one around" (CIB). Elsewhere, "There's voices in the night trying to be heard / I'm sitting here listening to every mind-polluting word" (MM). Most radically, "I was born here and I'll die here against my will" (NDY). According to internet postings by Martin Grossman and Ronnie Screiber, this line derives directly from the Talmud. It suggests the most fundamental self-division of all: the consciousness or will of the individual directed against the very conditions of its own existence.

Any solution to this division has to be postponed to a posited "next life," in which "Maybe . . . I'll be able to hear myself think" (MM).[36] The ideal of an undivided self, a self with the self-contained ability to hear and understand itself, is an ideal which must always be deferred " 'til everything becomes the same" (MM) and so (since the condition of language is that nothing ever does become the same) must always remain, in the phrase Dylan stresses later, "far away" (H).

This sense of disjunction infects even the platitudes of the weakest song on the album, "Make You Feel My Love." Here, the increasingly desperate nature of the singer's gestures—"crawl down the avenue," "go to the ends of the earth"—only serves to underline his inability to "make you feel" his love; that is, he cannot bring his words and his emotions together, cannot make things the same. It is not so much that the loved one cannot feel; the problem is that the singer thinks his lover has to be "made to" feel.

Projected into the sphere of social relations, disjunction is most memorably presented in the bleakly hilarious comedy[37] of the singer's encounter with the Boston waitress in "Highlands." It's a story of crossed purposes, misunderstood intentions, and arbitrary disruptions of social discourse. Roles are reversed and expectations frustrated. The waitress has to tell the customer what it is that he wants, and then the restaurant cannot supply even a menu item as basic as hard-boiled eggs. The waitress, as a figure of the audience, dictates what she wants the artist to do, and then refuses to accept his work. He insists on a resemblance that she rejects. The continuity of time is disrupted by the artist's insistence on regarding the present waitress as existing only in memory. Logical continuity is disrupted by the abrupt *non sequitur* of the question about women authors. Even the question is doubted: "At least that's what I think I hear her say." Her assumption that he is an ignorant male chauvinist is countered by his somewhat unexpected citation of Erica Jong.

And what of Erica Jong?[38] There are, in fact, echoes of her writing in this scene, though it may be suspected that the name was produced mainly by rhyme—directly to "way wrong," and indirectly (across seven minutes of playing time) to "Neil Young." The Jong/Young rhyme leads directly into the scene in which the singer looks at "people in the park," seeing them—like the "young in one another's arms" in Yeats's "Sailing to Byzantium"—as images of the youth he is alienated from. He would change places with them "in a minute if

I could"—a phrase that resonates all the way back to "Bob Dylan's Dream" in 1963. More directly, the scene echoes "Love Sick," the first song on the album, in which "I see / I see" (doubled, distanced) young lovers in the meadow as "silhouettes," mere shadows.

So far, so sad. And there is a tremendous sense of sadness to this album. All these images of the divided, uncertain self carry the emotional resonances of broken love affairs, lost confidence, abandoned dreams. There is a feeling of weariness and demoralization, at times stoic, at times bitter, at times merely resigned.

"What would it matter anyway?" he asks the waitress, just as, earlier, the drastic alternative of "kiss you or kill you" is dismissed with "it probably wouldn't matter to you anyhow" (SD). "It doesn't matter where I go any more," he sings (CW). At its most cynical, the album approaches a complete disavowal of moral responsibility: "If I had a conscience, well I just might blow my top / What would I do with it anyway? Maybe take it to the pawn shop" (H). But perhaps even this image hints at a concealed opposite—for things that are put in pawn can also be, in the technical word, *redeemed*. What prospects are there for redemption on *Time Out Of Mind*?

Looking at possible answers, I find again the same patterns of division and disjunction. Redemption does exist on *Time Out Of Mind*, but it is always equivocal, held at a distance, never assured. The singer is "praying for salvation" (DRB), but he "[doesn't] even hear the murmur of a prayer" (NDY). He "went to church on Sunday," but is immediately distracted when "she passed by" (CIB). He proclaims that "God is my shield, He won't lead me astray," but this faith affords no protection against the immediately following line, "Still I don't know what I'm going to do" (TIF). The singer is "trying to get to heaven"— again an image of a goal not yet attained—"before they close the door" (TGH).

Theologically, the only definitive "closing" of heaven's door would be at the Last Judgment; and familiar Dylan images of Apocalypse recur—in "Can't Wait," "the end of time has just begun;"[39] in "Not Dark Yet," "time is running away." Against this apprehension of time coming to a drastic end, the singer sets his pleas to "stop time." In "Love Sick" he hears the clock tick, and in "Highlands" he asks, "I wish someone would come and push back the clock for me." Time out.

The question of redemption may also be connected to the theme of abandoned love. When the singer tells us he is "sick of . . . this kind of love" (LS), he invites the question, *what* kind of love? Human or divine, erotic or spiritual? On *Time Out Of Mind*, the overwhelming majority of the "love songs" portray relationships which are failed or unreciprocated or definitively in the past. (Biographically, there is the temptation to read many of the songs as expressing still, twenty years on, the pain of the loss of Sara.) But love, of any kind, offers no assurance of redemption; love on this album is loss, pain, rejection, separation, despair.

Further images of possible redemption are bound up with two recurring puns: the familiar "eye/I," and a more conventional religious wordplay, characterized in Latin as "the Sol/Filius pun," *sun/Son*, in which references to the light of the sun also imply Christ as the second person of the Trinity. Both puns are used throughout the album, and they come together at its very end, in the last verse of "Highlands."

"I ain't lookin' for nothing in anyone's eyes," he sings in "Not Dark Yet." The vacancy of the eye/I is complete and reciprocal; no one's identity has anything to offer. The eye/I is the site of increasingly serious wounds: "heat rising in my eyes" (TGH); "my eyes begin to bleed" (DRB); "My eyes feel like they're falling off my face" (TIF). These wounds are presented as being beyond healing. "Nothing can heal me now," he sings, "but your touch" (TIF). As we have seen, however, "your touch" is unlikely to be given: the "you" of these songs is always absent. In "Not Dark Yet," "I've still got the scars that the sun didn't heal"—or, perhaps, that the Son didn't heal. The Son too, like the "you," is absent; there is no healing presence. The sun/Son is traditionally figured as redemptive, but on *Time Out Of Mind* its light is often obscured. Shadows fall, clouds pass over the sun, the light is dim: "You left me standing in the doorway crying / In the dark land of the sun" (SD). Not only is this world a "dark land," unilluminated by the sun/Son, it is the dark land *of* the sun. Darkness belongs to light; darkness is the shadow side of the Son Himself.

Eye/I and sun/Son come together in the last lines of the last verse of "Highlands":

> The sun is beginning to shine on me
> But it's not like the sun that used to be
> The party's over, and there's less and less to say
> I got new eyes, everything looks far away.

At first this seems like a clear statement of redemption: the sun/Son is once more beginning to shine. But the sun has changed. In some unspecified way, it is not what it "used to be." The next line suggests that this new sun only reinforces the singer's sense of despair and futility; the prophetic voice is left with "less and less to say." Similarly the new eye/I ought to be a sign of redemption, but it reads equally as a sign of alienation, the singer feeling "far away" from himself, and from any possibility of human contact.

However, any reading of "Highlands" must also take into account its choruses. While the verses of the song contain some of the album's bleakest and most despairing lines, the choruses contain some of its most hopeful. How are we to understand this juxtaposition? The most obvious symbolic reading of the word *highlands* would be to take it as "heaven," which is certainly the sense suggested by the line "That's where I'll be when I get called home." In that case perhaps the choruses simply present the contrast between sin and salvation, between the fallen "world gone wrong" and the paradise to come. But I don't think that it's quite that simple. In contrast to earlier albums, Dylan chooses not to use an explicitly Christian vocabulary; instead, his "highlands" have other, and quite complex, intertextual sources.

Firstly, the line "My heart's in the Highlands" is a direct quotation from Robert Burns, from a song of that name first published in 1790:

> My heart's in the Highlands, my heart is not here;
> My heart's in the Highlands a-chasing the deer;
> Chasing the wild deer, and following the roe;
> My heart's in the Highlands, wherever I go.

I'm not sure whether Dylan knows anything about this song other than its first line[40]—but the effects of intertextuality always spin beyond the author's control. In Scotland, Burns's song is usually regarded as somewhat sweet and sentimental, a genteel exercise in nostalgia for an idealized "highlands" that never truly existed in the first place. The very fact that it is written in standard English, with no admixture of Scots, gives it (for Burns) an artificial and stilted flavor. What is interesting is that the same effect is reproduced in Dylan's chorus. His highlands are "far from the town" and far from the gritty urban reality of the vocabulary everywhere else on the album. The choruses are full of slightly archaic expressions: "gentle and fair," "the horses and hounds," "the twang of the arrow and the snap of the bow." (This last phrase surely recalls the even more artificial, sentimental, and idealized evocation of Sara as "Glamorous nymph with an arrow and bow" [L, 391].) The highlands are, in the nursery-rhyme phrase, "over the hills and far away." Whether consciously or not, then, the Burns quotation serves to reinforce the idea that there is something false and idealized in this image of the "highlands." It is an artificial idyll, existing only in sentimental fancy.

Even more interesting is another set of intertextual resonances, which are set off by the obvious comparison of "Highlands" to "Sad-Eyed Lady of the Lowlands." The titles echo each other; the length and placing of the songs on the albums echo each other; the more recent song even has a reference to two blondes. More crucially, the imagery of eyes is repeated. "I got new eyes," "Highlands" concludes—and who cannot respond: "Sad-eyed lady of the Lowlands / Where the sad-eyed prophet says that no man comes" (L, 239)?

Consider also the possible puns on *highlands,* in terms of the images we have already seen at work in this song. "Eye-lands" is obvious, and leads to both "I-lands" and "islands." Put *island* alongside *no man,* and what emerges is John Donne: "No man is an island entire of itself; every man is a piece of the continent, a part of the main. . . . Any man's death diminishes me, because I am involved in mankind, and therefore send not to know for whom the bell tolls; it tolls for thee." If you think this quotation has led us too far astray from *Time Out Of Mind,* remember "Standing in the Doorway," where we find: "I can hear the church bells ringing in the yard / I wonder who they're ringing for." Them bells, one might say, are ringing for thee.

What I would argue, then, is that the image of the "highlands" is as split and equivocal as any of the other possible images of redemption on *Time Out Of Mind.* The allusion to Burns underlines the artificiality of the language used in the choruses, while the reading of *highlands* as "I-lands" returns us to the notion of the isolated and divided self. "Highlands" reinscribes the wounded eye/I into the center of its image of salvation. The "I" here is the voice which throughout the album has been continually undermined and denied authority or integrity, presented instead as an intertextual composite. It is the I that doesn't know, which isn't sure, which can't remember but can only "wonder."

Yet at the same time it is an "I" which, for all its professions of alienation, nevertheless is "involved with mankind" and remains part of a community. I return to the double effect of the phrase "time out of mind." I said originally that it signified both continuity and a disjunction within that continuity. My analysis has been heavily stressing the disjunction, but now, in closing, it is time to return to the continuity.

The singer of *Time Out Of Mind* remains part of a community, if only by virtue of the simple fact that he *is* a singer. He belongs to a tradition. And it is this point which Dylan has been making, emphatically, in the so-called Never Ending Tour, in his continued commitment to live performance. In the years since *Time Out Of Mind* came out, Dylan has worked most of its songs into his repertoire,[41] and has continued to interweave his own songs with classic songs from the American tradition: traditional folk songs, bluegrass-gospel by the Stanley Brothers, even Willie Dixon's "Hoochie Coochie Man"! And, in the fall of 2002, he gave us not only Neil Young (as in "Highlands"), but also a quite wonderful series of tributes to his fellow singer-songwriter Warren Zevon.

This sense of community is there to be heard also in the sound of the album: in those wonderful Daniel Lanois arrangements, in the sense that here are a dozen or more great musicians gathered in a great, echoing barn of a studio, feeding off each other's contributions, weaving a texture of sound round this worn, ancient, magical voice at the center. However much the singer insists that he has "less and less to say" (H), the very existence of the songs belies him. *Time Out Of Mind* is an album with a lot to say, and it says it memorably. But perhaps the most important thing that it says is that here is a singer who can embody within himself all these doubts and contradictions, all this faith and all this despair, and out of them still make great art. Here is a singer who can align himself with a great tradition of song in which he simultaneously loses himself and finds himself. Here is a singer, Bob Dylan, who is beginning to appear as if he had always existed, time out of mind.

"Love and Theft"

The release of Bob Dylan's *"Love and Theft"* (2001) was greeted by a good deal of both love and theft. The love was obvious in the ecstatic reviews the album received in most of the mainstream media. *Rolling Stone* gave the album a rare five stars and described Dylan as "relaxed, magisterial, utterly confident in every musical idiom he touches" (September 27, 2001; 65). The Toronto *Globe and Mail* said that it reached "a new level of maturity." The *Washington Post* called it "a triumphant return to his inspirations." And so on: the conventional wisdom is definitely that Dylan is back "in" and that *"Love and Theft"* confirms, or even surpasses, the achievement of *Time Out Of Mind.*[1]

But there was also a fair amount, if not of "theft," at least of advance borrowing. Several of the songs were broadcast on radio in advance of the official release, and MP3s of these songs were swiftly spread through the internet. Also, as sample copies sent to reviewers, journalists, and sales representatives began to circulate, so too did leaked CD-Rs. Many hardcore Dylan fans had complete copies of *"Love and Theft"* well in advance of its official release date—which was perhaps just as well, since the official release date was September 11, 2001, a day on which very few people had either the time or the inclination to listen to a new CD.[2]

Indeed, *"Love and Theft"* seems almost *too* neat and programmatic a title for a Dylan album, speaking directly to his love for all forms of American music, as well as to his tendency to express that love by direct quotation, borrowing, or "theft." I have already referred (in the section "Quotation/Citation/Recitation" in Chapter 2) to the fact that the quotation marks, the graphic sign of citation-ality, are built into the title. As with *Time Out Of Mind*, the album is saturated with quotations, both musical and verbal. Its musical styles range over the whole history of twentieth-century American music, from the blues to jazz, from Western swing to melodious pop. Echoes shift abruptly from the crooner Bing Crosby to the primitive blues singer Charley Patton. The instrumental accompaniment to the album's opening track, "Tweedle Dee and Tweedle Dum," is taken almost note for note from a 1950s pop song by Johnny and Jack, "Uncle John's Bongos."

Altogether, *"Love and Theft"* is a much more eclectic album than *Time Out Of Mind*, which was dominated by the influence of the blues and by the atmospheric production values of Daniel Lanois. On *"Love and Theft"* you never know from one track to the next what musical idiom you're going to end up in, although you can be sure that, whatever idiom it is, Dylan will handle it with virtuosic ease and mastery—aided by the expertise of his road-honed backing band.

The literary references in the lyrics are no less far-ranging. "Summer Days" lifts one of its most spectacular lines from F. Scott Fitzgerald. Shakespeare is travestied (in the manner of the minstrel shows); Virgil is quoted straight; a contemporary Japanese novelist, Jamichi Saga, is extensively stolen from. John Donne's "for whom the bell tolls" puts in a repeat appearance, doubling *Time Out Of Mind*. "High Water" includes a character called Bertha Mason, the madwoman in the attic of *Jane Eyre*, who, in the words of "Summer Days," "set fire to the place as a parting gift." This mid-nineteenth-century reference resonates, in "High Water," with mentions of Charles Darwin and of George Lewes, the husband of George Eliot—unless, of course, Dylan intends "George Lewis," a 1920s jazz clarinet player. It's been many years since Dylan so thoroughly ransacked his library.

The title *"Love and Theft"* has been widely understood as referring to Eric Lott's scholarly study of the American tradition of blackface minstrelsy. If so, the essential reference is to disguise, pastiche, the mask, deferred identity—all of which are essential thematic features of Dylan's whole work. All of *"Love and Theft"* operates in blackface: none of its narrative positions can be taken at face value. (Indeed, the narrative voice on most of the songs is more openly fictionalized than in any other Dylan album.) The voice always echoes other voices; the multiple personae inhabit all the intertextual traces of both musical and literary allusion, without ever coalescing into a single coherent stance. It's Dylan's ultimate trickster incarnation, or, as Richard Lodge wrote on rec.music.dylan, in as neat a summary as I have yet seen: "It's Huck Finn's album."

The strongest initial impression of *"Love and Theft"* is its generosity of invention, its overflowing quality. (In this way it really problematizes my initial division of Dylan's work. *"Love and Theft"* is not so much the culmination of the Years of Performance as it is a sudden, exhilarating throwback to the Years of Creation.) Everything about this album is a little too much. Every song seems to go on for two or three stanzas too long,[3] and many individual lines seem stuffed with an impossible number of extra syllables. Only Dylan's virtuosic command of rhythm and vocal delivery could have got away with presenting, as a single line: "She says 'You can't repeat the past,' I say, 'You can't? What do you mean you can't? Of course you can!' " (This line is also the Fitzgerald quote referred to above.) At every point, the writing seems to be exceeding its own limits, joyously ignoring any constraints of formal or thematic coherence. There is simply too much of everything on *"Love and Theft":* its overwhelming gift is sheer, unstinted *abundance.*

One aspect of this abundance is the jokes. As if he is truly working from within a minstrelsy music-hall tradition, Dylan serves up on this album a whole series of corny jokes—"I'm sitting on my watch, so I can be on time"—culminating in the knock-knock routine in the climactic stanza of "Po' Boy"—"Freddie or not, here I come." From one point of view, the jokes are simply further signs of throwaway excess, a reaction against the grim and controlled classicism of *Time Out Of Mind.* They suggest that Dylan is having fun again, and that perhaps the lyrics should not be taken altogether too seriously.

But from another point of view, the jokes are part of the album's whole rhetorical strategy of sneaking up very dark and ominous images under a cover of apparent innocuousness. "Bye and Bye" opens in the saccharine mode of a 1940s crooner, with Dylan's almost melodious voice issuing vacuous clichés like "I'm singing love's praises with sugar-coated rhyme"; yet somehow, by the end of the song we have arrived at "I'm gonna baptize you in fire so you can sin no more / I'm gonna establish my rule through civil war." A similarly sinister undertone undermines the "sugar-coated rhymes" of the album's other crooner, "Moonlight," which starts out with "the songbird's sweet melodious tone," and ends up with John Donne's tolling bell. The megalomaniac implications of "civil war" resurface even more startlingly in "Honest With Me": "I'm here to create the new imperial empire / I'm gonna do whatever circumstances require." Writing about "Tweedle Dee and Tweedle Dum," another rec.music.dylan correspondent, Glynn Walley, commented: "It's as if God had sent down two destroying angels and they turned out to be Laurel and Hardy." Or vice versa.

Abrupt transitions of tone are everywhere in these lyrics. In "Po' Boy" a knock-knock joke is followed, in the next line, by an allusion to the Parable of the Prodigal Son. Charley Patton transmutes into Charley Darwin, pursued down Highway 5 by a creationist sheriff. The narrator of a dark vision of the apocalypse as a Mississippi flood pauses to say "Jump into the wagon, love / Throw your panties overboard." Even within a single line, widely divergent tonal registers coexist: in "Cry Awhile," "Don Pasquale" is simultaneously an image of the sacrificial Lamb of Easter, a character in a Donizetti opera, and a local mafia hoodlum calling up his pimp. Whereas *Time Out Of Mind* was relatively homogeneous in tone, and created a coherent (if rather sombre) figure of its narrator, *"Love and Theft"* is wildly diverse and inconsistent, taking a gleeful delight in defying any possibility of pinning it down. In this respect, and also in its extreme musical eclecticism, the Dylan songs it most resembles are the Basement Tapes.

Nevertheless, despite all this diversity, *"Love and Theft"* clearly continues, in a different tone, many of the thematic concerns of *Time Out Of Mind*. However tricksterish the new album may appear on the surface, the prophetic worldview is never far away. This is still a world gone wrong: a world of violence, empire, and civil war, in which military captains aren't bothered by how many of their friends get killed; a world in which fire falls from the sky and floodwaters rise; a world in which "every moment of existence seems like some dirty trick." It's a world in which the singer remains divided from himself—"not even acquainted with my own desires"— and separated from any promise of love or consolation. Including religious consolation.

While *Time Out Of Mind* still included some ambiguous references to Christian redemption, *"Love and Theft"* is almost entirely bereft of any such allusion.[4] This is Dylan's least explicitly Christian album for several decades. All that remains are a few moments of human contact and love amidst the wreckage. Thus, even the doom-ridden and apocalyptic landscape of "High Water" does manage to end on the (decidedly tentative) note "I just can't be happy, love, unless you're happy too." In the last resort, only the sheer joy and verve of the music-making keeps this album from being one of Dylan's darkest and most oppressive works.

The same thing might, of course, be said about *Time Out Of Mind*. My first, knee-jerk reaction was that the two albums are so different from each other that comparisons might be of very limited value. Gradually I'm beginning to see the continuities. What does remain the same is that both albums, so vastly different from each other, struck me even on first hearing as absolutely authoritative: definitive statements of a songwriting and song-performing intelligence which is undiminished in its originality and brilliance. Bob Dylan still has the gift both of coming up with the unexpected and of making the unexpected seem inevitable. His genius is always somewhere else, an alibi or an alias; yet the alias is always somehow familiar, an echo or a ghost, bringing it all back home, revisited.

Preface

1 "Hull Rust Mahoning Mine: a national historic landmark," pamphlet distributed by the Hibbing Historical Society. Since the first edition of *Alias Bob Dylan,* a new source has provided a vast amount of information about the history of Hibbing and about Bobby Zimmerman's childhood there: Dave Engel, *Just Like Bob Zimmerman's Blues: Dylan in Minnesota* (Mesabi, WI: River City Memoirs, 1997). I acknowledge a tremendous debt to this book, especially in my more imaginative and speculative revisioning of the Hibbing years in Stephen Scobie, *And Forget My Name* (Victoria, BC: Ekstasis Editions, 1999).

2 The exact date of this performance and the names of the other band members are still subjects of historical disagreement. Robert Shelton, for instance, claims that the band consisted of "Chuck Nara on drums, Bill Marinec on bass, and Larry Fabbro on electric guitar, with Bob on piano, guitar, and lead vocals" *(No Direction Home,* 42). But this line-up more probably pertains to a later grouping, the Shadow Blasters. Dave Engel and Clinton Heylin both argue that the band, one version of the Golden Chords, consisted of Monte Edwardson on lead guitar and LeRoy Hoikkala on drums. Heylin *(Dylan)* dates the show as Winter 1957; Engel suggests February 6, 1958. My account draws on the standard biographical sources, and also on comments, such as that from Bill Marinec, which were passed on to those attending the "Mixed Up Confusion" Bob Dylan convention at Hibbing in October 1989.

Chapter One: Prophet and Trickster

1 In the late 1990s and early 2000s, this reaction has changed a little. The conventional wisdom of casual reviewers is now that Dylan puts on tremendous shows. But the basic presuppositions remain unaltered. In my local newspaper, the Victoria *Times-Colonist,* a review by Mike Devlin of Dylan's May 1998 concert in Vancouver began with these words:

> If his performance on Thursday night is anything to judge him by, Bob Dylan is in the process of making one of the biggest comebacks in rock 'n' roll history. Sure, there are some fans that would argue that Dylan has never left; but in reality, Dylan hasn't been a prominent musical force since his 1975 landmark album, *Desire.*

Later in the review, Devlin writes: "Dylan ditched his trademark acoustic guitar for much of the evening, forsaking his folk roots for his electric sound"—a comment at least thirty years out of date, but illustrative of the persistence of the popular image of the early Dylan.

2   In a 1997 interview with David Gates, Dylan specifically points to a concert at Locarno, Switzerland, in October 1987, as his "breakthrough" ("Dylan Revisited," 66).

3   One possible synthesis of the prophet and trickster figures may be found in the concept of the "shaman." For a magnificent poetic exploration of this synthesis, see Anne Waldman's poem about Dylan, *Shaman/Schamane:*

> shaman's shouting yeah for you
> & singing your sorrow
> . . . .
> shaman touches the ocean
> shaman don't drown
> shaman echoes himself
> . . . .
> shaman you're wily
> there's a sham in shaman.
>
> (10, 12, 22)

4   See Stephen Scobie, "No Prophet's Son," *The Bridge* 2 (Winter 1999): 7–20. In this article I discuss the background of the biblical citation from Amos 7:14, as well as the uses of similar phrases in traditional blues songs. I conclude that the form of the disclaimer is ambiguous, both in the biblical original and in Dylan's use of it.

5   Usually. Biblical tradition does allow for the possibility of female prophets, but all the canonical prophets in the Old Testament are male.

6   The "catastrophic situation" evoked in "A Hard Rain's A-Gonna Fall" has long been understood to be the Cuban missile crisis. Nat Hentoff's liner notes to *The Freewheelin' Bob Dylan* explicitly state that the song was written during the crisis, and Hentoff quotes Dylan as saying: "Every line in it is actually the start of a whole song. But when I wrote it, I thought I wouldn't have enough time alive to write all those songs so I put all I could into this one." Unfortunately, "A Hard Rain's A-Gonna Fall" had already been written at least a month before the major events of the crisis. Dylan performed it at Carnegie Hall on September 22, 1962. So, while its general prophetic evocation of a catastrophic situation remains valid, its specific connection to the Cuban missile crisis must be seen as another instance of retrospective myth making.

7   "How many people here are aware that we're living in the end of times right now? . . . You just watch your newspapers, you're going to see—maybe two years, maybe three years, five years from now you just wait and see. Russia will come down and attack in the Middle East. China's got an army of two million people. . . . There's gonna be a war called the Battle of Armageddon which is like something you never even dreamed about. And

Christ will set up His Kingdom and He'll rule it from Jerusalem" (Bob Dylan, November 1979, as quoted in Heylin, *Saved!*, 42, 46–47). Fortunately, Dylan's vision of imminent Apoclypse in the Middle East did not come true, at least not then.

8   Harry Smith was an artist, filmmaker, and musicologist associated with the Beat movement and especially with Allen Ginsberg. The *Anthology of American Folk Music* is a collection he put together for Folkways Records in 1952 (reissued in a deluxe CD boxed set by Smithsonian Folkways in 1997). It is a highly personal selection of recordings, mostly from the 1920s, of traditional American music: folk, blues, gospel, bluegrass, country. It was accompanied by Smith's idiosyncratic notes and marked by his conspicuous refusal to identify the race of the musicians. In the late 1950s and early 1960s, it became the "bible" for the emerging American folk music revival; young singers in Greenwich Village knew it by heart. From his earliest album in 1961 to *World Gone Wrong* in 1994, Dylan has continually returned to the Harry Smith *Anthology* as a source for his versions of traditional songs, and also for lines and images in his original work. For example, the line "All those railroadmen just drink up your blood like wine," from the 1966 "Memphis Blues Again," is taken directly from Bascom Lamar Lunsford's "I Wish I Was a Mole in the Ground," selection 63 on the *Anthology*.

9   Hyde's book, *Trickster,* also contains an extended treatment of Allen Ginsberg as trickster.

10   Dylan's songs contain many other echoes, and even direct quotations from Jack Kerouac, from "the perfect image of a priest" in "Desolation Row," to "Mexico City blues" in "Something's Burning, Baby." Ginsberg has repeatedly stated that it was Kerouac's *Mexico City Blues* which first "turned Dylan on" to poetry.

11   Ironically, Dylan has also been the subject of what is arguably the same kind of Promethean theft, in the form of the vast number of unauthorized "bootleg" recordings of his work. While there are undoubtedly a few bootleggers trying to make money from stolen property, the vast majority of those who circulate tapes of Dylan concerts are trickster-thieves, doing so out of a genuine love for the music and a desire that it should be shared as widely as possible.

12   It is perhaps tempting to see this interplay also as an extended interaction, in Dylan, between the movements generally designated as "modernism" and "postmodernism." Modernism, for all its play of fragmented surfaces, always yearns for the stability of the prophetic, as T. S. Eliot moved from shoring up the ruins of his Waste Land to the crystalline certainties of *Four Quartets,* whereas postmodernism has embraced the trickster's delight in instability and constantly shifting identity. Dylan's writing often seems deeply indebted to modernism—especially to Eliot: Dylan's "Desolation Row" can easily be seen as a variation on Eliot's *The Waste Land*—but he is also *post*modernist, not only in his reliance on performance, but also in his ironic attitude toward his own modernism, his awareness that he stands at the *end* of a twentieth-century tradition in poetry, if not in music. As a prophet, Dylan is perhaps the last of the century's great modernists; as a trickster, he is perhaps one of its first postmodernists.

Chapter Two: Glossary

1   "Waggoner's Lad" is a traditional American song. A version by Buell Kazee appears on Harry Smith's *Anthology of American Folk Music*. It was part of Joan Baez's early repertoire and appears on her second album. Dylan sang it a few times in 1988–90; the version from New York, October 1988, is quite stunning.

2   For an excellent discussion of this topic, see Daniel Karlin's essay, "Bob Dylan's Names," in Corcoran, 27-50.

3   Entertainers and movie stars were especially likely to have changed their names. Watching movies during the 1950s in Hibbing, at the Lybba Theater, which was owned by his maternal relatives the Edelsteins, Bobby Zimmerman would have seen, among many others, Emmanuel Goldenberg (Edward G. Robinson), Bernard Schwartz (Tony Curtis), and Issur Danielovitch (Kirk Douglas). He may even have listened to Ethel Merman, without realising that she too was a Zimmerman, and that she had, in Robert Shelton's words, "simply lopped off the first syllable" (49)!

4   Sometimes spelt with an extra *n:* Gunnn. In his early years, Dylan continued to use pseudonyms, from the obvious "Bob Landy" to the archetypal "Blind Boy Grunt" and the debatable "Roosevelt Gook."

5   There is, admittedly, little evidence in Bob Dylan's later work of any interest in American football. Sports references in Dylan songs tend to be either to boxing or to baseball. The most obvious reference to football is in a boxing song: the journalist in "Who Killed Davey Moore?" defends himself by claiming that "There's just as much danger in a football game" (L, 76). But Bobby Zimmerman was a teenage boy growing up in North America in the 1950s, and it's hard to believe that he was totally unaware of football. A photograph in Dave Engel's *Just Like Bob Zimmerman's Blues* shows two of Bob's erstwhile bandmates, Larry Fabbro and Chuck Nara, playing for a Hibbing High School football team (140). And I have heard some, unsubstantiated, rumours about Bobby Zimmerman trying out for the team.

6   Bobby Dillon still, to this day, holds the record for the Most Pass Interceptions by a Green Bay Packer over an entire career: 52, from 1952 to 1959. The record for the most interceptions in a single season is held by Irv Comp, with 10 in 1942, but Bobby Dillon comes in second with 9, a feat he achieved in 1953, 1955, and 1957. The 1953 total was helped by 4 in a single game (against Detroit), which also remains, to this day, a Green Bay Packers record. (All these statistics are taken from the Green Bay Packers website: www.packers.com.)

7   The name is also a legal fact, a "work of art" certified by law, signed and countersigned by the power of the state. Robert Allen Zimmerman legally changed his name to Bob Dylan on August 2, 1962.

8   For what little it's worth, there certainly are biographical anecdotes and indications of tensions between Bobby and his father, but no more than might quite normally be expected in the relationship between a middle-class 1950s father and a restless teenage son interested in music and motorcycles.

9 This phrase carries with it an enormous load of cultural association. In religious terms, the Name of the Father is the name of God; in specifically Christian terms, the name of the First Person of the Trinity. In psychoanalytic terms, writers like Jacques Lacan have utilized the French pun *nom/non* to reinforce the idea that *le Nom du Père* is also *le Non du Père:* the father's archetypal forbidding the son sexual access to the mother. This denial, it is argued, leads to the repression of desire into the unconscious and gives the son access instead to the symbolic order of language and the name: thus the *non* leads back to the *nom*, which indeed the son will eventually inherit from the father.

10 By "divisions" I intend to suggest here the whole problematics of language and reference proposed by Jacques Derrida under the term *différance.* Derrida, of course, would not agree that the proper name is exempt from *différance,* and this is precisely the point I now go on to argue, both here and in the sections on "Signature" and "Self Portrait" later in this chapter. For a fascinating discussion by Derrida on the implications of the assumption of an alias, see his *On the Name,* especially pp. 12–13.

11 I admit that I have no evidence of the extent of Bob Dylan's knowledge of German, though I think it highly unlikely that he would not, at some stage in his life, have become aware of *Zimmermann* as "carpenter" and *Zimmer* as "room." However, here as elsewhere, I do not regard my reading as dependent on conscious authorial intention.

12 For a more detailed discussion of this song, and especially for the implications of the lover being a ghost, see the section "Ghost" later in this chapter.

13 The change from "carpenter" to "truckdriver" was not a simple, once-and-for-all decision, although 1978 (the year of the divorce) does seem to be the main transition. *Truckdriver* appears as early as 1975, and the occasional *carpenter* as late as 1984. The fully revised lyrics sung in 1984 omitted the line altogether. From 1988 on, through hundreds of performances, "truckdriver" has been constant.

14 For a more detailed discussion of the Christ parallels in this song, see Christopher Rollason, " 'Tangled Up In Blue' and the Never-Ending Search," on the Bob Dylan Critical Corner website, www.geocities.com/Athens/Oracle/6752/magazine.html.

15 "Mark of orginality" was thus reprinted correctly by McGregor, *Bob Dylan* (18). Benson, *The Bob Dylan Companion* (12), reprints the incorrect "mask."

16 The lines come from one of the speeches Dylan gave between songs on his "gospel" tours: Hartford, May 8, 1980 (quoted from Heylin, *Saved!,* 74–75). This is a particularly notorious speech, in which Dylan goes on to assert that "either one-third or two-thirds" of the population of San Francisco is homosexual.

17 The *persona* or classical mask also acted as a mini-megaphone, amplifying the actor's voice through the carved mouth-hole. One etymological theory, now disputed, held that this feature was the origin of the Latin word for "mask": *per-sona* (through-sound).

18 See *Biograph,* liner notes, side 7. Dylan's comment comes, ironically, on a song called "Up To Me." Rimbaud's line (from a letter to Georges Izambard, dated May 13, 1871) has been widely quoted in support of the postmodern sense of the self not as a metaphysical entity but as the product of multiple and interlocking systems of discourse. It

can serve as a motto not only for Dylan but for a whole theory of the divided self, or rather, of the impossibility of an undivided self. Its use of the third person *is* instead of the first person *am* further serves to dislodge *I* from its privileged position as syntactic and ideological subject.

19 "Interview with Bob Dylan," *Maclean's* (March 20, 1978): 4–6.

20 Dave Percival's concordance *Love Plus Zero,* which covers all the lyrics up to *Under the Red Sky* (but does not include *Tarantula*), lists 132 instances of *eye* or *eyes* in Dylan's songs. By contrast, *ear(s)* produces only 27 references.

21 Derrida discusses "signature" in several of his books. The most pertinent instance here would be *Limited Inc.*

22 "Only the name can inherit," Derrida writes, "and this is why the name, to be distinguished from the bearer, is always and *a priori* a dead man's name, a name of death" *(Ear of the Other,* 7). For Derrida this link between death and the signature is so strong that he can state, "When I sign, I am already dead" *(Glas,* 19bi).

23 Michael Gray's initial discussion is in *Song and Dance Man* (1st ed., 279–81); his retraction is in *Telegraph* 29 (Spring 1988). Dylan's claim to authorship was made only on the record label; the sheet music credited him only with the arrangement, and the words do not appear in *Lyrics.*

24 These lines, in "Tomorrow is a Long Time" (L, 42), hold other echoes too. "Echo" was the name of Bobby Zimmerman's girlfriend in Hibbing, Echo Hellstrom. It may not be too fanciful to trace some of Dylan's obsession with images of identity at one remove— the self defined by the other—to his early love for a woman whose very name displaced her presence into an echo. As for the "footsteps," recall the early nuclear-protest song "Let Me Die in My Footsteps" (L, 21). To be in someone's footsteps is, idiomatically, to follow him (like the page of Good King Wenceslas), to put your foot in the trace of the other. So the expressed desire of this song is for the singer to live (and to die) in his own footsteps, in the trace of himself that he has already left behind. The footstep, like the signature, is a sign of presence which can be read only in the signer's absence.

25 The facts about Dylan's Minnesota background as Bobby Zimmerman were first widely publicized in an article in *Newsweek* (November 4, 1963).

26 At the same concert, Joan Baez joins in the game. Introducing "Silver Dagger," a traditional folk song that had been the first track on her first Vanguard album, she describes it as "an old Bob Dylan song."

27 The Name of the Father (the paternal signature rejected by an alias) is also, in Christian terms, the First Person of the Trinity. So, for an orthodox Jew, "there is no Second person" (T, 134): that is, Jesus is not a "Second person" of the divinity.

28 "You may call me R. J., you may call me Ray" (L, 424) is quoted from the comedian Ray Johnson. These lines formed, as it were, his signature.

29 Dylan's name does appear in a couple of *titles,* such as "Bob Dylan's Dream."

30 Dylan's album is clearly called *Self Portrait,* two words without hyphen. I have also adopted that usage in my own text, and write "self portrait." However, the Derrida text I

am quoting uses "self-portrait," so that is the form that occurs within quotations. And I use the hyphen within the word "self-portraiture."

31 Only fourteen songs, since two of them appeared twice, in different takes.

32 Was "All the Tired Horses" always intended this way? Again, I have no way of knowing. Was the existing text originally intended as a refrain, with more words to come? Did Dylan originally intend to sing the lines himself, over a track of backing vocals? Did he then listen to the backing track and say, Hey, that sounds neat, let's leave it as it is? I don't know. I can only deal with the text as we have it, as it is presented to us, as the first track of an album called *Self Portrait*.

33 Nothing in the published credits allows us to identify the singers.

34 In conversation, Thomas Dutoit suggested to me that the *riding/writing* pun is mediated through the mythological figure of Pegasus. He cites John Keats's final letter, dated November 30, 1820: "Yet I ride the little horse, and, at my worst, even in quarantine, summoned up more puns, in a sort of desperation, in one week than in any year of my life." Here Keats not only puns on *riding/writing*, but also self-reflexively comments that the writing produces puns. Consider also the other pun in Dylan's lines: *the tired/retired*. Dylan had at the time certainly "retired" from his public life and career. It would be another four years before he returned to the concert stage.

35 Dylan's interest in painting became much more serious and focused in the early 1970s, when he took a series of lessons from Norman Raeben. In 1994 Dylan published a book of his sketches entitled *Drawn Blank* (New York: Random House). Perhaps the most appreciative critical response is that of Richard Holt:

> In the sketches [by] musicians [such as Dylan] . . . the notational mark is constantly present; the quick, forceful rendition that captures the rawness and immediacy of rock. Coupled with an eye for social observation, the pictures reveal much of the quality of a rock song; raw insightful commentary in a precise package. . . . Dylan's drawings use a similar line to Lennon. His Thurberesque characters inhabit landscapes which are sparse yet often rich with the symbolic layers that typify his lyrical style.
>
> ("Lyrical Abstractions," 75)

36 Derrida puns between *autobiography* and *otobiography;* one of his major works on the subject of self-portraiture is entitled, in English, *The Ear of the Other*. The 'other,' then, may be identified precisely in terms of the ear, the receptive sense, of the listener.

37 I have already touched on the song "House Carpenter" (in the section "Alias" earlier in Chapter 2) in connection to the translation of *carpenter* from the German *Zimmermann*. The most extensive treatment of the history and traditional origins of "House Carpenter" is found in Heylin, *Dylan's Daemon Lover*, and in Christopher Rollason's online review of Heylin at the Bob Dylan Critical Corner (www.geocities.com/Athens/Oracle/6752/magazine.html). My discussion of the ballad's history is deeply indebted to Heylin, though we reach somewhat divergent conclusions in terms of its relation to Bob Dylan.

38 This is one of the points where I disagree with Heylin. In a private e-mail to me, Heylin emphasizes that "elements of the devil original reside in the 'ghost' version and the devil version is the original. . . . What I'm saying is that the clues about the demon lover's original nature reside in the ghost versions." Fair enough, but I still find it significant that Dylan chooses to say *ghost* and not *demon*.

39 Derrida also links the ghost and the demon: "The demon is that very thing which *comes back*. . . . The demon is the *revenance* which repeats its entrance, coming back from one knows not where . . . inherited from one knows not whom, but already persecutory, by means of the simple form of the return, indefatigably repetitive" *(Post Card,* 341). Derrida is actually discussing Freud and the pleasure principle, but he might as well be giving a plot summary of "House Carpenter."

40 A double remove actually: it's not that Angel *is* a ghost but that he *looks like* a ghost. This double remove is also characteristic of Dylan. As late as *Time Out Of Mind* (1997), in "Tryin' to Get to Heaven" we find the lines: "I'm going to sleep down in the parlour / And relive my dreams." The dream, already at one remove from waking reality, is distanced one step further: it must not only be dreamed but redreamed (reslept, relived). The "angel" is also at one remove: a messenger, bearing someone else's words.

41 For a magnificent realization of this image of the ghost, see Marilynne Robinson's novel *Housekeeping:* "Every spirit passing through the world fingers the tangible and mars the mutable, and finally has come to look and not to buy" (73). I rather doubt that Dylan has ever read *Housekeeping,* but he would certainly understand Robinson's evocation of the ghost as sorrow, the song as revenant:

> For families will not be broken. Curse and expel them, send their children wandering, drown them in floods and fires, and old women will make songs out of all these sorrows and sit in the porches and sing them on mild evenings. Every sorrow suggests a thousand songs, and every song recalls a thousand sorrows, and so they are infinite in number, and all the same.
>
> (194)

42 "Abandoned Love" is also the song which contains, two verses later, the lines about eyes and disguise discussed earlier in this chapter in the section "Mask."

43 The discussion here focuses on personal identity, but a similar argument could be made on the historical, national level. Ghosts are associated (obviously) with the past, and with the violence of the foundations of American history. The early song "The Death of Emmett Till" describes the Ku Klux Klan as "ghost-robed" (L, 20), while much later "Blind Willie McTell" includes a vision of "the ghost of slavery ships." It is precisely out of these ghostly images—slavery and the Klan—that filmmaker D. W. Griffith created the myth of *The Birth of a Nation.*

44 A point he would return to, a few years later, in the more conventionally religious formulation of "Death Is Not the End."

45 For a comparable effect, consider the work of another great innovator of the 1960s, one with many parallels to Dylan, the French film director Jean-Luc Godard. All of Godard's films are similarly saturated with quotations. Indeed, he boasts that the screenplay of his 1990 film *Nouvelle Vague* contains not a single line not drawn from a literary source. One could easily say the same thing about Dylan's recent albums. Indeed, the phrase "a history of love and theft" occurs in a 1981 poem by Douglas Dunn about nouvelle vague films (my thanks to Sarah Poynting for this reference).

Chapter Three: Contexts

1 The best website for information on Dylan's set lists is Bill Pagel's "Bob Links" (www.execpc.com/~billp61/dates.html). All Bob Dylan fans owe Bill Pagel an immense debt of gratitude for his exemplary work at this site.

2 Theorists like Jacques Derrida would argue that there is, strictly speaking, no such thing as a fully self-present "intention" but that the structure of language ensures that intention is always divided and deferred. Given these limitations, however, Derrida still concludes: "The category of intention will not disappear; it will have its place, but from this place it will no longer be able to govern the entire scene and the entire system of utterances" *(Margins, 326).*

3 See, for instance, Andy Gill's *Don't Think Twice, It's All Right: Bob Dylan, the Early Years (The Stories Behind Every Song),* which assumes even in its subtitle that there is a "story behind" each song, and which relentlessly identifies such stories in terms of identifying the biographical subjects. For example, "It Ain't Me, Babe" is straightforwardly described as "yet another song inspired by Suze Rotolo" (63), while "I Threw It All Away" is denied any biographical relevance on the grounds that "Bob had by then settled into the loviest and doviest of contentment with his wife Sara and their burgeoning brood" (139). Whether positively or negatively, biographical correspondence remains Gill's primary interpretive criterion. The result is an extremely limited book.

4 Bear in mind also the curious biographical incident of the young Dylan trying to visit Carl Sandburg, and being rather rudely rebuffed. On the whole question of influence, there is a marked similarity between T. S. Eliot and Dylan. Compare Eliot: "A poet cannot help being influenced, therefore he should subject himself to as many influences as possible, in order to escape from any one influence" ("Tradition and Practice," 877), with Dylan: "I can't tell you the influences 'cause there's too many to mention an' I might leave one out. . . . Open up yer ears an' eyes an' yer influenced an' there's nothing you can do about it" ("My Life in a Stolen Moment," L, 72).

5 The poet Anne Waldman appears in *Renaldo and Clara,* which also quotes her "Fast Speaking Woman" (1975). But Waldman is, as it were, an honorary Beat, and Dylan knew her because of her association with Allen Ginsberg.

6 Simon Frith, *Performing Rites,* cites some entertainingly embarrassing examples (176). It will be evident that a good deal of my discussion here is influenced by Frith's careful and comprehensive articulations.

7   In a 1966 radio interview, Phyllis Webb asked Leonard Cohen, "When is a poem *not* a song?" It's still a good question.

8   Similarly, Neil Corcoran (Professor of English at my own alma mater, the University of St Andrews) writes: "if Dylan's songs are not always, exactly, poems, they almost always have poetry in them, and the varied techniques of literary criticism and interpretation may be satisfactorily and illuminatingly applied to them" (13).

9   "Poems set to music" is a curious hybrid category. Sometimes they work splendidly (the musical setting of Blake's *Jerusalem),* but more often than not, I think they end up as unsatifactory in-between creations (the Philip Glass settings of Allen Ginsberg poems in *Hydrogen Jukebox).* Further, most poems are set to music by composers, not by "songwriters." As Frith says, "a Schubert song is a Schubert song, regardless of whose words he has set to music and which singer is singing them" (184).

10 It is in this respect that Dylan seems to anticipate later musical styles such as rap ("Subterranean Homesick Blues" has often been cited as a proto-rap song) or poetic styles like dub, slam, or performance poetry, which are often heavily dependent on rhyme.

11 A correspondent on the internet newsgroup rec.music.dylan, Lloyd Fonvielle, argues that such a view of quotations belongs to a postmodern worldview in which everything must be seen through irony. Post-postmodernism, he speculates, will "dispense with the pose of irony altogether. Much of *Time Out Of Mind* foreshadows this. Dylan uses the old folk and blues formulas without quotation marks around them, as though they were still operative—and thereby makes them operative." An interesting view—but I don't think it's so easy to dispense with quotation marks. You can't just pretend that the past, and the disruptions between the past and the present, don't exist; cultural history can be transcended, but it can't be ignored. If there is a "pose" on *Time Out of Mind,* I would say it is the pose of there being no quotation marks. But I agree that the end result is, indeed, to render the formulas once more operative.

12 Some parts of this section ("Performance") originally appeared in the first edition of *Alias Bob Dylan.* They were then revised and expanded, and adapted to the context of Leonard Cohen; see Stephen Scobie, "Racing the Midnight Train: Leonard Cohen in Performance," *Canadian Literature* 152/153 (Spring/Summer 1997): 52–68. They are here further revised and returned to their original context.

13 The exceptions are that rare breed who have the means and leisure to follow Dylan around to ten, thirty, or sixty concerts a year. I have never approached that level. But on the rare occasions when I did manage to attend a number of concerts in quick succession, I found it fascinating to observe the changes in my reactions on second and subsequent nights. See Stephen Scobie, "Three More Nights: Dylan in Germany," *On the Tracks* 15 (January 1999): 36–39, which describes my experience of seeing Dylan on three consecutive nights in three different cities (Leipzig, Berlin, Rostock) in June 1998.

14 Similar points are made—though with different conclusions—by Roy Kelly in his article "Songs Have Changed": "All singers are involved in a pretence: they're acting their

relationship to a song, usually a song they've delivered hundreds of times. That's what we want and expect. We've heard it lots of times before as well, but it can still move us. That's what songs do" (52). Kelly proceeds to a comparison with actors performing a pre-existing text: "No one would think an actor would be right to express his creativity by doing every production of Hamlet differently." But I am not persuaded that the analogy is either exact or helpful.

15 I'm always intrigued by the French use of the word *repetition* to mean "rehearsal"—so that even before the first performance, the piece has already been repeated. Before the song can be heard for the first time, it needs to have already happened.

16 In between these two modes are such mixed modes as the recording of a live concert—which may further vary, depending on whether the recording derives from a direct line recording from the soundboard or from an open microphone in the midst of a noisy audience. A fuller reading of all modes of performance would have to account for a wide range of listener response. How does one's response to a recording change from the first listening to subsequent listenings? (Another set of variations on sameness and difference.) How does one's reponse to a recording of a live concert change depending on whether or not one was present at the original concert? See also, in internet newsgroups, endless discussions about whether audiences should sit and listen, or get up and dance.

17 Internet newsgroups are full of stories of fans who made it to the front two or three rows of a concert and are convinced, rightly or wrongly, that the singer looked directly at them, or responded to their applause, or flirted with the pretty girls. The situation becomes more complex when fans are permitted (within limits) to climb up onstage and transgress into the performance space. On one famous occasion Dylan allowed a young woman to sing into his microphone, and stood back in amusement as she floundered through a chorus of "Mr. Tambourine Man." I confess that my most intense experience of a Dylan concert was in Rostock, 1998, when I made it all the way to the front row—though I don't think he ever looked at me!

18 This controversy resurfaced briefly in 1999 with allegations that Celine Dion had lip-synched some of her supposedly live concert performances. In defense of Dion the *Vancouver Sun* (October 12, 1999) quoted Paul Grace, a Toronto producer, as saying that the practice was "not unusual at all," especially in numbers that required energetic dancing. It is the visual spectacle, not the sound, which attracts today's concertgoers, Grace claims. "If you want to hear just the performance, stay home and listen to the album," he says—a comment which reveals that he cannot conceive of any value in a live concert performance that sounds *different* from the album. In any case, Grace concludes, it's only the media who make a fuss on this point: "They remember Woodstock and think that everyone should be like Bob Dylan. Well, not everyone is Bob Dylan." At which point, finally, Mr. Grace and I reach agreement—despite the fact that Bob Dylan did not perform at Woodstock!

19 For instance, "really pleased to be here tonight."

20 See my article on Leonard Cohen (cited in note 12, above) for a striking instance of this effect in relation to a performance of "Suzanne."

21 In the summer of 1999 Dylan *did* start telling funny stories between songs, with rather odd results. "I almost didn't make it here tonight. The bus had a flat tire. There was a fork in the road." Or: "Charlie [Sexton, the guitarist] went to see his cousin today at the Hamilton County Jail. He brought him a cell phone." This phase of Dylan's concert performativity has proved mercifully short. Similarly, in 1999, there was an odd instance (mistaken if deliberate) of an attempt to acknowledge the locality of a concert. When singing "Mr. Tambourine Man," Dylan changed "dance beneath the diamond sky" to "dance beneath the *German* sky"—unfortunately the concert in question took place in Zürich, Switzerland!

22 He did it in 2000 with "If Dogs Run Free," and the results were amazing!

23 In February 1994, a few months after I wrote this letter, Dylan revitalized "Masters of War" once again, dropping the electric rock arrangement he had used for several years and returning to an acoustic version—in which, apart from anything else, the words are more clearly audible. The site of this new arrangement was also significant: he first sang it in a concert at Hiroshima. Another instance of sameness and difference in live performance: the "same" song can sound completely "different" in a new context, either of place (Hiroshima) or of time (the Gulf War/Wars). In 1999, throughout the Kosovo conflict, "Masters of War" was a constant part of Dylan's repertoire. He also featured it in concerts in early 2003, during the most intensive phase of the Bush administration's build-up to war with Iraq. On the other hand, Dylan has always maintained that the song is directed not against war as such (he is not a pacifist), but rather against those who control and profit from war—what Eisenhower, in his last year in office, identified as "the military-industrial complex."

24 In 1996 Dylan authorized the use of a new set of lyrics to "Knockin' on Heaven's Door" on a recording put out in memory of the victims of the Dunblane school massacre.

25 Posting to rec.music.dylan; August 17, 1999.

26 In fact, debates on "the mirror" still recur regularly on the internet, with *Vermeer* as another possible version. Among recent Dylan mondegreens, my favourite is the (not entirely serious) hearing of "My sense of humanity" (in "Not Dark Yet") as "my sensitive manatee"!

27 Printed lyrics did appear with *Bob Dylan at Budokan* (1978), but the album was initially intended for Japanese release only. The lyrics are printed on the sleeve of *Under the Red Sky* (1990) but not on any subsequent albums.

28 It is the text from Dylan's 1985 *Lyrics* which is used on the CD-ROM *Highway 61 Interactive* and on the website bobdylan.com. A third, updated edition was promised in 1998 but then withdrawn; at the time of writing, it has still not appeared. It seems that a new edition of *Lyrics* is contractually tied to the appearance of the reputed autobiography, *Chronicles*. As Dylan works more and more on *Chronicles* (to the point where one wonders whether it is ever actually going to appear), so too does the (highly desirable) appearance of an updated, reliable text of *Lyrics* recede.

29 See Clinton Heylin, *"Lyrics, 1962–1985:* A Collection Short of the Definitive," in *All Across the Telegraph,* ed. Michael Gray and John Bauldie, pp. 229–42.

30 Such considerations inevitably raise the question of the extent to which *Lyrics* presents an "authorized" text. Can we be sure that Dylan made all these changes, or could they be the result of editorial decisions by other people? Researching this point for a Ph.D. dissertation, Craig Snow reports:

> Martha Kaplan, who worked on *Writings and Drawings* and *Lyrics, 1962–1985* as an editor with Alfred A. Knopf, Inc., the publisher of both books, told me in a phone interview that "all material" came from Dylan and that the editors at Knopf dealt with him as they would with any author. Pressed further, she clarified her contention, pointing out that the material for the two books came "from [Dylan's] office," but the editors did not alter the text of the lyrics.
>
> ("Folksinger and Beat Poet," 49)

This account still leaves open the possibility that someone else "from his office" made editorial changes—but the likelihood is that the oddities of the *Lyrics* text can be attributed to Dylan himself.

31 Collectors of Dylan bootlegs insist on the terminological distinction between "bootlegs" and "pirate" or "counterfeit" recordings—though it is a distinction which the music industry and its law enforcement arm have been reluctant to recognize. A "pirate" album or CD is the unauthorized release of previously available material, and is thus a deliberate attempt to deprive artists and publishers of due royalties, and to make an illegal profit by selling cut-price versions of existing hit records. A "counterfeit" attempts to duplicate also the original packaging, and to fool the buyers into thinking that what they are purchasing *is* the official album. A "bootleg," by contrast, contains previously *un*released material, such as live concert recordings or studio outtakes. It supplements but does not replace the official releases. Bootlegs are thus of interest primarily to those who already own the official recordings. At their best, bootlegs do not harm the artist financially, but rather preserve and extend his artistic legacy.

32 The definitive history of the bootleg phenomenon is Clinton Heylin's *Bootleg: The Secret History of the Other Recording Industry* (New York: St. Martin's Press, 1995). The nature of the bootleg economy has changed with changing technologies, from vinyl to cassette to CD to CDR to MP3, each new technology transforming the conditions under which bootlegs are circulated.

33 In recent years Dylan's security has succeeded in stemming the flow of studio outtake material. Much to the chagrin of collectors, none of the studio outtakes from *Time Out Of Mind* or *"Love and Theft"* has been bootlegged.

Moments & Milestones 3: *"Like a Rolling Stone"*

1 For the fullest account of this concert, see C. P. Lee, *Like the Night*. Most listeners now seem to agree that what Dylan says is "Get fucking loud!" though some listeners still hear

"Play it fucking loud!" or even "You're a fucking liar!" A minority school of opinion holds that the line is actually spoken by Robbie Robertson rather than by Dylan.

2   Similarly, when Dylan at this time sang "It Ain't Me, Babe," the context clearly implied that it ain't me you're looking for, babe—it's Him.

3   In recent concerts (2001–02), audience reaction has been rather cynically encouraged by a very manipulative lighting effect—the sweeping of floodlights over the crowd in time to the climax of "How does it feel?" Well, it feels great the first time you see it, but it wears thin in a hurry.

Chapter Four: Genres

1   This question is also central to the work of Leonard Cohen. See especially *The Energy of Slaves* (1972), where the lines "I can't write a poem anymore / You can call me Len or Lennie now / like you always wanted" (112) seem quite strikingly to prefigure Dylan's "You may call me Bobby, you may call me Zimmy" (L, 424) seven years later.

2   This effect is increased for a recorded song, which is always there to be played again. The "eternal circle" is also a turntable, or a compact disc.

3   The performance history of this stanza in "Mr. Tambourine Man" is interesting. For many years, Dylan in concert has sung only three of the song's four stanzas, and usually it was this third stanza that was omitted. But for a year or so in the mid-1990s, he restored the third stanza and instead omitted the second—which is, of course, the *only* stanza included in The Byrds' famous recording. Recently the second stanza is back in, and the "ragged clown" has again disappeared.

4   See Bill Allison, "She Belongs To Me: One Possible Hearing," *The Telegraph* 19 (Spring, 1985): 58–70.

5   This list is by no means exhaustive. It is confined to singers, and one stand-up comedian. (For a discussion of more "literary" intertextual influences on Dylan, see the section "Poetry" in Chapter 3.) This list also excludes the untitled poem Dylan wrote as liner notes for *Joan Baez in Concert, Part 2* (L, 78–85). Most of this poem is an extended and rather heavy-handed compliment to Baez, but she does not appear as an image *for* Dylan, as do Guthrie, Bruce, and McTell. Instead, the poem presents a series of romantic images of the young Dylan as "a demon child . . . a saddened clown . . . an arch criminal who'd done no wrong . . . a lonesome king . . . a scared poet . . . a rebel wild." The images remain unconvincing, precisely because they are unmediated and have not been reflected through the persona of another artist.

6   In 1999 and 2000 "Song to Woody" reentered Dylan's concert repertoire, in a beautiful, heartfelt arrangement.

7   The argument of Dylan's poem takes the form of a vastly extended sentence: When you're in an extreme state (many parallel examples), and there's something you need (examples), you won't find it in these places (examples), but there are two places you can go to (the two final possibilities).

8   The odd half-rhyme of *once* and *months* found in "Lenny Bruce" is repeated in "Million Miles" on *Time Out Of Mind*.

9   Biographically Robert Zimmerman does have a brother—David—but here the word is meant in a more symbolic sense.

10   When Dylan finally, in 1997, began singing "Blind Willie McTell" in concert, he used the version of the final lines of each verse first heard on a recording by The Band: "I know one thing / nobody can sing / the blues like Blind Willie McTell." In 1999 this version was modified into "I can tell you one thing. . . ." So the *tell* did finally make it into the song.

11   Ironically, "Blind Willie McTell" was, for many years, the only original Bob Dylan composition to contain the word *bootleg*. A second instance finally appeared in 2001, when "Sugar Baby," on *"Love and Theft,"* proclaimed: "Some of these bootleggers, they got pretty good stuff." When it was delivered in concert, this line always drew knowing applause from the audience.

12   Suze Rotolo sailed for Italy on June 8, 1962, and Dylan recorded "Down the Highway" on July 9 (Dundas, *Tangled Up in Tapes,* 8). The second *Italy* in this line is added almost as an afterthought, a quizzical puzzlement at the woman's choice of destination. This doubling of *Italy* was later to acquire an added irony, since in January 1963 Dylan also went to Italy, in search of Suze, only to find that she had already returned to New York.

13   The instrumental piece usually referred to as "The Cough Song," recorded in 1963, appears on *The Bootleg Series* under the title "Suze."

14   See Michael Gray, *Song and Dance Man,* 2d ed., p. 158. The phrase about wallpaper falls victim to what Gray calls "a small amount of pruning" in the third edition.

15   Dylan retrospectively claimed that the song was written for Sara: "Stayin' up for days in the Chelsea Hotel, / Writin' 'Sad-Eyed Lady of the Lowlands' for you" (L, 390). Of course, he also claimed that "Sara," the song in which he made this claim, was not written for his wife! Some critics have seen a problem in reconciling this claim with the well-documented statements by studio musicians that he was still writing the song in the Nashville studio immediately prior to recording it. But there seems to me little difficulty in accepting that he might have begun a first draft in New York and still been working on revisions in Nashville. More ingeniously, Neil McKinlay has questioned whether the two lines from "Sara" necessarily refer to the same event, rather than being part of a list of separate events occurring at separate times. Critics who accept Dylan's claim point to the line about "your magazine-husband" as referring to Sara's previous husband, Hans Lownds, a fashion photographer. Others claim that "Lowlands" itself is a version of the name "Lownds." Those other critics who persist, despite Dylan's denial, in thinking that the "Sad-Eyed Lady" was Joan Baez have equally plausible evidence in the text: "Spanish manners," for instance, or even, in a different sense, the word "Lowlands" again. The traditional British folk song "The Lowlands of Holland" was part of Baez's repertoire in the early 1960s. On the basis of "Sad-Eyed Lady" itself, it is impossible to state definitely who Dylan had in mind when he wrote it. However, from 1975 on, the claim made in "Sara" becomes an inescapable part of the song's intertext.

16   Nothing in this reading rules out the possibility of an alternative interpretation of these lines as drug references, in which the "warehouse eyes" are dilated pupils, the "Arabian

drums" are amphetamines, and the "gate" is the entry point of a hypodermic needle. But combing Bob Dylan songs of the mid-1960s for drug references is always too easy, and too reductive.

17 Gray points out that "lowlands" could also refer to "the lowlands of the Mississippi Delta . . . which imperiled people down in the floods" (274). This interpretation seems fully consonant with the reading I am advancing here.

18 After "You're the other half of what I am, you're the missing piece," any Hallmark greeting-card versifier could have produced "And I love you more than ever with that love that doesn't cease" (L, 350). Curiously, *Lyrics* flattens out some of the few interesting lines in "Wedding Song." On record, Dylan sings "Love you more than madness, more than dreams upon the sea," but the printed text in *Lyrics* gives a more conventional "waves upon the sea."

19 This line is one of the few direct references in Dylan's work to the town in which he was born. Duluth had been recalled in "11 Outlined Epitaphs," and it also appears in the *Planet Waves* liner notes: "Duluth—where Baudelaire lived & Goya cashed in his chips, where Joshua brought the house down!"

20 Whatever the emotional truth of "Tangled Up In Blue," it can definitely be stated that Bob Dylan never worked on a fishing boat out of Delacroix! On the other hand, he has sometimes in concert introduced "Simple Twist of Fate" as "a true story."

21 *Blood on the Tracks* was originally recorded in New York in September 1974, but several tracks were rerecorded in Minneapolis that December. Some critics have speculated that Dylan felt the New York versions were *too* revealing, and that the later versions retreat behind a more familiar mask.

22 Bob Spitz claims that Dylan recorded the song without warning, springing it on Sara in the studio. Spitz quotes one of his many unnamed sources as saying that Dylan "turned and sang the song directly at Sara, who sat through it all with an impervious look on her face" (466).

23 For a discussion of the failure of patriarchal authority on *Desire*, see "Outside the Law" (Chapter 4). For a discussion of Isis, see "Summation 2" (Chapter 7).

24 Especially, it must be said, by those seeking to justify the "outside the law" activities of bootleggers. The phrase is perhaps more often quoted than precisely defined.

25 Some writers claim that the outlaw John Wesley Hardin was a distant relative of the folksinger Tim Hardin, author of "If I Were A Carpenter" *(Zimmermann* again!).

26 Without wanting to reopen these internet debates, I must say that I remain unconvinced by religious readings of "Señor." They seem to be based almost entirely on interpreting the word *Señor* as an address to Christ, and they fail to account for the narrative details of the situation between the two central characters.

27 A less successful example is "Joey," the song on *Desire* which attempts to transform the New York mobster Joey Gallo into a "moral outlaw." But the events of Gallo's career were too recent (less than five years before the song was written) for the ballad-making process to be able to transform their moral ambiguities.

28　In 1963 Dylan outraged some of his audience by speculating on the possibility of imaginative identification with Lee Harvey Oswald. His lament for Medgar Evers, "Only a Pawn in Their Game," also concentrates on the equivocal figure of the killer rather than the martyred victim.

29　The usual problems of narrative indeterminacy are compounded in "Lily, Rosemary and the Jack of Hearts" because there are two slightly different versions of this song. The version released on *Blood on the Tracks* omits one stanza, which is included in both the earlier studio recording and the printed *Lyrics*. The extra stanza makes a crucial difference to the reading of the narrative.

30　In performance Dylan emphasizes the *d* and slurs the *r*, so that one almost hears "the Dylan in the wall."

31　The combination of "diamond mine" and "silver cane" may also recall William Zanzinger, "With a cane that he twirled around his diamond ring finger" (L, 102).

32　Later, Lily does say "I've missed you so," but this comment occurs in the "missing" stanza 12. (See note 29, above.)

33　The structure of the final lines—thinking about A, B, and C, but especially about D—is repeated in the final lines of "Tweeter and the Monkeyman": "Sometimes I think of Tweeter, sometimes I think of Jan / Sometimes I don't think about nothing but the Monkeyman."

34　The line of association was further extended by Lawrence Ferlinghetti in a broadsheet entitled "The Jack of Hearts (for Dylan)," published in 1976: "the Jack of Hearts / the black-eyed one who sees all ways / the one with the eye of a horse / the one with the light in his eye / the one with his eye on the star named Nova . . . when all is said and all is done / in the wild eye the wide eye / of the Jack of Hearts."

35　This widely quoted phrase first appeared in an interview with Robert Hilburn, printed in the *Los Angeles Times* in November 1980. For the fullest account of Dylan's conversion, see Ricketts, "Bob Dylan's Church," together with the accompanying interview with Pastor Larry Myers, both of which appear in *On the Tracks* 4 (Fall 1994): 30–47.

36　For many, but not for all. A quick scan of internet resources will show many listeners who strongly approve of Dylan's religious songs precisely *because* they use a rhetoric which can be straightforwardly explicated in terms of its biblical references. Biblical quotations had long been a staple of Dylan's writing—as is shown in Bert Cartwright's *The Bible in the Lyrics*—but now the songs became saturated in quotation. For some commentators, the simple fact that a line can be traced back to a scriptural source is itself an adequate defense of the line's poetic quality. The liner notes to *Gotta Serve Somebody: The Gospel Songs of Bob Dylan,* a 2003 CD of cover versions of Dylan's gospel songs, conveniently provide biblical chapter-and-verse citations for the title phrases of all the songs.

37　Especially in live performance. Whatever one's view of the theological implications of the lyrics, there is no doubt that the concerts of 1979–80 featured some of Dylan's most intense and passionately committed singing. Dylan originally intended to issue *Saved* as a live album, and many critics still think that the concert performances are superior to the studio versions of the songs.

38 "Strengthen the things that remain" is an apocalyptic phrase, from Revelation 3:2.

39 Again, vindictiveness can also be found in early works. The "Masters of War" are told that "Even Jesus would never / Forgive what you do" (L, 56)—theologically, a dubious proposition.

40 Though it does appear, bizarrely, that he recorded versions (uncirculated) of "Silent Night" and "Glory to the King" during the recording sessions for *Infidels!*

41 The Crucifixion may also be alluded to, punningly, in a phrase from "Idiot Wind"—"I been double-crossed now for the very last time and now I'm finally free" (L, 368). In German director Wim Wenders's film *Im Lauf der Zeit / Kings of the Road* (1975), one of the characters stands in front of a roadside crucifix, spreads out his own arms to double the cross, and quotes Dylan's line—in English.

42 Any such inhibition loosens up in later years. In 1999, for example, Dylan regularly sang in concert a bluegrass-gospel song by Ralph Stanley called "I Am the Man, Thomas," in which the first-person dramatic speaker is quite explicitly Christ.

43 See the entry on "Judas" in the *Supplement* to the *Oxford English Dictionary*, which gives 1914 as its earliest citation for the phrase "Judas Priest."

44 These are the words on the original *Shot of Love* recording. In performance Dylan has consistently revised the line to read "I am hanging in the balance of a perfect, finished plan." I still prefer the earlier version, partly because of the slight redundancy in "perfect, finished," but also, no doubt, because I prefer the secular context of "the reality of man."

45 *Shot of Love* has an extended and complicated recording history, and the studio sessions, extending from September 1980 to May 1981, include a lot of songs, some partial and some complete, which didn't make it to the final album. There are fascinating, unresolved fragments like "Hallelujah" and "On a Rocking Boat," which might well have evolved into major songs. "Caribbean Wind" exists in several versions, with widely variant lyrics, especially a live performance in San Francisco on November 12, 1980. The studio outtake was subsequently issued on *Biograph*, and its text is included in *Lyrics*. "The Groom's Still Waiting at the Altar" was released as the B-side of the single "Heart of Mine" and was later included on reissues of *Shot of Love* and on *Biograph*. A text is included in *Lyrics*, but it differs from the released version. "Angelina" was not released until *The Bootleg Series* in 1991, and its text is not included in *Lyrics*. With the exception of that one San Francisco performance, Dylan has not returned to any of these songs in concert.

46 The "pale white horse" conflates two different, indeed opposing, references in Revelation—"behold a pale horse: and his name that sat on him was Death" (6:8), and "behold a white horse; and he that sat upon him was called Faithful and True" (19:11). The latter reference immediately follows the description of the marriage of the Lamb, a key image both in these songs and in the later "Ring Them Bells."

47 Bert Cartwright *(Bible in the Lyrics,* 56) suggests that the woman who "owned the world" is the Queen of Sheba, and he cites 1 Kings 11:1, "King Solomon loved many strange women."

48 Some contributors to rec.music.dylan point to Dylan's repeated singing of these songs as evidence of his continuing Christianity. Others point out that he also sings in concert,

with equal enthusiasm, songs which are rather hard to reconcile with Christianity, such as "Friend of the Devil," and that he still frequently tells his audience that "everybody must get stoned." On the whole, however, I would conclude that the frequency of the gospel songs suggests, at the very least, that he is not uncomfortable with their message.

Chapter Five: Intertexts

1   These comments are astute self-criticism of *John Wesley Harding*.

2   Quoted by Michael Schumacher, *Dharma Lion* (304, 307). Dylan and Ginsberg were introduced by Al Aronowitz, who was also responsible for introducing Dylan to The Beatles in August 1964.

3   None of the Ginsberg biographies is precise on this point; the date might have been 1965. Ginsberg says, in a note in his *Collected Poems*, that Dylan didn't actually give him the typescript until 1968, but "it passed into his hands years earlier" (813). If, as I speculate here, the title is a possible source for Dylan's "Gates of Eden," then the earlier date is necessary, since the song was written in October 1964.

4   None of the Dylan biographies specifies a date for these photographs. Ginsberg said that the concert was in Princeton, quite shortly after his first meeting with Dylan; Barry Miles follows this account *(Ginsberg,* 334). But there is no record of a Dylan concert at Princeton in 1964. Dylan did give a concert at Princeton in March 1965, but at that time Ginsberg was in Czechoslovakia. It is also possible that the concert in question was not in Princeton at all, but was one given in Philadelphia in late 1964. However, in the recent collection of photographs *Early Dylan* (Feinstein et al.), Daniel Kramer includes one photo—an interesting mirror-shot in a crowded dressing room, also featuring Peter Orlovsky and Barbara Rubin—obviously taken at the same time, and he again dates it as "Princeton 1964" (89).

5   Another cover photograph shows Dylan having his head rubbed by a woman with close-cropped hair; she was an experimental filmmaker called Barbara Rubin. Barry Miles describes how Ginsberg met Rubin and saw her film *Christmas on Earth*. Miles quotes Ginsberg as saying:

> It was a lot of porn, beauty, in which she made an art object out of her vagina. I thought that was in the right spirit. We got into a very funny rapport, we were just there alone, and we actually ended up screwing on the floor that very night. She was really young and pretty and I liked her.
>
> *(Ginsberg,* 334)

Schumacher records that Ginsberg and Rubin remained on excellent terms: indeed that "Rubin had believed she and Allen might eventually marry and settle down" (654). But in fact Rubin married someone else. In 1994, Gordon Ball, the editor of Ginsberg's journals, told me (in conversation) of attending her wedding, which was also attended by both Allen Ginsberg and Bob Dylan. Rubin died in December 1980.

6   In January 1993 Bob Dylan performed at the inauguration of Bill Clinton.

7   For a good account of this meeting, see Schumacher (445–46), and for an even more vivid description, see Faithfull (40–56)—one of the best available accounts of 1965 Bob Dylan. Ginsberg's tactic is, of course, a trickster's move. He was always willing to make himself appear vulnerable, or even ludicrous, as a means of advancing a situation.

8   For a detailed account of these photographs, see my interview with the photographers, Larry Keenan and Dale Smith, in Stephen Scobie, "A Conversation With Larry Keenan and Dale Smith," *On the Tracks* 14 (1998): 46–52. These are definitive images.

9   A version of Allen Ginsberg's *The Fall of America*, published in 1972, won the National Book Award. However, that book excludes some poems which had been published separately, such as "Wichita Vortex Sutra" and "Iron Horse." In Ginsberg's *Collected Poems* of 1984, these sections were inserted in their correct chronological sequence. The first poem of the sequence, "Beginning of a Poem of These States," was written before Ginsberg's meetings with Dylan in San Francisco in 1965, and thus before the gift of the tape recorder.

10 It is thus also a tradition that would prove highly relevant to Bob Dylan. "A rag-bag to stuff all [his] thoughts in"; "a form that wouldn't exclude something merely because it didn't fit"—what are these if not descriptions of *Renaldo and Clara?* Indeed, in many ways, Dylan's film could be regarded as the movie version of *The Fall of America.*

11 Happy Traum worked with Dylan on several occasions in the early 1960s. He is the back-up singer and musician on the so-called "Banjo Tape" from February 1963, and he takes the lead vocal on the version of "Let Me Die in My Footsteps" recorded for *Broadside* in January 1963. More immediately, he had played with Dylan in October 1971 on several tracks included on the album *Greatest Hits Volume 2.* Traum's 1988 release, *Buckets of Song,* includes a superb version of Dylan's "Buckets of Rain."

12 This account was written by Anne Waldman in 1993 for the booklet accompanying *Holy Soul Jelly Roll.* Only a brief extract was used (Ginsberg, *Holy Soul,* 30). I am grateful to Anne Waldman for sending me the full text, from which this extract is taken.

13 All quotations in this section from unpublished Ginsberg journals are my own transcripts from the original manuscript and are used with the permission of the Allen Ginsberg office.

14 Sam Shepard comments: "Ginsberg's religious, chanting finale has been cut from the show, and he sits with Peter [Orlovsky] in the front row [of Plymouth Memorial Hall] looking dejectedly up at the stage as the technicians prepare the sound check. Allen's general positive outlook though is a constant wonderment to me. He seems determined to roll with the punches and manages to bounce back every time without bitching or cutting someone apart in the process" (1977, 24).

15 In this context the fact that Rubin Carter also came from Paterson, New Jersey, is clearly more important than the fact that another "American poet," William Carlos Williams, was also from the same city as Ginsberg.

16 For a vivid, if somewhat dramatized, account of Ginsberg's performance, see Sam Shepard, *Rolling Thunder Logbook* (28–32). It is this reading of "Kaddish" that Dylan used in the film *Renaldo and Clara.*

17 Not that Dylan criticism has ever been short of controversy! The disputes that swirl around Greil Marcus are mild in comparison with some of the vituperation directed against, say, Clinton Heylin or Bob Spitz. But the purpose here is not to enter into any of these disputes, except insofar as this section could be read as a defense of Marcus. Rather, I am using *Invisible Republic* as a convenient point of entry into my own discussion of the Basement Tapes.

18 "The Basement Tapes" is the name generally given to the recordings Dylan made with The Band during the spring and summer of 1967, in the basement of Big Pink, the Woodstock house in which The Band were living. These recordings formed the core of the first Dylan bootleg, *The Great White Wonder.* Since then, most of the original Dylan compositions from these sessions have been officially released: on *The Basement Tapes* (1975) and on compilations such as *The Bootleg Series.* However, most of the cover versions, and such essential Dylan works as "I'm Not There (1956)," have never been officially released and are available only on bootleg.

19 One of Marcus's quirks is a certain blindness to Ian and Sylvia. He makes several disparaging comments about them, and he fails to recognize that the song he calls "One Single River" is, in fact, Ian and Sylvia's "Song for Canada." (To be fair, it also seems unlikely that Bob Dylan valued this song for its political statement on Canadian bilingualism!)

20 At the time Marcus wrote, no complete translation of Walter Benjamin's *Passagen-Werk* had appeared in English. It finally appeared from Harvard University Press in 1999 as *The Arcades Project.*

21 Marcus was deeply involved with the 1997 Folkways/Smithsonian reissue of Smith's *Anthology,* whose liner notes reprinted a chapter from *Invisible Republic.* Marcus has also been influential in promoting reissues of recordings by some of the *Anthology* musicians, such as Dock Boggs.

22 To which one might add the further question: does Bob Dylan also make things "worse" when, in his performance of "The Coo Coo Bird" at the Gaslight Cafe, New York, in 1962, he changes "Willie" to "Mary"? Dylan has never repeated "The Coo Coo Bird" as part of his repertoire, but the song "High Water (for Charley Patton)," from *"Love and Theft"* (2001) does quote verbatim the opening line — "The cuckoo is a pretty bird, she warbles as she flies" — and then rather remarkably rhymes it with "I'm preaching the Word of God, I'm putting out your eyes."

23 It is difficult to overemphasize exactly how *weird* the Basement Tapes songs are. Works like "Yea! Heavy and a Bottle of Bread" or "Odds and Ends" truly defy explication. And while some of the songs aspire to the eschatological, others are simply scatological: "Please, Mrs. Henry," for instance, seems to be entirely concerned with defecation.

24 The significance of the parenthetical date in the title—"I'm Not There (1956)"—has never been satisfactorily explained.

25 For what it's worth, my ears hear "prize-forsaken" and "weighs"—both of which are interesting wordings—but poetically I prefer "Christ-forsaken" and "waits."

26 Dylan may quite literally have "breathe[d] the air around Tom Paine's." Paine spent several years towards the end of his life in lodgings in what is now Greenwich Village. Betrayal of trust is a continuous theme throughout *John Wesley Harding:* the eponymous hero endangering his "lady" by keeping her by his side in a gunfight; the complex, mutual betrayals of Frankie Lee and Judas Priest; St. Augustine condemned to death; the jury corrupting the court of justice in "Drifter's Escape"; the perfidy of the "Dear Landlord"; the "Lonesome Hobo" who "did not trust my brother [but] carried him to blame"; the "Poor Immigrant" whose visions of the new life in America "must shatter like the glass"; the "Wicked Messenger" blamed for the news he distorts, but also for the news he simply conveys. All of these are instances of "the inevitable betrayals that stem from the infinite idealism of American democracy" (Marcus, *Invisible Republic,* 89). It is interesting to note that in U.S. election year 2000, Dylan's concert repertoire featured blistering rock renditions of "Wicked Messenger" and "Drifter's Escape."

Moments & Milestones 5: "New Pony"

1 A performance of "Chestnut Mare" features prominently in the film *Renaldo and Clara,* which Dylan had been editing immediately prior to the composition of the songs for *Street Legal.*

2 Despite, it has to be said, Dylan's explicit denial of this interpretation.

Chapter Six: Movies

1 For lyrics quoted from *The Gunfighter,* see "Brownsville Girl." For lyrics quoted from *Shane,* the most direct reference is to the scene in which Joe Starritt asks Shane to leave his ranch, and Shane replies that he doesn't mind leaving, but "I'd like it to be my idea"—a line directly quoted in "Never Gonna Be the Same Again" (L, 494).

2 In one scene in *Major Dundee* that does survive, we see the major, played by Charlton Heston, lying in the gutter with a small dog licking his face—a possible source for Dylan's almost identical line in "Jokerman" (L, 471).

3 Let me pay particular tribute to a live concert version of "Ride, Billy, Ride" which I was privileged to hear, performed by an Austrian group, Die mit dem Italiener spielen, at the Dylan convention at Schloss Plankenstein in 1998. The group began their concert with this song and returned to it at the end, with the various instrumentalists, one at a time, stopping playing and walking off the stage, leaving in the end only a solo singer with acoustic guitar. It was truly memorable!

4 There is, however, a lovely cover version by Gillian Welch, which was played over the loudspeaker systems as a prelude to several Dylan concerts in 2002.

5 The title of the bootleg CD is indeed spelled *Peco's Blues.* Either the producers inserted a superfluous apostrophe into the place-name Pecos (Texas), or else it is a misspelling for *Paco.* In the film there is a character called Paco, who is sympathetic to Alias, and who is murdered by Chisum's men.

6   *The Tooth of Crime* premiered in London on July 17, 1972. The first American production was in Princeton in November of that year—by which time shooting for *Pat Garrett & Billy the Kid* had already begun. My thanks to Sandra Wynands for information about Sam Shepard.

7   Pat Garrett (or Ash Upson) here (in 1882) makes the same connection between the proper name and "legal property" which is discussed, in relation to Derrida one hundred years later, in the section "Signature" (see Chapter 2).

8   Thus it is possibly significant that the gun which Billy uses for his escape is concealed wrapped in old newspapers: could this be taken as a hint that Alias was in fact responsible for Billy's escape? I am indebted to Jacqueline Bitz for this suggestion.

9   Dylan has sometimes been described as left-handed, or at least ambidextrous. His name appears on lists of famous left-handers in history, and there are photographs of him signing his name with his left hand. But most of the time, Dylan does appear conventionally right-handed: he plays guitar right-handed, and when Alias displays his lethal ability with a knife in an early scene of *Pat Garrett & Billy the Kid*, the throw is right-handed.

10 Ginsberg's 1977 interview with Dylan was not published, however, until 1989; see Ginsberg, "It's Not Rational."

11 A similar collage is created in the one other major use of a spoken poem on the *Renaldo and Clara* soundtrack, Anne Waldman's "Fast Speaking Woman," which is overlaid with two gospel songs, "What Will You Do When Jesus Comes?" and "Little Moses."

12 I do not mean to suggest that Dylan shows any disrespect for Ginsberg's poem here— quite the opposite. The very precise and careful use of "Kaddish" in *Renaldo and Clara* is, in fact, the most explicit instance in Dylan's work of his love and respect for Ginsberg's poetry. It is his ultimate *hommage*.

13 Even an innocuous scene like that of roadies setting up equipment for a concert contains the line "There are two cables, one gold and one violet," while someone else complains that he has twin amps and the serial numbers don't match.

14 Another Leonard Cohen reference just misses being included. The performance of "Isis" begins, in the film, at the second verse. The full performance (recorded in Montreal and released on *Biograph)* begins with Dylan's dedication, "This is for Leonard, if he's still here."

15 The character of the young woman was played by Ruth Tyrangiel, who later attempted (unsuccessfully) to sue Bob Dylan, on the grounds that she had been his long-time companion, and that she deserved cowriter's credits on all his later songs. One ironic response suggested that Dylan now had the perfect "out" for any composition he might wish to disavow. Blame *her* for "Wiggle Wiggle," Bob!

16 The marble statue is located in the Grotto of St. Bernadette, near Lowell, Massachusetts. Stephen Ronan notes that the grotto was "quite important in Kerouac's childhood and *is* quite near the funeral home out of which he was buried." It is, however, separate from Edson Cemetery, the site of Kerouac's grave (though some of Dylan's editing obscures this distinction). My thanks to Stephen Ronan for this clarification.

17   The theme of ghosts has been tragically extended by the subsequent deaths of some of the major figures involved in the making of *Renaldo and Clara,* notably Howard Alk, David Blue, and Allen Ginsberg. Dead poets are a major theme of the film. English Romantic poets are evoked through Ginsberg's singing of Blake, and through references to the graves of Keats and Shelley. This scene, in which Ginsberg recalls leaving a copy of *Howl* on Baudelaire's grave, takes place at Kerouac's gravesite. Kerouac also bears a double name: the English "Jack" and the French *Ti Jean* inscribed on his tomb. At the end of this scene, Renaldo declares his idealistic desire to be buried in an unmarked grave, free of names.

18   Anne Waldman, however, has a more positive take on the scene. In a letter to me dated September 4, 1994, she wrote:

> The "sporting house" or brothel was my idea, suggested by the decor & feel of the Chateau Frontenac in Quebec City, the "Frenchness" of the atmosphere, red wallpaper, velvet curtains, plush sybaritic furniture. And the beauty of the damsels on the tour could be used to exotic measure. Buddhist notion of "Vajra Hell" plays in here as well, some inescapable realm you can't get out of, claustrophobic but very cutting & sharp. Also the "god realm" was another image, the lotus land associated with rock 'n' roll tours, where you can get whatever you want in the realm of senses & pleasure. But your seat starts to get too warm and you realize you're stuck with aging & death like everyone else. The scenes were pretty much improvised, everyone chipping in their two bits & into the parody mode. We were sort of charged by the whole possibility, a little giddy. We'd been traveling through snowstorms, arriving at the Chateau early morning to hot coffee, fresh buttery croissants and luxury & elegance of this older architectural site. I think we were picking up on the possible high "decadence" the place suggested. Our hotel/motels had been a bit on the mundane side up until then.

Moments & Milestones 6: "Female Rambling Sailor"

1   For a scholarly study of trouser songs, see Dianne Dugaw, *Warrior Women and Popular Balladry, 1650–1850* (Chicago: University of Chicago Press, 1996).

2   See Mark Gregory's website, "Australian Folk Songs" (www.crixa.com/muse/songnet/songs.html). Dylan first performed "Female Rambling Sailor" in Adelaide, and four of the six 1992 performances were in Australia. I am also indebted to Eric Debeck for his diligent research on this song.

Chapter Seven: Summations

1   At one early performance, Dylan introduced "Visions of Johanna" as "Mother Revisited," a title which may refer sarcastically to the aspect of Johanna as "Madonna," the mother goddess. In concert in 1999, on several occasions Dylan actually sang the title phrase as "Visions of Madonna."

2   A good deal of debate still surrounds the exact dates of these recordings.

3   Portland, Maine, February 25, 1999, is a particularly fine version.

4   This mental image was probably suggested by the photograph on the center-left of the inside sleeve of *Blonde on Blonde.*

5   In the interview which Joan Baez gave to Anthony Scaduto, she says that "Visions of Johanna" "sounded very suspicious to me, as though it had images of me in it," then adds "I mean, I can't ever say that publicly"—though that is precisely what she is doing, in speaking to Scaduto. Repeatedly Baez says that she does not want to claim that the song is about her, but says so in a way that does implicitly make that claim. She also tells how Allen Ginsberg asked her what she thought the song was about, trying (she supposes) to get her to say she thought it was about her.

> And I said, "I don't know, Ginsberg, your guess is as good as mine." He said, "No, no, what do you think it's about? Bobby says . . ." and then he reeled off this pile of crap that had nothing to do with anything. And I said, "Did Bobby say that or did you make that up, Allen?" I had the feeling the two of them were in sort of cahoots to make sure I never thought the song had anything to do with me.
>
> (Scaduto, *Bob Dylan,* 201)

Personally, I would be much more interested in hearing Ginsberg's "pile of crap that had nothing to do with anything"!

6   Pamela Thurschwell has some very interesting comments on these lines: "Louise makes a poor mirror for the singer—the absent Johanna is a better reflector for the singer's narcissism. Yet it is in that poor mirroring that Louise comes into her own; in those lines Louise manages to become a more interesting because inaccurate imitation of both the singer and Johanna" (Corcoran, 269).

7   In these lines Dylan places himself in a long tradition of poets who have written about painting, and who have offered in their poems creative interpretations of the meanings of paintings. (The technical term for this is "ekphrastic" poetry.) In twentieth-century poetry the most famous example is W. H. Auden's "Musée des Beaux Arts," with its reading of Pieter Breughel's painting *Landscape with the Fall of Icarus.* One could also mention Earle Birney's poem "El Greco: Espolio" (about that artist's painting *El Espolio).* All of these poems are verbal responses to nonverbal images—language rising to the bait, unable to resist the challenge to spell out in words what the painter has left implicit.

8   Note that there are two levels of nonverbal image in this discussion of the *Mona Lisa:* the smile itself (and interpreting facial expressions is an endlessly tricky business) and the painted sign of the smile. Two quasi-linguistic codes are at work: "body language" and the conventions of Renaissance portraiture. For a recent *ekphrasis* of Mona Lisa's smile, see Timothy Findley's novel *Pilgrim* (1999).

9   Of his painting *LHOOQ*, Marcel Duchamp also said, "I found that the poor girl, with a mustache and beard, became very masculine—which went very well with the homosexuality of Leonardo." (But let's not get into the controversial question of concealed references to homosexuality in Dylan's lyrics.) Duchamp was still alive, in New York, at the time that Dylan was hanging around Andy Warhol's Factory in 1965–66.

10 Yet another pun is lurking here: para-site/para-sight.

11 One obvious question is, why was the line deleted? Perhaps Dylan thought there were too many short rhyming lines piling up; even so, why choose this one to delete? Was Dylan perhaps wary of the scatological reading, that the "nightingale's code" might be no more than birdshit? In some of the "Basement Tapes" songs, Dylan does show a fondness for scatological humor (see note 23, Chapter 5, above), but he may well have seen it as inappropriate in this context.

12 Strictly speaking, "Brownsville Girl" (1986) comes later than my suggested dates (1973–83) for this phase, but it is the culmination of many of the images and motifs of the mid-1970s.

13 All quotations from Sam Shepard in this section are, unless otherwise indicated, taken from an interview in *Rolling Stone* 489–90 (December 18, 1986–January 1, 1987). All quotations from "Brownsville Girl" are transcribed from *Knocked Out Loaded* and annotated (BG). All quotations from "Danville Girl" are transcribed from the earlier (bootleg) recording and annotated (DG).

14 Shepard's account of the tour, *Rolling Thunder Logbook*, is surpassed only by Larry Sloman's *On the Road* and by passages in Allen Ginsberg's unpublished journals.

15 For a detailed account of the Dylan–Shepard affinities and collaborations, see Sandra Wynands, " 'A Face Like a Mask': Themes of Identity and Theatricality in Selected Works of Sam Shepard and Bob Dylan" (M.A. thesis, University of Victoria, 1998).

16 See Shepard, *Rolling Thunder Logbook*: "Shifty Jacques Levy, who blitzed off-off-Broadway some years back with his head-on Brechtian style" (117).

17 It is certainly foolish to treat *True Dylan*, as Clinton Heylin seems to do, as a "straight" reliable interview.

18 "Brownsville Girl" adds details from *The Gunfighter*—such as "riding across the desert"—which were not present in "Danville Girl," and also corrects the earlier song's erroneous "sheriff" to "marshall."

19 Especially in *The Right Stuff*, where he plays a pioneering astronaut, despite his own very public aversion to flying!

20 The transcription of Gregory Peck's speech appears in *On the Tracks* 13 (June 1998): 48–49.

21 Peggy is also, apparently, his wife or ex-wife. The exact relationship is never clarified in the film, but it seems unlikely that 1950s Hollywood would have countenanced such a sympathetic presentation of an illegitimate child.

22 Dylan once described "All Along the Watchtower" as being set in the Mojave Desert.

23 In the movie version of *Fool for Love*, The Old Man is played by Harry Dean Stanton, who also plays Travis in *Paris, Texas*. In the latter film, Travis comes out of the Mojave

Desert, reappearing after a four-year absence to reclaim his son and reestablish the family unit (or rather the mother-son unit) before disappearing again. During the crucial confrontation between Travis and Jane (the mother), the characters are both present and absent to each other, speaking by telephone through a two-way mirror. The mirror acts as screen within the screen, and the play of looks traversing it mirrors the role of the cinema spectator identifying with the camera as the apparatus of cinematic perception.

24 Note also that in the Song of Solomon, evoked by Dylan in several early 1980s songs, the bridegroom addresses the bride as his sister: "I am come into my garden, my sister, my spouse" (5:1).

25 Dylan also dedicated "Isis" to "Leonard, if he's still here." Leonard Cohen's work contains many parallels to the body of images discussed here: see the song "Where Is My Gypsy Wife Tonight?"; the crucial appearance of Isis in *Beautiful Losers;* and the version of "God said to Abraham, 'Kill me a son'" in "Story of Isaac."

26 Robert Shelton suggests that Robert Graves is a source for much of the imagery on *Desire,* but he does not specifically say that Dylan had been reading *The White Goddess.* See Shelton, *No Direction Home,* 463–65.

27 Often it is unclear whether the events depicted in "Brownsville Girl" have actually happened, whether they are figments of the characters' imaginations, or whether they are scenes from *other* movies, real or imagined.

28 Sam Shepard's play *La Turista* features an American couple in a motel in Mexico. The man falls sick, and the woman sends out for a doctor. The parallel is suggestive but not exact.

29 Critical commentary on the internet has suggested that the name "Henry Porter" could refer to the American short-story writer O. Henry. Possibly—but I think that the major point is simply the indeterminacy of the signature, its refusal to perform the proper functions of the proper name.

30 There is a much older tune, a nineteenth-century traditional American song, that is also called "Danville Girl," from which Dylan's "Danville Girl" (sometimes called "New Danville Girl") derives its title. There is a fine 1927 recording of the traditional song by Dock Boggs. The words have little in common with Dylan's, except for the obvious rhyme between *girl* and *curl.*

31 Brownsville, Texas, was the site of the last battle of the Civil War, fought by irregular Confederate troops a month after the surrender at Appomattox. In 1906 it was the site of a race riot, the aftermath of which developed into a major scandal for the Roosevelt administration.

32 The fatal encounter of Oedipus and Laius at a crossroads ("where three roads meet") is echoed in the mythology of the American blues by the tale of Robert Johnson selling his soul to the devil at a crossroads—a story obliquely referred to in Johnson's song "Crossroads," which was memorably performed by Dylan and Eric Clapton in 1999.

33 The earliest citation for "time out of mind" in the *Oxford English Dictionary* dates from 1407. Perhaps the most famous use in literature is in Mercutio's "Queen Mab" speech in *Romeo and Juliet:* "Time out o' mind the fairies' coachmakers."

34 *Time Out Of Mind* had a curiously mixed critical reception, with the strongest negative voices being those of Dylan fans and followers. The general press hailed it as a masterpiece, Dylan's best album since *Blood on the Tracks*. It won a Grammy Award as best album of the year. Other singers raved about it. But many Dylan fans held back—partly, I think, in reaction to the popular praise. To call *Time Out Of Mind* Dylan's best album since *Blood on the Tracks* is, all too easily, a way of dismissing everything that comes in between, suggesting that there is no longer any need to pay attention to *Desire* or *Street Legal* or *Shot Of Love* or *Oh Mercy*. And while I like *Time Out Of Mind* a great deal, I am certainly sympathetic to this reservation. Let me state quite firmly that I think *Time Out Of Mind* is Bob Dylan's best album since *World Gone Wrong!*

35 Throughout this section, quotations from individual songs on *Time Out Of Mind* are indicated by the following abbreviations:

> CIB "Cold Irons Bound"
> CW "Can't Wait"
> DRB "Dirt Road Blues"
> H "Highlands"
> LS "Love Sick"
> MM "Million Miles"
> MYFML "Make You Feel My Love"
> NDY "Not Dark Yet"
> SD "Standing in the Doorway"
> TGH "Tryin' to Get to Heaven"
> TIF "'Til I Fell in Love with You"

36 Readers of Derrida will be familiar with his deconstruction of the French phrase *s'entendre parler,* which is a fairly close approximation of "hear myself think."

37 For all its bleakness and despair, there is a good deal of comedy in *Time Out Of Mind* (as Christopher Ricks pointed out in a talk at Stanford University in January 1998). A lot of negative statements are given a wry and witty twist. "I know plenty of people who'll put me up," the singer protests, then adds, "for a night or two" (MM).

38 Erica Jong may be best known for *Fear of Flying*, but a more recent book is her *Fear of Fifty*. Dylan was fifty-five at the time he recorded these songs, and youth and age are very much to the point in this scene. But there is also a 1990 novel by Jong, *Any Woman's Blues*, which contains this passage: "I am looking now at one of the paintings I painted to his design (he had scribbled a rough sketch on a napkin; I, of course, had painted it), and there's no denying that it's an abortion, not my style at all"—a remarkably close parallel to the scene in Dylan's song "Highlands."

39 In one of the album's marvellous juxtapositions, this apocalyptic statement—"the end of time has just begun"—is immediately followed by a growled "Oh, honey. . . ."

40 It's possible that Dylan doesn't know the Burns song at all, but simply picked up the phrase from common usage, or from William Saroyan's 1939 play *My Heart's in the Highlands*. The other "Scottish" references in "Highlands" are far from geographically precise: there is no river called "Aberdeen," and the "border country" is far away from the Highlands.

41 The only song from *Time Out Of Mind* not yet performed live in concert is "Dirt Road Blues," though a concert version was filmed for the movie *Masked and Anonymous*.

Postscript: "Love and Theft"

1 Not that I am opposed to such views—I love to see Dylan get his due—but again, the very real achievement of the recent albums is all too easily used as an excuse for ignoring less easily appreciated phases of Dylan's career, such as the late 1980s or early 1990s.

2 There was, of course, the immediate temptation to read certain lines from *"Love and Theft"* as referring, prophetically, to the tragic events in New York and Washington: "Sky full of fire, pain pouring down," etc. This ahistorical reading repeats the widespread tendency to see *Time Out Of Mind* as referring to Dylan's near-fatal attack of histoplasmosis, which in fact occurred well *after* the album had been recorded.

3 Published reports suggest that Dylan was still writing extra stanzas in the studio, even as the songs were being recorded.

4 The only direct usage of Christian terminology comes in the last line of "Sugar Baby"— "Look up, look up, seek your Maker, 'fore Gabriel blows his horn"—and even here the implication is more of impending doom than of any expectation of redemption.

Barthes, Roland. *The Pleasure of the Text*. Translated by Richard Miller. London: Jonathan Cape, 1976.

———. *Image-Music-Text*. Translated by Stephen Heath. Glasgow: Fontana/Collins, 1977.

Bauldie, John. "The Oppression of Knowledge: No-one Can Sing the Blues Like Blind Willie McTell." In *All Across the Telegraph: A Bob Dylan Handbook,* edited by Michael Gray and John Bauldie. London: Sidgwick and Jackson, 1987.

Benjamin, Walter. *The Arcades Project*. Translated by Howard Eiland and Kevin McLaughlin. Cambridge: Belknap Press, 1999.

Benson, Carl, ed. *The Bob Dylan Companion: Four Decades of Commentary*. New York: Schirmer Books, 1998.

Bercovitch, Sacvan. *The American Jeremiad*. Madison: University of Wisconsin Press, 1978.

Bicker, Stewart P. *The Red Rose and the Briar: A Commentary on Bob Dylan's Film "Renaldo and Clara."* Privately published, 1984.

Blenkinsopp, Joseph. *A History of Prophecy in Israel*. Louisville, KY: Westminster John Knox Press, 1996.

Bowden, Betsy. *Performed Literature: Words and Music by Bob Dylan*. Bloomington: Indiana University Press, 1982.

Bowra, Maurice. *The Prophetic Element*. Oxford: Oxford University Press, 1959.

Carroll, Paul. *The Poem in its Skin*. Chicago and New York: Follett Publishing, 1968.

Cartwright, Bert. *The Bible in the Lyrics of Bob Dylan*. Rev. ed. Wanted Man Study Series, no. 4. Bury: Wanted Man, 1992.

Cavendish, Richard. *The Tarot*. London: Michael Joseph, 1975.

Clément, Catherine. *Opera, or the Undoing of Women*. Translated by Betsy Wing. Minneapolis: University of Minnesota Press, 1988.

Cohen, Leonard. *Stranger Music: Selected Poems and Songs*. Toronto: McClelland and Stewart, 1993.

Cohen, Scott. "Don't Ask Me Nothin' About Nothin' I Might Just Tell You The Truth: Bob Dylan Revisited." *Spin* 1, no. 8 (December 1985): 36–40, 80–81.

Crowe, Cameron. *Biograph* [booklet, liner notes, and interviews]. New York: Columbia Records, 1985.

Davidson, Robert. *Genesis 12–50*. Cambridge: Cambridge University Press, 1979.

Day, Aidan. *Jokerman: Reading the Lyrics of Bob Dylan.* Oxford: Basil Blackwell, 1988.

de Lauretis, Teresa. *Alice Doesn't: Feminism, Semiotics, Cinema.* Bloomington: Indiana University Press, 1984.

Derrida, Jacques. *Of Grammatology.* Translated by Gayatri Chakravorty Spivak. Baltimore and London: Johns Hopkins University Press, 1976.

———. *Margins of Philosophy.* Translated by Alan Bass. Chicago: University of Chicago Press, 1982.

———. *Signéponge / Signsponge.* Translated by Richard Rand. New York: Columbia University Press, 1984.

———. *The Ear of the Other: Otobiography, Transference, Translation.* Edited by Christie V. McDonald. Translated by Peggy Kamuf and Avital Ronell. New York: Schocken, 1985.

———. *Glas.* Translated by John P. Leavey, Jr. and Richard Rand. Lincoln and London: University of Nebraska Press, 1986.

———. *The Post Card.* Translated by Alan Bass. Chicago: University of Chicago Press, 1987.

———. *Limited Inc.* Translated by Samuel Weber and Jeffrey Mehlman. Evanston, IL: Northwestern University Press, 1988.

———. *Memoirs of the Blind: The Self-Portrait and Other Ruins.* Translated by Pascale-Anne Brault and Michael Naas. Chicago: University of Chicago Press, 1993.

———. *On the Name.* Translated by David Wood, John P. Leavy, Jr., and Ian McLeod. Stanford: Stanford University Press, 1995.

Dheilly, Joseph. *The Prophets.* Translated by Rachel Attwater. New York: Hawthorn Books, 1960.

Dugaw, Dianne. *Warrior Women and Popular Balladry, 1650–1850.* Chicago: University of Chicago Press, 1996.

Dundas, Glen. *Tangled Up in Tapes: A Recording History of Bob Dylan.* Thunder Bay, ON: SMA Services, 1999.

Dylan, Bob. *Tarantula.* New York: Macmillan, 1971.

———. *Lyrics, 1962–1985.* New York: Alfred A. Knopf, 1985.

Eliot, T. S. "Tradition and the Practice of Poetry." *Southern Review* 21, no. 4 (October 1985) [1936]: 873–88.

Engel, Dave. *Just Like Bob Zimmerman's Blues: Dylan in Minnesota.* Mesabi, WI: River City Memoirs, 1997.

Faithfull, Marianne, with David Dalton. *Faithfull: An Autobiography.* New York: Little, Brown and Company, 1994.

Feinstein, Barry, Daniel Kramer, and Jim Marshall. *Early Dylan.* Boston: Little, Brown and Company, 1999.

Ferlinghetti, Lawrence. *The Jack of Hearts (for Dylan).* San Francisco: City Lights Books, 1976.

Frith, Simon. *Performing Rites: On the Value of Popular Music.* Cambridge, MA: Harvard University Press, 1996.

Gans, Terry Alexander. *What's Real and What Is Not.* Munich: Hobo Press, 1983.

Gates, David. "Dylan Revisited." *Newsweek* (October 6, 1997): 62–68.

Gill, Andy. *Don't Think Twice, It's All Right: Bob Dylan, the Early Years (The Stories Behind Every Song)*. New York: Thunder's Mouth Press, 1988.

Ginsberg, Allen. "Songs of Redemption" [liner notes to Bob Dylan, *Desire*.] New York: Columbia Records, 1975.

———. *Collected Poems 1947–1980*. New York: Harper and Row, 1984.

———. " 'It's Not Rational But It's Logical': Allen Ginsberg interviews Bob Dylan." *The Telegraph* 33 (Summer 1989): 6–33.

———. *Holy Soul Jelly Roll: Poems and Songs 1949–1993*. CD/cassette and booklet. Rhino Records, 1994.

Graves, Robert. *The White Goddess*. London: Faber and Faber, 1961.

Gray, Michael. *Song and Dance Man: The Art of Bob Dylan*. 3d ed., London: Cassell, 2000. (1st ed., London: Hart-Davis, MacGibbon, 1972. 2d ed., New York: St. Martin's Press, 1981.) Quotations are from the third edition, unless otherwise noted.

Gray, Michael, and John Bauldie, eds. *All Across the Telegraph: A Bob Dylan Handbook*. London: Sidgwick and Jackson, 1987.

Herdman, John. *Voice Without Restraint: Bob Dylan's Lyrics and Their Background*. New York: Delilah Books, 1982.

Heylin, Clinton, ed. *Saved! The Gospel Speeches of Bob Dylan*. Madras and New York: Hanuman Books, 1990.

———. *Dylan: Behind the Shades*. London: Viking, 1991.

———. *A Life in Stolen Moments: Bob Dylan Day by Day 1941–1995*. New York: Schirmer Books, 1996.

———. *Dylan's Daemon Lover*. London: Helter Skelter Publishing, 1999.

Holt, Richard. "Lyrical Abstractions." *World Art* 9 (1998).

Hyde, Lewis. *Trickster Makes This World: Mischief, Myth, and Art*. New York: Farrar, Straus and Giroux, 1998.

"Interview [Sam Shepard]." *Rolling Stone* 489/490 (December 18–January 1, 1987).

Ions, Veronica. *Egyptian Mythology*. Feltham: Paul Hamlyn, 1965.

Kamuf, Peggy. *Signature Pieces: On the Institution of Authorship*. Ithaca and London: Cornell University Press, 1988.

Kaplan, Justin, and Anne Bernays. *The Language of Names*. New York: Simon and Schuster, 1997.

Kelly, Roy. "Songs Have Changed, But the Malady Lingers On." *The Bridge* 8 (Winter 2000): 40–60.

Kugel, James L., ed. *Poetry and Prophecy: The Beginnings of a Literary Tradition*. Ithaca: Cornell University Press, 1990.

Lee, C. P. *Like the Night: Bob Dylan and the Road to Manchester Free Trade Hall*. London: Helter Skelter Publishing, 1998.

Leggett, B. J. *Larkin's Blues: Jazz, Popular Music and Poetry*. Baton Rouge: Louisiana University Press, 1999.

Lott, Eric. *Love and Theft: Blackface Minstrelsy and the American Working Class.* Oxford: Oxford University Press, 1993.

Marcus, Greil. *The Dustbin of History.* Cambridge, MA: Harvard University Press, 1995.

———. *Invisible Republic: Bob Dylan's Basement Tapes.* New York: Henry Holt and Company, 1997.

———. "Real Life Rock Top 10" [column]. *Salon* [online] (February 7, 2000): <www.salon.com>.

McGregor, Craig, ed. *Bob Dylan: A Retrospective.* New York: William Morrow, 1972. (1990, rev. ed.; New York: Da Capo Press.) Page references are to the original edition.

Mellers, Wilfrid. *A Darker Shade of Pale: A Backdrop to Bob Dylan.* London: Faber and Faber, 1984.

Miles, Barry, ed. *Bob Dylan in His Own Words.* New York: Quick Fox, 1978.

———. *Ginsberg.* New York: Simon and Schuster, 1989.

Miller, James. *Flowers in the Dustbin: The Rise of Rock and Roll, 1947–1977.* New York: Simon and Schuster, 1999.

Nicholas, Tracy. *Rastafari: A Way of Life.* New York: Anchor Doubleday, 1979.

Pelikan, Jaroslav. *Jesus Through the Centuries: His Place in the History of Culture.* New York: Harper and Row, 1987.

Percival, Dave. *Love Plus Zero / With Limits.* Privately published, 1994.

Pichaske, David. "The Prophet and the Prisoner: Bob Dylan and the American Dream." *The Telegraph* 26 (Spring 1987): 36–98.

Pound, Ezra. "Vorticism." In *Ezra Pound: A Critical Anthology,* edited by J. P. Sullivan. Harmondsworth: Penguin, [1914] 1970.

Ricketts, Mac Linscott. "Bob Dylan's Church: The Vineyard Christian Fellowship." *On the Tracks* 4 (Fall 1994): 30–47.

Robinson, Marilynne. *Housekeeping.* New York: Bantam, 1982.

Scaduto, Anthony. *Bob Dylan: An Intimate Biography.* New York: Grosset and Dunlap, 1971.

Schumacher, Michael. *Dharma Lion: A Biography of Allen Ginsberg.* New York: St. Martin's Press, 1992.

Shelton, Robert. *No Direction Home: The Life and Music of Bob Dylan.* New York: William Morrow, 1986.

Shepard, Sam. *Rolling Thunder Logbook.* New York: Viking, 1977.

———. *Seven Plays.* New York: Bantam, 1981.

———. *Motel Chronicles.* San Francisco: City Lights Books, 1982.

———. *Fool for Love.* San Francisco: City Lights Books, 1983.

———. "True Dylan." *Esquire* 108, no. 1 (July, 1987): 59–68.

Sloman, Larry. *On the Road with Bob Dylan: Rolling with the Thunder.* New York: Bantam, 1978.

Snow, Craig. "Folksinger and Beat Poet: The Prophetic Vision of Bob Dylan." Ph.D. dissertation, Purdue University, 1987.

Sounes, Howard. *Down the Highway: The Life of Bob Dylan.* New York: Grove Press, 2001.

Southwell, Peter. *Prophecy*. London: Hodder and Stoughton, 1982.

Spitz, Bob. *Dylan: A Biography*. New York: McGraw-Hill, 1989.

Tatum, Steven. *Inventing Billy the Kid: Visions of the Outlaw in America, 1881–1981*. Albuquerque: University of New Mexico Press, 1982.

Waldman, Anne. *Shaman/Schamane*. Hannover: Apartment Editions, 1990.

Walker, Barbara G. *The Woman's Encyclopaedia of Myths and Secrets*. San Francisco: Harper and Row, 1983.

Whithouse, Chris. "Alias, Pat Garrett and Billy the Kid." In *All Across the Telegraph: A Bob Dylan Handbook*, edited by Michael Gray and John Bauldie. London: Sidgwick and Jackson, 1987.

Williams, Paul. *Performing Artist: The Music of Bob Dylan*. Vol. 1, *Volume One: The Early Years, 1960–1973*. Vol. 2, *Volume Two: The Middle Years, 1974–1986*. Novato, CA, and Lancaster, PA: Underwood-Miller, 1992.

Witt, R. E. *Isis in the Graeco-Roman World*. London: Thames and Hudson, 1971.

The Index to this book is dedicated to the memory of Allen Ginsberg, who expressed to me his disappointment that there was no such Index in the first edition. It is divided into two sections: the first lists names of people referred to in the text; the second lists titles (of songs, albums, books, movies) performed by and/or featuring Bob Dylan. Both sections are selective rather than comprehensive.

Titles

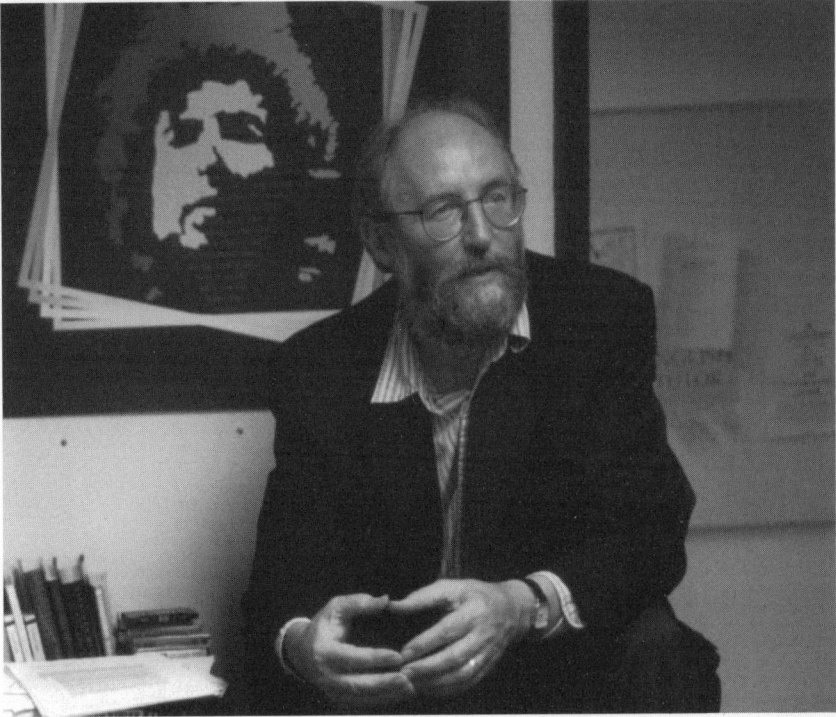

Stephen Scobie teaches literature at the University of Victoria, has published over twenty books and has won the Governor General's Award for *McAlmon's Chinese Opera*. He has lectured extensively on Bob Dylan's music in Canada, the United States, England and Austria. He has also published a poetic exploration of Dylan's childhood roots, *And Forget My Name*. His most recent publication is *The Spaces In Between: Selected Poems, 1965–2001*.